*Faith and the Founders
of the American Republic*

Faith and the Founders of the American Republic

Edited by

DANIEL L. DREISBACH
AND MARK DAVID HALL

OXFORD
UNIVERSITY PRESS

OXFORD
UNIVERSITY PRESS

Oxford University Press is a department of the University of Oxford.
It furthers the University's objective of excellence in research, scholarship,
and education by publishing worldwide.

Oxford New York
Auckland Cape Town Dar es Salaam Hong Kong Karachi
Kuala Lumpur Madrid Melbourne Mexico City Nairobi
New Delhi Shanghai Taipei Toronto

With offices in
Argentina Austria Brazil Chile Czech Republic France Greece
Guatemala Hungary Italy Japan Poland Portugal Singapore
South Korea Switzerland Thailand Turkey Ukraine Vietnam

Oxford is a registered trade mark of Oxford University Press
in the UK and certain other countries.

Published in the United States of America by
Oxford University Press
198 Madison Avenue, New York, NY 10016

© Oxford University Press 2014

Portions of Chapter 4 were originally published in Thomas S. Kidd, *American Christians and Islam: Evangelical Culture and Muslims from the Colonial Period to the Age of Terrorism* (Princeton, NJ: Princeton University Press, 2009). Reprinted with permission.

Portions of Chapter 9 have been adapted from Gregg L. Frazer, *The Religious Beliefs of America's Founders: Reason, Revelation, and Revolution* (Lawrence: University Press of Kansas, 2012) with the permission of the University Press of Kansas.

All rights reserved. No part of this publication may be reproduced, stored in a
retrieval system, or transmitted, in any form or by any means, without the prior
permission in writing of Oxford University Press, or as expressly permitted by law,
by license, or under terms agreed with the appropriate reproduction rights organization.
Inquiries concerning reproduction outside the scope of the above should be sent to the Rights
Department, Oxford University Press, at the address above.

You must not circulate this work in any other form
and you must impose this same condition on any acquirer.

Library of Congress Cataloging-in-Publication Data
Faith and the founders of the American republic / edited by Daniel L. Dreisbach and Mark David Hall.
p. cm.
Includes index.
ISBN 978–0–19–984333–6 (hardcover : alk. paper) — ISBN 978–0–19–984335–0 (pbk. : alk. paper)
1. Religion and politics—United States—History—18th century. 2. United States—Religion—To 1800.
3. Religion and state—United States—History—18th century. 4. Founding Fathers of the United States—
Religious life. I. Dreisbach, Daniel L. II. Hall, Mark David, 1966–
BL2525.F325 2014
200.973'09033—dc23
2013028786

*To Joyce, with gratitude for 25 wonderful years,
and to Mollie and Moriah.*
—D.L.D.

To Lydia, of whom I am very proud.
—M.D.H.

Contents

Contributors   ix

Introduction   DANIEL L. DREISBACH AND MARK DAVID HALL   1

PART I: *Religion and Political Culture in the American Founding*

1. Deism and the Founders   DARREN STALOFF   13

2. *Vindiciae, Contra Tyrannos*: The Influence of the Reformed Tradition in the American Founding   MARK DAVID HALL   34

3. Jews, Judaism, and the American Founding   DAVID G. DALIN   63

4. The Founders and Islam   THOMAS S. KIDD   84

5. Religion and the Loyalists   ROBERT M. CALHOON AND RUMA CHOPRA   101

6. The Antifederalists and Religion   DONALD L. DRAKEMAN   120

7. The Bible and the Political Culture of the American Founding   DANIEL L. DREISBACH   144

8. Religion, Race, and the Founders   JONATHAN D. SASSI   174

PART II: *Faith and the Founders*

9. Gouverneur Morris and Theistic Rationalism in the Founding Era   GREGG FRAZER   203

10. John Hancock: Congregationalist Revolutionary
    GARY SCOTT SMITH   228

11. Elias Boudinot, Presbyterians, and the Quest for a "Righteous
    Republic"   JONATHAN DEN HARTOG   253

12. The Quaker Contributions of John Dickinson to the Creation
    of the American Republic   JANE E. CALVERT   277

13. Isaac Backus and John Leland: Baptist Contributions
    to Religious Liberty in the Founding Era   JOE L. COKER   305

Index   339

Contributors

ROBERT M. CALHOON, Professor Emeritus of History at the University of North Carolina at Greensboro, is Adjunct Professor of History at Appalachian State University and, most recently, author of *Political Moderation in America's First Two Centuries* (2009).

JANE E. CALVERT is Associate Professor of History at the University of Kentucky, author of *Quaker Constitutionalism and the Political Thought of John Dickinson* (2009), and Director/Editor of the John Dickinson Writings Project.

RUMA CHOPRA is Associate Professor of History at San Jose State University and the author of, among other works, *Unnatural Rebellion: Loyalists in New York City during the Revolution* (2011).

JOE L. COKER is a Lecturer in the Department of Religion at Baylor University and the author of, among other works, "Sweet Harmony vs. Strict Separation: Recognizing the Distinctions between Isaac Backus and John Leland" in *American Baptist Quarterly* (September 1997), and *Liquor in the Land of the Lost Cause* (2007).

DAVID G. DALIN is Professor of History and Politics at Ave Maria University and the author or coauthor of, among other works, *Religion and State in the American Jewish Experience* (1997) and *The Presidents of the United States and the Jews* (2000).

JONATHAN DEN HARTOG is Associate Professor of History at Northwestern College (St. Paul, Minnesota). He is the author of *"Patriotism and Piety": Federalist Politics and Religious Struggle in the New Nation* (forthcoming).

DONALD L. DRAKEMAN is a Fellow in the Centre for Health Leadership & Enterprise at the Judge Business School of the University of Cambridge and the author of *Church, State, and Original Intent* (2010) and other works.

DANIEL L. DREISBACH is Professor of Justice, Law and Society at American University and the author of, among other works, *Thomas Jefferson and the Wall of Separation between Church and State* (2002).

GREGG L. FRAZER is Professor of History & Political Studies at The Master's College and the author of *The Religious Beliefs of America's Founders: Reason, Revelation, and Revolution* (2012).

MARK DAVID HALL is Herbert Hoover Distinguished Professor of Politics at George Fox University and the author of, among other works, *Roger Sherman and the Creation of the American Republic* (2013).

THOMAS S. KIDD is Professor of History at Baylor University and the author of, among other works, *Patrick Henry: First Among Patriots* and *American Christians and Islam* (2008).

JONATHAN D. SASSI is Professor of History at the College of Staten Island and the Graduate Center of the City University of New York and the author of, among other works, *A Republic of Righteousness: The Public Christianity of the Post-Revolutionary New England Clergy* (2001).

GARY SCOTT SMITH is the chair of the History Department and the Coordinator of the Humanities Core at Grove City College and the author of, among other works, *Faith and the Presidency: From George Washington to George W. Bush* (2006, 2009).

DARREN STALOFF is Professor of History at the City College of New York and the author of, among other works, *Hamilton, Adams, Jefferson: The Politics of Enlightenment and the American Founding* (2005).

*Faith and the Founders
of the American Republic*

Introduction

Daniel L. Dreisbach and Mark David Hall

RELIGION FIGURED PROMINENTLY in the identity and mission of English colonial settlements in the New World. An invocation of divine blessing and acknowledgment of a sacred mission to spread the Gospel were recurring themes in the colonial charters and other expressions of the colonists' political pursuits. The First Charter of Virginia in 1606 commended the colonists' "humble and well intended desires" to further, "by the providence of Almighty God," a noble work "in propagating [the] Christian religion to such people, as yet live in darkness and miserable ignorance of the true knowledge and worship of God."[1] The signatories to the Mayflower Compact in 1620 affirmed that they undertook their voyage "for the Glory of God, and Advancement of the Christian Faith, and the Honour of our King and Country."[2] The New England Puritans, especially, endeavored, in the words of Matthew 5:14, to build a "city set upon a Hill."[3] These pious settlers committed themselves to establishing Bible commonwealths and remaking the world in conformity with God's laws, as they understood them. The Bible was often the explicit basis of early colonial codes, including Virginia's "Articles, Laws, and Orders" (1610–1611) and the Massachusetts Body of Liberties (1641).[4]

Although the religious fervor of the first generation of settlers waned, starting in the 1730s and continuing for decades, there was a spiritual "awakening" or religious revival that swept up and down the Atlantic seaboard. The Great Awakening was, in fact, a series of revivals in a variety of locations throughout the colonies led by dynamic preachers such as the fiery Anglican evangelist George Whitefield, the cerebral Congregationalist minister Jonathan Edwards, and the dissenting Presbyterian preacher Samuel Davies. In some regions of the country, such as the central Virginia Piedmont, revivals continued with little interruption until the end of the century.[5]

Historians have long debated whether these revivals, which burned brightest in the first half of the eighteenth century, influenced the political culture, especially the movement for independence from Great Britain that dominated the second half of the century. The Great Awakening was a powerful and, to some extent, ecumenical (but Protestant) religious movement that demonstrated to many Americans that a rich, meaningful spiritual experience could take place outside the four walls of an established church. Insofar as these revivals involved a direct, unmediated relationship between God (especially the Holy Spirit) and humans, they unleashed diverse interpretations of the Bible and religious experiences, which further challenged the singular, unitary, authoritative articulation of religion imposed by an established church. The Great Awakening was a national phenomenon that helped create a national identity, breaking down geographical barriers and giving colonists in diverse communities a shared experience as Americans. This shared identity would prove significant in the confrontation that was to come with the mother country. Its attacks on *religious* establishments and elites were translated into attacks on *political* establishments and elites. This was an easy transition in those parts of the country where the religious establishment was the Church of England. Some historians have argued that the Great Awakening was an important precursor to the ideas and actions of the struggle for independence. The notion that God "awakens" people directly and empowers them to interpret His Word (the Bible) themselves challenged "top down" ecclesiastical authority. Moreover, the idea that salvation (and an unmediated relationship with God) was open to *all*—rich or poor, male or female—promoted a democratization of religion and suggested a broader democratization of civil society. These ideas were translated in the political realm into the consent of essentially *equal* people as the source of legitimate governance.[6]

And so the founding generation was born in a colonial culture shaped, in important respects, by Christianity. Even more specifically, the culture was profoundly influenced by *Protestantism*. Approximately 98 percent of white Americans in the late eighteenth century were Protestants of one stripe or another. Only about 1.9 percent were Roman Catholics—and even in Maryland, which was founded as a haven for Catholics, they were always a minority and the Church of England had been the colony's established church since 1692. There were also approximately two thousand Jews in the United States at this time.[7]

Few scholars question the notion that Christianity held sway in the lives of many eighteenth-century Americans. Yet some of the best-known and most influential founders—Benjamin Franklin and Thomas Jefferson, for two examples—were cosmopolitan in outlook and influenced by the rationalist philosophies of the Enlightenment. Even before they were dead and buried, the founders were the subjects of extraordinary—even obsessive—curiosity about their faith commitments (or lack thereof). The words and deeds of prominent founders, from church attendance to private correspondence, have been studied and debated for what they reveal about their commitment to or departure from Christianity. There is a consensus that most founders were self-identified "Christians," but were they orthodox in their beliefs? Did they attend church? Did they believe in a personal god who intervenes in the affairs of men and nations? Did they rely on reason or revelation or both? Did they believe faith should play a role in public life? For good or ill, answers to these questions have informed one of two metanarratives: America was founded as a Christian nation or America was founded as a secular republic.

Nineteenth century authors regularly portrayed the founders as pious, godly men.[8] An excellent example of this is Mason Locke Weems's popular account of George Washington kneeling in prayer in the snowy woods of Valley Forge.[9] This story was regularly retold throughout the century—most significantly in McGuffey's *Eclectic Reader* where it was read by millions of school children. That the event almost certainly did not happen as described by Parson Weems was not a problem for nineteenth century hagiographers.

History texts in the nineteenth century regularly portrayed American history in providential terms and asserted that the founders were pious Christians.[10] Robert Baird, for example, wrote in the 1840s that "[a]ll the leading men" at the Constitutional Convention "were believers in Christianity."[11] Stephen Colwell similarly contended a decade later that the founders "acknowledged the revelation of [God] contained in the Holy Scriptures; they derived the sanctions of their institutions, and the morality of their legislation and of their whole social system, from these Scriptures."[12] Most impressively, B. F. Morris compiled an 831 page collection of documents aimed at demonstrating that America was founded as a Christian nation and that it remained so to the present day (1864).[13] Such religious hagiography remains popular among Christian writers and publishers in the twenty-first century.[14]

In the twentieth century academics, along with many popular authors, began to tell a very different story. In this account, the American founding, sandwiched between two great religious "awakenings," was an age of Enlightenment in which rationalist thought was in the ascendancy, especially among intellectual and political elites. Traditional Christian thought, by contrast, was in decline. The founders, according to this narrative, were

Deists who desired the separation of church and state and the establishment of a secular polity. For instance, Charles A. Beard and Mary R. Beard opined that "Jefferson, Paine, John Adams, Washington, Franklin, Madison, and many lesser lights were to be reckoned among either Unitarians or Deists. It was not Cotton Mather's God to whom the authors of the Declaration of Independence appealed; it was to 'Nature's God.'"[15] More recently, historian Frank Lambert has written that the "significance of the Enlightenment and Deism for the birth of the American republic, and especially the relationship between church and state within it, can hardly be overstated."[16] Law professor Geoffrey R. Stone similarly contended that "deistic beliefs played a central role in the framing of the American republic . . . [and the] founding generation viewed religion, and particularly religion's relation to government, through an Enlightenment lens that was deeply skeptical of orthodox Christianity."[17] "[T]he Founding Fathers," sociologist William Martin averred, "were cosmopolitan intellectuals devoted to the rationalism of the Enlightenment."[18] For a final example, and many more could be given,[19] the dean of American historians, Gordon S. Wood, asserted that "The Founding Fathers were at most deists—they believed God created the world, then left it alone to run. . . ."[20] Not surprisingly, given the weight of these opinions, religion's contributions to the political thought of the founders and of the American founding have often been relegated to the margins—or ignored altogether[21]—by scholars and popular authors alike.[22]

When scholars who claim the founding was a product of the Enlightenment are attentive to the religious beliefs of the founders, they are usually drawn to the views of some combination of the following men: Benjamin Franklin, George Washington, John Adams, Thomas Jefferson, James Madison, Thomas Paine, and Alexander Hamilton. On rare occasions they reach beyond this select fraternity to include another founder or two, and almost inevitably they concede that not *all* founders were as enlightened as the ones they profile. Thus they leave the distinct impression that most founders, and certainly the important ones, were Deists.

Perhaps the near exclusive focus on a handful of famous founders could be justified if they were, in fact, the only consequential founders. But even the casual observer of American history knows that this is not the case. There was a large company of now "forgotten founders" who made salient contributions in thought, word, and deed to articulating the rights of colonists, securing independence from Great Britain, and establishing the new constitutional republic and its political institutions. Take, for example, one of the founders profiled in this volume, John Dickinson of Delaware and Pennsylvania (serving both states as the elected chief executive). He was a delegate to the Stamp Act Congress, where he drafted the "Declaration of Rights and Grievances" (October 1765); a member of the First and Second Continental Congresses, where he was the principal draftsman of the "Declaration of the Causes and Necessity of Taking Up Arms" (July 6, 1775) and author of an initial draft of the "Articles of Confederation"; and one of Delaware's delegates to the Constitutional Convention of 1787. Early in the colonists' struggle, he championed the rights of Americans in a series of brilliant "Letters from a Farmer in Pennsylvania" (1767–1768), and he later wrote a series of letters, under the pen name Fabius, in defense of the proposed Constitution that some scholars regard as more persuasive and intelligent than the more famous *Federalist Papers*.[23] Dickinson is only one of a host of other Patriots—Samuel Adams, Elias Boudinot, Elbridge Gerry, John Hancock, John Jay, Richard Henry Lee, George Mason, Gouverneur Morris, Charles Pinckney, Edmund Randolph, Benjamin Rush, John Rutledge, Roger Sherman, James Wilson, and John Witherspoon, just to name a few—who made salient, if now largely forgotten, contributions to the new nation.

One possible argument for giving excessive attention to Franklin, Washington, Adams, Jefferson, Madison, Paine, and Hamilton in examinations of the founders' faiths is that they represent well the founding generation's religious views and their approach to church-state relations. Yet these founders are far from what social scientists call a "representative sample." Consider for a moment the backgrounds and experiences of these seven individuals. Washington, Jefferson, and Madison were southern Anglican plantation owners. Hamilton was born and raised in the British West Indies, and Paine was born and raised in England (and he lived only twenty of his seventy-seven years in America). In an era when few people traveled internationally, Jefferson and Adams spent significant time in Europe, and Franklin lived *most* of the last thirty-five years of his life in Britain and France. As adults, Franklin and Hamilton were nominal Anglicans, which means five of these seven founders (71 percent) were Episcopalians (compared to 16 percent of all Americans in that era).[24] Paine, the scion of a Quaker father and Anglican mother, became one of the few open Deists in America. Although 50 to 75 percent of Americans in the founding era may be reasonably classified as Calvinists, only one of these famous founders worshipped at a Calvinist church—and Adams is not a particularly good representative of this theological tradition.[25]

As well, this elite group of founders does not contain a single person who can reasonably be called an evangelical. Born of the revivalism of the Great Awakening of the 1730s and 1740s, evangelicals are orthodox Protestants who emphasize the need for a conversion experience, have a very high view of the Bible, and believe Christians should actively share their faith.[26] Many evangelicals remained in Reformed denominations (notably the New Light Congregationalists and New Side Presbyterians), but they were present in most denominations. The eighteenth century saw the beginning of the explosive growth of two evangelical denominations, the Baptists and Methodists, which would radically alter America's religious landscape in the nineteenth century and beyond. In the eighteenth century, evangelical challenges to established churches contributed to advancing religious liberty and, according to some scholars, helped pave the way for the War for American Independence.[27]

We agree that the views of prominent and influential American founders warrant careful study.[28] A major goal of this project, however, is to expand the conversation to include other figures who had a significant role in the American founding. We do not dispute that rationalism—including Deism—had influence in the era, but we do think it is often misunderstood and its impact overstated.[29] Moreover, we believe Deism and related terms are interjected into discussions of the American founding without adequate explanation for what these terms mean. Deism is difficult to define because it is a belief system without an explicit, agreed upon creed or authoritative text to articulate its fundamental tenets; consequently, the term encompasses a wide range of sometimes inconsistent beliefs. Also, we want this volume to cast a light on the interplay among diverse religious traditions in the political culture and thought of the founding, as well as religion's influence on the political thought of selected founders. The essays collected in this volume, we believe, provide compelling evidence that diverse religious traditions were among the intellectual sources that informed and animated the American founding.

The first section of the volume contains thematic essays on how different religious traditions informed the political culture of the American founding or were viewed by the founders. We include essays on well-known traditions: Deism and Calvinism, as well as on minority faiths: Judaism and Islam. Two essays consider the impact of faith on two groups from the "losing" side of American history: Loyalists and Antifederalists. Finally, two essays explore how Americans from a variety of denominations used the Bible in their political discourse, and how religion informed different founders' views of race—especially with regard to slavery. (Another religious tradition that, in our view, merits attention is Roman Catholicism. Having devoted a chapter to this topic in a previous volume, we chose not to revisit the topic in this collection, but we gladly direct readers to this essay on Catholicism in the founding era: James R. Stoner, "Catholic Politics and Religious Liberty in America: The Carrolls of Maryland," in *The Founders on God and Government* [2004], 251–271.)

The second section includes essays on individual founders deliberately selected because they come from and, perhaps, illustrate an important political or theological perspective or constituency in late-eighteenth-century America. For instance, an essay on Gouverneur Morris suggests a theological perspective that might describe the religious views of some prominent founders: theistic rationalism. Chapters on John Hancock and Elias Boudinot help illustrate how Calvinist convictions informed the political and economic activities of a significant number of founders. Similarly, the chapter on John Dickinson opens a window on the roles Quakers played in the American founding. Finally, a chapter on Isaac Backus and John Leland shines a light on the role of theology in shaping the political thought and engagement of Baptists.

The founders profiled in this volume came from traditions, some small and some large, that influenced the founding in various ways. Reformed Americans, for instance, were very well represented in every important civic body at the national level in the founding era. Baptists, on the other hand, were seldom represented in these bodies, but their numbers were increasing rapidly from the Connecticut River to the Shenandoah Valley. Moreover, their forceful opposition to religious establishments and advocacy for religious liberty had an important impact on the American political tradition. Quakers have never been numerous in America, but they have played significant roles in social reform movements—particularly with respect to racial and gender equality.

The contributors to this volume come from a variety of disciplines, and we afforded them the freedom to pursue their subjects according to the canons of their disciplines. We should note that the contributors themselves hold a variety of religious beliefs (including unbelief) and significantly different views on how church and state should relate in America today. Whether or how the founders' views should inform contemporary questions of jurisprudence and politics is a matter we leave for another day.

On a personal note, Daniel L. Dreisbach thanks American University for its continuing support of his research. He also thanks his research assistants Andrew Lewis, Michele Frazier, Ryan Ady, Elizabeth Bretz, and Nicholas Mueller for their work on this book. For their endless patience and good humor during the course of this and other projects, he thanks his wife, Joyce, and two daughters, Mollie Abigail and Moriah Esther. Mark David Hall is grateful for the support of George Fox University, the National Endowment for the Humanities, and the Earhart Foundation. He also appreciates the Institute for Studies of Religion at Baylor University, where he serves as a Senior Fellow. Research assistance from Jay Miller, Austin Schaefer, Sergio Cisneros, and Chelsea McCombs contributed significantly to the success of this volume. Richard R. Johnson and members of the Pacific Northwest Early Americanists colloquium and Tommy Kidd of Baylor University were kind enough to comment on his essay for this collection. As always, he is grateful for the loving support of Miriam, Joshua, Lydia, and Anna.

Notes

1. The First Charter of Virginia (1606), in William Waller Hening, ed., *The Statutes at Large; Being a Collection of all the Laws of Virginia, From the First Session of the Legislature, in the Year 1619* (Richmond, VA: J. & G. Cochran, 1821), 1: 58.
2. The Mayflower Compact (1620), in Daniel L. Dreisbach and Mark David Hall, eds., *The Sacred Rights of Conscience: Selected Readings on Religious Liberty and Church-State Relations in the American Founding* (Indianapolis, IN: Liberty Fund Press, 2009), 86–88.
3. John Winthop, "A Modell of Christian Charitie" (1630), in Dreisbach and Hall, eds., *Sacred Rights of Conscience*, 131.
4. See Dreisbach and Hall, *Sacred Rights of Conscience*, 84–86; *Colonial Origins of the American Constitution: A Documentary History*, Donald S. Lutz, ed. (Indianapolis, IN: Liberty Fund, 1998), 70–87.
5. See generally Thomas S. Kidd, *The Great Awakening: The Roots of Evangelical Christianity in Colonial America* (New Haven, CT: Yale University Press, 2009).
6. See, for example, Alan Heimert, *Religion and the American Mind: From the Great Awakening to the Revolution* (Cambridge, MA: Harvard University Press, 1966), and Gordon S. Wood, "Religion and the American Revolution," in *New Directions in American Religious History*, Harry S. Stout and D. G. Hart, eds. (New York: Oxford University Press, 1997), 173–205.
7. Barry A. Kosmin and Seymour P. Lachman, *One Nation Under God: Religion in Contemporary American Society* (New York: Harmony Books, 1993), 28–29; Roger Finke and Rodney Stark, *The Churching of America, 1776–1990: Winners*

and *Losers in Our Religious Economy* (New Brunswick, NJ: Rutgers University Press, 1992), 22–108.
8. In the heat of partisan battles of the 1790s and early 1800s, selected founders, such as Thomas Jefferson, were described by political opponents as infidels, Deists, or even atheists.
9. Mason Locke Weems, *The Life of Washington: A New Edition with Primary Documents*, Peter Onuf, ed. (Armonk, NY: M. E. Sharpe, 1996), 146–147.
10. See, for example, George Bancroft, *History of the United States: From Discovery of the American Continent*, 10 vols. (Boston: Little, Brown and Co., 1834–1874). On this literature generally, see John Fea, *Was America Founded as a Christian Nation: An Introduction* (Louisville, KY: Westminster John Knox Press, 2011), 3–76, and Steven K. Green, *The Second Disestablishment: Church and State in Nineteenth-Century America* (New York: Oxford University Press, 2010), esp. 91–103.
11. Robert Baird, *Religion in the United State of America* (Glasgow: Blackie and Sons, 1844), 259.
12. Stephen Colwell, *The Position of Christianity in the United States* (Philadelphia: Lippincott, Grambo, 1854), 11.
13. B. F. Morris, *The Christian Life and Character of the Civil Institutions of the United States* (Philadelphia: George W. Childs, 1864).
14. See, for example, Peter Marshall and David Manuel, *The Light and the Glory* (Grand Rapids, MI: Fleming H. Revell, 1977); John Eidsmoe, *Christianity and the Constitution: The Faith of Our Founding Fathers* (Grand Rapids, MI: Baker Book House, 1987); Tim LaHaye, *Faith of Our Founding Fathers* (Brentwood, TN: Wolgemuth & Hyatt, 1987); and Gary DeMar, *America's Christian Heritage* (Nashville, TN: Broadman & Holman, 2003).
15. Charles A. Beard and Mary R. Beard, *The Rise of American Civilization* (New York: Macmillan, 1930), 449.
16. Frank Lambert, *The Founding Fathers and the Place of Religion in America* (Princeton, NJ: Princeton University Press, 2003), 161.
17. Geoffrey Stone, "The World of the Framers: A Christian Nation?" *University of California Law Review* 56 (October 2008), 7–8.
18. William Martin, *With God on our Side: The Rise of the Religious Right in America* (New York: Broadway, 1996), 376.
19. See, for example, Edwin Gaustad, *A Documentary History of Religion in America*, 2nd ed. (Grand Rapids, MI: William B. Eerdmans, 1993), 1: 227 ("the founding fathers themselves, largely deists in their orientation and sympathy..."); Richard T. Hughes, *Myths America Lives By* (Urbana: University of Illinois Press, 2003), 50 ("most of the American founders embraced some form of Deism, not historically orthodox Christianity."); Brooke Allen, *Moral Minority: Our Skeptical Founding Fathers* (Chicago: Ivan R. Dee, 2006), xiii ("the Founding Fathers were... skeptical men of the Enlightenment who questioned each and every received idea they had been taught."); Harvey Kaye, *Thomas Paine and the Promise of America* (New York: Hill and Wang,

2005), 108 ("[m]any of the nation's original Founders subscribed to some version of religious rationalism"); and Green, *The Second Disestablishment*, 87 ("Although many of the nation's elites privately embraced deism, *The Age of Reason* and other works popularized irreligion among the laboring and working classes").

20. Frederic Smoler, "The Radical Revolution: An Interview with Gordon Wood," *American Heritage Magazine* 42 (December 1992), accessed at http://www.americanheritage.com/print/57789 on June 18, 2011.

21. For instance, Alan Gibson's excellent survey of the literature on political thought that informed America's founding has chapters dedicated to progressive, liberal, classical republican, Scottish, multiple traditions, and the politically correct interpretations of the founding. He mentions only in passing, however, the possibility that Protestantism may have had an influence on America's founders. Alan Gibson, *Interpreting the Founding: Guide to the Enduring Debates Over the Origins and Foundations of the American Republic* (Lawrence: University Press of Kansas, 2006), 3.

22. There are some notable exceptions to this tendency. See, for example, Ellis Sandoz, *A Government of Laws: Political Theory, Religion, and the American Founding* (Baton Rouge: Louisiana State University Press, 1990); Barry Alan Shain, *The Myth of American Individualism: The Protestant Origins of American Political Thought* (Princeton, NJ: Princeton University Press, 1994); James H. Hutson, *Religion and the Founding of the American Republic* (Washington, D.C.: Library of Congress, 1998); and Thomas S. Kidd, *God of Liberty: A Religious History of the American Revolution* (New York: Basic Books, 2010).

23. For more on the life and influence of John Dickinson, see Jane E. Calvert's chapter in this volume.

24. Finke and Stark, *The Churching of America*, 55.

25. Sydney E. Ahlstrom, *A Religious History of the American People* (Garden City, NY: Doubleday, 1975), 1: 426.

26. This definition is closely related to, but not exactly the same as, that offered by David W. Bebbington, *Evangelicalism in Modern Britain: A History from the 1730s to the 1980s* (London: Unwin Hyman, 1989), 2–17, and Mark A. Noll, *The Rise of Evangelicalism: The Age of Edwards, Whitefield, and the Wesleys* (Downers Grove, IL: InterVarsity Press, 2003), 15–21.

27. See Heimert, *Religion and the American Mind*; Kidd, *God of Liberty*.

28. We included essays on the role of faith in the political thought, words, and deeds of the most famous founders in Daniel L. Dreisbach, Mark D. Hall, and Jeffry H. Morrison, eds., *The Founders on God and Government* (Lanham, MD: Rowman and Littlefield, 2004) (Franklin, Washington, John Adams, Jefferson, and Madison), and Daniel L. Dreisbach, Mark David Hall, and Jeffry H. Morrison, eds., *The Forgotten Founders on Religion and Public Life* (Notre Dame, IN: University of Notre Dame Press, 2009) (Hamilton and Paine).

29. For more on the influence of Deism on the political thought of the founders, see Darren Staloff's chapter in this volume.

PART I

Religion and Political Culture in the American Founding

I

Deism and the Founders

Darren Staloff

OVER THE LAST several decades, the role of Deism in the American founding has become a highly charged question of public controversy. In particular, this debate has focused on the faith and practice of six extremely influential founding fathers: Benjamin Franklin, George Washington, Alexander Hamilton, James Madison, John Adams, and Thomas Jefferson. These figures have become vital proxies in the ongoing culture war between traditional and/or evangelical Protestants and their increasingly militant secular opponents. The champions of a role for religious values and beliefs in American politics have insisted on the centrality of Christianity to early American history and have argued that the nation was founded on Judeo-Christian principles. As evidence for the latter they note the regularity of Congressional prayer, national days of prayer and thanksgiving, and the invocation of God as the source of our "unalienable rights."[1] Secularists who wish to insulate public life from religion deny that Judeo-Christianity played any appreciable role in the founding. The American regime was based on Enlightenment rationalism as evident in the strict separation of church and state they find in the First Amendment, as well as in the absence of scriptural references in the principal founding documents. They also note the use of presumably "deistic" natural religious terms to refer to God in the Declaration of Independence. Although they do not dispute the prevalence of Christian belief in the early Republic, they argue that the principal founders listed above did not share that belief, and that it was deistic and secular rather than Christian principles that informed the constitutional and political order they founded.[2]

The focus on these half-dozen statesmen is hardly haphazard. While they are of course a miniscule fraction of those engaged in establishing the new republic, they are among the most important figures in that project. Including the first four presidents, the most celebrated American of his day and the chief diplomat of the Revolution, and the principal architect of the federal republic's fiscal and foreign policy, these men palpably dominated the new nation. These are the A-list founders whose ideas, writings, and policy decisions patterned the political and constitutional order of the United States long after they retired from office. If, as the secularists maintain, these men were really Deists, however secretly, and their public actions flowed from those convictions, then a reasonable case can be made that our founding principles drew far more from the Enlightenment than from traditional Christianity. Without the A-list founders on its side, the secularist case loses traction and we are left with a Christian founding.

Part of what makes this public debate compelling is the way it reflects a rather more subtle ongoing division within the scholarly community over the role of religion in the American founding. On the one hand, the dominant debate over the revolutionary and early national periods has been between those who see the centrality of a republican ideology that stressed classical civic virtue and their liberal opponents who claim a market oriented, Lockean individualism as the driving force behind the politics of the early republic. Neither of these interpretive schools sees much role for religion in the founding. They do not deny the Christianity of much of the American people, but they argue that "most of the Founding Fathers, enlightened men in an enlightened age, were not all that enthusiastic about religion, certainly not about religious enthusiasm."[3] While the A-list founders are not always described as Deists per se, Jon Butler has claimed that they at least "embraced Deist principles."[4] And it was their principles that informed the American founding.

On the other hand, over roughly the same period a scholarly countertradition has emerged that challenges the assumptions of both ideological schools. Rather than Classical, Renaissance, and Enlightenment doctrines, they have argued that a traditional Christian worldview was central to the American founding. Beginning with Alan Heimert almost fifty years ago, these scholars have stressed the importance of the evangelical anti-authoritarianism of the Great Awakening as the essential precondition for the revolutionary struggle for independence and the ensuing federal settlement.[5] For these scholars, American republican government drew far more from dissenting ideals and religious voluntarism than has usually been acknowledged. Others have argued that a providential view of history and millennial fervor were far more influential in the founding era than the writings of Montesquieu, Hume, or Harrington.[6] Even the purported heterodoxy of the most prominent founders has been questioned.[7] The result has been the reformulation of the disjunction posed by the popular disputants. Was the American founding predicated on shared Christian beliefs and a broad public religiosity, or was it instead a largely secular affair grounded in Enlightenment principles? Given such a stark choice, the only tenable answer must be *both*.

Deism

The product of seventeenth- and eighteenth-century "free thinkers," Deism was a form of rational theology resulting in a "religion of nature" which claimed human reason as its sole basis. All Deists shared at least two beliefs. The first was in the existence of God, a belief grounded in either the cosmological argument (the a priori claim that the universe must have a first cause) or the a posteriori argument from design. Deists also denied that revelation and scripture could serve as a legitimate source of religious authority and truth. Most further rejected the supernatural elements of revealed religion—miracles, prophecies, and acts of providential intervention—as mere superstition. The Deist God was a distant, if benevolent, creator whose creation ran itself with clocklike regularity. His primary demands were moral and social, not spiritual or ecclesiastical. All the received doctrines of traditional Christianity, from the incarnation and divinity of Christ to original sin and atonement, were denounced as the residues of priestcraft ancient and modern.

Beyond this broad portrait, however, it is very difficult to offer definitive generalizations about early modern Deism. In part this is because many Deists wrote in an esoteric fashion, shielding their most radical implications and inferences behind purportedly fideistic professions.[8] Indeed, there was good reason for such subterfuge; even in latitudinarian England the Toleration Act of 1689 specifically excluded all forms of antitrinitarianism; Thomas Woolston's critique of the biblical account of miracles and the resurrection of Christ earned him a substantial £100 fine and a year in prison. Even more challenging is the wide range of disagreements among Deists. While all rejected miracles, some nonetheless made room for providential interference in human affairs while others insisted on a purely necessitarian and materialist account of nature and history. Deists also disagreed whether the soul was immortal and immaterial with the more radical elements denying any grounds for belief in an afterlife with its divine rewards and punishments. Even attitudes toward revelation varied. Militant Deists generally ridiculed scripture as imposture while their more irenic colleagues accepted that much of its content, especially the message of Jesus, was morally salutary if not always literally true. Perhaps most striking is the way in which Deist thought evolved over time in both England and her North American colonies.

English Deism is normally traced to Lord Herbert of Cherbury, a prominent statesmen and thinker whose *De Veritate (On Truth, as It Is Distinguished from Revelation, the Probable, the Possible, and the False)* (1624) laid out a rational theology based on the cosmological argument. Herbert sought to quell the rising confessional strife that had been wracking Europe for over a century and would shortly envelop England, Ireland, and Scotland in civil war. Meant as a universal creed that all religious people could embrace, Herbert's Deism included human duties of worship and virtuous behavior that would be rewarded in an afterlife. Despite his best efforts, Herbert's irenic creed bore little fruit. Religious strife continued unabated in the British Isles as well as on the European continent, and his rational religion found few adherents.

Beginning in the last quarter of the seventeenth century, however, Deism did emerge as a formidable presence in English public life. A series of strikingly militant authors, the so-called major Deists—Charles Blount, John Toland, Anthony Collins, and (to a lesser extent) Mathew Tindal—raised the specter of a Deist challenge to orthodox belief that reverberated through much of the first half of the eighteenth century. In 1679, Blount published *Anima Mundi* with its thinly veiled mortalism which ridiculed the immortality of the soul and compared most Christian churches "to the Muskmelons from the Dunghill" that had grown "out of the filthy Corruptions and Superstition of Paganism."[9] Four years later, his *Miracles, no Violation of the Laws of Nature* denied any empirical basis for the accounts of miracles in the Bible, and his subsequent anonymously published *Oracles of Reason* (1693) rejected all revelation and scripture. John Toland's *Christianity Not Mysterious* (1696) purportedly claimed to merely limit the sense of scripture to the test of reason, although it too implied mortalism like Blount's work before it. His subsequent publications, however, took on a distinctly radical, anti-Christian hue "in the direction of materialism, pantheism, and a republican quasi-Spinozism."[10] Anthony Collins, a good friend of philosopher John Locke, rejected the latter's distinction between scriptural accounts and religious doctrines that were above reason and contrary to reason in *An Essay Concerning the Use of Reason in Propositions the Evidence Whereof Depends on Human Testimony* (1707). Scripture could simply not be read as literal truth by a rational person, a claim he extended to the prophecies of Christ in his *Discourse of the Grounds and Reasons of the Christian Religion* (1724). Like Blount and Toland, Collins embraced mortalism and added to it a strong necessitarian strain that precluded providential intervention and made any need for divine judgment superfluous.

Given the distinctly anti-Christian tenor of their work, it is hardly surprising that these early major Deists sparked animus and controversy. George Berkeley's *Alciphron, or the Minute Philosopher* (1732) sought to expose deistic freethinking as a cover for atheism and rank libertinism. Samuel Clarke denounced Deism as a sham: "Deists, in our Days, who obstinately reject Revelation when offered to them, are not such men as *Socrates* and *Tully* were; but, under pretense of Deism, 'tis plain they are generally Ridiculers of all that is truly excellent even in natural Religion itself."[11] These charges were neither hysterical nor hyperbolic. As David Berman has cogently argued, the esoteric mortalism of the major Deists clearly obviated the need for any God at all to either intervene providentially or reward virtuous behavior in an afterlife.[12] Jonathan Israel has concluded that the natural religion of these men was hardly, upon careful examination, "distinct from atheism."[13]

With the deaths of Toland and Collins in the 1720s (Blount died in 1693), the Deist controversy in England began to subside. In part this was due to the inroads made by Anglican invocation of Newtonian physico-theology that gave scientific legitimacy to supernatural intervention.[14] But much of the change came within Deism itself as its subsequent promoters returned to the more irenic posture of Lord Herbert and sought to reconcile the religion of nature and Christianity. Matthew Tindal seems to have been a transitional figure in this development. An important government official and author of the so-called "bible of Deism," *Christianity as Old as Creation* (1730), Tindal is sometimes classed among the "radicals" for his purported mortalism and his rejection of revelation as literal truth.[15] Yet Tindal embraced rather than ridiculed Christianity, arguing that the truth of revelation recapitulated the religion of nature and that the providential design of Christianity was to deliver men from superstition and awaken them to their universal moral duties. Like Tindal, William Wollaston also found grounds for a providential deity in his *Religion of Nature Delineated* (1722) as well as the immortality of the soul. The auto-didactic artisan Thomas Chubb may have denounced priestcraft and "superstitious practices," but he also did so in defense of the true, rational Christianity as originally taught by its divine progenitor.[16] Even Thomas Woolston, whose *The Moderator between an Infidel and an Apostate* (1725) and *Six Discourses* (1727–1730) attacked the miracles of the gospels and the resurrection of Christ, accepted both providence and immortalism. The rise of this more moderate freethinking represented an attempted reconciliation between providential Deism and revealed religion. The result was the extinction of any meaningful controversy by the middle of the eighteenth century in England.[17] Deism had evolved from a militant assault on Christianity to a minor theological peccadillo for an educated elite.

The history of Deism in early America took the exact opposite trajectory. For most of the eighteenth century, Deism was a generally private creed shared by a veritable "minority within a minority" of the wealthy and learned upper classes.[18] All forty-eight members of the American Philosophical Society in 1768 shared a belief in a transcendental God and an immortal soul and only Benjamin Franklin expressed doubts about the divinity of Christ.[19] Those who embraced Deism were decidedly not anti-Christian in tone like England's major Deists. To the contrary, most colonial free thinkers claimed Jesus as "the first great deistic preacher" and expressed great admiration for his moral and spiritual teachings.[20] When early American Deists did espouse more critical principles, they generally did so in an oblique and subterranean fashion. Robert Beverley buried his latent criticism of revealed Christianity and its clerical priestcraft in his largely fictional depiction of Amerindian religion in his *History of Virginia* (1705).[21]

Far more direct was Benjamin Franklin who reprinted freethinking tracts in his *Pennsylvania Gazette*. Yet even Franklin did so for the avowed purpose of combating "dogmatism and superstition" rather than revealed Christianity per se.[22] Perhaps the only person to publicly identify himself as a Deist before the American Revolution was the Boston radical activist Thomas Young, who drafted much of the subsequently published *Reason: The Only Oracle of Man* in the 1750s.[23] In response to charges of irreligion, he published a brief creed in *The Massachusetts Spy* in November 1772. Young offered no clear affirmation of either divine providence or an afterlife. Nonetheless, he claimed that his belief in one God and His injunction "To do justly, and to love mercy and to walk humbly" (quoting Micah 6:8) comprised the core tenets of Christianity and that his more orthodox critics should leave off quibbling over "Paul, Cephas, Luther and Calvin; and put on charity."[24] Fairly uncommon to begin with, Deism in colonial British America was decidedly moderate and accommodating to the larger Christian milieu.

In the years after independence, however, that began to change. The Revolutionary struggle had unleashed radical impulses in society and religion as well as politics, and the first evidence of this in the theological domain came in 1784 when Ethan Allen, the hero of Fort Ticonderoga and revolutionary leader of the Green Mountain Boys, published *Reason: The Only Oracle of Man*. Allen had drafted much of the work some twenty years earlier with Thomas Young (Young supplied the theology, Allen added biblical criticism and commentary). Allen rejected revelation (scriptural or otherwise), prophecies, miracles, and divine providence as well as such specifically Christian doctrines as the trinity, original sin, and the need for atonement.[25] Despite its radicalism, Allen's screed attracted few followers. Very few copies ever circulated and its cumbersome style kept readers at bay. Indeed, Allen's lengthy tome had little impact other than raising the ire of the New England clergy and the specter of homegrown freethinking.

Militant Deism did find a popular spokesman in the following decade with the able pen of Thomas Paine. The legendary author of *Common Sense* brought the same militancy and rhetorical flair to the struggle for Deism that he had for independence in the first volume of his *Age of Reason* (1794). Paine lambasted the superstitions of Christianity and vilified the priestcraft that supported it. Miracles, prophecies, and the incarnation and divinity of Christ were ridiculed, as was almost every other received Christian doctrine. More than simply irrational, Christianity was the last great obstacle to the coming secular chiliad, the Age of Reason. The whole "Christian theory," he charged, was "little else than the idolatry of the ancient mythologists, accommodated to the purposes of power and revenue." It remained to "reason and philosophy to abolish the amphibious fraud."[26] Only when it was vanquished could human happiness and perfectibility be achieved. Paine's impact was due as much to the punchy power of his prose as the extreme radicalism of his views, as evidenced by this denunciation of the Old Testament:

> Whenever we read the obscene stories, the voluptuous debaucheries, the cruel and tortuous executions, the unrelenting vindictiveness, with which more than half the Bible is filled, it would be more consistent that we called it the word of a demon, than the Word of God. It is a history of wickedness, that has served to corrupt and brutalize mankind....[27]

Paine was hardly less critical of the New Testament. Even his statement on the immortality of the soul was expressed as a mere "hope." Militant Deism had arrived in early America with a bang.

His good friend Elihu Palmer fanned the flame that Paine sparked. Palmer, a former Baptist minister, traveled along the Atlantic seaboard lecturing audiences large and small about the truths of natural religion as well as the absurdities of revealed Christianity and the clerical priestcraft that supported them. A skilled biblical casuist, Palmer exposed the irrationality of Christianity and its debased moral principles in *Principles of Nature* (1801). Like Paine, Palmer hurled invective at traditional Christian doctrines like the atonement of original sin by the sacrifice of Christ: "To teach mankind virtue, they are to be presented with the example of murder; to render them happy, it is necessary to exhibit innocence in distress."[28] A radical feminist and abolitionist, Palmer found the scriptures filled with an ethical code of intolerance and vengeful cruelty in sharp contrast to the benevolent humanitarianism of his own rational creed. Palmer spread the word in two Deist newspapers he edited, *The Temple of Reason* (1800–1801) and *The Prospect* (1803–1805). By the time he died in 1806, Palmer had founded Deist societies in several cities, including New York, Philadelphia, and Baltimore.[29]

Organized Deism did not survive Palmer's demise. In fact, the Revolution had sparked a wave of evangelical revival that swept across the new republic.[30] In retrospect it is clear that the militant Deism of Paine and Palmer never really threatened mainstream Protestantism in early America. But that was not the way many orthodox divines saw it. In the years after Paine and Palmer began spreading their message, many ministers (particularly in New England) angrily denounced the growing menace of godless Deism, French-inspired Atheism, and revolutionary and conspiratorial "illuminatism." These charges took on an increasingly shrill and partisan edge, so much so that they became a campaign issue in the presidential election of 1800, which several clergymen depicted as a choice between the Federalist Patriot John Adams and the Francophile anti-Christian Thomas Jefferson.

The Founders

If nothing else, the foregoing demonstrates that there were at least some Deists among the founding generation. More than merely a polemicist, Thomas Paine served as a secretary in the Continental Congress, while Ethan Allen was one of the most important revolutionary leaders in Vermont. Moreover, both publicly championed radical critiques of revealed Christianity every bit as militant as that of Blount, Collins, or Toland. To their number might be added Governor Stephen Hopkins of Rhode Island and Philip Freneau, the founding editor of the Jeffersonian *National Gazette*. A fairly plausible case could even be made for Virginia Governor Edmund Randolph who served as attorney general and secretary of state in the first two Washington administrations.

Despite their radicalism and prominence, however, the presence of these Deist founders will simply not support the claim that the founding was a purely Enlightened affair grounded in skeptical misgivings about revealed Christianity. First of all, they represent a tiny fraction of those leaders active in the politics of the early Republic, the vast bulk of whom were thoroughly orthodox in their religious lives. As Stephen Marini has shown, "a disproportionately large number of religiously active men served in the new nation's constituent assemblies," a pattern replicated in the ratifying conventions of the Federal Constitution.[31] Far more critically, however, their radical Deism had no impact on the imbrication of religion and politics in the new nation. By any measure, that imbrication was quite extensive. Like the Continental Army, the Congresses of the central government were routinely served by chaplains who just as routinely proclaimed days of prayer and thanksgiving. Many state governments continued to support church establishments and demanded professions of faith from potential officeholders. Most even included "preambulary references to God."[32] For that matter, clergymen and lay church elders were hardly a rarity in the political councils of both nation and states. Hence Marini's conclusion that "in a host of way" in the early Republic "the church served as a school for politics."³³ The case for an Enlightened founding in fundamental tension with traditional Christianity will simply not rest on the slender foundation of a handful of freethinking radicals.

It is precisely because of this weakness that those who argue for a purely secular Enlightened founding seek to claim the A-list founders. Although still a tiny fraction of those involved in the creation of the American Republic, these figures were arguably the six most critical actors in the political establishment of the nation. If it can be argued, as Brooke Allen has claimed, that these men's "religious views really differed very little from Paine's, if at all," and that those views informed their policies and practices, then a tenable case could be made for an Enlightened founding shorn of most Christian moorings.³⁴ If Benjamin Franklin, George Washington, Alexander Hamilton, James Madison, John Adams, and Thomas Jefferson were all Deists of the militant stripe, even surreptitiously, then surely the argument for the centrality of revealed Religion to early American politics must be doubted.

Of these founders, the case for Alexander Hamilton's Deism is the weakest. Hamilton was noticeably devout in his youth and remained so throughout his college years. His piety certainly seemed to lag during his active years in politics, but there are no instances of him criticizing revealed Christianity or expressing freethinking principles in any of his voluminous writings or correspondence. Later in his life, especially after the death of his son Philip in a duel, he became quite religious again, regularly leading his family in prayer and attempting to organize a national "Christian Constitutional Society." Although a consistent spokesman for Enlightened principles in politics, the sole evidence adduced for his Deism seems to be an adulterous affair as secretary of the treasury and his nonattendance at church through much of his twenties and thirties.³⁵ Obviously, neither a sinner nor a lapsed Christian does a Deist make.

The evidence of James Madison as a Deist is hardly more substantial than that for Hamilton. Madison too was a pious youth and spent a year reading theology—among other subjects—with John Witherspoon after his graduation from Princeton. Like Hamilton, he showed few signs of deep devotion during his active years in public life. Madison did not represent himself as a champion of public religion. Yet he did, albeit reluctantly, urge public days of prayer and thanksgiving as president. He also produced not a single page in defense of Deism or in opposition to Christian doctrine or revelation. The sole evidence for his Deism comes from his efforts on behalf of religious disestablishment in Virginia in the

1780s and in the First Amendment to the Constitution. The implication here seems to be that Madison sought to build what Jefferson called a "wall of separation" between church and state, and that the only possible motive for such an effort was an attempt to insulate an Enlightened republic from the baleful effects of religious dogma and superstition. Yet as Stephen Botein argued in the case of the Federal Constitution, the motivation behind "so secular a document" was an attempt to "forestall criticism from sectarians fearful of oppression by a national religious establishment."[36] Daniel Dreisbach has shown that the same logic applied to disestablishment in Virginia. Far from a Madisonian urge to separate church and state, the political impetus behind the legislation came from dissenting evangelical churches that feared a revived Anglican establishment and sought to create a "flexible church-state model that fosters cooperation between religious interests and the civil state."[37] As for the disestablishment clause of the First Amendment, Donald Drakeman has demonstrated that Madison's role as draftsman has been vastly exaggerated, and that those who took the lead in that endeavor sought to preclude a federal establishment rather than erect a wall of separation.[38] Madison may not have been a very fervent or orthodox believer, but there is simply no convincing evidence that he was a Deist.

The Deism of George Washington rests on an equally slender evidentiary base, although a bit more tantalizing. Notoriously private and stoic in his mien, there is little clear evidence of Washington's religious convictions. Although he attended church regularly as president and enjoined religious services on his soldiers, his church going in private life was intermittent and he was never seen to take communion or kneel at the name of Jesus in prayer (a traditional part of the Anglican liturgy). While his writings and correspondence are replete with references to God and Providence and are sprinkled with scriptural phrases, scholars have strained to find references to Jesus Christ. It is at least possible that Washington's refusal to commemorate or refer to Jesus was because he doubted his divinity. Even so, that would make him a Socinian or Unitarian rather than a Deist. There is certainly no evidence of anything distinctly Deist in his writings. His 1783 Circular to the States specifically praised "the pure and benign light of Revelation" as a principal cause of "the blessings of society," something no self-respecting Deist would do.[39] In his first inaugural, he explicitly offered his adoration and "supplications to that Almighty Being who rules over the universe" and whose "providential aid" had been so remarkably conspicuous in "every step" by which the American people had progressed in "the character of an independent nation."[40] Most famously, his farewell address included an encomium to religious belief as a necessary bulwark to social and moral order: "reason and experience both forbid us to expect that National morality can prevail in exclusion of religious principle."[41] Far from advocating a strict separation of church and state, Washington "consistently sought to use governmental authority to encourage religion and to foster the religious character of the American people."[42] If Washington did harbor Deist beliefs, they evidently had no impact on his public actions or pronouncements as commander in chief or chief executive of the new nation.

In stark contrast to Washington, Thomas Jefferson left a vivid corpus of heterodox religious opinions in letters and writings. By his collegiate years, Jefferson had become a veritable free thinker, rejecting the divinity of Christ and the biblical accounts of miracles as superstitious priestcraft. A lifelong reductive materialist of the most rigid sort, he considered talk of immaterial or spiritual entities mere nonsense; "to say that the human soul, angels, god, are immaterial, is to say they are nothings."[43] Yet while Jefferson's God may have been material, he was decidedly not mechanistic. Like most Newtonians of his day, Jefferson did not believe that the laws of nature were intrinsic to the universe any more than motion was inherent to matter. Jefferson's cosmos required a superintending Deity to intervene and hold chaos at bay.[44] Jefferson also believed in an afterlife with rewards and punishments and deeply admired the moral teachings of Jesus. This constellation of beliefs was fully consonant with the moderate Deism of the latter English free thinkers, and it is quite likely that for much of his life Jefferson would have accepted that label.[45] That certainly changed in the 1790s, however, when he became acquainted with the person and writings of the famed chemist, political radical, and Unitarian minister Joseph Priestley. From Priestley he learned that he had been a Christian all along.[46] Jesus never claimed divinity and taught the same materialistic worldview Priestley found in the Old Testament; according to Priestley, the immaterialism and spiritualist doctrines of the New Testament were intrusions of Platonic mumbo-jumbo in the ensuing centuries.[47] Although Priestley may have been a theological radical, he was certainly no Deist. His support for the French Revolution was predicated on his reading of the prophecies contained in the Book of Revelation.[48] Jefferson embraced his newfound Unitarian creed with great ardor and began compiling a redaction of the genuine teachings of Christ shorn of their subsequent Platonic trappings. His second iteration of this project—"The Life and

Morals of Jesus"—comprised forty-six pages of "the most sublime and benevolent code of morals which has ever been offered to man." These teachings were the core doctrines of the most radically and truly reformed Christianity, he insisted, "such as were professed and acted on by the *unlettered* apostles, the Apostolic fathers, and the Christians of the 1st century."[49] So obviously authentic and true was the Unitarian reformation of Christianity that Jefferson never doubted all Americans before too long would adopt it. In his own mind, at least, the mature Thomas Jefferson was a Christian and one of the few who truly understood the teachings of its founder.

If anything, John Adams was even less orthodox than Jefferson. A Unitarian since his adolescence, Adams had early kept company with all manner of free thinkers from Deists and skeptics to outright unbelievers. He never accepted the materialism of Jefferson and Priestly, but neither did he embrace the immaterialism of Jonathan Edwards or George Berkeley. Adams's usual position on most mysteries—metaphysical or theological—was a skepticism that alternated between fideism and agnosticism. The immortality of the soul seemed beyond reason and demonstration, but he humbly accepted the doctrine nonetheless. The divine purpose behind the biblical account of creation was not only inscrutable but also palpably inconceivable: "suppose an eternal self-existent Being existing from Eternity, possessed of infinite Wisdom, Goodness and Power, in absolute Solitude, Six thousand Years ago, conceiving the benevolent project of creating a Universe." Adams could find no rational purpose behind such a project, but he accepted it anyway.[50] But he drew the line at the doctrines of limited atonement and eternal damnation of the reprobate. Such a God would be a sadistic tyrant and Adams would have no part of such belief. "Howl, Snarl, bite, Ye Calvinistick! Ye Athanasian Divines, if You will," he wrote to his old friend Jefferson. "Ye will say, I am no Christian: I say Ye are no Christian: and there the Account is ballanced."[51] Adams, then, was a Universalist as well as a Unitarian who, like the Reverend Charles Chauncy of Boston, believed that a purely benevolent and unitary God would ultimately save all men. But he also decidedly considered himself a Christian and thought that the "general Principles of Christianity" were every bit as "eternal and immutable, as the Existence and Attributes of God."[52] For all his heterodoxy and skepticism, Adams was no radical Deist critic of revealed Christianity. "Without Religion this World would be Something not fit to be mentioned in polite Company," he declaimed, adding as if the point were not obvious, "I mean Hell."[53]

Among all the A-list founders, only Benjamin Franklin can be described as a Deist without qualification or cavil. Even as a teenager, Franklin was so outspoken in his Deism and "indiscrete Disputations about Religion" that his fellow Bostonians began to shun him "as an Infidel or Atheist."[54] While working in London at the age of nineteen, he published a truly radical tract, *A Dissertation on Liberty and Necessity, Pleasure and Pain*. Adopting the thorough determinism of Anthony Collins, he denied the existence of free will and inferred from the existence of an omnipotent and benevolent God that "Evil doth not exist," that talk of sin was mere superstition, and that such notions of right and wrong and virtue and vice were merely relative to pleasure and pain.[55] Franklin then went on to prove that the total quantity of pleasure and pain was balanced in each life, thus eliminating any grounds "for the future Existence of the Soul."[56] Three years later, he drafted his own private creed that posited that "the infinite" generated a variety of Gods, one for each solar system. Although each of these deities was "not above caring for us" and was worthy of praise and worship, Franklin was not convinced that they were immortal and conspicuously failed to endorse either an afterlife or providential intervention.[57] The young Franklin was thus a remarkably militant Deist, denying the immortality of the soul, divine intervention in the course of natural and human affairs, frankly contradicting the biblical account of creation, and offering a hedonistic reduction of morality that smacked of Mandevillean libertinism.[58] In many ways, Franklin's Deism was even more radically anti-Christian than that of Allen, Paine, and Palmer.

As Franklin matured, however, his militancy faded. By 1732, he was arguing before the Junto Club that God both could and did intervene directly in human and natural history through "special providences."[59] In the early 1750s, he explicitly rejected his previous determinism, claiming that God had endowed mankind with free will.[60] He came to see the publication of his Deist tract and its radical tenets as one of the great errors of his youth, particularly when he considered the immoral behavior it seemed to provoke in himself and his fellow freethinking comrades.[61] Franklin had come to appreciate that, as he warned his readers in *Poor Richard's Almanac*, "talking against Religion is unchaining a Tyger; The Beast let loose may worry his Deliverer."[62] From his mid-twenties until his death, Franklin had abandoned his radicalism and made peace with revealed Religion. He remained a Deist, but one of a decidedly moderate and irenic stripe. His final creed, communicated to Ezra Stiles in his last year of life, affirmed a providential God and an immortal soul that "will be treated with justice in another life respecting its conduct in this."[63] He had even quite famously called for prayers at the Federal Convention in Philadelphia.

Christianity and Enlightenment in the Founding

With the sole exception of Benjamin Franklin, then, all of the A-list founders were self-identified Christians. In this regard, they were no different than their less prominent colleagues. None tucked up their cudgels against the tenets of revealed Christianity, regardless of personal misgivings. Indeed, except for Jefferson, all supported public prayer both within political bodies and throughout the polity at large. And even Jefferson, the most outspoken champion of a strict separation of church and state, thought popular religion was vital to the survival of the experiment in republican government. "Can the liberties of a nation be thought secure," he wondered, if they did not rest on "their only firm basis, a conviction in the minds of the people that these liberties are the gift of God?"[64] If the convictions and practices of the most prominent statesmen is any index, the American founding drew on the moral and political authority of religion, and religion was critical to the political culture of the early Republic.

But if the regime the founders established was based on revealed religion, it was just as evidently built on an Enlightened republican foundation. Each of these prominent leaders articulated Enlightened ideals of constitutional government and practical policy. The federal constitutional order they established not only forbade any church establishment, it also explicitly rejected any religious tests for officeholders and utterly failed to mention or recognize the deity in its text. Moreover, the unabashed if privately held Unitarianism of the second and third presidents of the United States—a conviction possibly shared by the first—suggests that Enlightened convictions informed their religion every bit as much as religion underlay their Enlightened politics. These were, then, Enlightened Christians, a term that might well characterize a significant number of the leading political figures in a republic populated by a far more orthodox citizenry.

The apparent conundrum of a founding both secular and religious is based on a mistaken belief that the thrust of the Enlightenment in America was hostile to received Christianity. That may have been true in late eighteenth-century France, where the philosophes rallied to Voltaire's angry call to *ecrasez l'infame*, but it was decidedly not the case in early America. As most scholars have agreed, the tenor of the American Enlightenment was moderate rather than radical, and its exponents sought to reform existing institutions from within rather than criticize and uproot from without. This was certainly true with regard to religion. The Enlightened in America rarely rejected Christianity tout court; rather, they embraced those elements they found attractive and simply ignored and dropped those they did not. Given the ever-widening array of sects and tenets that proliferated, it was not too difficult to find a reasonably comfortable spiritual fit. Even the Deist Franklin, after all, was able to accommodate and even grudgingly appreciate American revealed Christianity.

If the Enlightened in America had little difficulty in making peace with revealed religion, that was in no small part due to the remarkable inroads Enlightened doctrine made in American Protestantism. In fact, one of the earliest and most powerful forces for Enlightenment in British America was the latitudinarianism of prominent low-church Anglicans like John Tillotson and Edward Stillingfleet. Their focus on a benevolent God and a beautiful harmonious universe, and their stress on moral virtue over doctrinal commitment found an appreciative audience among the wealthy, educated classes throughout the colonies, particularly among the Chesapeake gentry. It also garnered a following in Congregational New England. By the last quarter of the seventeenth century, a small but influential coterie of clergymen abandoned the themes of total depravity and ceased preaching for conviction. Instead they argued for the benevolence of God, the beauty of his cosmic order, and the duties of compassionate behavior.[65] By the early eighteenth century, this Enlightened seed had blossomed into a growing Arminian minority among the Congregational churches who rejected the Calvinist heritage in toto. Perhaps the ultimate fruit of this amalgamation of Enlightenment in New England Congregationalism was the endowment of the Dudleian Lectures in the 1750s. Patterned after the Boyle lectures in England, Dudleians used natural theology to support reformed ideals against their detractors, especially Roman Catholics. The result was the promulgation of a "specific strain of Protestantism that wedded low-church ideas with Enlightenment rationality."[66] Dudleian clergymen taught that reason was the handmaid of revelation, for when properly read in the light of reason, "the Gospel adopts the whole law of nature."[67] If the Enlightened did not feel the need to struggle against Christianity in early America, in part this was because so many established clergymen had preemptively declared a truce.

Even evangelical new lights, many of whose early endeavors to articulate a "new divinity" was meant to contain a creeping Arminian rationalism, ultimately could not resist the allure of the new learning. As their schismatic churches became more settled and they sought to establish colleges to fill new pulpits, they ineluctably were drawn to the tenets of Anglophone Enlightenment. Mark Noll has noted the particular affinity of American evangelicals for Scottish common sense philosophy.[68] Nowhere was this affinity more evident than among new side Presbyterians. By 1775, the evangelical wing of the Presbyterian Church had absorbed its old side foes and emerged as the most powerful denomination in the mid-Atlantic, assuming "effective direction" of the revolutionary cause throughout the region.[69] By that point, however, they had largely absorbed the core teachings of the Enlightenment, and their college at Princeton—once presided over by the immaterialist Calvinist Jonathan Edwards—was imbuing its charges with a Christianity laced with Scottish Enlightened teachings, including those of the notorious infidel, David Hume.[70] The same pattern persisted across the new nation after independence. As Gordon Wood has noted, the revivals of the early Republic did not produce a creed that repudiated "the ideals of the Enlightenment; instead, it absorbed and vulgarized them."[71]

This is not to say that every denomination, much less every Protestant believer, absorbed the Enlightenment without reservation. Given the inherently volatile, sectarian, and schismatic nature of American Christianity—the result of the longstanding absence of either powerful ecclesiastical authorities or governments willing and able to enforce established churches—it is surely impossible to look for anything like strict philosophical or doctrinal unity among the major denominations.[72] No doubt Wood is correct that many American Protestant believers endorsed a "vulgarized," watered-down version of the Anglophone Enlightenment. But the same is true on the other side. The Christianity of the Enlightened was every bit as diffuse and diluted as the Enlightenment of the more orthodox Christians in the nation as a whole. Any Christianity that included among its adherents men like President John Adams who doubted the miracles recounted in scripture and positively denied such fundamental doctrines as the eternal damnation of the reprobate and the divinity and resurrection of Jesus Christ was a faith so broad as to almost lack any meaningful boundaries. And it was this broad and diffuse religion and religiosity that underlay the American founding, not a narrow Calvinism or sweeping revivalism. It was this broad and diverse range of opinions among Christians that necessitated not only federal disestablishment, but also more pointedly the use of natural religious language in our founding documents and speeches. Only such ecumenical and vague phraseology and ecclesiastic neutrality could avoid giving offense to one sect or another in a nation where sectarian diversity and religious liberty was bred in the bone. But in practice such ecumenicism was hardly distinguishable from outright secularism. The Christianity that served as a founding creed in the new nation was a remarkably "big tent" affair, including Calvinists and Quakers, evangelicals and Universalists, and Unitarians and fundamentalists. Evidently, the tent was so capacious as to even comfortably accommodate the odd Deist.

Notes

1. See, for example, Gary T. Amos, *Defending the Declaration: How the Bible and Christianity Influenced the Writing of the Declaration of Independence* (Brentwood, TN: Wolgemuth and Hyatt Publishers, 1989) and John Eidsmoe, *Christianity and the Constitution: The Faith of Our Founding Fathers* (Grand Rapids, MI: Baker Book House, 1987).
2. Recent instances include Gary Kowalski, *Revolutionary Spirits: The Enlightened Faith of America's Founding Fathers* (New York: BlueBridge, 2008) and Brooke Allen, *Moral Minority: Our Skeptical Founding Fathers* (Chicago: Ivan R. Dee, 2006). For a more balanced popular treatment of religion in the American founding, see Steven Waldman, *Founding Faith: How Our Founding Fathers Forged a Radical New Approach to Religious Liberty* (New York: Random House, 2009).
3. Gordon S. Wood, "Religion and the American Revolution," in Harry S. Stout and D. G. Hart, eds., *New Directions in American Religious History* (New York: Oxford University Press, 1997), 173.
4. Jon Butler, "Coercion, Miracle, Reason: Rethinking the American Religious Experience in the Revolutionary Age," in Ronald Hoffman and Peter J. Albert, eds., *Religion in a Revolutionary Age* (Charlottesville: University Press of Virginia, 1994), 21. For a more popular and sustained treatment of "deistic" influences on the founders, see David L. Holmes, *The Faiths of the Founding Fathers* (New York: Oxford University Press, 2006).
5. Alan Heimert, *Religion and the American Mind: From the Great Awakening to the Revolution* (Cambridge, MA: Harvard University Press, 1966). Also see Rhys Isaac, *The Transformation of Virginia, 1740–1790* (Chapel Hill: University of North Carolina Press, 1982) and Patricia U. Bonomi, *Under the Cope of Heaven: Religion, Society, and Politics in Colonial America* (New York: Oxford University Press, 1986).
6. Ruth H. Bloch, *Visionary Republic: Millennial Themes in American Thought, 1756–1800* (New York: Cambridge University Press, 1985) and Nathan O. Hatch, *The Sacred Cause of Liberty: Republican Thought and the Millennium in Revolutionary New England* (New Haven, CT: Yale University Press, 1977).
7. Edwin S. Gaustad, *Faith of the Founders: Religion and the New Nation, 1776–1826* (Waco, TX: Baylor University Press, 2004).

8. See David Berman, "Deism, Immortality, and the Art of Theological Lying," in J. A. Leo Lemay, ed., *Deism, Masonry, and the Enlightenment: Essays Honoring Alfred Owen Aldridge* (Newark: University of Delaware Press, 1987), 61–78.
9. Quoted in Roger L. Emerson, "Latitudinarianism and the English Deists," in Lemay, *Deism, Masonry, and the Enlightenment*, 24.
10. Jonathan I. Israel, *Enlightenment Contested: Philosophy, Modernity, and the Emancipation of Man, 1650–1752* (New York: Oxford University Press, 2006), 123.
11. Samuel Clarke, *A Demonstration of the Being and Attributes of God, More Particularly in Answer to Mr. Hobbs, Spinoza, and Their Followers* (London, 1728), 170.
12. Berman in fact concludes that "the history of deism may turn out to be more like the history of covert atheism," in "Deism," 77.
13. Israel, *Enlightenment Contested*, 124.
14. Margaret C. Jacob, *The Newtonians and the English Revolution, 1689–1720* (Ithaca, NY: Cornell University Press, 1976).
15. See Berman, "Deism," 62 and 77.
16. Israel, *Enlightenment Contested*, 124.
17. Ibid., 352.
18. Jon Butler, "Coercion, Miracle, Reason," 20.
19. Harold E. Taussig, "Deism in Philadelphia During the Age of Franklin," *Pennsylvania History* 37:3 (1970), 217–236.
20. Herbert M. Morais, *Deism in Eighteenth Century America* (New York: Columbia University Press, 1934), 15.
21. J. A. Leo Lemay, "The Amerindian in the Early American Enlightenment: Deistic Satire in Robert Beverley's *History of Virginia* (1705)," in Lemay, *Deism, Masonry, and the Enlightenment*, 79–92.
22. A. O. Aldridge, "Benjamin Franklin and the Maryland Gazette," *Maryland Historical Magazine* 44:3 (1949), 182–184.
23. For more on Young's career, see Pauline Maier, "Reason and Revelation: The Radicalism of Dr. Thomas Young," in Joseph Ellis, ed., Special Issue *An American Enlightenment*, in *American Quarterly* 28 (1976), 229–249.
24. Quoted in A. O. Aldridge, "Natural Religion and Deism in America before Ethan Allen and Thomas Paine," *William and Mary Quarterly*, 3rd ser., 54:4 (1997), 847.
25. For a good treatment of Allen's Deist beliefs, see Kerry Walters, *Revolutionary Deists: Early America's Rational Infidels* (Amherst, NY: Prometheus Books, 2011), 87–112.
26. Thomas Paine, *The Age of Reason*, in *The Writings of Thomas Paine*, Moncure Daniel Conway, ed. (New York: G.P. Putnam's Sons, 1908), 4:25.
27. Ibid., 34.
28. Quoted in Walters, *Revolutionary Deists*, 192.
29. For a good account of Palmer's career as a Deist, see ibid., 179–211.
30. Stephen E. Marini, "Religion, Politics, and Ratification," in Hoffman and Albert, *Religion in a Revolutionary Age*, 196.
31. Marini, "Religion, Politics, and Ratification," 188–189.

32. Stephen Botein, "Religious Dimensions of the Early American State," in Richard Beeman, Stephen Botein, and Edward C. Carter II, eds., *Beyond Confederation: Origins of the Constitution and American National Identity* (Chapel Hill: University of North Carolina Press, 1987), 319.
33. Marini, "Religion, Politics, and Ratification," 188.
34. Allen, *Moral Minority*, 162.
35. Ibid., 123.
36. Botein, "Religious Dimensions," 320–321.
37. Daniel L. Dreisbach, "Church–State Debate in the Virginia Legislature: From the Declaration of Rights to the Statue for Establishing Religious Freedom," in Garret Ward Sheldon and Daniel L. Dreisbach, *Religion and Political Culture in Jefferson's Virginia* (Lanham, MD: Rowman and Littlefield, 2000), 148–155.
38. Donald L. Drakeman, "James Madison and the First Amendment Establishment of Religion Clause," in Sheldon and Dreisbach, eds., *Religion and Political Culture in Jefferson's Virginia*, 219–230.
39. George Washington, "Circular to the States," in William B. Allen, ed., *George Washington: A Collection* (Indianapolis, IN: Liberty Fund, 1988), 241.
40. George Washington, "First Inaugural Speech," ibid., 460–461.
41. George Washington, "Farewell Address," ibid., 521.
42. Vincent Phillip Muñoz, *God and the Founders: Madison, Washington, and Jefferson* (New York: Cambridge University Press, 2009), 50.
43. Thomas Jefferson to John Adams, August 15, 1820, in Lester J. Cappon, ed., *The Adams-Jefferson Letters: The Complete Correspondence Between Thomas Jefferson and Abigail and John Adams* (Chapel Hill: University of North Carolina Press, 1959), 567–568.
44. Edwin S. Gaustad, *Sworn on the Altar of God: A Religious Biography of Thomas Jefferson* (Grand Rapids, MI: Wm. B. Eerdmans, 1996), 36–37.
45. Kerry Walters has described Jefferson as a "deistic Christian," an apt label for someone who "endorsed what he took to be the rational heart of Christianity while jettisoning, in good Enlightenment style, its supernaturalist excesses." *Revolutionary Deists*, 17.
46. For a good treatment of Jefferson's "conversion" to Priestley's variant of Unitarianism, see Paul Conkin, "Priestley and Jefferson: Unitarianism as a Religion for a New Revolutionary Age," in Hoffman and Albert, *Religion in a Revolutionary Age*, 290–307.
47. On the biblical grounds for Priestley's materialism, see Ira V. Brown, "The Religion of Joseph Priestley," *Pennsylvania History* 24:2 (1957), 85–100.
48. Clarke Garrett, "Joseph Priestley, the Millennium, and the French Revolution," *Journal of the History of Ideas* 34:1 (1973), 51–66.
49. Thomas Jefferson to John Adams, October 12, 1813, in Cappon, *Adams-Jefferson*, 383–384.
50. John Adams to Thomas Jefferson, September 14, 1813, ibid., 374–375.
51. Ibid., 373–374.

52. John Adams to Thomas Jefferson, June 28, 1813, ibid., 340.
53. John Adams to Thomas Jefferson, April 19, 1817, ibid., 509.
54. *The Autobiography of Benjamin Franklin with Related Documents*, Louis P. Masur, ed., 2nd ed. (New York: Bedford/St. Martin's, 2003), 44.
55. Benjamin Franklin, *A Dissertation on Liberty and Necessity, Pleasure and Pain* (London, 1725), in *The Papers of Benjamin Franklin*, Leonard W. Labaree, ed. (New Haven, CT: Yale University Press, 1959), 1:59.
56. Ibid., 68–69.
57. Benjamin Franklin, "Articles of Belief and Acts of Religion," November 20, 1728, ibid., 102–105.
58. In fact, Franklin's tract was so radical that it earned him an introduction to Mandeville. See his account in *Autobiography*, 62.
59. Walters, *Revolutionary Deists*, 73.
60. *Poor Richard's Almanac*, in *Papers of Benjamin Franklin* (New Haven, CT: Yale University Press, 1961), 4:95.
61. *Autobiography*, 73–74.
62. *Poor Richard's Almanac*, in *Papers of Benjamin Franklin*, 4:96.
63. Quoted in Allen, *Moral Minority*, 24.
64. Thomas Jefferson, *Notes on the State of Virginia*, William Peden, ed. (Chapel Hill: University of North Carolina Press, 1982), 163.
65. John Corrigan, *The Prism of Piety: Catholick Congregational Clergy at the Beginning of the Enlightenment* (New York: Oxford University Press, 1991) and Michael P. Winship, *Seers of God: Puritan Providentialism in the Restoration and Early Enlightenment* (Baltimore, MD: Johns Hopkins University Press, 1996).
66. Leslee K. Gilbert, "The Alter of Liberty: Enlightened Dissent and the Dudleian Lectures, 1755–1765," *Historical Journal of Massachusetts* 31:2 (2003), 151.
67. Andrew Eliot, *A Discourse on Natural Religion* (Boston, 1771), xxxvii.
68. Mark A. Noll, "Common Sense Traditions and American Evangelical Thought," *American Quarterly* 37:2 (1985), 216–238.
69. Sheldon S. Cohen and Larry R. Gerlach, "Princeton in the Coming of the American Revolution," *New Jersey History*, 92:2 (1974), 69–92.
70. Mark A. Noll, "The Irony of the Enlightenment for Presbyterians in the Early Republic," *Journal of the Early Republic* 5:2 (1985), 149–175, and *Princeton and the Republic, 1768–1822: The Search for a Christian Enlightenment in the Era of Samuel Stanhope Smith* (Princeton, NJ: Princeton University Press, 1989).
71. Gordon S. Wood, "Religion and the American Revolution," in Stout and Hart, *New Directions in American Religious History*, 190.
72. On the volatile and diffuse nature of early American Christianity, see Patricia U. Bonomi, "Religious Dissent and the Case of American Exceptionalism," in Hoffman and Albert, *Religion in a Revolutionary Age*, 31–51, and *Under The Cope of Heaven: Religion, Society, and Politics in Colonial America* (New York: Oxford University Press, 1986).

2

Vindiciae, Contra Tyrannos:
The Influence of the Reformed Tradition in the American Founding

Mark David Hall

IN *ORIGINAL MEANINGS*, Jack Rakove observes that the "larger intellectual world within which the Constitution is often located—the Enlightened world of Locke and Montesquieu, Hume and Blackstone, plain whigs and real whigs, common lawyers and Continental jurists—has been the subject of extensive analysis." Significantly, he does not mention religion in this context. Historians are better than political scientists and law professors at recognizing that faith mattered to many Americans in the founding era, but even they have a tendency to treat America's founders as Deists who embraced a rationalist approach to politics and who produced secular documents such as the Declaration of Independence, Constitution, and Bill of Rights. Although there are important exceptions, scholars are still too prone to neglect the significant influence of Christianity, generally, and the Reformed theological and attendant political traditions, more specifically, on the founding generation.[1]

One reason Calvinism is neglected is that students of the founding often view the era through the eyes of southern Anglican gentlemen: Thomas Jefferson, James Madison, and George Washington; men born outside America: Alexander Hamilton and Thomas Paine; and the cosmopolitan Benjamin Franklin, who lived most of the last thirty-five years of his life in Europe. The only member of a Congregational or Presbyterian church among the famous founders is John Adams, but like some of his fellow Congregationalists (especially in and around Boston) he was moving rapidly toward Unitarianism. These men were brilliant and influential, but they are not representative of the many American leaders who were firmly rooted in the Reformed tradition.[2]

Sydney Ahlstrom, in his magisterial history of religion in America, estimates that the Reformed tradition was "the religious heritage of three-fourths of the American people in 1776." Similarly, Yale historian Harry Stout states that prior to the War for Independence "three out of four colonists were connected with Reformed denominations (mostly Congregational and Presbyterian)." These figures may be high—neither scholar explains or defends them—but numerous studies make it clear that Calvinist churches dominated New England and were well represented throughout the rest of the nation. Although some scholars have asserted that few Americans attended these or other churches in the founding era, as we shall see this claim does not survive close scrutiny.[3]

Not only were well over a majority of all Americans in the founding era associated with Calvinist churches, adherents of this tradition exercised significant influence through a variety of venues. New England was the intellectual and cultural center of America until well into the nineteenth century. Literally millions of Americans learned to read using the explicitly Calvinist *The New-England Primer* (more than two million copies were printed in the eighteenth century alone, and in spite of its name the text was used throughout America).[4] As well, many pedagogues throughout the nation were members of Reformed faiths. For instance, James Madison was educated by the Scottish Presbyterian minister Donald Robertson (about whom he later said, "all that I have been in life I owe largely to that man"), the Anglican rector Thomas Martin (a graduate of the Presbyterian College of New Jersey), and the Presbyterian minister John Witherspoon. Under President Witherspoon, the College of New Jersey produced "five delegates to the Constitutional Convention; one U.S. President (Madison); a vice president (the notorious Aaron Burr); forty-nine U.S. representatives; twenty-eight U.S. senators; three Supreme Court Justices; eight U.S. district judges; one secretary of state; three attorneys general; and two foreign ministers." It is noteworthy that only two of the 178 students who studied under Witherspoon between 1769 and 1775 became Loyalists.[5]

The primary purpose of this chapter is to introduce readers to the Reformed political tradition, show how the tradition manifested itself in colonial American politics (especially in New England), and demonstrate that Calvinism was still a vibrant and influential force in late-eighteenth-century

America. I conclude by suggesting that shifting our focus from a handful of elites to a broader range of founders (emphasizing for the purposes of this chapter members of Reformed congregations) helps scholars better understand key founding documents such as the Declaration of Independence, the Constitution, and the First Amendment.

Reformed Political Theory

Reformed political theory is a branch of Christian political theory, so it is not surprising to find significant overlap between how Calvinists and other Christians view politics. General Christian propositions with implications for politics include the ideas that humans are created in the image of God, men and women are sinful, and God has established different institutions for various purposes: notably, the family, church, and state. Virtually all Christian political thinkers have recognized that civil authorities are ordained by God and that there is a biblical obligation to obey them, but that the obligation is not absolute. Although generalizations can be dangerous, it is fair to say that between Constantine and the Protestant Reformation most Christians who thought about politics assumed that monarchy was the preferred form of government, saw rulers as playing an important role in promoting the common good, and paid little attention to subjective individual rights. While they believed that Christians should refuse to obey an unjust law, virtually none of them contended that the people had a right to revolt against unjust rulers.

Reformed political theory broke in significant ways from previous Christian views. Of course Reformed thinkers borrowed from earlier thinkers, and the tradition evolved over time. However, in the same way that scholars are comfortable speaking of a "liberal tradition" that includes John Locke, John Stuart Mill, John Rawls, and, according to numerous scholars, many founders, so too is it possible to speak of a Reformed tradition that includes John Calvin, John Knox, Samuel Rutherford, John Winthrop, and many of America's founders. Because some readers may be unfamiliar with this tradition, I offer a brief introduction to it below. Obviously a few pages on a tradition that spans centuries and involves a contentious and wordy people cannot do it justice, but it does allow me to introduce key themes that had a significant impact on American political ideas.

The Protestant Reformation was a wide-ranging movement opposed to perceived abuses by the Roman Catholic Church. It may be conveniently traced to 1517, when Martin Luther nailed his *Ninety-Five Theses* to the Wittenberg castle church door. For our purposes, the work of John Calvin is of particular interest. Calvin was born in France but lived most of his adult life in Geneva, Switzerland, which he helped govern from 1536–1538 and 1541–1564. In 1536, he published the first edition of his *Institutes of the Christian Religion*, a volume he revised several times until the final 1559 edition. The work, along with his voluminous biblical commentaries, has proven enormously influential among his followers, who were represented most prominently in America by the Puritans.

Calvin's work echoed the great battle cries of the Reformation, such as *sola fide* and *sola scriptura*, and it reinforced the seminal notion of the priesthood of all believers. Reformers rejected the idea that the church and her priests were necessary intermediaries between common persons and God, and that the Church as an institution possessed the authority to speak for God. Individuals were told that they were responsible for their relationship with God, and that His will for them is most clearly revealed in the Holy Scriptures. This belief led to widespread male literacy and a commitment to translating and printing the Bible in the vernacular. These views and practices helped undermine existing hierarchies and nurtured a desire for self-government. Although ecclesiastical structures varied, Reformed churches leaned heavily toward republican forms of government, and nowhere was this more true than among the Separatists and Puritans who immigrated to America. New England Calvinists debated the relative merits of pure congregationalism versus more presbyterian forms of church governance, but under both models church members played critical roles in governing themselves.[6]

Particularly significant within the Reformed tradition is the insistence that God is sovereign over all creation. Reformers attempted to apply their faith to all elements of life, including activities such as raising children, conducting business, and participating in politics. This "sanctification" of every aspect of life contributed to the tremendous economic and social development that marked most countries in which Reformed Protestants became a majority. From their earliest days in power, Calvinists were concerned with creating Christian political institutions and practices. Yet they were not theocrats, and they even expanded contemporary distinctions between church and state. Reformers believed that both church and civil state were divinely mandated institutions and that the two should work closely together to create a Christian society. They believed, however, that those functions divinely delegated to the church should not be exercised by the civil state or vice versa. Because only God is sovereign, and because of their commitment to the doctrine of total depravity, they insisted that both ecclesiastical and civil authority be limited. As well, Calvinist thinkers retained the traditional Christian idea that governments should promote the common good.[7]

Calvinist movements sprang up throughout Europe, and they were particularly successful in Switzerland, Holland, Scotland, and England. In these and other countries—notably France, where the Huguenots were a persecuted minority—they faced hostile regimes. Although the Reformers initially advocated passive obedience, they rapidly developed a resistance theology unlike anything ever seen on a widespread level in Christendom. Calvin, one of the most politically conservative of the Reformers, cautiously contended that in some cases inferior magistrates might resist an ungodly ruler. However, Reformers such as John Knox (1505–1572), George Buchanan (1506–1582), and Samuel Rutherford (1600–1661) of Scotland; Theodore Beza (1519–1605) of France and Switzerland; David Pareus (1548–1622) of Germany; and Christopher Goodman (1520–1603) and John Ponet (1516–1556) of England argued that inferior magistrates should resist unjust rulers, and even permitted or *required* citizens to do so.[8]

Among the most famous pieces of resistance literature is Stephanus Junius Brutus's *Vindiciae, Contra Tyrannos* (1579). Written by a Huguenot, probably Philippe du Plessis Mornay (1549–1623) or Hubert Languet (1518–1581), the *Vindiciae* contends that men originally exist in a state of natural liberty, and that "the natural law [*ius Naturale*] teaches us to preserve and protect our life and liberty—without which life is scarcely life at all—against all force and injustice." Humans are "free by nature, impatient of servitude," and they create civil governments to promote the common good. Legitimate rulers are established only by virtue of a twofold covenant (*duplex foedus*). The first of these, between God, king, and people, commits the people and ruler to obey God. If either the king or the people turn from God and so violate this covenant, it is void. The second covenant, which is between the ruler and the people, stipulates that the consent of the people is necessary for government to be legitimate. The people promise to obey the king as long as he rules justly. Rulers who are illegitimate, negligent, unjust, or tyrannical break this covenant and forfeit their right to rule. When the people resist ungodly or unjust rulers, they are "procuring that which is their natural right [*droit naturel*]."[9]

For Reformers, families, churches, and civil governments should be grounded in agreements between humans that are witnessed and enforced by God. Of course, they did not invent covenants, but they emphasized their use and significance—particularly with respect to civil and ecclesiastical authorities. Moreover, as represented well by Brutus's first covenant, they believed that God makes covenants with peoples, much as He did with the ancient Jews. These covenanted people then have an important role to play in God's plan to bring about His kingdom on earth. Failure to keep these covenants, clergy routinely warned in sermons known as jeremiads, would result in God's punishment. The rights and responsibilities associated with such covenants would have an important influence in America.[10]

One might object that nothing in the preceding section is *distinctive* to the Reformed tradition. Indeed, Quentin Skinner has argued that even works like *Vindiciae* are not "specifically Calvinist at all," but that ideas contained in them were borrowed from Scholastic authors.[11] As a matter of the genealogy of ideas this may be the case, but what is critical for the purposes of this chapter is that these ideas were most extensively developed, defended, and applied within the Reformed tradition. Within a generation of Calvin, virtually every Reformed civil and ecclesiastical leader was convinced that the Bible taught that governments should be limited, that they should be based on the consent of the governed, that rulers should promote the common good and the Christian faith, and that unjust or ungodly rulers should be resisted or even overthrown. Whether or not these ideas are inherently connected to Calvinism, the Reformed tradition became a major means by which they became a part of American political culture.

The Reformed Tradition in America

Protestantism's progress began inauspiciously in England when Henry VIII severed ties with Rome and created an independent Church of England in 1534. This institution, however, remained too "popish" for many Calvinists, who became known as Puritans because of their desire to purify completely this church. Some Separatists, known today as the Pilgrims, eventually gave up hope for reformation of the English church and, facing increasing persecution in their homeland, fled to Holland in 1608 and then to America in 1620. Before they disembarked from the Mayflower, they created a covenant that represents important aspects of early Puritan political thought. This agreement, known today as the

Mayflower Compact, committed the people and the rulers to "the Glory of God, and the Advancement of the Christian Faith, and the Honour of our King and Country." Its legitimacy stemmed from the consent of the 41 men heading households on the Mayflower, and it required rulers to govern justly.[12]

The Mayflower Compact is the most famous early civil covenant made in America, but it is not unique. As David A. Weir illustrates in his exhaustively researched book, *Early New England: A Covenanted Society*, hundreds of ecclesiastical and civil covenants were created whereby people joined together before the eyes of God to pursue different projects ultimately aimed at glorifying God.[13] Each of these covenants reinforced the idea that governments are legitimate and binding because they were established by the consent of the governed. This view is reflected well by Henry Wolcott's notes of a 1638 election sermon by one of Connecticut's founders, Thomas Hooker:

> Doctrine. I. That the choice of public magistrates belongs unto the people by God's own allowance.
> II. The privilege of election, which belongs to the people, therefore must not be exercised according to their humors, but according to the blessed will and law of God.
> III. They who have the power to appoint officers and magistrates, it is in their power also to set the bounds and limitations of power and place unto which they call them.
> Reasons. 1. Because the foundation of authority is laid, firstly, in the free consent of the people.[14]

Not only did the people consent to the original form of government, but also most men could participate in town meetings and freemen elected representatives to the colonial legislatures. Of course there was an expectation that citizens would elect and defer to godly, talented magistrates. John Winthrop famously lectured Massachusetts Bay's General Court on this point in 1645, and thirty-five years later Connecticut's Samuel Willis reiterated the sentiment with a greater emphasis on class when he declared that "[t]he making of rulers of the lower sort of people will issue in contempt, let their opinion be what it will." Such statements have led some scholars to overemphasize the importance of social class in the era, but others such as Joy and Robert Gilsdorf have persuasively argued that eighteenth-century Connecticut citizens were more concerned with competence (and, I would add, godliness) than social standing or wealth. Moreover, the colonies, led by those in New England, clearly grew more democratic in the seventeenth and eighteenth centuries.[15]

Early Puritan societies are often described as theocracies, and their founders and leaders undoubtedly attempted to create thoroughly Christian social and political institutions. This mission is illustrated well by a 1672 declaration by the Connecticut General Court that "[w]e have endeavoured not only to ground our capital laws upon the Word of God, but also all other laws upon the justice and equity held forth in that Word, which is a most perfect rule." Within these societies, however, the institutions of church and state were kept separate and distinct. In early Massachusetts, clergy could not hold political offices or otherwise serve in a civil capacity (this restriction was eventually lifted), and the Massachusetts Body of Liberties (1641) specifically banned European practices such as ecclesiastical courts and made it clear that ecclesiastical sanctions such as excommunication had no impact upon holding civil office. Civil magistrates were to be "nursing fathers" to the church (a phrase taken from Isaiah 49:23), by creating a society that encouraged true Christianity. Throughout New England (with the exception of Rhode Island), the Congregational church was supported financially through taxation, there were religious tests for officeholders, and statutes required church attendance and punished vice. Protestant dissenters in the region were tolerated if they remained quiet and did not disturb the public order. However, vocal and disorderly dissenters such as the Quakers and perceived troublemakers, including Roger Williams (1635) and Anne Hutchinson (1638), were banished, exiled, or, on rare occasions, hanged.[16]

The Puritan conviction that rulers should promote true religion might suggest a powerful state, but this possibility was tempered by the view that civil power should be strictly limited. Fear of arbitrary power exercised by fallen human actors led the Puritans to devise and adopt a variety of democratic institutions and checks on rulers. For instance, the 1641 Massachusetts Body of Liberties contained many protections later found in the American Bill of Rights, including prohibitions against double jeopardy, torture, and "in-humane Barbarous or cruell" bodily punishments. Seven years later these laws were revised and published as *The Book of the General Lawes and Liberties Concerning the Inhabitants of Massachusetts*. This was one of the first times a legal code had ever been printed in the Western world—a practice that made it possible to distribute the laws more widely than if they were copied by hand.[17]

More broadly, Puritans believed the power of the state also was constrained by what John Davenport called in 1669 "the Law of Nature," which is "God's law."[18] Rulers who violated natural law could legitimately be resisted. A striking expression of this idea is found in a 1678 sermon by Massachusetts's Samuel Nowell entitled "Abraham in Arms," in which he contended that the "Law of nature . . . teachth men self-preservation." Moreover, he proclaimed that there "is such a thing as Liberty and Property given to us, both by the Laws of God & Men, when these are invaded, we may defend our selves."[19] Puritans were less likely to make natural rights arguments than later Calvinists, but the essential elements for such arguments were all present in earlier Reformed political theory.[20]

Long before the War for Independence, Reformed Americans had experience resisting tyrannical political power. New England Puritans supported Parliament against abuses of the British Crown during the English Civil War, and John Cotton even preached a sermon defending the execution of Charles I. After the Restoration, England attempted to "improve" the governance of New England by combining all of the colonies into a single entity know as the Dominion of New England (1686–1689). The first governor of the new entity, Sir Edmund Andros, immediately made himself unpopular by demanding that a Congregational Meeting House in Boston be made available for Anglican services and by restricting town meetings. On April 18, 1689, shortly after news of the Glorious Revolution reached Boston, colonial leaders arrested Andros and returned him to England for trial. The new monarchs and Lords of Trade wisely abandoned the Dominion, but the new Massachusetts charter did require toleration of other Protestants.[21]

Like their descendants, Puritans were concerned with "liberty." David D. Hall argues in *A Reforming People: Puritanism and the Transformation of Public Life in New England* that these Calvinists had an "animus against 'tyranny' and 'arbitrary' power that pervaded virtually every sermon and political statement." But it is critical to recognize that they never understood the concept to include the excessively individualistic idea that men and women are free to do anything except physically harm others. They distinguished between liberty and personal license. Puritans were primarily interested with freedom from sin, but they also understood liberty as the ability of a people to govern themselves and to do what God requires. They came closest to embracing modern notions of liberty with respect to freedom of conscience, but even here religious *actions* judged by the community to be disruptive could still be restricted. As Barry Alan Shain has demonstrated, this constrained understanding of liberty remained dominant in America until well into the eighteenth century.²²

Few scholars question the influence of the Reformed tradition on the Puritans, but some have argued it declined rapidly. Clearly, the way New England colonists thought about society and politics changed in response to increased prosperity and events like the English Civil War, the Restoration, the Glorious Revolution, and the English victory in the Seven Years' War. The First Great Awakening was particularly significant as it led to discord between supporters of the revivals (e.g., New Light Congregationalists and New Side Presbyterians) and their more traditional coreligionists. These tensions led to a weakening of religious establishments in New England and, according to some scholars, helped pave the way for the War for Independence. But in spite of a variety of significant changes, both civic and ecclesiastical leaders in the Reformed tradition remained committed to the political principles discussed above, and many became even more convinced that America had a special role to play in God's advancing kingdom.²³

The Bible and Reformed Literature in the American Founding

As one would expect of a people who believed in the principle of *sola scriptura*, the Bible was virtually omnipresent in New England. Connecticut even required households to possess a Bible, and selectmen were instructed to provide one to families who could not afford the Holy Scriptures. In his chapter for this volume, Daniel L. Dreisbach shows that founders from throughout the nation looked to the Bible for guidance and regularly used it in their writings and speeches. Indeed, the political literature of the era contains more references to the Bible than the works of all Enlightenment thinkers combined (34 percent to 22 percent).²⁴

In addition to the Bible, books containing the essential elements of Reformed political thought were accessible to political and ecclesiastical elites from the colonies' inception. A thorough and systematic study of which Reformed books were available at what time has yet to be attempted, but Herbert D. Foster has documented the availability of classic texts by John Calvin, John Knox, Theodore Beza, Stephanus Junius Brutus, Peter Martyr, and others.²⁵ The respect Puritan leaders had for their European predecessors is reflected well by John Cotton's statement that "I have read the fathers and the school-men, and Calvin too; but I find that he that has Calvin has them all." Yet, as Perry Miller pointed out, "[i]f we were to measure by the number of times a writer is cited and the degrees of familiarity shown with his works, Beza exerted more influence than Calvin, and David Pareus still more than Beza."[26] This is significant for our purposes because the latter two thinkers expressed significantly more radical theories of resistance than did John Calvin.

Moving to the founding era, political leaders generally, but particularly those from New England, often owned or referred to Reformed literature. It is not surprising that Princeton President John Witherspoon owned Calvin's *Institutes*, Beza's *Rights of Magistrates* (1757) and Buchanan's *The Law of Scottish Kingship* (1579). More intriguing is that John Adams declared that John Poynet's *Short Treatise on Politike Power* (1556) contains "all the essential principles of liberty, which were afterwards dilated on by Sidney and Locke." Similarly, late in life he wrote, "I love and revere the memories of Huss Wickliff Luther Calvin Zwinglius Melancton and all the other reformers how muchsoever I may differ from them all in many theological metaphysical & philosophical points. As you justly observe, without their great exertions & severe sufferings, the USA had never existed."[27]

Unlike his cousin, Samuel Adams was a latter-day Puritan. In 1740, well before John Locke's *Second Treatise* was popular in America, he returned to Harvard to defend the thesis that "it is lawful to resist the Supreme Magistrate, if the Commonwealth cannot be otherwise preserved" in order to receive his master's degree. Twenty-eight years later he wrote three essays for the *Boston Gazette* under the pseudonym of "a Puritan." In them, he urged Americans to guard their rights carefully and to beware of British attempts to appoint a Bishop for America lest the nation be subjected to "Popery." The following year the famous political cartoon "An Attempt to Land a Bishop in America" was published in *The Political Register*. It depicted an erstwhile bishop who is not allowed to disembark in America because of a rioting mob wielding works by Locke and Sidney. Notably, the fleeing bishop is about to be struck in the head by a copy of "Calvin's Works," which had apparently been thrown at him by a member of the mob. In 1766, George Buchanan's *De Jure Regni: or the due right of Government* was reprinted in Philadelphia—seven years before the *Second Treatise* was first published in America. Finally, at the Constitutional Convention Luther Martin (who, in spite of his name, was hardly an exemplar of the Protestant Reformation) read passages from "Locke & Vattel, and also Rutherford [presumably *Lex, Rex*]" to show that states, like people, are equal. In short, there is no shortage of evidence that civic leaders in the founding era were aware of Reformed political thinkers and their major doctrines.[28]

Adherence Rates, Calvinism, and the American Founding

A significant argument made by scholars who dismiss the influence of Christianity, generally, or Reformed theology, specifically, in the founding era is that the founding generation was not particularly religious. In recent years, the most important advocates of this position are the sociologists Roger Finke and Rodney Stark, who claim that on "the eve of the Revolution only about 17 percent of Americans were churched." Such assertions have made their way into polemical literature, as evidenced by Isaac Kramnick and R. Laurence Moore's statement that "Americans in the era of the Revolution were a distinctly unchurched people. The highest estimates from the late eighteenth century make only about 10–15 percent of the population were church members." Although all of these authors acknowledge that "adherence" rates varied by region, Finke and Stark still conclude that New England adherence rates were no more than 20 percent of the total population.[29]

James H. Hutson, chief of Manuscripts Division at the Library of Congress, has demonstrated that Finke and Stark make numerous factual, methodological, and historical errors. For instance, they misstate Ezra Stiles' estimate of the population of New England in 1760, and they ignore the best calculations of the American population in 1776. More significantly, by relying on church membership rates in an era when it was difficult to join many churches (particularly in New England), they grossly undercount the number of Americans who were "churched." As well, Hutson notes that many of Finke and Stark's data come from decades after the era about which they write, and that some of the data comes from fledgling denominations such as the Methodists.[30] Using their methodology but the more reliable data offered by Ezra Stiles, Hutson contends that 82 percent of New Englanders were involved in Congregational churches—and this does not include New Englanders who were active in Baptists, Anglican, or other churches.[31] Patricia U. Bonomi and Peter R. Eisenstadt similarly conclude that in late-eighteenth-century America "from 56 to 80 percent of the [white] population were churched, with the southern colonies occupying the lower end of the scale and the northern colonies the upper end."[32]

In New England, citizens overwhelmingly attended churches firmly within the Reformed tradition. In 1776, 63 percent of New England churches were Congregationalist, 15.3 percent were Baptist, and 5.5 percent were Presbyterian. Virtually all Baptists were Calvinists in this era, so approximately 84 percent of the region's churches were in the Reformed tradition. Moreover, the Congregational churches generally had the largest congregations. In Connecticut, for instance, Bruce Daniels estimated that in 1790 "dissenting societies comprised about one-third of the total number, [but] they were only about 20 percent of the population." And members of Congregational churches tended to have more influence in their communities and states than did dissenters.[33]

It is worth noting as well that 95 percent of Congregational ministers were college graduates—usually from Harvard or Yale—and they were among the most educated and influential members of their communities. Within these churches, congregants would gather twice on Sunday to hear theologically and exegetically rich sermons lasting about one-and-a-half hours and to engage in other acts of worship. Where possible, congregations would gather on Thursday as well for an additional sermon. Harry S. Stout calculated that the "average 70-year old colonial churchgoer would have listened to some 7,000 sermons in his or her lifetime totaling nearly 10,000 hours of concentrated listening. This is the number of classroom hours it would take to receive ten separate undergraduate degrees in a modern university, without even repeating the same course!"[34]

Outside of New England, Calvinism was less dominant, but by 1776 Reformed congregations accounted for 51 percent and 58 percent of the churches in the middle and southern colonies respectively. Particularly noteworthy in these regions were Scottish and Scotch-Irish immigrants, most of whom were Presbyterian. In Pennsylvania, for instance, Presbyterians accounted for 30 percent of the population by 1790 and held 44 percent of the seats in the state legislature by the late-1770s. In the South, most political elites were Anglicans, but in the late-eighteenth century Presbyterianism was the fastest growing faith in the region and its adherents were rapidly becoming a significant factor in state politics. J. C. C. Clark points out that well over a majority of the leaders of North Carolina's militia were Presbyterian elders.[35]

Case Studies

Because scholars and popular writers have tended to focus on founders who were not part of the Reformed tradition, and because they often simplistically attribute any reference to natural rights, government by consent, and the right to resist tyrannical authority to a secularized Locke, they have neglected the influence of Calvinist political thought on the American founders. However, if we take the tradition seriously and look beyond a few elite founders, a more complete and textured picture of the founding era comes into focus. Within the academy, historians have done a better job of doing this than have political scientists and law professors. The latter two groups are far more likely to focus on a few texts, such as the Declaration of Independence, the Constitution, *The Federalist Papers*, and the Bill of Rights. Moreover, they tend to interpret public documents in the light of the privately held views of a few elites rather than as a product of communities—for our purposes, communities that included a significant number of Reformed Christians. In the following sections I indicate ways that taking this tradition seriously can help scholars better understand key public documents, such as the Declaration, Constitution, and Bill of Rights. Each study is necessarily brief and is meant only to be suggestive.

The Declaration of Independence

Puritans and their descendants had always been in the precarious position of maintaining what was in effect a dissenting establishment. One of their chief fears was that an Anglican bishop would be sent to America to take over all colonial churches and set up oppressive ecclesiastical courts. The Stamp Act's reference to courts "exercising ecclesiastical jurisdiction within the said colonies" was taken by many to imply that a bishop would be sent shortly, and that for the first time ecclesiastical courts would operate in the American colonies. In retrospect this possibility seems unlikely, but it is important to recognize that Calvinists had often struggled against unfriendly governments and the Puritans had come to New England precisely because they were unable to reform completely the Church of England. Moreover, some Anglicans continued to argue that Congregationalist and Presbyterian churches were not "true" churches because bishops had not ordained their ministers. The extent to which Church of England leaders supported the plans of Americans who desired a bishop has been extensively debated; but there is little reason to doubt that Reformed Christians genuinely feared an Anglican episcopate. Ill-conceived actions by the Church of England, such as founding a "mission" in Cambridge, Massachusetts, in 1759, did little to calm their fears.[36]

Calvinists were troubled by the possible appointment of a bishop, but they were incensed by the Quebec Act of 1774. From Parliament's perspective, this innocuous piece of legislation simply provided for the efficient governing of territory won from France after the Seven Years' War. The act, however, extended the colony of Quebec into what is now the American Midwest, permitted the use of French civil law, and allowed Catholics to practice their faith freely and take oaths without reference to Protestantism. To many Protestants, these steps constituted a significant retreat for the kingdom of God in North America. Reformed Protestants of the era considered Roman Catholics to be, at best, seriously deceived and, at worst, in league with Satan. Connecticut minister Samuel Sherwood reflected the views of many Calvinists when he interpreted the Quebec bill as attempting "the establishment of popery" and as part of a pattern of "violent and cruel attempts of a tyrannical and persecuting power," the main goal of which is the destruction of Protestant Christianity.[37]

Calvinists had long been on their guard against tyrannical rulers desiring to stamp out the true gospel. Although they believed that God is sovereign, they were haunted by events such as the massacres of French Huguenots, where "evil" rulers seemed to succeed. When tyrannical rulers had failed it was, from a human perspective, because Protestants had resisted them with arguments, laws, and force. As Reformed Americans began to perceive a pattern of tyranny by Parliament and the Crown, they reacted forcefully against the threat.

The influence of Reformed political ideas on Americans is often ignored because students of the era focus on the Declaration of Independence as *the* statement of why separation from Great Britain was justified. Moreover, they read the document in the light of the views of its primary drafter, Thomas Jefferson, who was more heavily influenced by the Enlightenment than virtually any other American.[38] The Declaration of Independence deftly employed language and arguments that resonated with diverse constituents and traditions, one of which was the Reformed tradition. Although the Declaration of Independence is compatible with the Reformed political theory, this tradition's influence is more evident in other public documents stating the Patriots' case. These latter texts are not narrowly Reformed—indeed, they might be better characterized as articulating Protestant concerns. However, a large majority of Protestants in America at the time were, in fact, Calvinists, and these Protestants were more likely to support the Patriot cause and use such language than, say, Anglicans.

On September 17, 1774, Paul Revere delivered the Suffolk Resolves to the Continental Congress. The Resolves recognized the sovereignty of King George, but challenged the legality of recent acts and practices by the British Parliament. They proclaimed

> [t]hat it is an indispensable duty which we owe to God, our country, ourselves and posterity, by all lawful ways and means in our power to maintain, defend and preserve those civil and religious rights and liberties, for which many of our fathers fought, bled and died, and to hand them down entire to future generations.

As well, they condemned

> the late act of parliament for establishing the Roman Catholic religion and the French laws in that extensive country, now called Canada, [because it] is dangerous in an extreme degree to the Protestant religion and to the civil rights and liberties of all America; and, therefore, as men and Protestant Christians, we are indispensably obliged to take all proper measures for our security.[39]

The Suffolk Resolves played a significant role in encouraging congressional delegates to take a strong stand against Parliament. Shortly after receiving the Resolves, they adopted the "Declaration of Rights," which asserted the colonists' constitutional and natural rights. They objected specifically to the act passed

> for establishing the Roman Catholick Religion in the province of Quebec, abolishing the equitable system of English laws, and erecting a tyranny there, to the great danger, from so total a dissimilarity of Religion, law, and government of the neighbouring British colonies, by the assistance of those whose blood and treasure the said country was conquered from France.[40]

Congress's "Appeal to the People of Great Britain," approved at the same time, expanded on the significance of the Quebec Act and challenged

Parliament's ability "to establish a religion, fraught with sanguinary and impious tenets, or, to erect an arbitrary form of government, in any quarter of the globe." These and other congressional documents highlight concerns that are only vaguely represented in the Declaration of Independence's charge that the king abolished "the free System of English Laws in a neighboring Province. . . ." The difference had something to do with the person who drafted the latter document, but even more relevant was a critical audience for the text—Roman Catholic France. The eventual intervention of France on the Patriots' side did much to diminish the vehement anti-Catholicism of many Americans in this era, but suspicion of "papists" remained a powerful force in the American imagination well into the twentieth century.[41] On July 4, 1776, Congress approved the Declaration of Independence. Its most famous lines proclaim that

> all men are created equal; that they are endowed by their Creator with certain unalienable rights; that among these are life, liberty, and the pursuit of happiness; that, to secure these rights, governments are instituted among men, deriving their just powers from the consent of the governed; that whenever any form of government becomes destructive of these ends, it is the right of the people to alter or to abolish it, and to institute new government, laying its foundation on such principles, and organizing its powers in such form, as to them shall seem most likely to effect their safety and happiness.[42]

These words reflect arguments long made by Patriots, relatively few of whom read Locke and many of whom were active Calvinists. Of course their primary drafter, Thomas Jefferson, definitely read Locke and was most certainly not a Calvinist, but he later acknowledged that he was not attempting to "find out new principles, or new arguments" and that the Declaration's authority rests "on the harmonizing sentiments of the day." Jefferson indisputably borrowed language from Locke, but the ideas to which he referred predated Locke by years. There is simply no evidence that signers from Reformed backgrounds such as Josiah Bartlett, William Whipple, Matthew Thornton, John Hancock, Samuel Adams, John Adams, Robert Treat Paine, William Ellery, Roger Sherman, William Williams, Samuel Huntington, Oliver Wolcott, William Floyd, Philip Livingston, Richard Stockton, John Witherspoon, John Hart, Abraham Clark, James Smith, James Wilson, Thomas McKean, and Lyman Hall understood the

"Creator" to be "nature" or thought they were approving a document that mandated a strictly "secular politics," as some scholars have claimed.[43]

With the exception of John Witherspoon, no active clergyman is listed above. Yet observers have long recognized that Reformed ministers were among the most important supporters of the Patriot cause. The Loyalist Peter Oliver railed against "Mr. *Otis's* black Regiment, *the dissenting Clergy,* who took so active a part in the Rebellion." King George himself reportedly referred to the War for Independence as "a Presbyterian Rebellion," and historians have recognized that there was an "almost unanimous and persistent critical attitude of the Congregational and Presbyterian ministers toward the British imperial policy." Indeed, before real bullets were exchanged at Lexington and Concord, the Congregationalist minister Jonathan Mayhew fired "the MORNING GUN OF THE REVOLUTION, the *punctum Temporis* when that period of history began." The gun in question was Mayhew's influential sermon "A Discourse Concerning Unlimited Submission and Non-Resistance to the Higher Powers," delivered and published in Boston in 1750. The sermon powerfully and eloquently reiterated arguments that governments are ordained by God, that their powers are limited, and that citizens have a duty to resist rulers who do evil. Mayhew is not a good representative of Calvinist theology, but his sermon is an excellent example of Calvinist political thought. And it is only one of many sermons preached, printed, and circulated that encouraged Reformed Christians to be wary of and to resist tyrannical governments.[44]

The Constitution

According to Isaac Kramnick and R. Laurence Moore, the Constitution is "godless." This observation would have come as quite a shock to Roger Sherman, Nathaniel Gorham, Caleb Strong, John Langdon, Nicholas Gilman, Abraham Baldwin, James Wilson, Gunning Bedford, James McHenry, William Livingston, William Paterson, Hugh Williamson, Jared Ingersoll, Oliver Ellsworth, John Lansing Jr., Robert Yates, James McClurg, William Blount, William Houston, William Davie, and Alexander Martin—delegates to the Federal Convention who were raised in the Reformed tradition. Not all of these men played significant roles at the Convention, and a few ended up opposing the Constitution. Yet some of them, notably Roger Sherman, James Wilson, William Paterson, and

Oliver Ellsworth, were intimately involved in key debates and served on important committees. Political scientist David Brian Robertson has recently demonstrated that in many respects Sherman was a more effective delegate than Madison, and he suggests that the "political synergy between Madison and Sherman . . . very well may have been necessary for the Constitution's adoption."[45]

At first glance the Constitution may appear to be "godless" as the deity is only referred to in Article VII—where the document is dated "in the Year of our Lord. . . ." Article I presumes that Congress will not conduct business on Sunday, but this provision is more than balanced by Article VI's prohibition on religious tests for national office.[46] Yet the argument for the influence of Reformed political ideas on the Constitution does not depend on explicitly religious references. It is more profitable instead to consider the ways in which Calvinist political thought may have influenced the men and women who wrote, debated, and ratified the document.

John Witherspoon's student James Madison wrote in Federalist 51 that "if men were angels, no government would be necessary." Almost to a person America's founders were convinced that humans are self-interested or, in theological language, sinful. Of course one can reach this conclusion for a variety of reasons, but it would seem likely that the 50–75 percent of Americans connected to Reformed traditions adhered to this idea because they heard it from the pulpit since childhood. It is true that every major Christian tradition in America in this era agreed that humans are sinful, but few emphasized it as much as the Calvinists who taught the doctrine of total depravity. In contrast, many Enlightenment thinkers believed that humans are basically good, and that through proper education they could be perfected. As Louis Hartz recognized, "Americans refused to join in the great Enlightenment enterprise of shattering the Christian concept of sin, [and] replacing it with an unlimited humanism."[47]

America's founders believed that because humans are sinful it is dangerous to concentrate political power. The Constitution thus carefully separates powers and creates a variety of mechanisms whereby each institution can check the others. Critically, the power of the national government itself was limited by Article I, section 8. Indeed, the very notion of federalism, some scholars have argued, was itself modeled after Reformed approaches to church governance (especially Presbyterianism) and New England civic arrangements which, as we have seen, were themselves heavily influenced by Calvinist political ideas. It is noteworthy that the authors of the Connecticut Compromise, Roger Sherman and Oliver Ellsworth, were both serious Reformed Christians who were leaders in their Congregational churches. Enlightenment thinkers, on the other hand, generally embraced unicameralism and the centralization of power in a national government.[48]

Federalism helps explain why religion is not mentioned in the Constitution. The founders recognized that it would be impossible to agree upon a single Christian denomination that could be established at a national level, and many feared giving the national government power in this area. Moreover, many founders were beginning to question the wisdom of establishments altogether (usually because they feared that they hurt rather than helped Christianity). There was almost complete agreement that if there was going to be an establishment it should be at the state or local level.[49]

The First Amendment

America's founders differed with respect to whether and/or how civic authorities should support Christianity. On balance, Reformed Christians were more sympathetic to significant state support for religion, as suggested by the survival of establishments in Vermont (1807), Connecticut (1819), New Hampshire (1819), Maine (1820), and Massachusetts (1833). Yet when Supreme Court justices have turned to founding era history to shine light on the meaning of the religion clauses, they have overwhelmingly relied on the views of two Southern Anglicans—Thomas Jefferson and James Madison. This approach is particularly ahistorical as Jefferson was not even involved in crafting or ratifying the First Amendment.[50]

In contrast to Jefferson, Roger Sherman—a latter-day Puritan if there ever was one—was intimately involved in framing the First Amendment. Sherman served on the committee of eleven that compiled the list of rights first debated by the House of Representatives (the only handwritten draft of the Bill of Rights is in his hand), he actively participated in debates over the amendments, and he served on the six-person conference committee that put the Bill of Rights into its final form. On some issues, such as whether amendments should be interspersed throughout the Constitution or attached to the original text, Congress sided with Sherman rather than Madison. Given Sherman's extensive involvement in drafting the First

Amendment and Jefferson's absence from the country at the time, it is striking that when US Supreme Court justices have used history to help them interpret the First Amendment's religion clauses they have made 112 distinct references to Jefferson but have mentioned Sherman only three times.[51]

James Madison may have been a driving force behind the Bill of Rights, but the document was ultimately a product of a community—a community that included the following members of Reformed churches: Roger Sherman, Oliver Ellsworth, John Langdon, Caleb Strong, Paine Wingate, Philip Schuyler, Abraham Baldwin, Jonathan Elmer, Elias Boudinot, Fisher Ames, Abiel Foster, Benjamin Huntington, James Jackson, Jeremiah Wadsworth, Nicholas Gilman, Egbert Benson, James Schureman, Henry Wynkoop, Daniel Hiester Jr., Daniel Huger, Benjamin Bourne, William Paterson, William Smith, and Hugh Williamson. Certainly these men were not all equally influential, but at least Sherman, Ellsworth, Huntington, Baldwin, Boudinot, Paterson, and Ames played important roles in key committees and/or debates. None of these seven men advocated anything like a wall of separation between church and state, and they all thought that states and localities should encourage Christianity. They agreed with their colleagues that the nation should not have an established church, but even at the national level they supported things like hiring congressional and military chaplains and requesting President Washington to issue a Thanksgiving Proclamation.[52]

Conclusion

Students of the American founding often view the era through the eyes of elites such as Thomas Jefferson, James Madison, George Washington, Alexander Hamilton, Thomas Paine, Benjamin Franklin, and John Adams. These men were brilliant, well educated, and influential, but they are not good representatives of the many Americans who were associated with Reformed congregations in the founding era. Franklin and Adams, the only founders in this group who were raised in the Reformed tradition, clearly came to reject basic tenets of orthodox Christianity—something that was rare for any American of that era. Yet even among this small, unrepresentative group a reasonable argument can be made that at least some of these men (most obviously Adams and Madison) were influenced by Reformed political ideas.

Tracing intellectual influence is a messy business. Different people may express similar ideas for completely different reasons, or they may use similar words but mean different things by them. Even within the realm of Christianity, members of different denominations may adhere to similar ideas, so it is problematic to label almost anything as *distinctively* Reformed. Yet if we recognize that Calvinists shared a basic set of political ideas, and that a large majority of Americans were steeped in this tradition, it is only reasonable to consider the impact of this tradition on America's founders. I suggest above how taking this tradition seriously might qualify the widespread view that the Declaration, Constitution, and First Amendment are fundamentally secular documents.

Let me reiterate that I am *not* arguing that America's constitutional order is simply and solely a product of Reformed political thought. There were clearly other intellectual influences at work in the era, and founders often acted for nonideological reasons. As well, although the Reformed tradition was dominant in New England, it was less influential in the middle and southern colonies. My point is simply that there are good reasons to believe many founding era Americans were influenced by Reformed political thought. If scholars can pull their eyes away from indisputably fascinating men like Washington, Adams, Madison, Jefferson, Hamilton, Paine, and Franklin long enough to consider the many members of the Continental Congress, Constitutional Convention, and First Federal Congress who were comparatively drab Calvinists, they will gain a fuller and richer understanding of this critical era in American history.

Notes

1. "Reformed" in this context means "Calvinist" and refers to the intellectual tradition developed by John Calvin (1509–1564) and his followers. Jack Rakove, *Original Meanings: Politics and Ideas in the Making of the Constitution* (New York: Alfred A. Knopf, 1997), 7, 18. The preface to Daniel L. Dreisbach, Mark David Hall, and Jeffry H. Morrison, eds., *The Forgotten Founders on Religion and Public Life* (Notre Dame, IN: University of Notre Dame Press, 2009), xiii–xxi, provides numerous examples of scholars who describe the founders as Deists dedicated to creating a secular commonwealth. I offer an extensive discussion of secondary literature related to this chapter in *Roger Sherman and the Creation of the American Republic* (New York: Oxford University Press, 2013). For reasons of space, I keep this discussion to an absolute minimum in this chapter.
2. Like Franklin, Jefferson and Adams lived for extended periods of time in Europe. Franklin was raised in the Reformed tradition but rejected it at an early age. For

details on the religious views of these founders, see Daniel L. Dreisbach, Mark David Hall, and Jeffry H. Morrison, eds., *The Founders on God and Government* (Lanham, MD: Rowman & Littlefield, 2004) and Dreisbach, Hall, and Morrison, *The Forgotten Founders on Religion and Public Life*.

3. Sydney E. Ahlstrom, *A Religious History of the American People* (Garden City, NY: Doubleday, 1975), 1: 426; Harry S. Stout, "Preaching the Insurrection,"*Christian History* 15 (1996), 17. Presumably, both figures are for white Americans. According to Charles O. Paullin, 56 percent of churches in America in 1776 were in the Reformed tradition. Paullin, *Atlas of the Historical Geography of the United States* (Washington, DC: Carnegie Institution, 1932), 50. Roger Finke and Rodney Stark rely heavily on his study when they discuss denominations in the era in *The Churching of America, 1776–1990: Winners and Losers in Our Religious Economy* (New Brunswick, NJ: Rutgers University Press, 1992), 25. According to Edwin Gaustad and Philip Barlow, 63 percent of the churches in 1780 were in the Reformed tradition. Gaustad and Barlow, *New Historical Atlas of Religion in America* (New York: Oxford University Press, 2001), 8. The two estimates for 1776 (56 percent and 75 percent) are not necessarily contradictory if Reformed churches had larger congregations than non-Reformed churches.

4. *The New-England Primer*, Paul Leicester Ford, ed. (1727; reprint, New York: Dodd, Mead, and Company, 1897); Stephanie Schnorbus, "Calvin and Locke: Dueling Epistemologies in *The New England Primer*, 1720–1790," *Early American Studies* 8 (Spring 2010), 250–287.

5. Ralph Ketcham, *James Madison: A Biography* (Charlottesville: University Press of Virginia, 1971), 17–50; Jeffry H. Morrison, *John Witherspoon and the Founding of the American Republic* (Notre Dame, IN : University of Notre Dame Press, 2005), 4; Joseph S. Tiedemann, "Presbyterianism and the American Revolution in the Middle Colonies," *Church History* 74 (June 2005), 339.

6. Kenneth A. Lockridge, *Literacy in Colonial New England* (New York: W.W. Norton & Co., 1974), 98. Lockridge calculates that 60 percent of males in New England were literate in 1660, and that this percentage rose to 85 percent by 1760 (13). James F. Cooper, Jr., *Tenacious of Their Liberties: The Congregationalists in Colonial Massachusetts* (New York: Oxford University Press, 1999) and David A. Weir, *Early New England: A Covenanted Society* (Grand Rapids: Eerdmans, 2005).

7. John Witte, Jr., *The Reformation of Rights: Law, Religion, and Human Rights in Early Modern Calvinism* (Cambridge: Cambridge University Press, 2007), 1–80. There is a debate among students of Reformed thought concerning the extent to which early Reformers believed civic government can be redeemed. David VanDrunen provides an excellent overview of this literature and makes a good, but in my mind not persuasive, case that the early Reformers adhered to the two kingdom doctrine of Augustine and Luther. VanDrunen, *Natural Law and the Two Kingdoms: A Study in the Development of Reformed Social Thought* (Grand Rapids: Eerdmans, 2010).

8. Quentin Skinner, *The Foundations of Modern Political Thought: vol. 2: The Age of Reformation* (Cambridge: Cambridge University Press, 1978), especially chapters 7–9.
9. Stephanus Junius Brutus, *Vindiciae, Contra Tyrannos*, George Garnett, ed. (Cambridge: Cambridge University Press, 1994), 149, 92, 37–40, 129–131; Skinner, *Foundations of Modern Political Thought*, 2: 329 (quoting Brutus).
10. The exact nature of these covenants was hotly contested among New England ministers. See Perry Miller, "From Covenant to the Revival," in Miller, *Nature's Nation* (Cambridge, MA: Harvard University Press, 1966); Sacvan Bercovitch, *The American Jeremiad* (Madison: University of Wisconsin Press, 1978); and Jonathan D. Sassi, *A Republic of Righteousness: The Public Christianity of the Post-Revolutionary New England Clergy* (New York: Oxford University Press, 2001), 19–83.
11. Skinner, *Foundations of Modern Political Thought*, 2: 321. But see Michael Walzer, *Revolution of the Saints* (Cambridge, MA: Harvard University Press, 1965).
12. Daniel L. Dreisbach and Mark David Hall, eds., *The Sacred Rights of Conscience: Selected Readings on Religious Liberty and Church-State Relations in the American Founding* (Indianapolis, IN: Liberty Fund Press, 2009), 86.
13. Weir, *Early New England*. See also Daniel J. Elazar, *The American Constitutional Tradition* (Lincoln: University of Nebraska Press, 1988).
14. Perry Miller, ed., *The American Puritans: Their Prose and Poetry* (New York: Columbia University Press, 1956), 89; Alice M. Baldwin, *The New England Clergy and the American Revolution* (1928; reprint, New York: Frederick Ungar, 1965), 26–27; and Richard L. Bushman, *From Puritan to Yankee: Character and the Social Order in Connecticut, 1690–1765* (Cambridge, MA: Harvard University Press, 1967), 154–159.
15. John Winthrop, "Speech to the General Court" (1645), in Miller, *The American Puritans*, 90–93; Bushman, *From Puritan to Yankee*, 12; Joy B. and Robert R. Gilsdorf, "Elites and Electorates: Some Plain Truths for Historians of Colonial America," in David D. Hall, John M. Murrin, and Thad W. Tate, eds., *Saints and Revolutionaries: Essays on Early American History* (New York: W.W. Norton: 1984), 207–244; David D. Hall, *A Reforming People: Puritanism and the Transformation of Public Life in New England* (New York: Alfred A. Knopf, 2011), 90; J. S. Maloy, *The Colonial American Origins of Modern Democratic Thought* (New York: Cambridge University Press, 2008), esp. 86–170; Robert E. Brown, *Middle-Class Democracy and the Revolution in Massachusetts, 1691–1780* (Ithaca, NY: Cornell University Press, 1955); and Perry Miller, "Hooker and Connecticut Democracy," in *Errand Into the Wilderness* (New York: Harper & Row, 1956), 16–47.
16. *The Public Records of Connecticut* (Hartford: Case, Lockwood & Brainard, 1894), 2: 568; Dreisbach and Hall, *Sacred Rights of Conscience*, 83–213; Edmund S. Morgan, *Puritan Political Ideas, 1558–1794* (Indianapolis: Bobbs-Merrill, 1965), xiii–xlvii; T.H. Breen, *The Character of the Good Ruler: A Study of Puritan Political Ideas in New England, 1630–1730* (New Haven, CT: Yale University Press, 1970).

17. Bruce Frohnen, ed., *American Republic: Primary Sources* (Indianapolis, IN: Liberty Fund Press, 2002), 15–22; Hall, *A Reforming People*, 107, 147–154, and passim; *The Laws and Liberties of Massachusetts* (1648; reprint, San Marino, CA: The Huntington Library, 1998), 46, 50.

18. John Davenport, "A Sermon Preach'd at The Election of the Governour" (Boston, 1670), 4. See generally Baldwin, *New England Clergy*, 13–21. Similarly, two years earlier Jonathan Mitchel declared in his election sermon that "the Law of Nature, is part of the Eternal Law of God." Mitchel, "Nehemiah on the wall in troublesome times . . ." (Cambridge, 1671), 11. Note that in these examples (and numerous others could be given) indisputably orthodox clergy appealed to "the law of nature" as a source of authority.

19. Samuel Nowell, "Abraham in Arms" (Boston, 1678), 10–11; Baldwin, *New England Clergy*; Martha Louise Counts, "The Political Views of the Eighteenth Century New England Clergy as Expressed in Their Election Sermons" (PhD diss., Columbia University, 1956).

    Some scholars consider any hint of a right of self-preservation to be evidence of the influence of Thomas Hobbes and/or John Locke. However, the right to protect oneself had long been a part of the natural law tradition, and it is clearly present in Reformed works written well before Hobbes's *Leviathan*.

20. Scholars differ as to the origin of the concept of subjective natural rights. John Witte provides a brief overview of this literature in *The Reformation of Rights* and argues persuasively that they were used well before Hobbes and Locke and that early Calvinists contributed significantly to their development. See also Georg Jellinek, *The Declaration of the Rights of Man and of Citizens: A Contribution to Modern Constitutional History*, Max Farrand, trans. (1901; reprint, Westport, CT: Hyperion Press, 1979).

21. Francis J. Bremer, "In Defense of Regicide: John Cotton on the Execution of Charles I," *William and Mary Quarterly* 3rd ser. 37 (1980), 103–124; John Cotton, *The Keyes to the Kingdom of Heaven* . . . (London, 1644; reprint Boston: Tappan and Dennet, 1843), 97–100; Richard Dunn, *Puritans and Yankees: The Winthrop Dynasty of New England, 1630–1717* (1962; reprint, New York: W.W. Norton, 1971), 30–36, 229–257.

22. Barry Alan Shain, *The Myth of American Individualism: The Protestant Origins of American Political Thought* (Princeton, NJ: Princeton University Press, 1994), esp. 155–288; Hall, *A Reforming People*, 193 and passim; Witte, *Reformation of Rights*, 1–37, 277–319.

23. *God of Liberty: A Religious History of the American Revolution* (New York: Basic Books, 2010); Alan Heimert, *Religion and the American Mind: From the Great Awakening to the Revolution* (Cambridge, MA: Harvard University Press, 1966); Thomas S. Kidd, *The Protestant Interest: New England after Puritanism* (New Haven, CT: Yale University Press, 2004); Nathan O. Hatch, *The Sacred Cause of Liberty: Republican Thought and the Millennium in Revolutionary New England* (New Haven, CT: Yale University Press, 1977).

24. *Acts and Laws Of His Majesties Colony of Connecticut in New-England* (New London, 1715), 207. For the 1784 version of this statute, see *Acts and Laws of the State of Connecticut, in America* (New London: Timothy Green, 1784), 258. Donald S. Lutz, "The Relative Influence of European Writers on Late Eighteenth-Century American Political Thought," *American Political Science Review* 78 (1984), 189–197, esp. 192–193; Clark, *Language of Liberty*, 26. There are a variety of problems with relying on citations, and accounts of which books were available at what time are woefully incomplete. Responses to arguments denying Locke's availability and influence in colonial America include Zuckert, *Natural Rights and the New Republicanism*, 18–25, and Steven M. Dworetz, *The Unvarnished Doctrine: Locke, Liberalism, and the American Revolution* (Durham, NC: Duke University Press, 1990).
25. Herbert D. Foster, *Collected Papers of Herbert D. Foster: Historical and Biographical Studies* (Privately Printed, 1929), 77–105.
26. Cotton Mather, *Magnalia Christi Americana* (Hartford: Silas Andrus and Son, 1885), 1: 274; Miller, *The New England Mind*, 1: 93.
27. Morrison, *John Witherspoon*, 81; Charles Francis Adams, ed., *The Works of John Adams* (Boston: Charles C. Little and James Brown, 1850), 6: 4; John Adams to F.C. Schaeffer, November 25, 1821, in James H. Hutson, *The Founders on Religion: A Book of Quotations* (Princeton, NJ: Princeton University Press, 2005), 15–16.
28. John Dunn, "The politics of Locke in England and America in the eighteenth century," in John Yolton, ed., *John Locke: Problems and Perspectives: A collection of new essays* (Cambridge: Cambridge University Press, 1969), 45–80, see esp. 69–71; Gary Scott Smith, "Samuel Adams: America's Puritan Revolutionary," in Dreisbach, Hall, and Morrison, *Forgotten Founders*, 40–64; Ira Stoll, *Samuel Adams: A Life* (New York: Free Press, 2008), 23; *The Writings of Samuel Adams*, Harry Alonzo Cushing, ed. (New York: G.P. Putnam's Sons, 1904), 1: 201–212; James B. Bell, *A War of Religion: Dissenters, Anglicans, and the American Revolution* (Houndmills, UK: Palgrave MacMillan, 2008), 100–101; Max Farrand, ed., *The Records of the Federal Convention of 1787* (New Haven, CT: Yale University Press, 1911), 1: 438.
29. William Warren Sweet, "The American Colonial Environment and Religious Liberty," *Church History* 4 (March 1935), 43–56; Finke and Stark, *The Churching of America, 1776–1990*, 15, 27; Isaac Kramnick and R. Laurence Moore, *The Godless Constitution: The Case Against Religious Correctness* (New York: W. W. Norton & Co., 1996), 17.
30. James H. Hutson, "The Christian Nation Question," in James H. Hutson, *Forgotten Features of the Founding: The Recovery of Religious Themes in the Early American Republic* (Lanham, MD: Lexington Books, 2003), 111–132. Scholars who argue for a lack of religiosity among Americans in the founding era are often led astray by laments about the lack of denominational commitments among Americans or jeremiads decrying what was perceived to be insufficient

attention to religious and moral concerns. The point applies with equal force to claims by Calvinists that other ministers, university professors, or parishioners were embracing "Arminianism" or "Arianism." Of course some of these laments were accurate, but often they were overstated. For further discussion, see Patricia Bonomi, *Under the Cope of Heaven: Religion, Society, and Politics in Colonial America* (New York: Oxford University Press, 1986), 1–127.

31. Hutson, "The Christian Nation Question," 118. Hutson also provides an excellent critique of historian Jon Butler's work, which purports to build upon and offer additional evidence for Finke and Stark's figures (120–125). See Jon Butler, "Why Revolutionary America Wasn't a 'Christian Nation,'" in James H. Hutson, ed., *Religion and the New Republic* (Lanham, MD: Rowman & Littlefield, 2000), 187–202, and *Awash in a Sea of Faith: Christianizing the American People* (Cambridge, MA: Harvard University Press, 1990).

32. Patricia U. Bonomi and Peter R. Eisenstadt, "Church Adherence in the Eighteenth-Century British Colonies," *William and Mary Quarterly*, 3rd ser., 39 (April 1982), 275.

33. Finke and Stark, *Churching of America*, 29; Bruce C. Daniels, *The Connecticut Town: Growth and Development, 1635–1790* (Middletown, CT: Wesleyan University Press, 1979), 104 and passim.

34. Finke and Stark, *Churching of America*, 45; Mary Latimer Gambrell, *Ministerial Training in Eighteenth-Century New England* (New York: Columbia University Press, 1937); Stout, "Preaching the Insurrection," 12. James Cooper notes that Congregational "ministers frequently addressed questions of church government in their sermons," which is significant as there are important similarities between Reformed approaches to ecclesiastical and civic government. Cooper, *The Tenaciousness of the Their Liberties*, 31.

35. Finke and Stark, *Churching of America*, 29; David Hackett Fisher, *Albion's Seed: Four British Folkways in America* (New York: Oxford University Press, 1989), 431, 606, 608; Howard Miller, "The Grammar of Liberty: Presbyterians and the First American Constitutions," *Journal of Presbyterian History* 54 (1976), 151–152; Clark, *The Language of Liberty*, 351–363.

36. Carl Bridenbaugh, *Mitre and Sceptre: Transatlantic Faiths, Ideas, Personalities, and Politics: 1689–1775* (New York: Oxford University Press, 1962), 207–287, 256; Frohnen, *American Republic*, 110; Bernard Bailyn, *The Ideological Origins of the American Republic* (Cambridge, MA: Harvard University Press, 1967), 95–96; Heimert, *Religion and the American Mind*, 351–352.

37. Kidd, *The Protestant Interest*, passim, and *God of Liberty*, esp. 67–74; Samuel Sherwood, "The Church's Flight into the Wilderness. . ." (1776), in Ellis Sandoz, *Political Sermons of the American Founding Era, 1730–1805*, 2nd ed. (Indianapolis, IN: Liberty Fund Press, 1998), 1: 514; Martin I. J. Griffin, ed., *Catholics and the American Revolution* (Rideley Park: self-published, 1907), 1: 1–40; 3: 384–392.

38. See especially Zuckert, *Natural Rights Republic*, 76, 141, and Alan Dershowitz's *Blasphemy: How the Religious Right is Hijacking Our Declaration of Independence* (Hoboken, NJ: John Wiley & Sons, 2007).
39. *Journals of the Continental Congress, 1774–1789*, Worthington C. Ford et al., eds. (Washington, DC, 1904–37), 1: 33–35 [hereinafter *JCC*].
40. Adams, ed., *Works of John Adams*, 2: 16; *JCC*, 1: 68–70, 72.
41. *JCC*, 1: 83, 87–88.
42. Adrienne Koch and William Peden, eds., *Life and Selected Writings of Thomas Jefferson* (New York: Random House, 1993), 24.
43. Thomas Jefferson to Henry Lee, May 8, 1825, in ibid., 656–657; Zuckert, *Natural Rights Republic*, 76, 141. Of course some of the founders listed above (and in the following lists) were better Calvinists than others—for example, John Adams was a lifelong Congregationalist, but privately he came to embrace Unitarian theology. On the other hand, he specifically claimed to be heavily influenced by Reformed political theory (*supra*, 21). As well, some joined other denominations later in life (e.g., Wilson eventually became an Anglican). I have compiled each list of Reformed founders myself, but where possible I cite a printed account of the denominational affiliation of the founders. William Stevens Perry, "The Faith of the Signers of the Declaration of Independence," *Magazine of History* (1926), 215–237.
44. Douglass Adair and John A. Schutz, eds., *Peter Oliver's Origin and Progress of the American Rebellion* (Stanford, CA: Stanford University Press, 1961), 41; Paul Johnson, *A History of the American People* (New York: HarperCollins, 1997), 173; Baldwin, *New England Clergy*, 91; JohnWingate Thornton, ed., *The Pulpit of the American Revolution*, 2nd ed. (Boston: D. Lothrop, 1876), 43; and Sandoz, *Political Sermons*, passim. By way of contrast, many Anglican ministers were Loyalists. Bell, *War of Religion*, 240, 244.
45. Kramnick and Moore, *The Godless Constitution*; M. E. Bradford, *Founding Fathers: Brief Lives of the Framers of the United States Constitution*, 2nd ed., rev. (Lawrence: University Press of Kansas, 1994); David Brian Robertson, "Madison's Opponents and Constitutional Design," *American Political Science Review* 99 (May 2005), 225–243, 242.
46. Article VI's ban on religious tests is often taken as evidence that the founders desired a secular civil order. For a different view, see Daniel L. Dreisbach, "The Constitution's Forgotten Religion Clause: Reflections on the Article VI Religious Test Ban," *Journal of Church and State* 38 (Spring 1996), 261–295. During the ratification debates and into the nineteenth century, some Calvinists warned that the Constitution's failure to acknowledge God would lead to, or was the cause of, disasters. See Dreisbach and Hall, *Sacred Rights*, 346–363.
47. Alexander Hamilton, James Madison, and John Jay, *The Federalist Papers*, Clinton Rossiter, ed. (New York: New American Library, 1961), 322; Hartz, *The Liberal Tradition in America*, 39.

48. Elazar, *American Constitutional Tradition*, 144; Shain, "Afterword," in Dreisbach, Hall, and Morrison, *The Founders on God and Government*, 274–277.
49. Mark David Hall, "Religion and the American Founding," in Richard A. Harris and Daniel J. Tichenor, eds., *A History of the U.S. Political System: Ideas, Interests, and Institutions* (Santa Barbara, CA: ABC-CLIO, 2010), 1: 99–112; Daniel L. Dreisbach, "In Search of a Christian Commonwealth: An Examination of Selected Nineteenth-Century Commentaries on References to God and the Christian Religion in the United States Constitution," *Baylor Law Review* 48 (1996), 927–1000.
50. Numerous scholars and jurists have asserted that Madison's Memorial and Remonstrance and Jefferson's Virginia Statute for Religious Liberty influenced the authors and ratifiers of the First Amendment. I demonstrate that there is little evidence to support this proposition in "Madison's Memorial and Remonstrance, Jefferson's Statute for Religious Liberty, and the Creation of the First Amendment," *American Political Thought*, forthcoming.
51. Mark David Hall, "Jeffersonian Walls and Madisonian Lines: The Supreme Court's Use of History in Religion Clause Cases," *Oregon Law Review* 85 (2006): 568–569. Of course Reformed Christians often opposed established churches if their churches were not established, but even then they seldom supported a strict separation between church and state. See, for instance, Thomas E. Buckley, *Church and State in Revolutionary Virginia, 1776–1787* (Charlottesville: University Press of Virginia, 1977), passim.
52. Dreisbach and Hall, *Sacred Rights of Conscience.* 426–433, 441–487; Hall, *Roger Sherman and the Creation of the American Republic,* chapter 6; Charlene Bangs Bickford et al., eds., *Documentary History of the First Federal Congress* (Baltimore: The Johns Hopkins University Press, 1992), 11: 1500–1501.

3

Jews, Judaism, and the American Founding

David G. Dalin

MUCH HAS BEEN written about the Jewish contribution to the American Revolution and the impact of the Revolution on American Jews.[1] The Revolution, Jonathan D. Sarna noted, ushered in a new era for American Jews in which "changes in law and in the relationship of religion to the state ... transformed American Jewish life forever after."[2] New constitutions, promulgated by almost every state after 1776, promised Jewish citizens a greater measure of religious freedom than they had heretofore enjoyed. Virginia's historic Statute for Establishing Religious Freedom, drafted by Thomas Jefferson in 1777 and enacted in 1786, proclaimed that "all men shall be free to profess, and by argument to maintain, their opinions in matters of religion, and that the same shall in no wise diminish, enlarge or affect their civil capacities."[3] The Northwest Ordinance, adopted by the Confederation Congress in 1787 and affirmed by the new national government in 1789, extended religious freedom into the territories north of the Ohio River. With the ratification of a new national Constitution forbidding religious tests for federal offices, and the First Amendment prohibiting Congress from making any law "respecting an establishment of religion, or prohibiting the free exercise thereof," the hopes of revolutionary-era American Jews for equal rights were finally being realized.[4]

By the time of American Independence, approximately two thousand Jews lived in the former British colonies. They were concentrated in five cities: New York, Philadelphia, Newport, Charleston, and Savannah. Many Jews supported the War for Independence and some were active in early national politics, but there were no Jewish delegates to the Continental Congresses, no Jewish signatories to the Declaration of Independence, and no Jewish members of the Federal Convention of 1787. As Sarna pointed out, "the Constitutional Convention, and most state discussions concerning the place of religion in American life, ignored Jews. The major American documents bearing on religious liberty do not mention them even once."[5]

Moreover, the promise of religious equality made by the founding fathers in the First Amendment to the US Constitution, and in other documents of the American founding, was not immediately translated into practice. At the time the national Constitution was ratified, "[a]ll but two states had religious tests banning Jews... from public office."[6] Jews, along with other taxpayers, were required to support Christian churches and ministers in Massachusetts, New Hampshire, Connecticut, New Jersey, Georgia, North Carolina, and South Carolina.[7] South Carolina's constitution of 1778 declared "the Christian Protestant religion... the established religion of this State."[8] As late as 1816, "more than half of the original thirteen states still denied Jews political equality."[9]

Hebrew, Hebrew Biblical Imagery, and the Founding Fathers

"Like their Puritan forebears," the founding fathers who led America's War of Independence "frequently compared their own struggle with Great Britain to that of Israel's contest against Egypt."[10] The founding generation encountered this theme in the sermons of Patriot clergymen, which "reveal that Old Testament analogues were frequently drawn by preachers in their efforts to justify or explain the common desire to break away from British rule."[11] For the American colonists fighting for their independence, "King George was viewed as Pharaoh" of the Old Testament and George Washington was compared to Moses, "who was called up by God to bring freedom to his nation."[12] Indeed, when John Adams, Benjamin Franklin, and Thomas Jefferson were asked by the Continental Congress to propose a new national seal, Franklin recommended a design depicting "Moses standing on the Shore, and extending his Hand over the Sea, thereby causing the same to overwhelm Pharaoh..." and Jefferson suggested a portrayal of the Children of Israel led through the wilderness by a pillar of a cloud by day and a pillar of fire by night. Both men agreed that the new national motto should be "Rebellion to Tyrants is Obedience to God."[13]

Many founders, like their Puritan ancestors, venerated the Hebrew language, the Old Testament, and the Jews of the Bible. As Shalom Goldman noted, "the founders of Harvard, Yale and Columbia, and the other early colleges were men for whom the Hebrew language was a source of inspiration and an essential component of a good education."[14] This was especially the case at Harvard, "where the first two college presidents were scholars of Hebrew," and where all freshmen were required to study the language until 1787. John Adams, for example, who pursued his undergraduate studies at Harvard between 1751 and 1755, studied under Judah Monis, a Jewish convert to Christianity, who taught Hebrew language and grammar at Harvard from 1722 to 1761. Monis also authored *A Grammar of the Hebrew Tongue*, the first Hebrew textbook published in the American colonies.[15] His conversion to Christianity in 1722, about which much has been written, was a prerequisite to his appointment as a Hebrew instructor at Harvard.[16]

While many founders studied Hebrew and admired the Jewish religion of the ancient Hebrews, the ambivalence of some civic leaders towards Jews and Judaism was evident in their political culture and law. A few founders crafted test oaths restricting the participation of Jews in politics and public life, while others appointed (or recommended the appointment of) Jews to civic and political office, forged cordial relationships with Jewish synagogues, and became friends with individual Jewish supporters of the Patriot cause. Some who studied and revered the Hebrew language of the Old Testament, and admired the Jews of the Hebrew Bible, never socialized with their Jewish compatriots or counted Jews among their neighbors and friends.

This chapter discusses the interaction and correspondence of four founders—George Washington, Alexander Hamilton, John Adams, and Thomas Jefferson—with individual Jews, and their views of Jews and Judaism. In addition to being among the most prominent founders, these men represent different approaches to, and engagement with, Judaism. Hamilton, who interacted more extensively with Jews than any major founder, had great admiration for the Jewish people. Similarly, Washington viewed American Jews positively and was an important advocate for religious equality. Adams was among the few founders who was clearly a Christian Zionist. Jefferson, by contrast, shared with other Enlightenment rationalists of his generation a decidedly negative view of the Jewish religion. Examining how these four men interacted with Jews and viewed Judaism shines a light on how America's founders were informed by this religious tradition, and on how they thought Jews should be treated in the new republic.

George Washington

President George Washington was the first leader of a modern nation to acknowledge openly the Jewish people as full-fledged citizens of the country in which they had chosen to settle. Although the Jewish community was small at the time of his inauguration, Washington was well aware of, and grateful for, the substantive contributions Jews had made to the cause of independence and to the founding of the new nation.

Washington's first personal contact with a member of the Jewish community came about as a result of a tragedy—the incurable illness of George and Martha's daughter Patsy, who suffered from epilepsy. "In an exasperating quest for a cure," biographer Ron Chernow recounted, the Washingtons "took Patsy to the leading physicians in Williamsburg, including eight visits to Dr. John de Sequeyra, the scion of a prominent family of Sephardic Jews in London."[17] Their encounter with Dr. Sequeyra was "the only time we know for sure that George Washington had contact with a Jew before the Revolution."[18]

During the War of Independence, Washington was impressed by the loyalty, courage, and devotion to the Patriotic cause of many Jews. For example, Benjamin Nones, a French Jew who had immigrated to America from Bordeaux in 1772, served as a major on General Washington's staff and distinguished himself for bravery during the siege of Savannah. Similarly, two Jewish members of Washington's regiment, Isaac Franks and Philip Moses Russell, shared the hardships of the bitter winter at Valley Forge. Franks, who would achieve the rank of colonel before his retirement from the military, "made a worthy name for himself as a brave and dedicated soldier in the Continental army and consequently enjoyed the personal friendship of George Washington."[19] Russell, a surgeon's mate on Washington's medical staff, served the suffering soldiers at Valley Forge with distinction. According to one account, "[h]is personal relationship with General Washington is attested to in [a] special commendation that he *ostensibly* received (but that cannot be documented in any of Washington's papers) from the commander in chief: 'for his assiduous and faithful attention to the sick and wounded, as well as his cool and collected deportment in battle.'"[20] Fritz Hirschfeld reported that, in the aftermath of the War of Independence, General Washington did not forget the Jewish soldiers serving in the Continental army "who had faithfully marched with him from the beginning to the end."[21] His friendship with Colonel Isaac Franks, who became a wealthy Philadelphia merchant, would continue throughout the years of his presidency. For two months in 1793, when a deadly yellow fever epidemic spread through the nation's capital in Philadelphia, President Washington rented Franks' home in the Philadelphia suburb of Germantown.[22]

Washington was especially indebted to the courage and devotion of the Polish-born Jew Haym Salomon. Salomon, a broker for the new Office of Finance of the United States, assisted Superintendent of Finance Robert Morris in funding the war effort. "As a broker," Beth S. Wenger recounted, "Salomon offered a valuable service to the Revolution by raising funds and negotiating bills of exchange with several foreign governments, particularly the French, with whom he had conducted considerable business and established reliable contacts."[23] Throughout the war, Washington repeatedly turned to Salomon because Congress and the state assemblies were not forthcoming in allocating sufficient monies for supplies, ammunition, and salaries. Salomon demonstrated great resourcefulness in securing the funds needed to maintain Washington's army.[24]

Although no Jews actively participated in the proceedings of the Constitutional Convention in Philadelphia in 1787, Jonas Phillips, a German-Jewish immigrant living in Philadelphia, petitioned the Convention delegates not to include in the document they were crafting a religious test for holding public office. This was the only petition concerning religious liberty submitted to the Constitutional Convention.[25]

Jews were among those in attendance at President George Washington's inauguration when he took the oath of office on April 30, 1789. The most notable of these was Gershom Mendes Seixas, the American-born spiritual leader of Congregation Shearith Israel, New York City's most venerable synagogue. Sexias, who "led his New York congregation in special services to mark the adoption of the new federal Constitution," was one of the fourteen clergymen who took part in the inaugural ceremonies.[26] In the fall of 1776, when the British occupied New York, Seixas, along with many members of his congregation, fled the city, "[t]aking their Torah scroll and other ritual objects with them," and relocated to Philadelphia.[27] The flight of Seixas and most of his Shearith Israel congregation to Philadelphia, Hasia R. Diner noted, demonstrated to many "Jewish support for the revolutionary cause."[28] In his sermons throughout the War of Independence, Seixas "regularly called on God to bless the Revolution, the Congress and George Washington."[29] When Seixas and his congregation returned to New York City at the war's end, he was acclaimed and admired by Alexander Hamilton, John Jay, and other prominent New Yorkers as the city's preeminent Jewish leader of the revolutionary cause. No other Jewish leader of this era mingled so easily with the Protestant leaders of the American founding.[30]

As Vincent Phillip Muñoz observed, "[m]ost scholars assume that on matters of religious liberty Thomas Jefferson and James Madison speak for the founding generation. . . . George Washington, however, was no less dedicated to securing religious freedom than his second and third presidential successors."[31] Indeed, religious liberty "was a cardinal principle of Washington's political philosophy."[32] In a 1783 letter, Washington wrote, "[t]he establishment of Civil and Religious Liberty was the Motive that induced me to the field [of battle]."[33]

When he became president in 1789, Washington gave public recognition to the active role of America's Jews in furthering the cause of American independence.[34] In the months following his inauguration, he received numerous congratulatory letters, including letters from six of the new republic's Jewish synagogues, to which he replied in correspondence that deserves to be included among the founders' most important statements on religious liberty and the prudential relationship between religion and the state. Washington's 1790 letter to the "Hebrew Congregation" of Newport, Rhode Island, today known as the Touro Synagogue, is the most significant.

The famed correspondence between George Washington and Jewish Americans, Jonathan D. Sarna noted, went far to define "the place of Judaism in the new nation."[35] It commenced with an address from the Hebrew congregation in Newport to the new president, "composed for his visit to that city on August 17, 1790, following Rhode Island's ratification of the Constitution." The Rhode Island Jews "noted past discrimination against Jews, praised the new government for 'generously affording to all liberty of conscience and immunities of citizenship,' and thanked God 'for all of the blessings of civil and religious liberty' that Jews now enjoyed under the Constitution."[36] Washington's eloquent reply is worth quoting at length:

> The Citizens of the United States of America have a right to applaud themselves for having given to mankind examples of an enlarged and liberal policy: a policy worthy of imitation. All possess alike liberty of conscience and immunities of citizenship. It is now no more that toleration is spoken of, as if it were the indulgence of one class of people, that another enjoyed the exercise of their inherent natural rights. For happily the Government of the United States,

which gives to bigotry no sanction, to persecution no assistance requires only that they who live under its protection should demean themselves as good citizens, in giving it on all occasions their effectual support.

It would be inconsistent with the frankness of my character not to avow that I am pleased with your favorable opinion of my Administration, and fervent wishes for my felicity. May the Children of the stock of Abraham, who dwell in this land, continue to merit and enjoy the good will of the other Inhabitants; while every one shall sit in safety under his own vine and figtree, and there shall be none to make him afraid. May the father of all mercies scatter light and not darkness in our paths, and make us all in our several vocations useful here, and in his own due time and way everlastingly happy.[37]

Washington's missive to the Hebrew Congregation in Newport is a foundation stone of religious liberty and equality in America. The new president "made history by extending the definition of American religious legitimacy beyond Christians[,] . . . declaring [in his correspondence with the Newport congregation] full religious equality for Jews."[38]

Alexander Hamilton

Alexander Hamilton was born in 1755 on the island of Nevis in the British West Indies. During the eighteenth century, according to Chernow, "Nevis had a thriving population of Sephardic Jews, many of whom had escaped persecution in Brazil and entered the local sugar trade."[39] By the 1720s, the Jews of Nevis had "created a synagogue, a school, and a well-kept cemetery that survives to this day."[40] Hamilton's mother, Rachel, was the daughter of physician John Faucette, "a French Huguenot who emigrated to the West Indies in consequence of the revocation of the Edict of Nantes."[41] Rachel Faucette's first marriage was to Johann Michael Lavien. Hamilton's biographer Ron Chernow noted that Lavien "can be a Sephardic variant of *Levine*."[42] "[B]ut if he was Jewish," as he is generally believed to have been, Chernow continued, Lavien may have hidden his origins from Rachel's family, who "would certainly have squelched the match in a world that frowned on religious no less than interracial marriage."[43]

Their marriage, never a happy one, lasted only a few years. After the couple separated, Rachel began living with a Scotsman, James Hamilton, whom she apparently never married, and subsequently gave birth to Alexander on January 11, 1755. Divorce, Hamilton's biographer observed, "was a novelty in the eighteenth century. To obtain one in the Crown colonies was an expensive, tortuous affair, and this deprived James and Rachel of any chance to legitimize their match."[44] Hamilton's birth was thus viewed as illegitimate by the Anglican Church, which "could not offer full acceptance of the situation . . . [and] denied Alexander membership or education in the church school on Nevis."[45] With his illegitimate birth thus barring him from an Anglican school, Hamilton was educated by Jewish teachers in the small Sephardic Jewish school on Nevis, where he was tutored in Hebrew and, as his son would later recall, even "taught to repeat the Decalogue in Hebrew, at the school of a Jewess."[46]

"Perhaps from this exposure at an impressionable age," Chernow suggested, "Hamilton harbored a lifelong reverence for Jews."[47] In later years, Hamilton would write admiringly that the Jews were a people whose history was "entirely out of the *ordinary course* of human affairs" and "the effect of some great providential plan."[48] He later argued, "Why distrust the evidence of the Jews? Discredit them and you destroy the Christian religion. . . . Were not the [Jews] witnesses of the pure and holy, happy and heaven-approved faith, converts to that faith?"[49]

In 1784, when Hamilton drafted the new charter of his *alma mater* King's College (which soon came to be known as Columbia College), he "saw to it that all clergymen" were on its new Board of Regents, including "the local rabbi" Gershom Mendes Seixas, whom Hamilton had come to know and admire during the War of Independence.[50] In his appointment as a Columbia College Regent, Seixas became the first American Jew to serve on the governing board of an American university.[51] Moreover, in drafting Columbia College's new charter, Hamilton, who supported the Jewish quest for religious liberty and freedom of conscience in the new nation, "had hoped that Columbia College would not compel its students to study religious works," such as readings in Protestant theology, "to which they could not conscientiously subscribe."[52]

Hamilton's respect for Judaism and for Jews is also attested to by the fact that he was one of the only lawyers among the founding fathers—and many of the founders were lawyers—to serve Jewish clients in his law practice.[53] One of Hamilton's notable Jewish clients, and a member of Gershom Seixas's congregation, was Isaac Moses, a Philadelphia merchant and Patriot who served in the Philadelphia militia during the American Revolution and who, during the 1770s and early 1780s, was "unquestionably the wealthiest Jew in Philadelphia."[54] A close associate and business partner of Robert Morris during the Revolution, Moses "bought bills of credit from Robert Morris to assist the Treasury, then in dire need of ready funds."[55]

Moses moved to New York in 1783, where he joined "a group of some thirty merchants who addressed the New York legislature, proposing that the state reward their patriotism and compensate them for their losses by selling the Loyalists' estates."[56] Among his business ventures in New York "was a partnership with the international trading firm of Samuel and Moses Myers and Marcus Elcan of Richmond, which did business with Amsterdam."[57] In 1785, when the Myers' firm was "in financial trouble, threatening the credit and solvency of its partner, Isaac Moses," Moses retained Hamilton as his counsel. Hamilton interceded on Moses's "behalf with the New York creditors, assuring them that Moses was solvent" and saving Moses from a precarious financial situation.[58] With Hamilton continuing as his attorney, Moses emerged from the financial crisis, becoming a charter stockholder of the Bank of New York, and one of the most respected Jewish business leaders in the city.[59]

When he was fatally wounded by Aaron Burr in 1804, Hamilton was mourned by Isaac Moses and his other clients and friends in Seixas's synagogue. Seixas, too, in the aftermath of the Burr-Hamilton duel, mourned Hamilton's tragic death, lamenting the fact that "prejudices, whether political or civil[,] . . . have a tendency to foment evil in the land."[60]

John Adams

Much has been made of John Adams's admiration for Judaism, his appreciation for Jews, and his interest in Jewish books. Isidore S. Meyer showed that Hebrew biblical and post-biblical sources about the ancient Hebrews influenced Adams's writings about American legal and constitutional thought. In Adams's *Defence of the Constitutions of the Government of the United States of America*, for example, "copious references are made to the seventeenth-century writings of Algernon Sidney and James Harrington who drew many of their ideas about government from biblical and post-biblical Jewish sources."[61] Also, the extensive correspondence between John Adams and his wife Abigail, in the years preceding and during the American Revolution, is replete with allusions to the Hebrew Psalms and "to the other books of Jewish Scriptures during this critical period of American history."[62]

Adams's interest in Jews and the Hebrew Bible stemmed in part from his association with the Reverend George Duffield, a prominent Presbyterian minister of French Huguenot descent who served as one of the two chaplains to the Continental Congress. During the sessions meeting in Philadelphia in 1776, Adams and other delegates listened regularly to the Reverend Duffield's sermons. As Meyer noted, "[i]t is interesting to observe how Duffield made use of Jewish Scriptures and how he alluded to the experience of the Jews in his discourses before the signing of the Declaration of Independence and with the advent of peace in 1783."[63] In a May 17, 1776, letter to Abigail, Adams observed: "I have this morning heard Mr. Duffield, upon the signs of the times. He ran a parallel between the case of Israel, and that of America; and between the conduct of Pharaoh, and that of George . . . He concluded, that the course of events indicated strongly the design of Providence, that we should be separated from Great Britain, &c."[64] With the coming of peace in 1783, Duffield preached an oft-quoted sermon of thanksgiving in which he referred to the American states as the tribes of Israel and George Washington as the Joshua of the day, and in which he viewed "the hand of God as guiding and guarding the way of the Americans" in their successful War of Independence.[65]

Adams's appreciation for Judaism and the contribution of Jews to the making of a better world are most evident in letters he wrote to the Dutch jurist Francis Van der Kemp, whom he had met while a US diplomat in Amsterdam during the early 1780s.[66] In a missive dated December 31, 1808, Adams stated that he was appalled by Voltaire's derogatory attitude toward the Hebrew Bible and the Jewish people. "How is it possible this old Fellow [Voltaire] should represent the Hebrews in such contemptible light?" asked Adams. "They are the most glorious Nation that ever inhabited this Earth. The Romans and their Empire were but a Bauble in comparison of the Jews. They have given Religion to three quarters of the Globe and have influenced the affairs of Mankind more, and more happily than any other Nation ancient or modern."[67]

In a subsequent letter to Van der Kemp dated February 16, 1809, Adams wrote:

> . . . in spite of Bolingbroke and Voltaire, I will insist that the Hebrews have done more to civilize men than any other nation. If I were an atheist, and believed in blind eternal fate, I should still believe that fate had ordained the Jews to be the most essential

instrument for civilizing the nations. If I were an atheist of the other sect, who believe, or pretend to believe that all is ordered by chance, I should believe that chance had ordered the Jews to preserve and propagate to all mankind the doctrine of a supreme, intelligent, wise, almighty sovereign of the universe, which I believe to be the great essential principle of all morality, and consequently of all civilization.[68]

Adams is perhaps the sole founder who is on record supporting the restoration of the Jews to their own land in Judea. Aware of Adams's favorable attitude towards Jews, the American Jewish newspaper editor, politician, diplomat, and playwright Mordecai Manuel Noah initiated a correspondence with the former president.[69] In 1818, Noah delivered an address at the consecration of the new synagogue building erected by his own Congregation Shearith Israel, in New York City. Noah's "Discourse" focused on "the universal history of Jewish persecution at the hands of nondemocratic governments and their nations, and declared that the Jewish people could only live free of oppression when they were reestablished in their own home and could govern themselves."[70] Noah sent a copy of his "Discourse" to Adams, who replied encouragingly, expressing his personal wish that "your Nation may be admitted to all Privileges of Citizens in every Country of the World. This Country has done much, I wish it may do more, and annul every narrow idea in Religion, Government and Commerce. . . . It has pleased the Providence of the 'first Cause,' the Universal Cause, that Abraham should give Religion, not only to the Hebrews, but to Christians and Mahometans, the greatest Part of the Modern civilized World."[71]

The following year, Noah sent Adams a copy of his recently published book, *Travels in England, France, Spain and the Barbary States*. In a letter of thanks acknowledging the gift, Adams praised it as "a magazine of ancient and modern learning of judicious observations and ingenious reflections," and expressed regret that Noah had not extended his travels to "Syria, Judea and Jerusalem." Had Noah done so, Adams wrote, he would have attended "more to [his] remarks than to those of any traveler I have yet read," adding, "Farther I could find it in my heart to wish that you had been at the head of a hundred thousand Israelites . . . & marching with them into Judea & making a conquest of that country & restoring your nation to the dominion of it. For I really wish the Jews again in Judea an independent nation."[72]

Thomas Jefferson

Throughout his life, Thomas Jefferson advocated religious equality and freedom for members of all faiths, including Jews, to whom he frequently referred. Jefferson's advocacy of civic equality for American Jews began as early as 1776, when he cosponsored a Bill for the Naturalization of Foreigners that, had it been enacted by the Virginia legislature, would have permitted Jews, Catholics, and other non-Protestants to be naturalized as Virginia citizens. Despite Jefferson's strong endorsement, the bill was not passed by the Virginia Assembly.[73]

Jefferson eventually won the day when the state legislature passed his famous Statute for Establishing Religious Freedom, which guaranteed "that no man shall be compelled to frequent or support any religious worship . . . but that all men shall be free to profess, and by argument to maintain, their opinions in matters of religion, and that the same shall in no wise diminish, enlarge or affect their civil capacities."[74] He came to regard his authorship of the Virginia Statute as an achievement "second in importance only to his authorship of the Declaration of Independence."[75] This historic Virginia statute "not only gave full legal equality to Virginia's Jews (one of whom, two years later, was elected to municipal office), it also set the stage for the Constitution's provisions on religious freedom."[76]

By the time Jefferson assumed the presidency in 1801, his contact with individual Jews and connections with the Jewish community had been minimal. Nonetheless, during his presidency, he appointed Reuben Etting, a Jewish political supporter from Baltimore, US Marshall from Maryland. In doing so, he became the first American president to appoint a Jew to a federal government position.[77]

After leaving the presidency, Jefferson corresponded with a few Jews, "although there is no indication that Jefferson developed a strong friendship with any of them."[78] In 1818, Mordecai Manuel Noah sent Jefferson a copy of the same "Discourse" he had sent to Adams. In his response to Noah, Jefferson wrote:

> I thank you for the discourse on the consecration of the Synagogue in your city, with which you have been pleased to favor me. I have read it with pleasure and instruction, having learned from it some valuable facts in Jewish history which I did not know before. Your sect by its sufferings has furnished a remarkable proof of the universal spirit of religious intolerance inherent in every sect. . . . Our

laws have applied the only antidote to this vice, protecting our religious, as they do our civil rights, by putting all on an equal footing. But more remains to be done, for although we are free by the law, we are not so in practice. Public opinion erects itself into an inquisition, and exercises its office with as much fanaticism fans the flames of an Auto-de-fe.[79]

In 1820, Jefferson wrote to Dr. Jacob De La Motta, the prominent Savannah physician and Jewish community leader, that "religious freedom is the most effectual anodyne against religious dissention," and he expressed the hope that American Jews would be afforded equal rights and "will be seen taking their seats on the benches of science as preparatory to their doing the same at the board of government."[80] Jefferson's genuine concern for the religious freedom of Jews also found expression in a letter, written on January 6, 1826, six months before his death, apparently referring to the then-common practice of reading the King James Bible in schools. Imposing on Jewish youth "in our public seminaries . . . a course of theological reading which their consciences do not permit them to pursue," Jefferson wrote, was "a cruel addition to the wrongs" that Jews had suffered throughout history.[81]

Of all the major founders, Jefferson was the most critical in his attitude toward Judaism. "A product of the eighteenth-century Enlightenment, Jefferson considered himself a 'rational Christian,'" calling himself, among other things, a Unitarian.[82] Jefferson's support for Jewish religious and political equality did not mean that he approved of Judaism as a religion. On the contrary, he shared with other Enlightenment rationalists of his generation a decidedly negative view of the Jewish religion. Although he read widely, his knowledge of Judaism was minimal, and he believed that Judaism had not changed significantly since the time of Moses. As Egal Feldman pointed out, Jefferson was "[c]ritical of Judaism's claim to a divine revelation, . . . considered its biblical history distorted, its God and law cruel, its form of worship meaningless, and it morality ethnocentric. He attributed to his own Unitarian faith a moral superiority to that of Judaism."[83]

Jefferson's antipathy towards Judaism is reflected in an 1813 letter to John Adams, in which he quoted with approval a scholarly work that asserted: "Ethics were so little understood among the Jews, that in their whole compilation called the Talmud, there is only one treatise on moral subjects. . . . What a wretched depravity of sentiment and manners must have prevailed, before such corrupt maxims could have obtained credit! It is impossible to collect from these writings a consistent series of moral doctrine."[84] Similarly, the "vicious ethics" of the Jews,[85] Jefferson wrote, "were 'irreconcilable with the sound dictates of reason & morality,' encouraged poor relationships among people, and were downright 'repulsive and anti-social, as respecting other nations.'"[86] As Jonathan D. Sarna aptly put it, Jefferson "continued to think Jews morally depraved."[87]

Jefferson's complaints extended even to the Jewish conception of God. In his *Syllabus of an Estimate of the Merit of the Doctrines of Jesus*, he described the Jewish idea of God and his attributes as "degrading and injurious."[88] Elsewhere in his correspondence, he depicted the Jewish God as "cruel, vindictive, capricious, and unjust."[89] Finally, in a letter to Ezra Stiles, the noted Hebraist and president of Yale University, he attacked Jewish theology, "which supposes the God of infinite justice to punish the sins of the fathers upon their children, unto the third and fourth generation."[90]

"To an extent rarely acknowledged," Steven Waldman opined, Jefferson "despised . . . the Jews of the Old Testament and the religion it seemed to spawn."[91] Although his "negative attitude about Judaism seemed mostly confined to antiquity, he occasionally revealed an up-to-date bias."[92] It is not clear that Jefferson was anti-Semitic per se, given that he was critical of all but Enlightened forms of religion. In any case, he departed from the admiration most of his colleagues had for Judaism.

Conclusion

George Washington was the first president to visit a synagogue and correspond with American Jews. When, in his historic 1790 response to the Rhode Island Jews, Washington issued the stirring assurance that "the government of the United States . . . gives to bigotry no sanction, to persecution no assistance," he "acknowledged not only the principle of religious freedom, but also that Jews were citizens—the first time anywhere for a head of state to do so."[93] In visiting a synagogue, Washington set a precedent that future presidents—including Ulysses S. Grant, William McKinley, William Howard Taft, Lyndon Johnson, Ronald Reagan, and Bill Clinton, among others—would follow.

The relationship of the founders to America's Jews was one of both admiration and ambivalence. With the exception of George Washington and Alexander Hamilton, none of the famous founders knew Jews personally, socialized with Jews, or counted Jews among their close acquaintances or friends. "John Adams's interest in the Jewish people," Egal Feldman asserted, "grew out of his knowledge of their biblical past, somewhat tempered by democratic ideas of the revolutionary age."[94] His affection for Jews apparently was a product of his reverence for the ancient Hebrews and their three thousand years of history. For Adams, as for some of the other Christian leaders of the new American republic, it was the idealized or "mythical" Jew of Hebrew Scripture, rather than the contemporary reality, that inspired his admiration for Judaism and its people. Adams knew no Jews personally, had no Jewish clients in his Boston law practice, and had no Jewish neighbors or friends.[95] To be sure, he was a Christian Zionist who expressed support for a Jewish homeland in Palestine. And yet, Adams's well-known sympathy for Zionism, as articulated in his correspondence with Mordecai Noah, was predicated on the theological hope and presupposition that a Jewish homeland in Palestine would hasten the conversion of Jews to Christianity. "Once restored to an independent government and no longer persecuted," wrote Adams, the Jews "would soon wear away some of the asperities and peculiarities of their character & possibly in time become liberal Unitarian Christians."[96]

Although a champion of religious liberty for Jews and other religious minorities and a staunch defender of the wall of separation between church and state, Thomas Jefferson, of all the founders, had the least favorable—indeed, most harshly critical—view of Judaism. In his *Syllabus*, which he sent to Benjamin Rush in 1803, Jefferson accused Jews of having a "degrading and injurious" understanding of God and contended that their view of ethics was "imperfect" and "irreconcilable with the sound dictates of reason and morality."[97] Jews "needed reformation . . . in an eminent degree," Jefferson wrote, a view implicitly shared by others in the founding generation.[98] Jefferson never invited Jews to his home, Monticello. Like Adams, Jefferson had no Jewish neighbors or friends.

Of all the founders discussed in this essay, Alexander Hamilton had the closest connection to Jews, a connection that went back to his childhood. More than any prominent founder, he had an admiration for Judaism and for the contribution of Jews to civilization. "For Alexander Hamilton, an Episcopalian who had learned to read Hebrew in his youth," Michael Oren remarked, "the destiny of America was not unlike that of the Jews."[99]

While a great deal has been written about the history of the American Jewish political experience generally, comparatively little has been written about the relationship between the founding fathers and America's Jews. Both as individuals and as a community, Jews play a relatively insignificant role (when they play any role at all) in the standard biographies of most founders.[100] Indeed, in some of the most-acclaimed biographies of the founding fathers, Jews are not mentioned at all.[101] Ron Chernow's recent prize-winning biographies of Hamilton and Washington are welcomed exceptions to this pattern. This writer hopes that future scholarship will give more attention to and analysis of the founders' views on Jews and on Judaism, and on the relationship between the American founders and Jews.

Notes

1. Jewish contributions to the American Revolution are discussed in Samuel Rezneck, *Unrecognized Patriots: The Jews in the American Revolution* (Westport, CT: Greenwood Press, 1975); Richard Morris, "The Jewish Role in the American Revolution in Historical Perspective," in Gladys Rosen, ed., *Jewish Life in America* (New York: The American Jewish Committee, 1978), 8–17; Leon Huhner, "Francis Salvador: A Prominent Patriot of the Revolutionary War," in Abraham J. Karp, ed., *The Jewish Experience in America* (Waltham, MA: American Jewish Historical Society, 1969), 1:276–291; and Alf J. Mapp, Jr., "Haym Solomon," in *The Faiths of Our Fathers: What America's Founders Really Believed* (Landham, MD: Rowman and Littlefield, 2003), 146–152; and Fritz Hirschfeld, *George Washington and the Jews* (Newark: University of Delaware Press, 2005). The best analysis of the impact of the Revolution on American Jews is Jonathan D. Sarna, "The Impact of the American Revolution on American Jews," in Jonathan D. Sarna, ed., *The American Jewish Experience* (New York: Holmes and Meier Publishers, 1986), 18–28.
2. Jonathan D. Sarna, *American Judaism: A History* (New Haven, CT: Yale University Press, 2004), 36.
3. Daniel L. Dreisbach and Mark David Hall, *The Sacred Rights of Conscience: Selected Readings on Religious Liberty and Church-State Relations in the American Founding* (Indianapolis, IN: Liberty Fund Press, 2009), 251.
4. Jonathan D. Sarna and David G. Dalin, *Religion and State in the American Jewish Experience* (Notre Dame, IN: University of Notre Dame Press, 1997), 3, 62.
5. Sarna, *American Judaism*, 37.
6. Steven Waldman, *Founding Faith: How Our Founding Fathers Forged a Radical New Approach to Religious Liberty* (New York: Random House, 2008), 132.

7. Ibid., 132–133.
8. Dreisbach and Hall, *Sacred Rights*, 244.
9. Jacob Rader Marcus, "The Handsome Young Priest in the Black Gown: The Personal World of Gershom Seixas," *Hebrew Union College Annual* 40–41 (1969–1970), 424.
10. Egal Feldman, *Dual Destinies: The Jewish Encounter with Protestant America* (Urbana: University of Illinois Press, 1990), 37.
11. Ibid.
12. Ibid., 38.
13. Dreisbach and Hall, *Sacred Rights*, 229.
14. Shalom Goldman, "Introduction," in Shalom Goldman, ed., *Hebrew and the Bible in America* (Hanover, NH: Brandeis University Press and the University Press of New England, 1993), xxi.
15. Francis Russell, *Adams: An American Dynasty* (New York: American Heritage Publishing Co., 1976), 18–19. Goldman, *Hebrew and the Bible in America*, 201–202. Monis's textbook was also used in a number of New England colleges during the eighteenth century. Ibid., 202.
16. See, for example, Goldman, *Hebrew and the Bible in America*, xxi and 108–109; Feldman, *Dual Destinies*, 16–17; Arthur Hertzberg, *The Jews in America: Four Centuries of an Uneasy Encounter: A History* (New York: Columbia University Press, 1997), 29–31; and Jonathan D. Sarna and Ellen Smith, eds., *The Jews of Boston* (Boston: Combined Jewish Philanthropies of Greater Boston, Inc., 1995), 30–34.
17. Ron Chernow, *Washington: A Life* (New York: Penguin Press, 2010), 153.
18. Ibid.
19. Hirschfeld, *George Washington and the Jews*, 71.
20. Ibid., 75.
21. Ibid., 130.
22. Rezneck, *Unrecognized Patriots*, 36; and Chernow, *Washington*, 702.
23. Beth S. Wenger, *History Lessons: The Creation of American Jewish Heritage* (Princeton: Princeton University Press, 2010), 183.
24. David G. Dalin and Alfred J. Kolatch, *The Presidents of the United States and the Jews* (Middle Village, NY: Jonathan David Publishers, 2000), 6; Jacob Rader Marcus, *United States Jewry, 1776–1985* (Detroit: Wayne State University Press, 1989), 1: 66–77.
25. Dreisbach and Hall, *Sacred Rights*, 374–375; Sarna and Dalin, *Religion and State in the American Jewish Experience*, 72–74.
26. Feldman, *Dual Destinies*, 83.
27. Hasia R. Diner, *The Jews of the United States, 1654 to 2000* (Berkeley: University of California Press, 2004), 47–48.
28. Ibid., 48.
29. Michael Feldberg, ed., *Blessings of Freedom: Chapters in American Jewish History* (Hoboken, NJ: KTAV Publishing House, in association with the American Jewish Historical Society, 2002), 25.

30. Seixas was the most prominent Jewish religious leader in America and "more fully integrated into New York society than any Jewish clergyman was ever to be until the twentieth century." Arthur Hertzberg, *The Jews in America*, 71.
31. Vincent Phillip Muñoz, "Religion and the Common Good: George Washington on Church and State," in Daniel L. Dreisbach, Mark D. Hall, and Jeffry H. Morrison, eds., *The Founders on God and Government* (Lanham: Rowman and Littlefield, 2004), 1.
32. Lee M. Friedman, "George Washington and Jews of His Day," in Lee M. Friedman, ed., *Jewish Pioneers and Patriots* (Philadelphia: The Jewish Publication Society of America, 1942), 20.
33. George Washington to the Ministers, Elders, Deacons, and Members of the Reformed German Congregation of New York, November 27, 1783, in John C. Fitzpatrick, ed., *The Writings of George Washington*, 37 vols. (Washington, DC: Government Printing Office, 1931–1940), 27:249.
34. Hirschfeld, *George Washington and the Jews*, 15.
35. Sarna, *American Judaism*, 38. This correspondence is also discussed in Sarna and Dalin, *Religion and State in the American Jewish Experience*, 77–78.
36. Sarna, *American Judaism*, 38.
37. George Washington to the Hebrew Congregation in Newport, Rhode Island, August 18, 1790, in Dreisbach and Hall, *Sacred Rights*, 464.
38. Waldman, *Founding Faith*, 163–164.
39. Ron Chernow, *Alexander Hamilton* (New York: Penguin Press, 2004), 17.
40. Ibid.; see also Malcom H. Stern, "Some Notes on the Jews of Nevis," *American Jewish Archives* (October 1958), 151–159.
41. Chernow, *Alexander Hamilton*, 8, quoting Hamilton.
42. Ibid., 10.
43. Ibid.
44. Ibid., 16.
45. Yitzchok Levine, "The Jews of Nevis and Alexander Hamilton," *The Jewish Press*, May 2, 2007.
46. John C. Hamilton, *Life of Alexander Hamilton* (Boston: Houghton, Osgood, 1879), 1: 42.
47. Chernow, *Alexander Hamilton*, 18.
48. Ibid., quoting Hamilton.
49. Ibid.
50. Marcus, *United States Jewry, 1776–1985*, 1: 120.
51. Sarna, *American Judaism*, 40–41.
52. Marcus, *United States Jewry, 1776–1985*, 1: 120–121.
53. Marcus, "The Handsome Young Priest in the Black Robe," 426, footnote 36.
54. Rezneck, *Unrecognized Patriots*, 70.
55. Ibid.
56. Ibid., 71.

57. Ibid., 71–72
58. Ibid., 72.
59. Ibid.
60. Marcus, "The Handsome Young Priest in the Black Robe," 425.
61. Isidore S. Meyer, "John Adams Writes a Letter," *Publications of the American Jewish Historical Society* 37 (October 1947), 187.
62. Ibid., 186.
63. Ibid., 189.
64. John Adams to Abigail Adams, May 17, 1776, quoted in Ibid., 192.
65. Ibid., 195–196. See also George Duffield, *A Sermon Preached in the Third Presbyterian Church, in the City of Philadelphia, on Thursday, December 11, 1783. The day appointed by the United States in Congress assembled, to be observed as a day of thanksgiving, for the restoration of peace, and establishment of our Independence, in the enjoyment of our rights and privileges* (Philadelphia: F. Bailey, 1784).
66. David McCullough, *John Adams* (New York: Simon and Schuster, 2001), 608.
67. John Adams to F. A. Van Der Kemp, December 31, 1808, in Meyer, "John Adams Writes a Letter," 200; Dalin and Kolatch, *The Presidents of the United States and the Jews*, 13.
68. John Adams to F. A. Van Der Kemp, February 6, 1809, in Norman Cousins, ed., *"In God We Trust": The Religious Beliefs and Ideas of the American Founding Fathers* (New York: Harper and Brothers, 1958), 102–103.
69. The definitive biography of Noah is Jonathan D. Sarna, *Jacksonian Jew: The Two Worlds of Mordecai Noah* (New York: Holmes and Meier Publishers, Inc., 1981).
70. Feldberg, ed., *Blessings of Freedom*, 202–203.
71. John Adams to Mordecai M. Noah, July 31, 1818, quoted in ibid., 203.
72. John Adams to Mordecai M. Noah, March 15, 1819, quoted in ibid.
73. Bill for the Naturalization of Foreigners, October 14, 1776, in Julian P. Boyd, ed., *The Papers of Thomas Jefferson* (Princeton, NJ: Princeton University Press, 1950), 1: 548, 558–559; Robert M. Healey, "Jefferson on Judaism and the Jews," *American Jewish History* 73 (1984), 360; and Feldberg, ed., *Blessings of Freedom*, 60.
74. Dreisbach and Hall, *Sacred Rights*, 251.
75. Feldman, *Dual Destinies*, 42. James Madison, who, as Daniel L. Dreisbach has noted, had "shepherded" Jefferson's Virginia Statute for Religious Freedom "through the Virginia legislature in the dramatic and rancorous church-state battles of the mid-1780's," described the Virginia Statute as "a true standard of Religious Liberty" that "circumscribes governmental infringements on religious liberty and rights of conscience." Daniel L. Dreisbach, *Thomas Jefferson and the Wall of Separation between Church and State* (New York: New York University Press, 2002), 86.
76. Sarna and Dalin, *Religion and State in the American Jewish Experience*, 66–67.
77. Jefferson's appointment of Reuben Etting is discussed in Dalin and Kolatch, *The Presidents of the United States and the Jews*, 19.

78. Feldman, *Dual Destinies*, 43.
79. Jefferson to Mordecai M. Noah, May 28, 1818, in Dalin and Kolatch, *The Presidents of the United States and the Jews*, 19–20.
80. Jefferson to Jacob de la Motta, August 1820, in Dreisbach and Hall, *Sacred Rights*, 596.
81. Thomas Jefferson to Isaac Harby, January 6, 1826, in Joseph L. Blau and Salo W. Baron, eds., *The Jews of the United States, 1790–1840: A Documentary History*, 3 vols. (New York: Columbia University Press, 1963), 3:704–705.
82. Feldman, *Dual Destinies*, 42. "In keeping with his rational outlook," Feldman noted, "Jefferson was disdainful of Presbyterians and unsympathetic toward the Roman Catholic or Anglican priesthood, whom he considered to be the corruptors of the moral message of Jesus." Ibid.
83. Ibid., 44.
84. Jefferson to John Adams, October 13, 1813, in Adrienne Koch and WilliamPeden, eds., *The Life and Selected Writings of Thomas Jefferson* (New York: The Modern Library, Random House, 1972), 631.
85. Jefferson to Charles Thomson, January 9, 1816, in Andrew A. Lipscomb and Albert Ellery Bergh, eds., *The Writings of Thomas Jefferson*, 20 vols. (Washington, DC: The Thomas Jefferson Memorial Association, 1903–1904), 14:386 [hereinafter *Writings of Jefferson*].
86. Waldman, *Founding Faith*, 75, quoting Jefferson to Benjamin Rush, April 21, 1803, *Syllabus of an Estimate of the Merit of the Doctrines of Jesus*, in Koch and Peden, *Life and Selected Writings of Thomas Jefferson*, 569.
87. Jonathan D. Sarna, "American Anti-Semitism," in David Berger, ed., *History and Hate: The Dimensions of Anti-Semitism* (Philadelphia: The Jewish Publication Society of America, 1986), 121.
88. Jefferson to Benjamin Rush, April 21, 1803, *Syllabus of an Estimate of the Merit of the Doctrines of Jesus*, in Koch and Peden, *Life and Selected Writings of Thomas Jefferson*, 569.
89. Jefferson to William Short, August 4, 1820, in *Writings of Jefferson*, 15:260.
90. Jefferson to Ezra Stiles, June 25, 1819, in *Writings of Jefferson*, 15:203; Jonathan D. Sarna, "The 'Mythical Jew' and the 'Jew Next Door' in Nineteenth Century America," in David A. Gerber, ed., *Anti-Semitism in American History* (Urbana: University of Illinois Press, 1986), 59.
91. Waldman, *Founding Faith*, 75.
92. Ibid.
93. Eli Faber, *The Jewish People in America: A Time for Planting: The First Migration, 1654–1820* (Baltimore: The Johns Hopkins University Press, 1992), 129.
94. Feldman, *Dual Destinies*, 47.
95. This point has been suggested by Peter Grose in *Israel in the Mind of America* (New York: Alfred A. Knopf, 1983), 6, and Jonathan D. Sarna in "The 'Mythical Jew' and the 'Jew Next Door.'"

96. John Adams to Mordecai M. Noah, March 15, 1819, quoted in William Pencak, "Anti–Semitism, Toleration, and Appreciation: The Changing Relations of Jews and Gentiles in Early America," in Chris Beneke and Christopher S. Grenda, eds., *The First Prejudice: Religious Tolerance and Intolerance in Early America* (Philadelphia: University of Pennsylvania Press, 2010), 260.
97. Jefferson to Benjamin Rush, April 21, 1803, *Syllabus of an Estimate of the Merit of the Doctrines of Jesus*, in Koch and Peden, *Life and Writings of Thomas Jefferson*, 569.
98. Ibid.
99. Michael B. Oren, Power, *Faith and Fantasy: America in the Middle East, 1776 to the Present* (New York: W.W. Norton, 2007), 85.
100. This important point has been made, with particular reference to biographies of Thomas Jefferson, by Healey in his article, "Jefferson on Judaism and the Jews," 361.
101. To cite but a few examples: Joseph J. Ellis, *Passionate Sage: The Character and Legacy of John Adams* (New York: W.W. Norton and Company, 1993); Joseph J. Ellis, *American Sphinx: The Character of Thomas Jefferson* (New York: Vintage Books, 1998) (winner of the National Book Award); and Joseph J. Ellis, *His Excellency: George Washington* (New York: Vintage Books, 2004); Richard Norton Smith, *Patriarch: George Washington and the New American Nation* (Boston: Houghton Mifflin Company, 1993); and Richard Brookhiser, *Alexander Hamilton, American* (New York: The Free Press, 1999).

4

The Founders and Islam[1]

Thomas S. Kidd

IN THE LAST public act before his death, Benjamin Franklin parodied a proslavery speech in Congress by comparing it to a fictitious proslavery address by a North African Muslim pirate named Sidi Mehemet Ibrahim. Like proslavery southerners, the Algerian argued that he could not accept the end of Christian slavery because it would hurt the interests of the Algerian state, unfairly deprive Muslim slave masters of property, and release dangerous slaves into a vulnerable society. Franklin's salvo against slavery was published in 1790 in major northern newspapers.[2] His polemical use of a Muslim character is one of the most famous from eighteenth-century America, but it was not unique. Islamic references peppered the public documents of early America, demonstrating that many of the founders—both the well-known and the largely forgotten—were not only aware of Islam, but also ready to use it as a rhetorical tool.

There were actual Muslims living in America during the founding period, too, but the vast majority of them were toiling as slaves in the South. Of course, Muslim traders and sailors also passed through American ports on occasion, but most American Muslims were Africans forcibly imported to work on American plantations. The exact number of Muslims is hard to discern, but historian Michael Gomez has estimated that perhaps 200,000 slaves came from African regions with significant Muslim influences. This does not mean that all of these were Muslims, but it does suggest that hundreds of thousands of slaves may have been at least marginally familiar with Muslim beliefs.[3]

But the typical Muslim appearing in Anglo-American writing during the Revolutionary period was not an African slave; more likely he would have been a Barbary pirate or a Middle Eastern despot. A close look at the uses of Islam in the founding period and early republic shows that Ben Franklin's appropriation of a North African Muslim character represented a well-established tradition: citing the similarities between an opponent's views and the "beliefs" of Islam as a means to discredit one's adversaries. Over the course of the eighteenth century, Americans' uses of Islam became increasingly secularized. Early in the century, Islam was typically used for religious purposes in religious debates, while later commentators often implemented knowledge of despotic Islamic states to support political points. Real fears of Islam as a religion continued, however, appearing in episodes such as the ratification debates of the late 1780s, when the lack of a religious test in the Constitution theoretically opened a door to the election of Muslims to American political offices. Although one should hesitate to describe early Americans as conversant with Islam, they certainly conversed about Islam regularly. In doing so, they helped to establish views of Muslims that would persist, in very different contexts, through our own day.

Benjamin Franklin's *Poor Richard* once wondered, "is it worse to follow Mahomet than the Devil?" For most early American observers, no such question was necessary: to follow the former meant following the latter. Before the period of the American and French Revolutions, Anglo-Americans typically used categories from Islam as rhetorical tools to discredit opponents, or as players in eschatological speculation. The Revolutionary era saw significant changes in the uses of Islam, however. In addition to using images of Islam for religious purposes, polemicists often used Islam and Muslim nations as the world's worst examples of tyranny and oppression, the very traits that the Revolutionaries meant to fight.[4]

A representative example of the prophetic understanding of Islam came from Samuel Buell, one of the key young preachers of the First Great Awakening in New England, and pastor at Easthampton, Long Island, the scene of a major new revival in the mid-1760s. That later excitement at the church led some to turn their thoughts earnestly toward the last days. Buell, in a conventional pairing of Roman Catholicism and Islam, argued that "the Pope in the West and Mahomet in the East, with their Powers will be utterly ruined," and perhaps soon. In a revival narrative published in 1766, in the midst of the turmoil over the Stamp Act crisis, Buell told his readers that the sixth vial of God's wrath, referenced in Revelation 16:12 as being "poured out upon the great River Euphrates," would fall "upon the Mehomitan antichristian Power in the East." This would prepare the way for the mass conversion of Muslims to Christianity.[5]

Buell's fellow Calvinist minister Nathanael Emmons of Connecticut revealed the subtleties of the transition to more political uses of Islam in his sermon *The Dignity of Man* (1787). Emmons lifted up the potential of man to enlighten the world through reason and the gospel, and gave the Revolution a key place in Christian teleology. Charting the progress of reason and the gospel briefly through human history, Emmons noted Luther's Reformation, Newton's scientific discoveries, and included "Franklin in the cabinet, and Washington in the field, [who] have given independence and peace to America." Emmons thought these were only part of a greater process, as the "kingdom of Antichrist is to be destroyed, the Mahomedans are to be subdued, the Jews are to be restored, . . . and the whole face of things in this world, is to be beautifully and gloriously changed." Here, the subjugation of the Muslims was only part of a reasonable, millennial process. This reflected the borrowing of traditional eschatological categories for America's republican ends, what historian Henry May has called "secular millennialism."[6] The main difference from earlier American uses was that Islamic categories now often served primarily political principles.

Defenders of Revolutionary ideals pointed regularly to Muslim states as models of tyranny that crushed essential freedoms. Key texts undergirding the founders' political vision bolstered this notion. John Trenchard and Thomas Gordon's highly influential *Cato's Letters* (1723) made much of Islamic governments' prohibitions on the free press and free exchange of ideas. Montesquieu's *The Spirit of the Laws*, also influential among many Revolutionary leaders in America, depicted the Turkish state as uniquely despotic. A number of Americans picked up on Montesquieu's formulation that all governments fell somewhere on the continuum between absolute despotism and absolute democracy. The Baptist leader Enos Hitchcock quoted "the great Montesquieu" at length in his *Oration in Commemoration of the Independence* in 1793, arguing that a "state, in which the will of an individual is most frequently a law, and decides on the life or death of the subject, is called a despotic state. Such is the Turkish empire."[7]

William Blackstone's *Commentaries on the Laws of England* likewise argued that civil and religious tyranny often went together. When a society embraced "perverted and erroneous" religious principles, they have become "the cloak and the instrument of every pernicious design that can be harboured in the heart of man." Muslim history bore out this claim, wrote Blackstone, as the "terrible ravages committed by the Saracens in the east, to propagate the religion of Mahomet" confirmed the tendency of religious oppression to foster political tyranny.[8]

In his 1776 best-seller *Common Sense*, leading Patriot Thomas Paine denounced the evils of monarchy and called on America to become the world's new "asylum for . . . liberty." To make the case against kings, Paine drew on America's wells of anti-Catholic and anti-Islamic thought. "[Monarchy] in every instance is the Popery of government," he wrote. He considered the doctrine of divine right a fable. It was a "superstitious tale, conveniently timed, Mahomet like, to cram hereditary right down the throats of the vulgar." It was high time for Americans to throw off all such superstition, according to Paine, and enter a new era of enlightened democracy. Islam proved one of the most readily available foils for that envisioned American republic.[9]

Some Americans used the example of Islam to campaign for freedom of religion and the end of state-established denominations. The Presbytery of Hanover, Virginia, called on the legislature to disestablish the Anglican Church in 1776, as they set about making new laws for the independent state. As in the eschatological speculation regarding Islam, the presbytery paired Roman Catholicism and Islam as tyrannical faiths that required official state backing to survive. "[T]here is no argument in favor of establishing the Christian religion but what may be pleaded for establishing the tenets of Mahomet by those who believe the Alcoran," they insisted. They thought that pure Christianity would flourish in the absence of an established church. Baptist leader John Leland also argued against state establishment of religion by saying that it was more fit for Islamic nations, because "Mahomet called in the use of law and sword to convert people to his religion; but Jesus did not, does not." Reverend Richard Price, a leading English dissenting minister and friend of several major founders—Jefferson, Adams, and Franklin among them—noted in a tract circulated in America that in Muslim countries, "civil magistrates have a right to silence and punish all who oppose the divine mission of Mahomet," but that this was only another example of civil power supporting bad doctrine and illegitimately intruding upon spiritual matters.[10]

These points touched a nerve among those who supported the continuation of established churches. In Connecticut, where the Congregational Church remained established well into the 1800s, the *New Haven Gazette* argued in 1788 that a government could reasonably make a distinction between the salutary effects of established Christianity, and the crippling effects of established Islam. "The faith of Mahomet, wherever it is established, is united with despotic power. On the banks of the Ganges, and on the shores of the Caspian . . . it is still found accompanied with servitude and subjection; every free, and every gallant people, whom it has involved in the progress of its power, have abandoned their rights when they enlisted themselves under the banner of the prophet. . . . The religion of CHRIST, on the contrary, is found to exist and to flourish under every variety of political power. In the different periods of its history it has been united with every form of government—and . . . has operated in so striking a manner to limit the progress of tyranny." Christianity was uniquely compatible with liberty and moral refinement; therefore, it was the ideal established faith, as opposed to the degrading effects of Islam.[11]

Defenders of religious test oaths for officeholders also used the specter of Islam to argue against Leland and other advocates of full religious liberty. They insisted that disestablishment could allow non-Christians of all kinds, including Muslims, to serve in government. Polemicists in favor of religious tests undoubtedly used the threat of Islam as a logical extreme—in the 1780s it did not seem likely that Americans would elect an actual Muslim any time soon. Nevertheless, writers such as John Swanwick, a resident of Philadelphia and opponent of the principles encapsulated in Thomas Jefferson's Bill for Establishing Religious Freedom, claimed that Jefferson's Bill would open office holding to "men professedly atheists, Mahometans, or of any other creed, however unfriendly to liberty or the morals of a free country."[12]

This kind of argument failed to convince the legislature in Virginia, which passed Jefferson's bill in 1786. Although a number of other states maintained religious tests for officeholders, the trend toward full religious liberty likely influenced the framers of the Constitution, too, who in Article VI, clause 3, ensured that "no religious test shall ever be required as a qualification to any office or public trust under the United States." This decision generated consternation among many Antifederalist opponents of the Constitution, including Maryland delegate Luther Martin, who noted that there were some at the Constitutional Convention "so unfashionable as to think that a belief of the existence of a Deity, and of a state of future rewards and punishments would be some security for the good conduct of our rulers, and that in a Christian country it would be at least decent to hold out some distinction between the professors of Christianity and downright infidelity or paganism."[13]

Some Antifederalists also wished to make a distinction between Christians and non-Christians; to them, only Christians should serve in American political office. Amos Singletary of Massachusetts was doubly concerned that the new government wielded great powers and that it opened the door to non-Christians in office. He feared, the stenographer at his state ratifying convention noted, that the new government "will destroy all power in this of raising taxes, and we have nothing left—the only security is, we may have an honest man, but we may not have—we may have an atheist, pagan, Mahommedan—must take care of posterity—few nations enjoy the liberty of Englishmen. Is for giving up some power, but not every thing—no bill of rights—civil and sacred privileges will all go."[14]

The editorialist "Curtiopolis," writing in a New York newspaper, lampooned the objections of Antifederalists such as Singletary, sarcastically stating that the new Constitution wrongly "admits to legislation" just about every objectionable group imaginable: "1st. Quakers, who will make the blacks saucy, and at the same time deprive us of the means of defense--2dly. Mahometans, who ridicule the doctrine of the trinity--3dly. Deists, abominable wretches—4thly. Negroes, the seed of Cain--5thly. Beggars, who when set on horseback will ride to the devil--6thly. Jews, etc. etc." Curtiopolis seemed to imply that the Antifederalists' bigotry would make room for no group to be represented but themselves.[15]

More seriously, North Carolina Federalist James Iredell spoke for many when he portrayed the religious test issue as a choice between liberty and persecution. "It is objected," he noted, "that the people of America may, perhaps, choose representatives who have no religion at all, and that pagans and Mahometans may be admitted into offices. But how is it possible to exclude any set of men, without taking away that principle of religious freedom which we ourselves so warmly contend for?" No one involved with the framing of the Constitution particularly wished for Muslims to be elected to public office, but many like Iredell were willing to accept what then seemed a far-fetched scenario in order to ensure religious liberty for all. In any case, Iredell believed, like many Federalists, that Americans were unlikely to elect someone of a non-Christian faith, especially a Muslim or pagan. (Ironically, North Carolina voters would quickly elect a Jew, Jacob Henry, to their legislature in 1809, even though the state constitution banned non-Christians from holding office.) After all, just because the Constitution did not impose a religious test did not mean that voters could not employ one themselves.[16]

North Carolina governor Samuel Johnston agreed with Iredell, but went a small step further, making an indirect argument that Americans should, in theory, be allowed to elect a non-Christian to office if they chose to do so. But the only scenarios in which he could envision "Mahometans" or other non-Christians being elected president were, first, if "the people of America lay aside the Christian religion altogether." The second, more tantalizing prospect, was if "any persons of such descriptions should, notwithstanding their religion, acquire the confidence and esteem of the people of America by their good conduct and practice of virtue." Johnston apparently believed that Jews, and even Muslims, could conceivably reach that level of acceptance by their moral qualities, so he thought it best to leave the possibility open.[17]

The prevailing view of religious freedom did mean, in theory, that liberty, and even office holding, was open to "Mahometans," and that the government should not prefer one denomination or tradition over another. Yet many Americans continued to express doubts about this arrangement, well beyond the Revolutionary era and early national period, especially with regard to religious liberty in the states. In an 1811 New York blasphemy case, for example, the state high court argued that the state government (not yet constrained by the First Amendment, as the states would be in the twentieth century) could indeed prefer Christianity over skepticism, Islam, or other religious contenders.

> The free, equal, and undisturbed, enjoyment of religious opinion, whatever it may be, and free and decent discussions on any religious subject, is granted and secured; but to revile, with malicious and blasphemous contempt, the religion professed by almost the whole community, is an abuse of that right. Nor are we bound, by any expressions in the constitution, as some have strangely supposed, either not to punish at all, or to punish indiscriminately the like attacks upon the religion of *Mahomet* or of the grand *Lama;* and for this plain reason, that the case assumes that we are a christian people, and the morality of the country is deeply ingrafted upon christianity, and not upon the doctrines or worship of those impostors.

As late as the 1868 New Hampshire case *Hale v. Everett*, a state court declared that Protestantism was the preferred religion, and that by definition this category did not include "the believer in Judaism, the Mohammedan, the pagan, the atheist, deist, theist, free religionist or any other class of infidels."[18]

The fact remained, however, that in principle the ban on religious tests had raised the possibility that one day a Muslim could serve in political office. This was one of many reasons why some Americans continued to express doubts about the wisdom of the Constitution, long after its adoption. The Confederate Constitution of 1861, its supporters believed, at least rectified the Constitution's failure to mention God, as southerners explicitly invoked the "favor and guidance of Almighty God." Yet the Confederates too banned any religious test. One South Carolina newspaper editor complained in 1864 that the Federal Constitution "could have been passed and adopted by Atheists or Hindoes or Mahometans."[19] The writer's complaint reflects the fact that, while the specter of Muslim and other non-Christian office holders haunted many Antifederalists and later critics of the Constitution, the framers of the Constitution overcame that fear to endorse real religious liberty in the ban on religious tests, and in the First Amendment's religion clauses.

Americans of the founding era typically did not reflect at length on the merits of Islam itself, but instead, like Tom Paine, referred to Islam to make political points about the Revolution, the Constitution, or other domestic concerns. An excellent example was the Antifederalist satire by "A Turk" in Philadelphia's *Independent Gazetteer* in October 1787. In it, the writer said, "I have read without spectacles the proposed federal constitution, and I see with the most heartfelt pleasure the resemblance that it bears to that of our much admired SUBLIME PORTE [the court of the Ottoman Empire]— Your president general will greatly resemble in his powers the mighty Abdul Ahmed, our august Sultan . . . What do you say, you Christian dog?" This editorial employed common impressions of Muslim tyranny to indict the Constitution—presumably no American wished to have a government like that of the Ottomans.[20]

Again, this represented the use of Muslim imagery for political commentary on domestic concerns. Few major founders engaged with Islam directly as a religion. An exception to this rule was Elias Boudinot, who commented on Islam in religious writings published after 1800. Boudinot was a prominent New Jersey lawyer who served in a variety of positions in the early national government, including president of the Continental Congress and director of the US Mint. That Boudinot would reflect upon Islam was not surprising, as he was an evangelical Christian engaged in apologetics against anti-Christian critics such as Paine.

In his *The Age of Revelation*, a response to Paine's *Age of Reason*, Boudinot asserted that "Mahomet aimed to establish his pretensions to divine authority, by the power of the sword and the terrors of his government." Boudinot, following earlier sources such as English theologian Humphrey Prideaux's widely read *The True Nature of Imposture Displayed in the Life of Mahomet*, cast the Prophet Muhammad as a religious fraud. Muhammad assiduously avoided performing his supposed miracles in the presence of his followers, and he tailored his revelations to the tastes of his prospective recruits. Showing that prophetic interpretations regarding Islam still held sway, even among some elites, Boudinot added in his 1815 *The Second Advent* that the overthrow of "the Turkish and Mahometan empires, to make way for [the] converted Jews or Kings of the East—This, it may be, will introduce the vintage, or that cruel slaughter of the kings of Europe at the battle of Arma Geddon, or the great day of God Almighty."[21]

The post-Revolutionary uses of Islam followed the pattern of appropriating Islam and Islamic societies to make political points about America. This tendency was illustrated by the second American printing of Humphrey Prideaux's *The True Nature of Imposture* by James Lyon of Fairhaven, Connecticut. Lyon was the son of Congressman Matthew Lyon, who was languishing in jail for violation of the Sedition Act, which in 1798 prohibited American citizens from writing or speaking maliciously against the national government. James Lyon tellingly omitted Prideaux's original preface that had discussed English Deism, and let the book speak for itself about the dangers of centralized power and religious zeal in silencing dissent. To the Lyonses, President John Adams, who signed the Sedition Act, was the new Muhammad. Conversely, John Adams had worried in his "Discourses on Davila" that the excesses of the French Revolution would eventually lead to tyranny and people would "follow the standard of the first mad despot, who, with the enthusiasm of another Mahomet, will endeavor to obtain them." John Quincy Adams, similarly, once compared Jefferson to "the Arabian prophet," and imagined Jefferson's followers bellowing, "There is but one Goddess of Liberty, and Common Sense is her Prophet."[22]

Anti-Muslim texts continued to foster these kinds of uses of Islam and the Prophet. A new biography of Muhammad by an anonymous British author, *The Life of Mahomet; or, The History of that Imposture Which was Begun, Carried on, and Finally Established by Him in Arabia*, was published in American editions in Worcester, Massachusetts, in 1802, and New York in 1813. This aggressively anti-Islamic and anti-Arabian text starkly contrasted the pure rationality of Christianity with the violent duplicity of Islam. The author portrayed Muhammad as a fiend of deception, who intentionally crafted a false religion suited to "ignorant barbarians, to whose lusts it promised to administer everlasting fuel." The growth of Islam came by the sword, as "rapine and murder were the darlings of

[Muhammad's] soul." Although he produced little evidence confirming his prophetic office, the Arabians' reception of Muhammad's religion proved "the stupidity of the multitude, in believing the very worst of crimes can be the offspring of religion." Nothing less than "the conquest of Mahometan countries, by which the sentiments of men may be freed from their fetters, will ever be the destruction of that system of blasphemy and iniquity by which they are at present enslaved," the writer proclaimed. The author doubted that sending missionaries would help Muslim countries, as this would only be "conducting [the missionaries] to a slaughterhouse." Before Christian power alone "the monstrous blasphemy and absurdities of Mahomet must fall.... The contest is between barbarity and benevolence, between Jehovah and a monster in the shape of a man." Anticipating late twentieth century American opinions, *The Life of Mahomet* asserted that the global clash between Christianity and Islam was inevitable.[23]

The anti-Islamic rage behind publications such as *The Life of Mahomet* can be partially explained by the post-Revolutionary renewal of Barbary piracy in the Mediterranean. Incursions against American ships became one of the first great foreign policy challenges of the early republic, and a considerable source of anxiety about America's military impotence. Some leaders even feared that Barbary spies were infiltrating American cities. Patrick Henry, as governor of Virginia, wrote an official letter to the House of Delegates in 1785, reporting ominously that "Certain persons from the coast of Barbary are now in this city [Richmond]. There appears ground to suspect them of designs unfavorable to this country." Henry asked for guidance about whether his office, or perhaps the assembly, possessed the police powers requisite to track the suspected spies. Ultimately, the state detained three suspects, but they professed to be Moors from Spain, not agents of the Barbary states.[24]

Immediately after the American Revolution ended, North African corsairs began attacking newly vulnerable American vessels. (The British navy had protected American shipping prior to the war, and America's French allies had done so through much of the Revolution. Once the War for Independence was over, the American government was unable to secure new European protection for its merchant fleet.) In 1786, John Adams and Thomas Jefferson attempted to negotiate with the envoy of the sultan of Tripoli, a man named Abdrahaman. Adams believed that if they could not come to an agreement, the Americans would face "a universal and horrible War with these Barbary States, which will continue for many Years." Adams tried to charm the ambassador by smoking a hookah in his presence, leading Abdrahaman to cry out "in Extacy, 'Monsieur vous etes un Turk!'" But when it came down to business, the charm offensive did not work. Jefferson explained that "We took the liberty to make some inquiries concerning the Grounds of their pretentions to make war upon Nations who had done them no Injury, and observed that we considered all mankind as our friends who had done us no wrong, nor had given us any provocation." The envoy's reply—as recorded by the ambassadors—fulfilled their worst suspicions about the Barbary states' religious motivations. "The Ambassador answered us that it was founded on the Laws of their Prophet, that it was written in their Koran, that all nations who should not have acknowledged their authority were sinners, that it was their right and duty to make war upon them wherever they could be found, and to make slaves of all they could take as Prisoners, and that every Musselman who should be slain in battle was sure to go to Paradise." In the short term, Adams argued that all the United States could realistically do to address the crisis was pay off the Barbary states for protection from the pirates.[25]

American diplomatic and naval weakness allowed the North Africans repeatedly to embarrass the new nation. Algerian raiders seized two American ships in 1785, and eleven more in 1793. A 1796 agreement to free eighty-eight American sailors in Algiers cost the federal government one million dollars, or about one-sixth of the national budget. When the ruler of Tripoli declared war on the United States in 1801, President Jefferson ordered a blockade of the North African port. A new disaster came in 1803 when the US frigate *Philadelphia* ran aground and was captured by Tripolitans. This delivered more than three hundred American sailors into the North Africans' hands. A fiercer naval assault eventually forced Tripoli to concede victory to the Americans for a modest payoff of sixty thousand dollars in 1805. Algerian corsairs resumed attacks on American merchantmen during the War of 1812, and James Madison began a new war against Algiers in 1815. A formidable American fleet forced not only Algiers, but all the Barbary states, to give up piracy and ransoms against American interests by the end of 1815. This impressive victory signaled America's emergence as an independent commercial power in the broader Atlantic world.[26]

One can make the case that the conflict between the Barbary pirates and the United States did not originate in religious differences, but rather in the Barbary states' economic and military opportunism in the face of American weakness. But American diplomats had reasons not to emphasize the religious factor in these wars. In a 1797 treaty with Tripoli, in fact, the United States specifically pronounced that "As the Government of the

United States of America is not, in any sense, founded on the Christian religion; as it has in itself no character of enmity against the laws, religion, or tranquility, of Musselmen; . . . no pretext, arising from religious opinions, shall ever produce an interruption of the harmony existing between the two countries." Given Abdrahaman's hostile statements in 1786, the 1797 treaty may have represented wishful thinking by the United States that religion did not divide them from Tripoli. It was certainly the tactful thing to say in an attempt to defuse religious controversy. Regardless, the blunt religious language of the treaty apparently generated little controversy, as the Senate unanimously ratified it.[27]

Thirty years of struggle against the Barbary pirates led to renewed popularity for captivity narratives, further refining American images of ostensibly typical North African Muslims. One American captive in Algeria, John Foss, kept a journal of his experience that was published in his hometown of Newburyport, Massachusetts, in 1798. Foss's narrative supplied lurid details of the horrific violence committed against Christian slaves in Algeria, and painted Islam as a bloodthirsty religion. The corsairs who boarded Foss's ship were "like a parcel of ravenous wolves" who stripped the Americans of all their belongings and clothes. One "old Turk" offered Foss a shirt to cover himself, but Foss thought that "[t]his was the only Mahometan I ever met with, in whom I had the least reason to suppose the smallest spark of humanity was kindled." The pirates' captain told the captives that they must be treated as slaves because of their "bigotry and superstition, in believing in a man who was crucified by the Jews, and disregarding the true doctrine of God's last and greatest prophet, Mahomet."[28]

Foss emphasized the Muslims' brutal treatment of Christian slaves, explaining at length the excruciating means of torture and execution their tormentors used. He noted that a Christian slave found in the company of a Muslim woman would be beheaded, while the woman would be tied into a sack with heavy rocks and thrown into the sea. Similarly, for speaking ill of the "Mahometan Religion," a slave would be burnt or impaled. These and many other horrors revealed the desperate situation of those slaves "persecuted by the hands of merciless Mahometans." Their demoralizing confinement stood in sharp contrast to the liberty these whites would enjoy in America.[29]

On a popular level, Americans certainly seem to have viewed the contest with the North Africans as a spiritual battle. Foss and other interpreters saw the clash that way. The Christian slaves were subjected to religiously inspired persecution, and told that they would be treated viciously because, as Christians, they deserved no better. The North Africans acted as they did because they were "genuine children of Ishmael," given to violence against God's chosen people. A poem published with Foss's narrative, "The Algerine Slaves," wondered:

> *Ye sons of Ishmael, how long shall ye remain*
> *The scourge of Christians, robbers of the main?*
> *How long, ye vile, ye worse than savage crew,*
> *Must all the world bow down and stoop to you?*

Strikingly, the poet called not just on the Christian God, but on *America's* God to destroy this Muslim threat:

> *Columbia's God! unsheath thy glitt'ring sword,*
> *Ride on and conquer—speak, O speak the word . . .*
> *Send quick destruction on this cursed land,*
> *This more than vile, this worse than murd'rous band.*

To supply even more background on the North Africans' faith, James Wilson Stevens' *An Historical and Geographical Account of Algiers* (1800) included an extended biographical account of Muhammad, who, as usual, was "styled the Impostor" and who made "his disciples swallow whatever he pleased to impose on them." Between the leaders of the North African states and American politicians, the conflict revolved around money and America's weak national defense. But in American popular imagery, the contest seemed equally to involve religion. In American Christian views of Islam, spiritual images have often supplanted secular realities as the shapers of opinion.[30]

As negative as popular images of Islam were in the early republic, they could also be employed to call for political and moral reform. One of the most obvious examples of this tactic was using Islamic images to argue against slavery, as Ben Franklin did in this chapter's opening anecdote. Barbary captivity narratives were all the rage in the 1790s and early 1800s, but some narratives focused less on the religious and moral failings of the Islamic captors and more on the political and social lessons to be learned from Barbary slavery. These captivity narratives, and the burgeoning popular literature based on slavery in North Africa, sometimes assisted the early American abolitionist movement. Susannah Rowson's play *Slaves in Algiers* (1794), for instance, featured an Algerian master, converted to democratic principles by his American slaves' bravery, who decided to end slavery in Algiers.[31]

The anonymous poem *The American in Algiers* (1797) juxtaposed the enslavement of a Revolutionary War veteran in Algiers with the enslavement of a West African man in America. After the war, the veteran was captured on a merchant ship and transported to Algiers, where he was presented to the "Dey,"

> *A wretch austere! whose haughty looks, denote*
> *A soul more savage than the forest brute.*

The Dey told the sailor that,

> *My God commanded, and Mahomet gave*
> *Full leave to make each infidel a slave;*
> *But if you'll turn Mahometan at once . . .*
> *My princely favor shall to you extend,*
> *And break the chains that o'er your limbs impend.*

Here the Muslim Dey of Algiers was presented as a savage slave master, and the poem called for the United States to exact harsh retribution against the Barbary pirates and to free the American captives. In the poem's second canto, however, a "sable bard" sought to "trump the inconsistency of those Feign'd friends to liberty, feign'd slavery's foes." How could white Americans express outrage at their own sons' enslavement in the Barbary states when they enslaved Africa's sons and daughters in their own land? The United States' "Vile Christians perpetrate [murders] to serve their God," the poet raged. In a country devoted to the proposition that "all men are created equal," "Afric's sons continue slaves." In this poem, African Muslims were used as a brutish mirror image to shame Americans about their own sin of slave owning.[32]

Royall Tyler's *The Algerine Captive* (1797) was the most popular of the anti-slavery novels based on Barbary captivity, and it posited that the Algerian masters were no worse than those in the American South. If anything, they were probably more benevolent, despite being Muslims. Tyler's narrator, Updike Underhill, visited a southern church before his captivity and noted with bewilderment how the pastor beat and cursed his slave just before mounting the pulpit to preach on the text, "I said I will take heed unto my ways, that I sin not with my tongue" (Ps. 39:1).[33] After he was taken captive, Underhill confronted a very bright and rational "mollah," who insisted that his faith "disdained the use of other powers than rational argument," and that he would not use the tactics of Rome—namely torture—to convert him. The mullah proceeded to bring into serious question the divine inspiration of the Bible, the peaceful nature of Christianity, and the clear distinction between the two religions. Underhill was befuddled, writing that "[a]fter five days' conversation, disgusted with his fables, abashed by his assurance, and almost confounded by his sophistry, I resumed my slave's attire, and sought safety in my former servitude."[34] Despite Tyler's later protests to the contrary, he used Islam to undermine Christianity's divine sanction. This was a far cry theologically from the typical American usage of Islam, but Tyler still meant primarily to contribute to intra-Protestant debates.[35]

By the election of Jefferson in 1800, the founders had set general patterns for American Christians' discussions of Islam. It was an emblem of political tyranny, a foil for American liberty, and a convenient tool for bludgeoning one's opponents. Occasionally, Muslims, actual and fictional, became a means to criticize America, too, for failing to live up to its stated principles of liberty, as seen in Ben Franklin's attack on slavery. Some Christian founders, such as Elias Boudinot, maintained older theological understandings of Islam as a spiritual antagonist and player in the events of the last days. Most remarkably, though, America's substantive commitment to religious liberty theoretically made Muslim political participation in America possible, even if the first Muslim (Keith Ellison) did not win a seat in Congress until 2006 (Ellison took his oath of office on a Qur'an owned by Thomas Jefferson). To be sure, early national America was rife with anti-Muslim rhetoric and stereotypes of a sort surpassed only by the vehemence and pervasiveness of its anti-Catholicism. Yet the refusal to adopt a religious test in the Constitution did set the stage for the fulfillment of the vision—or apprehension—of North Carolina governor Samuel Johnston that establishing real religious liberty might one day result in the election of a Muslim to national public office.

Notes

1. Portions of this chapter were originally published in Thomas S. Kidd, *American Christians and Islam: Evangelical Culture and Muslims from the Colonial Period to the Age of Terrorism* (Princeton, NJ: Princeton University Press, 2009). Thanks to Paul Matzko for his help in researching this chapter.
2. Reprinted in "Benjamin Franklin and Freedom," *Journal of Negro History* 4, no. 1 (Jan. 1919): 48–50; see also Joseph J. Ellis, *Founding Brothers: The Revolutionary Generation* (New York: Alfred A. Knopf, 2000), 111–112; Robert J. Allison, *The Crescent Obscured: The United States and the Muslim World, 1776–1815* (New York: Oxford

University Press, 1995), 104–106; David Waldstreicher, *Runaway America: Benjamin Franklin, Slavery, and the American Revolution* (New York: Hill and Wang, 2004), 238.
3. Michael A. Gomez, "Muslims in Early America," *Journal of Southern History* 60, no. 4 (Nov. 1994): 682.
4. *Poor Richard, 1741* (Philadelphia, 1740), May; Timothy Marr, *The Cultural Roots of American Islamicism* (New York: Cambridge University Press, 2006), 20–21.
5. Samuel Buell, *A Faithful Narrative of the Remarkable Revival of Religion* (New York, 1766), 24–25.
6. Nathanael Emmons, *The Dignity of Man* (Providence, RI, 1787), in Ellis Sandoz, ed., *Political Sermons of the American Founding Era, 1730–1805*, 2nd ed. (Indianapolis, IN: Liberty Fund, 1998), 1: 893; Henry May, *The Enlightenment in America* (New York: Oxford University Press, 1976), 153.
7. Enos Hitchcock, *An Oration, in Commemoration of the Independence of the United States of America* (Providence, RI, 1793), in Sandoz, *Political Sermons*, 2: 1176–1177. On Montesquieu's influence, see May, *Enlightenment in America*, 40–41.
8. William Blackstone, *Commentaries on the Laws of England: Book the Fourth* (Philadelphia, 1771–1772), 102–103.
9. Thomas Paine, *Common Sense and Related Writings*, Thomas P. Slaughter, ed. (Boston: Bedford/St. Martin's, 2001), 82–83, 88.
10. "Memorial of the Presbytery of Hanover," *Journal of the House of Delegates of Virginia* (Williamsburg, VA, 1776), 33; John Leland, *The Rights of Conscience Inalienable* (New London, CT, 1791), in Sandoz, *Political Sermons*, 2: 1090–1093; Richard Price, *Observations on the Importance of the American Revolution*, 2nd ed. (Philadelphia, 1785), 13–14; Allison, *Crescent Obscured*, 47.
11. *New Haven Gazette*, May 1, 1788, 1–2.
12. "A Citizen of Philadelphia" [John Swanwick], *Considerations on an Act of the Legislature of Virginia, Entitled, An Act for the Establishment of Religious Freedom* (Philadelphia, 1786), iii.
13. Luther Martin, *The Genuine Information* (Philadelphia, 1788), 80.
14. John Kaminski and Gaspare Saladino, eds., *Documentary History of the Ratification of the Constitution* (Madison, WI: State Historical Society of Wisconsin, 2000), 6: 1296.
15. "Curtiopolis," in *The Daily Advertiser* (New York), January 18, 1788.
16. Jonathan Elliott, ed., *The Debates in the Several State Conventions, on the Adoption of the Federal Constitution* (Washington, DC, 1836), 4: 194.
17. Elliott, ed., *Debates*, 4: 198–199.
18. *People v. Ruggles*, 8 Johnson 290 (N.Y. 1811), in Daniel L. Dreisbach and Mark David Hall, eds., *The Sacred Rights of Conscience: Selected Readings on Religious Liberty and Church-State Relations in the American Founding* (Indianapolis, IN: Liberty Fund, 2009), 560; *Hale v. Everett*, 53 N.H. 9 (1868), in Isaac Grant Thompson, ed., *The American Reports* (San Francisco, 1876), 187.
19. George C. Rable, *God's Almost Chosen Peoples: A Religious History of the American Civil War* (Chapel Hill: University of North Carolina Press, 2010), 338.

20. *Independent Gazetteer*, October 10, 1787.
21. Elias Boudinot, *The Age of Revelation* (Philadelphia, 1801), 36; Elias Boudinot, *The Second Advent* (Trenton, NJ, 1815), 345.
22. Allison, *Crescent Obscured*, 39–41.
23. *The Life of Mahomet; or, The History of that Imposture Which was Begun, Carried on, and Finally Established by Him in Arabia* (Worcester, MA, 1802), 37, 60, 83–84, 98.
24. Patrick Henry to the Speaker of the House of Delegates, November 17, 1785, in William Wirt Henry, *Patrick Henry: Life, Correspondence, and Speeches* (New York: Charles Scribner's Sons, 1891), 3: 337; William Foushee to Patrick Henry, December 6, 1785, in William P. Palmer, ed., *Calendar of Virginia State Papers* (Richmond, VA, 1884), 4: 71.
25. John Adams to Thomas Jefferson, February 17, 1786, John Adams to Thomas Jefferson, February 21, 1786, and American Commissioners to John Jay, March 28, 1786, in Barbara B. Oberg and J. Jefferson Looney, eds., *Papers of Thomas Jefferson Digital Edition* (Charlottesville, VA, 2009); Kevin J. Hayes, *The Road to Monticello: The Life and Mind of Thomas Jefferson* (New York: Oxford University Press, 2008), 309, 315–316.
26. Allison, *Crescent Obscured*, xv, 31; Paul Baepler, ed., *White Slaves, African Masters: An Anthology of American Barbary Captivity Narratives* (Chicago: University of Chicago Press, 1999), 8–9; Frank Lambert, *The Barbary Wars: American Independence in the Atlantic World* (New York: Hill and Wang, 2005), 198–202; Martha Elena Rojas, "'Insults Unpunished': Barbary Captives, American Slaves, and the Negotiation of Liberty," *Early American Studies* 1 (Fall 2003): 161.
27. "Treaty of Peace and Friendship between the United States of America and the Bey and Subjects of Tripoli, of Barbary" (1797), in Dreisbach and Hall, *The Sacred Rights of Conscience*, 475–476.
28. John Foss, *A Journal, of the Captivity and Sufferings of John Foss*, 2nd ed. (Newburyport, MA, [1798]), 10–12; Baepler, *White Slaves, African Masters*, 71–72.
29. Foss, *Journal*, 32–33, 122.
30. Foss, *Journal*, 141, 182–183; James Wilson Stevens, *An Historical and Geographical Account of Algiers*, 2nd ed. (Brooklyn, NY, 1800), 170, 176; Lambert, *Barbary Wars*, 118.
31. Benilde Montgomery, "White Captives, African Slaves: A Drama of Abolition," *Eighteenth-Century Studies* 27, no. 4 (Summer 1994): 629–630; Baepler, *White Slaves, African Masters*, 30–31, 47.
32. *The American in Algiers* (New York, 1797), 14–16, 21, 23–24; Lambert, *Barbary Wars*, 114.
33. Royall Tyler, *The Algerine Captive* (London, 1802), 1: 136–139.
34. Ibid., 2: 37–53, quote on 53.
35. Cathy Davidson, *Revolution and the Word: The Rise of the Novel in America* (New York: Oxford University Press, 1986), 208–209; Timothy Marr, *The Cultural Roots of American Islamicism* (New York: Cambridge University Press, 2006), 57–58; Baepler, *White Slaves, African Masters*, 46–47; Montgomery, "White Captives, African Slaves," 616–617.

5

Religion and the Loyalists

Robert M. Calhoon and Ruma Chopra

DURING THE AMERICAN Revolution, every Protestant denominational community, and even Jewish synagogues and Roman Catholic parishes, harbored Patriots, Loyalists, and neutralists. Even among staunchly Whiggish Presbyterians, there were more than a handful of Loyalists. Among the laity of the colonial Church of England, especially in the Chesapeake and Carolina lowcountry, a majority of planter elites were Whigs. In the thirteen rebellious colonies, approximately 101 politically active Anglican priests were Loyalists, 76 were Patriots, and 59 kept their allegiance to themselves so that they could continue to minister to divided Episcopal parishes.[1] There were Whig and Loyalist Dutch and German Reformed; some neutralist Quakers leaned toward Loyalism while others wished the American cause well. Methodism appealed to African Americans and to poor whites who lived in fear of Patriot elites on the Eastern Shore of the Chesapeake Bay. One German pacifist family in Pennsylvania refused to acknowledge the legitimacy of any state because God had not yet bestowed victory on either the British or American armies.[2] Behind these statistics and rumored political affiliations stood a myriad of personal dilemmas and torn allegiances.

Issues that sparked antagonism between American revolutionaries and the British led to resentment towards the religious institution which came to exemplify British despotism. In the upheaval of the 1770s, the revolutionaries portrayed the Church of England in America as symptomatic of British tyranny over the colonies, and the Anglicans as expansive and militant. They crafted an explicit link between Anglicanism and British oppression and imbued the Anglican Church with much greater authority than it actually exercised in the colonies.

In 1701, a royal charter founded a new organization, the Society for the Propagation of the Gospel in Foreign Parts (SPG), for the spread of the Church of England in overseas territories acquired by England. The growing expansion of English territories by the latter part of the seventeenth century encouraged religious enterprise. The English began the settlement of Calcutta in 1690, and soon established the colonies of Carolina and Georgia in North America. With the Treaty of Utrecht in 1713, they would gain Nova Scotia and Newfoundland, and receive Gibraltar and Minorca from Spain. Emboldened by these gains, the Church saw itself as having new missionary responsibilities, an implicit assumption that the SPG should support British sovereignty. The Church sent Anglican clergymen—men who took an oath to the Church of England and to the reigning monarch—to their newly acquired territories.[3]

The SPG was meant to reinvigorate Anglicanism in the American colonies outside of Virginia, Maryland, and the Carolinas where it was already legally instituted. By exporting English identity along with English religion, it would secure the loyalty of American colonists and promote the interests of the expanding empire. Within a year of its inauguration, the SPG established a tradition of distributing annual sermons which included extracts from SPG ministers based in North America. Historian Rowan Strong regards the SPG exchanges between England and the North American colonies as the "first official Anglican construction of English-British imperialism."[4] By 1783, the SPG had sent more than six hundred clergymen who founded three hundred Anglican churches in northern colonies.[5]

The Church of England shared in the growing religious pluralism of the American colonies. During most of the eighteenth century, there was little widespread hostility to the Church. An important explanation for why the Anglicans did not become targets of abuse until 1775—unlike stamp act agents, admiralty judges, and royal governors—was the wide acceptance of the Anglican Church as a colonial one.[6] During the years of the Great Awakening, the Church presented itself as an oasis in a sea of enthusiasm and disorder. The clergymen's goal was "neither to call the elect out of the world into a pure church nor to prepare individuals for conversion by God."[7] They promoted a calm and predictable religious style in contrast to an emotional one.[8] In 1742, New England minister Timothy Cutler attributed the preference for the Anglican Church to a desire for "quiet and order."[9]

Opposition to revivalism in the Great Awakening of 1739–1742 anticipated the rise of religiously inspired Loyalism in 1776–1777. Fueled by economic growth and population growth, the revivals appealed to the newly prosperous while traditional elites were suspicious of religious innovation and its underlying cause of "enthusiasm." New England Congregationalists split first into Old Light and New Light factions and then split again as some Old Light church members defected to the Church of England and some New Light to the Separate Baptists. After the Great Awakening, New Englanders had four main religious choices: Old Light, New Light, Anglican, or Separate Baptist. This religious pluralism anticipated the conflicts of the 1760s and 1770s over political allegiance.

Critically, no official mechanism linked Anglican theology to British constitutionalism. During the eighteenth century, the British state was less interested in imposing Anglicanism than in expanding the colonial population and securing commercial gains; it hoped that loyalty would follow prosperity. Hence, by the time of the Revolution, more than 75 percent of Americans were non-Anglicans in comparison with the English population where less than 10 percent were dissenters from the Church of England.[10]

The repercussions of the British focus on population and commerce were especially obvious in the southern colonies. During the eighteenth century, the British—along with the southern gentry—hoped to increase the white populace to serve as a buffer against the Native Americans, and to counterbalance the large slave population in the south. The incentive of inexpensive land drew thousands of settlers into the backcountry between the 1750s and 1770s. These immigrants shared a desire to acquire fertile land but were otherwise heterogeneous in nationality and religion. Few were Anglican.[11]

The arrival of diverse immigrants weakened an already weak Anglican presence in the southern colonies. Although the Church of England was the establishment in every colony in the south, the authority of the Anglicans had long been curbed by the southern laity and legislatures.[12] Wealthy planters protected their political and economic interests by acting as vestrymen and maintaining the social authority of the Anglican Church. The clergymen, in turn, saw their salaries and standing best protected by an alliance with the planters.[13]

In the Chesapeake, the Church of England in Virginia metamorphosed into the Church of Virginia. The Anglican establishment was casually integrated into the daily lives of Virginians. The Church conducted marriages and asked justices of the peace to punish moral offenses such as unlicensed preaching. Colonial Virginians found strength in their congregations, their clergymen, their families, and their beliefs. The lack of theological disputes produced a low incidence of religious violence and a higher tolerance for diversity. The violent episodes against some Baptist preachers were extreme responses and not reflective of the society at large.[14] The Church's moderation, in part, shielded Virginians from political instability and religious volatility. Indeed, historian Brent Tarter asserts that the "Church of England in Virginia was a perfect fit for the colony and without it the colony would not have been what it was."[15]

The southern clergymen's loyalty to colonial interests extended to their silent support for the institution of slavery. Although the Church of England had a virtual monopoly on missionary work in the plantation colonies during the first half of the eighteenth century, it played only a modest part in the conversion of African-Americans. Because the clergymen received limited funds from the Bishop of London, they became dependent upon prominent local planters who controlled the vestries. Unwilling to challenge slaveholders, most Anglican clergymen focused on ameliorating the living conditions of slaves and did not promote slave emancipation. During the course of the century, the Anglican ministers turned their focus to Anglicizing white settlers instead of Christianizing black slaves. A serious challenge to southern slaveholders would come with the Great Awakening, but from Baptist and Methodist ministers, not from Anglicans.[16]

Despite the catholic spirit of Anglicanism, clergy in the southern colonies offered little spiritual comfort to Native American communities.[17] In 1702, the SPG claimed that its purpose with respect to the American colonies was "toward the conversion of the Natives."[18] In South Carolina, the early missionaries showed a sincere interest in the culture and lifestyle of the natives and tried to win over native families when they resisted sending their children to live amongst the missionaries. The Yamasee War in 1715 ended these conversion efforts. The Indians moved further west, and the ministers, understanding the work required in learning native languages and the time needed to win natives' trust, abandoned their attempts.[19]

Amongst the Mohawks in New York colony, the missionaries carried on their work with more success. After the crushing of Pontiac's Rebellion in 1766, Sir William Johnson, Indian superintendent and a member of the SPG, pointed out the importance of establishing the Church among the Indians.[20] In March, 1770, New York's Reverend Charles Inglis also voiced the implicit link between loyalty and religion. He explained that the most effective way of securing Iroquois loyalty was by "proselytizing them to Christianity, as professed by the Church of England."[21] If neglected, they would "naturally grow alienated from the Government."[22]

For some Mohawks, the Anglican Church signified a critical middle ground, and the Church's continual presence represented their successful negotiation in preserving their homeland from colonial squatters. In 1712, the SPG had established an Anglican mission in Tryon County in upstate New York, about thirty miles northwest of Albany. Referred to interchangeably as Fort Hunter or Tionondderoga, this community comprised of two hundred Mohawks who lived in close interaction with Anglican ministers as well as their colonial neighbors. In August 1775, when rebel leaders in the county punished the region's most prominent Loyalists, one Mohawk leader, Little Abraham, sought to ensure the safety of the Anglican minister, arguing that "the King sent him to them, and they [the Mohawks] would look upon it as taking away one of their own body."[23]

About twenty miles west of Tionondderoga, Canajoharie was home to Joseph Brant, one of Britain's strongest Mohawk allies.[24] Joseph Brant grew up in the home of the Indian superintendent, William Johnson, of Anglican faith. Brant's faith may have been reinforced under the missionary teachings of Reverend John Stuart in the 1770s. He would translate the Book of Common Prayer and a doctrinal primer in 1787.[25] His sister, Molly Brant, widow of William Johnson, mobilized Indian warriors to support the British cause. Significantly, when Molly Brant died in 1796, the bell in the tower of the local Anglican Church at Cataraqui (Ontario) tolled for her. The extent to which Molly Brant's Loyalism was influenced by her faith in the Anglican Church is hard to determine: the Anglican Church, however, clearly recognized her as an important ally.[26]

Anglican Persuasions

By no means were Anglican colonists uniformly loyal to Britain during the rebellion. If the Church of England supplied more Loyalist spokesmen than any other single denomination, it must also be observed that the signers of the Declaration of Independence included more men of Anglican faith than any other.[27] Furthermore, Anglican ministers varied greatly in the intensity of their involvement. Dependent on the British government for their livelihood, and loyal to the Church from which they derived their sense of meaning, some Anglican clerics in the northern colonies associated loyalty to the Church with loyalty to the empire. They equated the rebel argument for the natural rights of man with the state of nature, and painted a picture of terrifying, unbridled, and unending social chaos. These Loyalist writers expressed fear, hatred, and a rising hysteria about the effects of rebellion. They feared not the loss of British constitutionalism but the disruption of the social fabric. The American rebellion represented disloyalty to the crown and disobedience to God.

New Englanders's Loyalist religious discourse fairly crackled with exasperation, grief, frustration, and yearning for spiritual solace. "I am far from considering the colonists . . . a warlike people," Massachusetts Attorney General Jonathan Sewall wrote, in May 1775, to General Frederick Haldimand, a Swiss born mercenary officer in the British Army and discerning observer of colonial folkways. "But," Sewall confided, "there is an enthusiasm in politics like that which religious notions inspire that drives men on with an unnatural impetuosity that baffles and confounds all calculation based on rational considerations."[28]

Sewall's prose betrayed his divided religious and political soul. Descended from the Puritan Sewalls, he had grown up in strained circumstances following his father's business failure and early death. He had advised his young friend, John Adams, son of an obscure farmer, to combine law and politics as a tribune of the people—a career path he could not afford to pursue because he needed short term wealth and security as a Loyalist ally of the Crown. That vantage point gave him an insight into rebel ideology. "Liberty," he explained to Haldimand, "is a word whose very sound carries a fascinating charm. The colonists fancy this precious jewel in danger of being ravished from them. They will not, they cannot examine or question the truth of it [a very intoxicating experience] until they are affrighted" by a convincing display of British military force.[29]

Less than a year later, SPG missionary, John Wiswall, with his wife and three daughters, sought refuge in Boston where British troops maintained order in a port city cut off from the rest of the empire by the Coercive Acts, closing Boston until its inhabitants paid for the tea destroyed by the Tea Party. Driven from his Falmouth parish after Wiswall prayed for protection of his loyal parishioners from "all sedition, privy conspiracy, and rebellion," the Wiswall family came down with a violent intestinal disorder then sweeping Boston. John tried to make biblical sense of his plight. Only "the God who stilleth the raging of the seas, the noise of the waves, and the *madness* of the people" (paraphrasing Psalm 89) could "restore peace, order, and government to this distracted continent" because, as Wiswall sensed intuitively, America was "too free and happy" ever to be "contented with its happiness."[30] Wiswall, who inspired novelist Kenneth Roberts's character, Oliver Wiswell, here anticipated by six months Jefferson's understanding of a pursuit of happiness that was almost unbearably intense.

Another SPG missionary in New England, Samuel Andrews in Wallingford, Connecticut, protested against a day of prayer and fasting on behalf of the American cause, by preaching on that occasion from the text in Amos 5:21, "I hate, I despise your feast days, and I will not smell of your solemn assemblies." The "unruly," "vindictive," and "ungodly spirit" exhibited toward those who happen to disagree with the Patriots "in things civil or religious" utterly discredited the movement's pretension to penitence. Amos condemned practitioners of false religion "who drew nigh to God while their hearts were removed far from him." Andrews fashioned a religious ethic which could match his Congregationalist adversaries in communal discipline and social realism: "Only . . . if we . . . repent of our vileness as a people and reform our manners—live in strict piety toward God and charity towards men, and perform all the duties of our stations as good Christians and faithful subjects, without controversy—[will] our light break forth as the morning . . . and the glory of the Lord be our reward." Then, in a remarkable change of tone, Andrews conceded that the spirit of political resistance he had been denouncing was for many a natural and appealing mode of belief and expression. "I know there are many who talk a language different from me in these matters; they are extremely confident of success and brand those who show the least diffidence . . . as enemies or cowards. They are girding on the harness. . . . But in my opinion, such confidence is an ill omen of success. However, just [as] it may be to struggle for our rights when they are invaded and however strong and well prepared for war we may be, yet we are to consider that the battle is the Lord's and that it is alike easy with Him to save or punish many or few. I am not so much afraid of the power of England as I am of the sins of America."[31] Andrews here recognized that the existence of new political language, the grim confidence of girding for battle, and disagreement as to the will of God in these things represented an institutionalization of the politics of resistance.

Andrews knew political mobilization when he saw it because Anglican Loyalism in New England, as in neighboring New York City, had, since the 1750s, sought to institutionalize obedience to British authority through worship and learning. One of the marks which separated the Church of England from other religious groups in America was its insistence that a church needed to have bishops and that clergy should be episcopally ordained. The institutional core of this enterprise was King's College, nominally nondenominational but increasingly dominated by Anglican administrators beginning with its founder, Samuel Johnson, who as a Yale Congregationalist student doubted the efficacy of Congregational ordination and with two companions sailed to London to seek Anglican ordination. Johnson's timing was right. Prosperity and cosmopolitanism of the mid-eighteenth century made Anglicanism attractive, not only to the elite such as William Franklin but also to the poorest colonial farmers entranced by the beauty of *The Book of Common Prayer*. "In the Church of England," Johnson taught, "worship consists of a most serious and solemn address to the great creator, preserver, and governor of the world, testifying from the bottom of our hearts our dependence upon . . . and submission to Him, praising Him for everything we enjoy, praying to him for whatsoever we want, and devoting ourselves . . . [to] his Service." Anglican churches sprang up throughout New England as fast as Separate Baptist churches did for radical dissenters.[32]

Johnson was the first president of King's College, and his protégé, Myles Cooper, who led King's from 1763 to 1776, sought to make it a bastion of Tory orthodoxy. He raised funds in England and persuaded the Anglican hierarchy that King's would be an "instrument" for "cementing between Great Britain and the Colonies" by producing students renowned for their "loyalty, learning, and Virtue."[33] That very reputation for high Toryism alienated the non-Anglicans, especially Dutch Reformed Trustees, and narrowed the base of support in New York at the same time it brought funds and royal patronage from London. Institutionalization thus cut both ways. The only way to shore up colonial support for Anglicized education and colonial submission to the Crown was through polemical writing employing the same medium of highly charged pamphlets that served Whig politicians so well.

As in New England, the core group of New York writers who protested the vigilantism of the rebel mobs between 1774 and 1776 were Anglican clergyman. These pamphleteers had forged their defense about the supremacy of the Crown in the controversy over Anglican bishops in America. In 1774, they turned their eyes to new targets. Under the leadership of Samuel Seabury, Thomas Bradbury Chandler, and Charles Inglis, New York and New Jersey clerics objected to the extremist demands for ideological conformity, asserted their right to dissent from popular opinion, and emphasized the need for tolerance.

Between November 1774 and January 1775, New York printer, James Rivington, published four pamphlets authored by Seabury that assailed the Continental Congress's economic boycott of British goods. Scion of an old New England family, a Yale graduate, and an ardent pamphleteer, Seabury posed as a simple farmer to lash out against the Continental Congress. Like other Anglican clergy, Seabury's Loyalism reflected his church's conviction that society should be hierarchic, that ordinary human beings required the supervision of kings and bishops, and that Presbyterianism would lead to revolution. He condemned the Congress for rending the bonds of civil society and threatening the rule of the king with a "parcel of upstart, lawless, committee-men." In the fourth pamphlet, entitled *An Alarm to the Legislature of the Province of New York*, Seabury warned that the Continental Association and its boycott would set up "a new sovereign power in the province and plunge it into all the horrors of rebellion & civil war."[34]

Chandler was the foremost Anglican polemicist in the pre-Revolutionary controversy. His two famous pamphlets, *American Querist* (1774) and *Friendly Address to All Reasonable Americans* (1775), went to the heart of issues of liberty and authority that Whig writers had raised in their denunciations of British colonial policy. *Querist* presented one hundred questions culminating in this sweeping vindication of hierarchy and obedience: "Whether some degree of respect be not always due from inferiors to superiors, and especially from children to parents; and whether the refusal of this on any occasion be not a violation of the general laws of society, to say nothing here of the obligations of religion and morality?" And was not Great Britain the parent of her colonies and entitled to punish "disrespectful and abusive treatment from [her] children?"[35]

Chandler's profound question about social hierarchy brought together two great traditions of political thought, one deeply conservative and the other prophetically liberal. His conservative root was the divine right of kings theory popularized by Robert Filmer in the Court of James I in the early seventeenth century. John Locke had pilloried Filmer in his *Two Treatises of Government*, positing a hopeful compact between ruler and ruled, but Locke had discreetly not rebutted the more formidable contract theory of Thomas Hobbes, written during the English Civil War of the 1640s, a compact based on fear of anarchy. Chandler's source was the revival of Hobbes by the Jacobite theorist Charles Leslie who declared in 1711 that "I think it most natural that authority should descend . . . from a *superior* to an *inferior*, . . . from *kings* and *fathers* to *sons* and *servants*." Little noted is the liberal element of

Chandler's famous query invoking "general laws of society." That phrase anticipated the French Enlightenment writer, Marquis de Condorcet, writing from prison during the French Revolution in the early 1790s, twenty years *after* Chandler turned it against the American Whigs. Both Condorcet *and* Chandler learned of the existence of general or immutable laws of human behavior from Rousseau's *Social Contract* (1762).[36]

Inglis echoed Chandler. He described the rebellion as "one of the most causeless, unprovoked, and unnatural that ever disgraced any country... a rebellion marked with peculiarly aggravated circumstances of guilt and ingratitude."[37] When Inglis responded to Thomas Paine's *Common Sense* with *The True Interest of America Impartially Stated*, his pamphlet was seized from the printer and burned, and his house was plundered by the rebels. Addressing himself to the "passions of the populace," Inglis warned that Paine's "scheme" of a republican empire was "new as it is destructive." It invited "uncommon phrenzy" and would prove ruinous to America. By rashly inviting the Continental Congress to move toward a "romantic and untried scheme," argued Inglis, Paine furthered the breach between Great Britain and the colonies. Instead of proposing reconciliation with Britain on "solid constitutional principles," the fanatical Paine proposed "cutting off a leg because the toe happened to ache." Insisting that he belonged to no party and cared only about the welfare of America, Inglis pleaded for the avoidance of "blood and slaughter."[38]

By 1774–1775, what Bernard Bailyn characterized as "this ancient, honorable, and moribund philosophy" of high Tory Anglicanism appeared too cumbersome, and too weighted down by old scars and scores, to confront effectively the ideological (and violent) origins of the American Revolution. To be sure, Chandler tried to concede the legitimacy of opposition politics, but in terms that stripped it of all effectiveness. "If the supreme power of any state, from want of due information or attention, should adopt measures that are wrong or oppressive, the subjects may complain and remonstrate against them in a respectful manner, but they are bound by the laws of heaven and earth not to behave undutifully.... *The ill-consequences of open disrespect to government are so great that no misconduct by the administration can justify or excuse it.*"[39]

On religious grounds, then, the pre-Revolutionary controversy in New York and New England was inconclusive. The high Anglican vindication of hierarchy smashed like a cresting wave against the rocky shore of the Tea Act and Coercive Acts. The ideological storm abated and resumed in 1776 as a military conflict of arms. On hearing the news (on June 8, 1776) that the British had recruited Hessian mercenaries, William Smith, Jr., a moderate Presbyterian politician in New York, confided to his diary that "the clouds grow very dark. My hopes for conciliatory negotiation almost fail me." Almost, but not entirely. There remained just a chance of peaceful resolution if only the colonists reconsidered the theoretical requirements of peace: Great Britain had the right to frame colonial governments and to punish treason, but at the same time the colonists derived their political system from Parliament as well as the Crown, and this hybrid colonial constitution thus constituted a "compact" or an imperial constitution. "Neither of the contracting parties may dissolve this compact as long as their joint aim in the union, to wit, their mutual prosperity, can be attained by it." Negotiation was therefore a moral imperative because the alternative of a rebellious war was "beyond all controversy, a Satanical maxim."[40]

During the imperial crisis of 1774–1775, what kept many colonial merchants and politicians loyal to Britain was not just a principled and abstract confidence in the stability of monarchy or the moderation of the Church, but the turbulence in the streets and the violence against those who shared different views. William Franklin, governor of New Jersey, son of Benjamin Franklin, and ardent Loyalist, belonged to the Church of England. On January 3, 1775, he associated the rebellion with "Anarchy, Misery, and all the Horrors of a Civil War."[41] To the Anglican Church in New York City belonged the governor and lieutenant-governor, many members of the Council, and some of the richest families.[42] Prosperous merchants such as Elias Desbrosses and politicians such as Councilor James De Lancey, and Thomas Jones, Chief Justice of New York, were drawn to the moderation of Anglican faith.[43] Chief Justice Jones supported the meeting of the First Continental Congress but opposed the Continental Association which permitted local committees to harass respectable inhabitants in the name of maintaining unity. The Association represented a menace, an illegal threat to the fabric of society. For his views, Jones suffered four months of imprisonment in 1776, was captured by a rebel raiding group in 1779, and, in the same year, attainted by the state of New York.[44]

The individual Anglican voices became even weaker when the revolutionaries seized control of the press. Of the forty-two newspapers in the colonies, not one of them openly supported reunion before 1774.[45] Furthermore, when Anglican ministers protested revolutionary violence, their stance transformed them from mere antagonists into enemies. In 1776, Reverend Inglis wrote that the ill-treatment suffered by the Anglican clergy "could fill a Volume."[46]

Loyalism extended across denominational lines. One of the most courageous was the Swiss-born, Presbyterian minister in Georgia, John Jacob Zubly, whose essays under the pseudonym "Helvetius" (that is, "A Swiss") in the *Royal Georgia Gazette* castigated southern Patriots for their violence and cruelty. Recalling the history of the Thirty Years' War, Zubly predicted that justice to Loyalist victims of Patriot violence would come at the Last Judgment, "when all the ghosts of the slain, every drop of innocent blood you [Patriots] have spilt, every act of violence you concurred in or committed, all the confederates of your crime whom you have forced or seduced, every injured widow's groan and every orphan's tear whom you have ruined, the spoils of the honest and innocent whom you have robbed, every friendly warning which you rejected, will at once arise in judgment against you and render you as completely miserable as you have rendered yourselves distinguishedly wicked." In that moral and religious indictment, Zubly captured much of the complexity and tragedy of the American Revolution and underscored the troubling phenomenon of religion and ideology in America's first civil war.[47]

Between 1776 and 1777, the Loyalists—Anglicans as well as Presbyterians—expressed confidence in British military victory. When the British Army entered New York City in September 1776, Smith decided to abandon his country home and place himself under the protection of British arms, hoping that conciliatory politicians in the mother country "will discern the propriety of negotiating for a pacification."[48] Unlike the estimated two-thirds of the clergymen directly employed by the SPG who left the colonies during the revolution, Reverend Inglis stayed.[49] He took his loyalty seriously and worked hard to encourage more colonists to remain friends of the Crown. During the war, he wrote pro-British essays for *The New York Gazette and Weekly Mercury* and the *The Royal Gazette*.[50] After the Continental Congress issued the Declaration of Independence, Inglis sent his family seventy miles up the Hudson River but stayed in the city himself to visit the sick, baptize the children, and offer support to the poor. At the request of the New York governor, William Tryon, he also gave sermons to Loyalist militia to rally colonists to the cause of reunion with the empire.[51] In September 1777, he exhorted the soldiers to oppose the rebellion:

> It is the cause of Truth against Falsehood, of Loyalty against Rebellion, of Legal Government against usurpation, of constitutional freedom against Tyranny—in short it is the cause of human happiness of millions against outrages and oppression.[52]

On the death of Dr. Samuel Auchmuty in March 1777, Inglis became rector of Trinity Church in New York City and continued in this role until 1783.[70]

The active persecution of Anglicans did not play a central role in the revolution. Indeed, the reputation earned by Anglican clerics—their association with moderation—meant a general escape from revolutionary persecution. The Anglicans—clergy and laity—who did not loudly and publicly assert their loyalty or participate actively in the cause of reunion were left unharmed. But Inglis's active support of empire did not go unnoticed. In 1779, the state of New York declared fifty-nine persons guilty of felony and ordered them to forfeit their property to the state. Included in the list were Mrs. Inglis and two other wives.[53] Given the limited autonomy of women in public life and their circumscribed role in church structure, it is surprising that any women were included.[54] Although women participated in family worship and religious education, men dominated as church leaders (with the exception of women in the Quaker faith). Yet, during the rebellion, as Mrs. Inglis's case illustrates, some women became politicized through their association with Anglican Loyalists who were their husbands or fathers. Revolutionary statutes that defined treason spoke of "persons" instead of men alone.[55]

The Quakers confronted different treatment than the Anglicans. The clumsy and untested coercive machinery of the Revolutionary regime revealed the tone deafness of Patriot administration of justice. In the summer and autumn of 1777, in the midst of British military occupation of Philadelphia, the Continental Congress directed Pennsylvania and Delaware to institute a repressive campaign against those "who have not manifested their attachment to the American cause"—an ill-disguised description of Quakers in the middle colonies. This initiative culminated in the arrest and imprisonment in Winchester, Virginia, of eleven prominent members of the Society of Friends for no other reason, according to spokesman Henry Drinker, than their "endeavoring steadily to adhere to what I believed to be my Christian duty of refusing to join any of the prevailing seditions and tumults." Though released after a few months when searches turned up no incriminating evidence, the harassment stunned the entire Quaker community. As a result, by 1783, the Society of Friends, according to historian Sydney V. James, altered its entire confessional identity as a primitive sect living in anticipation of the Christian promise of a Peaceable Kingdom into being simply one more Protestant denomination, thus finding a way to "reconcile their beliefs with the pluralism of the American religious scene."[56]

The French alliance with the revolutionaries in 1778 led to Loyalist frenzy. Shaken by the news, the Anglicans' renewed rhetoric shifted to attack the menace of French Catholicism. Conceding French power, Loyalists turned it to meet their own ends. They argued that France would transform free American colonists into French dependents.[49] In the summer of 1778, they bitterly crusaded against the "universal establishment of Popery" that would extinguish every "spark" of civil and religious liberty in the world. They contrasted the natural ties of consanguinity, language, manners, and religion that bound the colonies to the British Empire against the "unnatural alliance with perfidious Frenchmen." By allying themselves with the "ambition" and "duplicity" of the "inveterate foes" of Britain, the colonists would enter into league with those who wished to overturn the Protestant faith. The Catholic enemy was perfidious, restless, and enterprising. Warning colonists of French cunning, the Loyalists constructed the French as a Proteus that entered like a "lamb," transformed into a "fox," and treacherously became the "devouring wolf." The colonies would be sold to a French king and live under "wretched submission" to French despotism and popish superstition.[57]

Further, the clergymen explained the ruthless power politics of Europe as a seething cauldron of opportunism and deceit, and predicted accurately that French officials would jump at a favorable opportunity to make peace with Britain and leave the rebellious colonists to suffer the consequences. There was, however, a pro forma tone to these anti-Catholic, anti-French polemics in the Loyalist press. The French alliance was the best target garrison town Loyalists would ever enjoy, and by 1780–1781 the New York populace knew that the tide had turned in the military struggle. Accordingly, the Loyalist press in 1782 prepared for British withdrawal and the prospect of making peace with the Patriot regime. Here their Protestant heritage became a useful source of guidance. Garrison town moderates recalled the heroic role of Sir William Davenant, a peacemaker in England in the 1650s who paved the way for royalist-Puritan reconciliation and who, on the eve of the Restoration of Charles II, persuaded Oliver Cromwell's followers not to "despair" for that was "the last thing that should enter into the heart of wise and honest men."[58]

Conclusion

The British Empire, it seems, had learned important lessons from the success of the American rebellion. In the Loyalist refuge of British North America, the government hoped to employ the Church of England to foster loyalty and discourage civil disobedience. In 1787, Reverend Inglis was appointed Bishop of Nova Scotia. He had jurisdiction over not only Nova Scotia, but also Canada, Newfoundland, and New Brunswick. In 1789, Bishop Inglis promoted the idea of an Anglican seminary for American refugees. Inglis linked Anglican theology with British constitutionalism. The church would assure "diffuse salutary effects" so "pure religion, virtue, order and loyalty may prevail."[59] Nova Scotia would be an "asylum of Loyalists who wish to have their children educated in constitutional principles."[60] If proper encouragement was not given to Anglican establishments, Inglis warned, the next generation would not be indoctrinated in constitutional principles. They would go to churches run by Methodists who "get drunk and blaspheme like atheists."[61]

There was no general agreement amongst Loyalist refugees about the role of the Church of England in British North America. For instance, William Smith, Jr. did not share Inglis's view on the centrality of the Church of England. Over twenty years earlier, Inglis and Smith had clashed over the question of an American bishopric. Ten years before that, Smith had promoted a secular state university (King's College) for New York. In British North America, Smith appealed to his patron, Lord Dorchester, to establish schools where no theology was taught while Inglis appealed to the church hierarchy in England to promote an Anglican educational establishment. Instead of religion serving as a binding glue, Smith anticipated that British "liberal government . . . without any contracted preference or religious discriminations" would help to assimilate the French in Quebec and to create a bicultural region protected by English law.[62]

In the thirteen rebel colonies, the war was more than a regime change; it also ushered in a new political and religious culture. In so doing, it wounded relationships within religious communities and disrupted fellowship and discipleship within church bodies. Anglican disestablishment and the status and privileges of new Episcopal churches were an early consequence of American independence. Even among staunchly Patriot Presbyterians, there were religious and political conservatives who distrusted rebellion as tainted with Cromwellian and Jacobite extremism. A substantial minority of Calvinist Dutch Reformed, who looked to church authorities in Holland for spiritual guidance and political orthodoxy, abstained from supporting the Revolution or intentionally did business with the British military. Some Lutherans honored their old world ties to the Electors of Hanover, now kings of Great Britain. The novel religious radicalism of Methodists looked askance at Patriot politicization of civil society and religious order. Peace churches—Quakers and

German pietists—agonized over the violence and brutality of revolutionary warfare. And efforts by Episcopalians in South Carolina and Virginia to secure public funding for well-behaved Protestant churches raised, for Patriot leaders like James Madison as well as most Baptists and Presbyterians, the specter of churches becoming "engines of civil policy."

Though not enflamed or grotesque, these wounds still took time to heal. Methodists (in 1784) and Presbyterians and Episcopalians (in 1787) drafted denominational constitutions in order to insure legitimacy within the new nation. Quakers and Moravians redefined themselves as Protestant denominations rather than as apolitical prophetic witnesses. The Virginia religious settlement of 1786 enacted Jefferson's Statute for Religious Freedom and, at the same time, protected Anglican glebe lands. That trade-off prefigured the religion clauses of the First Amendment, ratified in 1791, proscribing establishment of any national church and protecting free exercise of religion by the citizenry. During the early decades of the nineteenth century, a spirited discussion of separation of church and state helped define the meaning of republican citizenship.

Just as the Christian God was a trinity of divine manifestations, so Loyalism took on three guises: principled Loyalists concerned with law and public policy, moderate Loyalists searching for compromise and accommodation, and doctrinaire Tories transfixed with the evil of rebellion. In each sphere, religion played a part. Principled Loyalism made respect for law a religious imperative; moderate Loyalism held that only mutual forgiveness could save the empire from dismemberment; and Tory doctrine considered the worship prescribed in *The Book of Common Prayer* the epitome of beauty and order.

Notes

1. James B. Bell, *A War of Religion: Dissenters, Anglicans and the American Revolution* (New York: Palgrave Macmillan, 2008), 240.
2. Henry J. Young, "The Treatment of the Loyalists in Pennsylvania" (Unpublished dissertation, Johns Hopkins University, 1955), 82–93.
3. Rowan Strong, *Anglicanism and the British Empire, c.1700–1850* (New York: Oxford University Press, 2007), 63.
4. Strong, *Anglicanism and the British Empire*, 10.
5. Boyd Stanley Schlenter, "Religious Faith and Commercial Empire," in P. J. Marshall, ed., *The Oxford History of the British Empire: Eighteenth Century* (New York: Oxford University Press, 1996), 131.

6. Frederick V. Mills, *Bishops by Ballot* (New York: Oxford University Press, 1978), 134.
7. Quoted in Brent Tarter, "Reflections on the Church of England in Colonial Virginia," *The Virginia Magazine of History and Biography* 112, no. 4 (2004), 343.
8. S. Charles Bolton, *Southern Anglicanism: The Church of England in Colonial South Carolina* (Westport, CT: Greenwood Press, 1982), 5; Strong, *Anglicanism and the British Empire*, 45.
9. Quoted in Frank Lambert, *The Founding Fathers and the Place of Religion in America* (Princeton, NJ: Princeton University Press, 2003), 155.
10. Schlenter, "Religious Faith and Commercial Empire,"145–146; in contrast, Roger Finke and Rodney Stark note that 85 percent were non-Anglicans. See *The Churching of America, 1776–2005: Winners and Losers in our Religious Economy* (New Brunswick, NJ: Rutgers Press, 2005).
11. Bolton, *Southern Anglicanism*, 13–14.
12. Religious establishment of the Anglican Church in Georgia, South Carolina, North Carolina, Virginia, Maryland, and in the southern counties of New York fell under the jurisdiction of the colonial assemblies as did the Congregational Church in New England.
13. Bolton, *Southern Anglicanism*, 5–6.
14. Rhys Isaac, *The Transformation of Virginia, 1740–1790* (Chapel Hill, NC: Omohundro Institute, 1982), 177.
15. Tarter, "Reflections on the Church of England," 347–348, 352, 354, quote from 353.
16. Bolton, *Southern Anglicanism*, 114, 120; note that this is in contrast to the efforts of the Anglican Church in Philadelphia. See Gary B. Nash, *Forging Freedom: The Formation of Philadelphia's Black Community, 1720–1840* (Cambridge, MA: Harvard University Press, 1988), 20–24; Sylvia Frey and Betty Wood argue that the clergy were unable to offer a compelling reason for slaves to abandon their traditional beliefs in favor of those espoused by the clergymen. See Frey and Wood, *Come Shouting to Zion: African American Protestantism in the American South and British Caribbean to 1830* (Chapel Hill: University of North Carolina Press, 1998), 75.
17. They interacted with at least forty-six native communities. See "Red, Black, and White—the Society in Mission," in Daniel O'Connor, ed., *Three Centuries of Mission: The United Society for the Propagation of the Gospel, 1701–2000* (London: Continuum Books, 2000), 32.
18. Quoted in Bolton, *Southern Anglicanism*, 104.
19. Bolton, *Southern Anglicanism*, 105–108.
20. Charles Inglis, March 8, 1770, in John Wolfe Lydekker, ed., *The Life and Letters of Charles Inglis: His Ministry in America and Consecration as First Colonial Bishop, from 1759 to 1787* (London: Society for Promoting Christian Knowledge, 1936), 92.
21. Charles Inglis, June 15, 1770, in *The Life and Letters of Charles Inglis*, 101.
22. Charles Inglis, March 8, 1770, in ibid., 94.
23. Quoted in Caitlin A. Fitz, "'Suspected on Both Sides': Little Abraham, Iroquois Neutrality, and the American Revolution," *Journal of the Early Republic* 27 (Fall 2008), 314.

24. Fitz, "Suspected on Both Sides," 304.
25. Milledge L. Bonham, Jr., "The Religious Side of Joseph Brant," *The Journal of Religion* 9, no. 3 (July, 1929), 403, 414.
26. Carol Berkin, *Revolutionary Mothers: Women in the Struggle for America's Independence* (New York: Knopf, 1995), 114.
27. John Frederick Woolverton, *Colonial Anglicanism in North America* (Detroit: Wayne State University Press, 1984), 232.
28. J. P. Greene, ed., *Colonies to Nation, 1763–1789* (New York: McGraw Hill, 1967), 266–268.
29. Ibid.
30. Robert M. Calhoon, *The Loyalists in Revolutionary America, 1760–1781* (New York: Harcourt Brace Jovanovich, 1973), 258.
31. Ibid., 261–262.
32. Ibid., 210–211.
33. David C. Humphreys, *From King's College to Columbia University, 1746–1800* (New York: Columbia University Press, 1976), 141.
34. Seabury, quoted in Tiedemann, *Reluctant Revolutionaries* (Ithaca, NY: Cornell University Press, 1997), 208–209; see also Samuel Seabury, *Letters of a Westchester Farmer, 1774–1775*, Charles H. Vance, ed. (White Plains, NY: Westchester Historical Society, 1930), 30.
35. Bernard Bailyn, *The Ideological Origins of the American Revolution* (Cambridge, MA: Harvard University Press, 1967), 313.
36. Ibid., 310–319; David Williams, *Condorcet and Modernity* (Cambridge, Eng.: Cambridge University Press, 2004), 172–174.
37. Charles Inglis, October 31, 1776, in *The Life and Letters of Charles Inglis*, 159.
38. Charles Inglis, "The True Interest of America Impartially Stated, in Certain Strictures on a Pamphlet Intitled Common Sense," in Edward Larkin, ed., *Common Sense: Thomas Paine* (Toronto: Broadview Editions, 2004), 151, 155, 157, 152.
39. Calhoon, *Loyalists in Revolutionary America*, 217.
40. Ibid., 103–104.
41. Quoted in David J. Toscano, Ronald M. McCarthy, and Walter H. Conser, Jr., "A Shift in Strategy: The Organization of the Military Struggle," in Walter H. Conser, Jr. et al., eds., *Resistance, Politics, and the American Struggle for Independence, 1765–1775* (Boulder, CO: Lynne Rienner Publishers, 1986), 439.
42. Tiedemann, *Reluctant Revolutionaries*, 23.
43. Thomas Jefferson Wertenbaker, *Father Knickerbocker Rebels: New York City During the Revolution* (New York: C. Scribner's Sons, 1948), 50; Roger J. Champagne, "Thomas Jones of New York, a Loyalist Historian of the American Revolution," in Lawrence H. Leder, ed., *The Colonial Legacy: Historians of Nature and Man's Nature* (New York: Harper and Row, 1973), 315.
44. Champagne, "Thomas Jones," 318–320.
45. Mills, *Bishops by Ballot*, 148–149.

46. Charles Inglis, October 31, 1776, in *The Life and Letters of Charles Inglis*, 159.
47. Calhoon, *Loyalists in Revolutionary America*, 153–154.
48. Ibid., 104.
49. Schlenther, "Religious Faith and Commercial Empire," 147.
50. Charles Inglis, in *The Life and Letters of Charles Inglis*, 211.
51. William Tryon to Charles Inglis, September 12, 1777, in *The Life and Letters of Charles Inglis*, 187.
52. Charles Inglis, September 1777 sermon, in *The Life and Letters of Charles Inglis*, 257.
53. Linda K. Kerber, *Women of the Republic: Intellect and Ideology in Revolutionary America* (New York: W.W. Norton, 1980), 127.
54. Maya Jasanoff, *Liberty's Exiles: American Loyalists in the American World* (New York: Knopf, 2011), 147.
55. Berkin, *Revolutionary Mothers*, 100–101.
56. Calhoon, *Loyalists in Revolutionary America*, 388–399.
57. *The Royal Gazette*, June 13, July 1, June 6, June 24, and August 22, 1778.
58. Timothy M. Barnes and Robert M. Calhoon, "Loyalist Discourse and the Moderation of the American Revolution," in *Tory Insurgents: The Loyalist Perception and Other Essays*, Revised and Expanded Edition (Columbia: University of South Carolina Press, 2010), 186–187.
59. Charles Inglis to Macarmick, May 1, 1789, MG1 Vol. 479a, in Nova Scotia Archives, 152.
60. Charles Inglis to Archbishop, April 20, 1789, MG1 Vol. 479a, in ibid., 147.
61. Charles Inglis to Archbishop, March 18, 1789, MG1 Vol. 479a, in ibid., 144.
62. Quoted in Oscar Zeichner, "Documents: William Smith's 'Observations on America,'" *New York History* XXIII (1942), 339.

6

The Antifederalists and Religion

Donald L. Drakeman

Introduction

IN THE LATE summer of 1789, Elbridge Gerry interrupted the congressional debate over what would become the First Amendment's religion clauses. The feisty Massachusetts congressman wanted to speak up for those who had joined him in trying to defeat the ratification of the Constitution, a group that had often been derided as "Antifederalists" by the generally pro-ratification, "Federalist" press. His comments came at a time when Congress was considering a proposed amendment that would read, "no national religion shall be established by law."[1]

Two years earlier, Gerry had played an active role at the Constitutional Convention, but, dissatisfied with the outcome, he was one of three delegates who refused to sign the resulting document. Then, while serving in the First Congress, he objected to the language of the proposed nonestablishment amendment because it contained the controversial word "national." Gerry and his fellow opponents of ratification were worried that the new Constitution improperly "consolidated the union"—that is, they made it a "national" government—rather than a federal one, as had existed under the Articles of Confederation, where the states were the central focus of political power.

"Those who were called antifederalists," noted Gerry, "complained that they had injustice done them by [that] title." In fact, he told the Federalist-dominated Congress that the so-called Antifederalists were the ones who were "in favor of a federal government," while their opponents, who had bestowed upon themselves the name Federalist, were actually "in favor of a national one." The Federalists "were for ratifying the Constitution as it stood," while Gerry and his compatriots did not want ratification "until amendments were made." And so, Gerry cleverly concluded, their "names . . . ought not to have [been] federalists and antifederalists, but rats and antirats."[2]

Gerry has a point. Despite the presence among the "antirats" of such distinguished revolutionary heroes and American statesmen as Gerry, Patrick Henry, Richard Henry Lee, and George Mason, the people we now call Antifederalists have routinely suffered from bad press. As James Hutson notes, historians have often seen the Antifederalists and the Loyalists as "Revolutionary America's two most conspicuous groups of losers."[3] Even the "first searching investigation of the political ideas of the Antifederalists undertaken by . . . any historian," which did not appear until the 1950s, was titled "Men of Little Faith," a reference to their pessimistic views of government.[4]

More recently, the Antifederalists' ideas—including their thoughts about religion—have become matters of both historical and constitutional importance.[5] Beginning in the 1940s, a series of Supreme Court cases created national standards for how church and state should relate to each other in states, cities, towns, and schools around the country. These decisions have generally been based upon the Supreme Court's view of the framers' original understanding of the First Amendment's religion clauses.[6] And since that amendment only came to pass because those opposed to ratification insisted upon a Bill of Rights, the Antifederalists' views on religion and government have been increasingly scrutinized. The balance of this chapter will focus both on what we know about the Antifederalists and religion, and on how those views have been described by scholars.

Religious Affiliations of the Antifederalists

It is difficult to draw any sharp distinctions between the Federalists and the Antifederalists on the basis of their religious affiliations. The vast majority of Americans eligible to vote at the time of ratification were Protestants, and there were considerable differences of opinion about the new Constitution within the various Protestant denominations.[7] As Jackson Turner Main has pointed out, while the New England Congregationalist ministers were in favor of ratification, "there does not seem to have been any clear-cut alignment of Congregationalists behind the Constitution: thus while Connecticut favored adoption, central and western Massachusetts did not."[8] Meanwhile, the Baptists in Philadelphia, eastern North Carolina, and South Carolina were Federalists, and "a convention of Baptists of the middle states recommended ratification," while "the Virginia Baptist Association voted unanimously against ratification."[9] Massachusetts Baptists were split, with Antifederalists prevailing "in the interior," and Federalists, "including the prominent Isaac Backus," in the coastal part of the state.[10] The Presbyterians were divided as well—Federalists dominated in "southern New York, eastern Pennsylvania, and the Shenandoah Valley," but not elsewhere.[11] Pennsylvania Quakers and Episcopalians were "fairly consistent in their Federalism . . . yet in the west they were often in the opposite camp," and the "German sects divided irregularly."[12] Since there is no easy way to categorize the Antifederalists based on their denominational affiliations, it would be difficult to assess their constitutional views on religion by reference to any particular religious doctrine or theological tradition.[13]

The Antifederalists on Religion

Scholars writing about the Antifederalists are immediately confronted with the problem that this "disparate group of critics of the proposed government" did not always agree with each other.[14] How do we know, for example, whether a particular argument made in an Antifederalist essay fairly represents the views of ratification's opponents, and is not just a reflection of one individual's idiosyncratic outlook? The answer, in short, is that it is hard to know with certainty. Scholars have generally taken one of two approaches to trying to identify those ideas that represent the thinking of the Antifederalists. One method, seen especially in the work of Saul Cornell, concentrates on those writings that were reprinted most often, and were thus likely to have been read by the most people. The other, pioneered by Herbert J. Storing, who compiled a seven volume collection called *The Complete Anti-Federalist*, has sought to identify the most sophisticated arguments, those that Storing deems to be the most "fundamental" in articulating a coherent political philosophy.[15] This chapter will take advantage of both approaches. It will focus primarily on the Antifederalist writings collected by Storing, and it will identify those materials that were reprinted most frequently, and may therefore have been most influential.

If we ask what the Antifederalists said about religion and the Constitution, the answer is: not very much. This is not to say that religion was unimportant to the lives of individual Antifederalists. Many Antifederalists were church members, and some were prominent church leaders.[16] But in the extensive collection of essays and other writings published by the Antifederalists about the ratification of the Constitution, the discussions of religion—or even of political issues relating to religion—are remarkably infrequent compared to much more regularly articulated concerns about the risks entailed in having a strong central government.

Gerry's statement explaining his "Objections to Signing the National Constitution" is one of the most important antiratification documents, and his "criticisms were appropriated and elaborated by a wide variety of authors."[17] Gerry's principal concerns were that "there is no adequate provision for a representation of the people . . .— that some of the powers of the legislature are . . . indefinite and dangerous—that the Executive . . . will have an undue influence over the Legislature—that the judicial department will be oppressive . . .—and that the system is without the security of a bill of rights."[18] Gerry pointed out that the "Constitution has proposed few, if any *federal* features, but is rather a system of *national* government"; it has, nevertheless, "great merit, and by proper amendments, may be adapted to the 'exigencies of government,' and preservation of liberty."[19] His short statement does not describe those amendments, nor does he mention religion at all.

A few weeks later, George Mason's "Objections to the Constitution of Government Formed by the Convention" was first published. Mason, the highly regarded author of Virginia's Declaration of Rights, had also been a delegate at the Convention but had refused to sign the Constitution. His "Objections," which were widely reprinted, had much in common with Gerry's, but he provided additional detail about the liberties that should be included in a "Declaration of Rights": the "Liberty of the Press, the Trial by Jury in civil Causes" and the need to protect against the "Danger of standing Armys in time of Peace."[20] Religion was not mentioned.

Another prominent and oft-reprinted Antifederalist document—the "Reasons of Dissent" by Robert Yates and John Lansing, two New York delegates who left the Constitutional Convention before its work was completed—not only failed to mention religion, but, as Storing notes, "there is no objection to the absence of a bill of rights" at all.[21] Similarly, Edmund Randolph, another delegate who refused to sign, but who later joined the Federalist ranks, listed a number of potential amendments in a frequently reprinted letter, none of which related to a Bill of Rights in general or to religion in particular.[22]

Among the Convention delegates who refused to sign the Constitution, the only one to mention religion in his explanation was the loquacious Luther Martin of Maryland, who was described by one contemporary as "so extremely prolix, that he never speaks without tiring the patience of all who hear him."[23] Martin's essay was over twenty times the length of Gerry's objections, which may explain why it was reprinted far less often.[24] After nearly fifty pages detailing the defects in Articles I, II, and III of the Constitution, Martin turned to a series of what Storing calls "miscellaneous" concerns.[25] One involved Article VI's provision that there should be "*no religious test . . . required as a qualification to any office or public trust. . . .*"[26] Martin noted that this clause had not been controversial; it was "adopted by a great majority of the convention, and without much debate. . . ."[27] Some delegates, presumably including Martin himself, were "*so unfashionable* as to think that a *belief of the existence of a Deity*, and of a *state of future rewards and punishments* would be some security for the good conduct of our rulers. . . ."[28] Moreover, argued Martin, "in a Christian country it would be at *least decent* to hold out some distinction between the professors of Christianity and downright infidelity or paganism."[29]

Perhaps the most prominent Antifederalist who had not served as a delegate to the Convention was Declaration of Independence signer Richard Henry Lee of Virginia. He wrote a letter to Governor Randolph that was reprinted twenty times, making it one of the most widely circulated Antifederalist essays. Both in the body of the letter and in the "postscript" that detailed his proposed amendments, Lee cited the need to protect several fundamental rights, including "the rights of conscience." There should be, he argued, "a declaration or bill of rights, clearly and precisely stating the principles upon which this social compact is founded, to wit: That the rights of conscience in matters of religion ought not to be violated—That the freedom of the press shall be secured," and so on through about a dozen proposed amendments that overlap considerably with the final version of the Bill of Rights.[30]

Altogether, there were seventeen essays by individual Antifederalists that were reprinted at least ten times or that were published in a nationally circulated periodical.[31] These documents were typically printed shortly after the Constitutional Convention in an effort to influence the various state ratifying conventions. Nearly 80 percent of these writings were silent on the topic of religion. The others mentioned religious freedom only as part of a much longer list of proposed amendments, and opposition to the no-religious-test language came solely from Maryland's Luther Martin.

As the focus shifted to the state conventions, religious issues arose only occasionally. The Constitutional Convention had ended in September 1787, and by December Delaware's ratifying convention unanimously approved the Constitution. There was spirited debate in Pennsylvania, but the Federalists won in the end and were able to successfully block consideration of amendments.[32] Unable even to get their suggestions recorded in the convention's proceedings, the Pennsylvania minority published their proposed amendments as a "Minority Dissent" that was signed by twenty-one of the twenty-three delegates voting against ratification.[33] Although the Dissent was primarily about "the issue of representation," it contained numerous "unalienable and personal rights of men, without the full, free, and secure enjoyment of which there can be no liberty . . . [the] principal of which are the rights of conscience . . ., habeas corpus, jury trial . . .; and the liberty of the press. . . ."[34] These Pennsylvania dissenters further proposed that no branch of the federal government "shall have authority to alter, abrogate, or infringe any part of the constitution of the several states, which provide for the preservation of liberty in matters of religion."[35] Finally, in a state containing many Quakers and others who were theologically opposed to military service, the report noted that "the rights of conscience may be violated, as there is no exemption of those persons who are conscientiously scrupulous of bearing arms."[36]

These concerns about religious liberty had also been expressed in several essays published around the time of Pennsylvania's convention. In an essay reprinted eleven times, Centinel described a number of liberties that should be protected, including "that all men have a natural and unalienable right to worship Almighty God, according to the dictates of their own consciences and understanding. . . ."[37] The rights of conscience were also highlighted by the less frequently reprinted Pennsylvanians Old Whig and Philadelphiensis, both of whom also supported religious exemptions from military service, a topic that appears more often in Pennsylvania than elsewhere.[38]

Centinel also had a negative view of religious establishments: "no man ought, or of right can be compelled to attend any religious worship, or erect or support any place of worship, or maintain any ministry, contrary to, or against his own free will. . . ."[39] Old Whig expressed similar worries about a "religious establishment for this country,"[40] and fellow Pennsylvanian Deliberator echoed these concerns in an essay published after the convention, saying "Congress may establish a uniformity in religion throughout the United States. Such establishments have been thought necessary, and have accordingly taken place in almost all the other countries in the world, and will, no doubt be thought equally necessary in this."[41] Although the concerns about liberty of conscience and religious exemptions from the military were reflected in the Dissent, these anti-establishment views were not.

New Jersey (in December) and Georgia (early in January 1788) ratified unanimously. In Connecticut, the Federalists dominated both the convention and the press, leading to an overwhelming majority vote for ratification just a few days later.[42] Although not included in Storing's collection, a letter by Declaration of Independence signer William Williams expressed his unhappiness at the lack of a religious test and the absence of "an explicit acknowledgment" in the Constitution "of the being of a God. . . ."[43]

The first state formally to "recommend," but not require, amendments was Massachusetts, where the Antifederalist challenge was formidable. Although dozens of the delegates were Protestant ministers, religion was not a major issue. The topic did come up periodically in published essays and in the debates, however. The religious issue that most animated Antifederalists was the Constitution's lack of a religious test. In a February 1788 essay, A Watchman complained first that "there is no religious liberty given to the people to perform religious worship" and then, in the following sentence, that "a door [is] opened for the Jews, Turks, and Heathen to enter into publick office. . . ."[44] An essay by Samuel also appears to argue for a religious test because "[i]f civil rulers won't acknowledge God, he won't acknowledge them."[45] His question as to whether "there [was] ever any State or kingdom, that could subsist, without adopting some system of religion"[46] found expression by Charles Turner on the floor of the Massachusetts convention, where he stated that "without the prevalence of *Christian piety, and morals*, the best republican Constitution can never save us from slavery and ruin."[47] In the end, the prefatory clause of Massachusetts' ratification resolutions "acknowledge[d] . . . the goodness of the Supreme Ruler of the universe in affording the people . . . an opportunity . . . to form a more perfect union" through the new Constitution. But the proposed amendments themselves did not mention religion.[48]

Massachusetts ratified in early February, and over two months went by before another state followed suit. In the meantime, Rhode Island's referendum vote opposed ratification. It would not change its mind until 1790. Maryland was next to ratify, and its decision was rarely in doubt. After the ratification vote, Declaration of Independence signer William

Paca proposed to establish a committee to recommend amendments.[49] That committee agreed upon thirteen amendments, but a minority of the committee sought fifteen additional ones. The only one relating to religion was on this extended list. It read, "That there be no National Religion established by Law; but that all Persons be equally entitled to protection in their religious Liberty."[50] The complete list of amendments was published separately as "Amendments Proposed by William Paca in The Maryland Convention," and it was one of the most frequently reprinted Antifederalist documents.[51]

South Carolina was the next to ratify and, following Massachusetts' example, it recommended amendments. A bill of rights was rejected, but four amendments were approved, one of which would modify Article VI's no-religious-test language so that "it would say that 'no *other* religious test' would be required, understanding that an oath is a form of religious test."[52]

New Hampshire became the ninth state to ratify, but not without considerable effort. There was a great deal of opposition to the Constitution at the New Hampshire convention when it first assembled in February 1788. At that time, an essay by A Friend to the Rights of the People feared that "we may have a Papist, a Mohomatan, a Deist, yea an Atheist at the helm of Government. . . ."[53] For this essayist, "no man is fit to be a ruler of protestants, without he can honestly profess to be of the protestant religion."[54] The convention then adjourned for several months, while Maryland and South Carolina ratified, and only in June did New Hampshire reconvene and ratify with recommended amendments, but, unfortunately, without a record of the proceedings.[55] The lack of further commentary about religion is disappointing because the Granite State recommended an amendment specifically relating to religion: "Congress shall make no law touching religion, or to infringe the rights of conscience."

We have better records from the Virginia convention than from any other state. With respect to religion, Governor Randolph acknowledged that "[f]reedom of religion is said to be in danger. . . . It has been said that, if the exclusion of the religious test were an exception from the general power of Congress, the power over religion would remain," but he argued that "no power is given expressly to Congress over religion." In fact, "there are now so many [sects] in the United States, that they will prevent the establishment of any one sect."[56] Patrick Henry, speaking at great length on many topics, countered that "religious liberty . . . ought not to depend on constructive logical reasoning"; moreover, he thundered, "Holy Religion . . . will be prostituted to the lowest purposes of human policy."[57]

A letter from Denatus was published as the Virginia convention met. Denatus asked the delegates for amendments because "in the general bustle ... they forgot to put a bill of rights to it."[58] Denatus' principal proposal was for the Constitution to establish "academies ... throughout the United States for the education of youth in morality, - the principles of the Christian religion without regard to any sect ...: The principles of ... law ...: And the art of defending and conquering nations in battle...."[59] Denatus' letter appears to have had no effect on the Convention, which ultimately ratified the Constitution with recommendations for numerous amendments as well as a "Declaration of Rights" that included:

> 19th. That any person religiously scrupulous of bearing arms ought to be exempted, upon payment of an equivalent to employ another to bear arms in his stead.
> 20th. That religion, or the duty we owe to our Creator, and the manner of discharging it, can be directed only by reason and conviction, not by force or violence, and therefore all men have an equal, natural and unalienable right to the exercise of religion according to the dictates of conscience, and that no particular sect or society ought to be favored or established by law in preference to others.

The preamble of Virginia's declaration of ratification also said "that among other essential rights, the liberty of conscience and of the press cannot be cancelled, abridged, restrained or modified by any authority of the United States."

Attention then turned to New York. Months before the New York convention met, Federal Farmer published a series of influential essays pointing out defects in the Constitution. In the fourth, he listed the "free exercise of religion" as one of numerous items that should be included in the bill of rights, noting that "we are not disposed to differ much, at present, about religion; but ... we are making a constitution, it is to be hoped, for ages and millions yet unborn...."[60] A month later, a series of essays by Cincinnatus, probably Richard Henry Lee's brother, Arthur, appeared in a New York newspaper. He also mentioned the need to protect "liberty of conscience," along with numerous other rights. He argued that the no-religious-test provision, which he did not oppose, "implies, that in all other cases whatever liberty of conscience may be regulated. [Although] no such power is expressly given, yet it is plainly meant to be included in the general powers, or else this exception would have been totally unnecessary. . . ."[61] Similarly, A Countryman, in his fifth essay, argued, "surely it would have been of more importance, to have provided against Congress, making laws to take away liberty of conscience . . . than against . . . ex post facto laws, or even their making lords."[62] In fact, "in most of the old countries, their rulers . . . have thought it for the general welfare to establish particular forms of religion, and make every body worship God in a certain way . . . [;] there has been a great deal of mischief done by rulers in these particulars [but] I have never . . . heard of any great mischief being done by ex post facto laws. . . ."[63]

As the New York convention approached, a group of Antifederalists in Albany circulated a list of many objections to the Constitution, including the fact that "[m]en conscientiously scrupulous of bearing arms, [are] made liable to perform military duty" and it fails to "secur[e] the rights of conscience in matters of religion, [and] of . . . the liberty of worshipping God . . ., whereas the experience of all ages proves that the benevolence and humility inculcated in the gospel, are no restraint on the love of domination."[64]

Ultimately, in June, New York recommended numerous amendments, one of which said "That the People have an equal, natural and unalienable right, freely and peaceably, to exercise their religion according to the dictates of conscience, and that no religious sect or society ought to be favored or established by law in preference of others." This language fairly closely resembles Virginia's proposals about religion.

Storing's *Complete Anti-Federalist* does not include any North Carolinians on the subject of religion, but the topic was raised in the Convention by the Reverend David Caldwell who argued that "even those who do not regard religion, acknowledge that the Christian religion is best calculated, of all religions to make good members of society, on account of its morality."[65] Two Antifederalists are reported also to have expressed concerns that "one particular religion, including its 'ecclesiastical courts' [will] be established by the national government."[66] In the end, North Carolina did not ratify until November 1789, after the First Congress adopted the Bill of Rights. North Carolina's ratification included a series of recommended amendments based on Virginia's proposals, including those relating to religion.

Finally, six months passed before Rhode Island reversed its earlier decision and ratified the Constitution. By that point, its recommendation of an amendment on religion, which tracked North Carolina's language, was a moot point.

What Scholars Have Said about the Antifederalists' Views of Religion

Over the last few decades, a number of prominent scholars have focused considerable attention on the Antifederalists' views on religion, despite Jackson Turner Main's dismissive assertion that the "Antifederalists were not greatly concerned about religious freedom...."[67] Perhaps the most lively commentary has related to the First Amendment's establishment clause—"Congress shall make no law respecting an establishment of religion"—because the Supreme Court has relied on the views of James Madison and Thomas Jefferson to conclude that the Constitution erected a "wall of separation" between church and state.

Gary Glenn dislikes those decisions because they rely on "the thought of Madison and Jefferson who supported the original Constitution . . . ," and did not campaign for amendments.[68] Glenn instead seeks to identify the religion clauses' "forgotten purposes" by studying the Antifederalists, whose political actions brought about the First Amendment. That is, "the meaning of the religion clauses must be sought, at least initially, in what [the Antifederalists] had to say about religion during the ratification debates."[69] Glenn argues that the Antifederalists believed that religion provides a vital moral foundation for society. They were, therefore, more supportive of links between religion and government than what he calls the "standard historiography" or the Supreme Court's "conventional view."

Glenn notes that the "anti-Federalists were not primarily concerned about omission of guarantees of 'religious liberty. . . .'"[70] Rather, they were worried about "the actual or potential consequences of [the no religious test] clause."[71] He acknowledges that there may not have been "one neatly defined anti-Federalist position," but he believes that he has identified a "cluster of arguments" pointing to "a central fear that this clause was . . . harmful to religion itself" and "to religion's beneficial . . . influence on public life and public order."[72] Thus, the desire for a religious test was not driven simply by the fact that "non-Protestants, non-Christians, and even 'avowed atheists' were permitted to govern," but, more importantly, by "concerns related to the fate of the new government if it was indifferent or hostile to that religiously grounded moral virtue which anti-Federalists thought was useful or indispensable. . . ."[73]

Glenn's revisionist history is based on the documents found in Storing's *Complete Anti-Federalist*, and Storing himself made similar arguments. "[M]any Anti-Federalists," according to Storing, "were concerned with the maintenance of religious conviction as a support of republican government."[74] In considering a Bill of Rights, "[t]ypically they favored both governmental encouragement of religion and liberty of individual conscience."[75] To bolster this interpretation, Storing includes in his collection of Antifederalist writings two documents that clearly link religion to civic virtue: one is a local Virginia document that Storing describes as "unconcerned with the new proposed Constitution," and the other is a letter by Massachusetts writer David that, Storing notes, is "not explicitly Anti-Federal. . . ."[76]

That Storing would need to include two not-necessarily-Antifederalist writings to describe a "typical" view held by "many Anti-Federalists" raises the question of how much evidence actually supports his conclusion that it is a core component of "What the Anti-Federalists Were For." For additional support, Storing reaches outside even his own canon of Antifederalist writings. He cites a letter about a Virginia bill written by Richard Henry Lee three years before the Constitutional Convention; Antifederalist Mercy Warren's history of the revolution, which was published fifteen years after ratification; and, finally, an Antifederalist speaking at a state ratifying convention, Charles Turner, who said that "without the prevalence of Christian piety and morals, the best republican Constitution can never save us from slavery and ruin."[77]

Storing needs to cite this array of documents because Turner's comment is, in fact, a rare instance of an Antifederalist who voices the need to link religion, virtue, and the government in a debate about the Constitution.[78] This topic does not typically appear when Antifederalists discuss the federal government. Similarly, Glenn invokes a fairly small number of complaints about the lack of a religious test for public office—none of which led to a formally proposed amendment[79]—and, in the absence of further explanation, they could have been based as much on prejudices against "Jews, Turks and Heathen" as on a philosophy of civic republicanism. Whatever may have motivated the handful of Antifederalist comments about the lack of a religious test, it is difficult to conclude, based on the documents relating to ratification, that the Antifederalists, as a group, "favored . . . governmental encouragement of religion."[80]

Much as recent scholarship has shown that the historical evidence supporting the Supreme Court's "conventional" view is quite weak,[81] the Storing-Glenn interpretation of the Antifederalists rests on less firm ground than their broad statements may suggest. To be sure, Glenn and Storing can cite a small handful of Antifederalists who spoke of the importance of religion for government. But, it seems that the critical question to be contemplated by scholars who write with Supreme Court cases in mind is not what might be included in an exhaustive summary of the diverse and sometimes contradictory opinions expressed by the people opposing ratification. It should be, instead, what "The Antifederalists" believed—that is, the common viewpoints that we can reasonably attribute to enough people whose political power forced the issue of amendments such that we can identify those views as important motivations (or "forgotten purposes") for the Bill of Rights. By this standard, the Storing/Glenn civic republicanism interpretation is not supported by enough evidence to consider it a likely understanding of "The Antifederalists'" conception of the federal government.

Other leading scholars, also writing in opposition to the "conventional view," have identified a separate concern of the Antifederalists on the subject of religion. According to Phillip Muñoz, the "primary criticism the Anti-Federalists leveled [about religion and the Constitution] was that the proposed Congress, through its power to make all laws 'necessary and proper,' could impose uniformity of religious practice through the establishment of a national religion."[82] He cites concerns by Deliberator and A Countryman about a "national religious establishment," as well as Agrippa's statement that uniformity is undesirable because people in his state of Massachusetts are different from "our Southern brethren," and "no state can be happy, when the laws contradict the general habits of the people."[83]

Muñoz employs these Antifederalists' comments about a fear of a nationally mandated uniformity of religion to interpret the establishment clause—barring laws "*respecting* an establishment of religion"—as designed solely to allocate decision-making about religious establishments to the states rather than to Congress. According to Muñoz, the First Amendment is not based on a principle of nonestablishment; rather, it simply reinforces the principle of federalism. That is, it recognizes religion as being within the sole domain of the states, which would remain free to choose whether to have established churches.[84]

Addressing Muñoz's full argument would go beyond the scope of this chapter, but it is possible to consider the strength of the evidence relating to his conclusions that (1) national religious uniformity was a "primary" concern of the Antifederalists, and (2) the Antifederalists did not believe in nonestablishment as a principle.

As to the fear of the federal government usurping state prerogatives, Muñoz is surely right that the basic principle of federalism is a consistent theme throughout the Antifederalists' writings: If there is a unifying theme among Antifederalists, it is that the federal government should have very limited power to do anything at all. Much less clear, however, is whether that viewpoint can be extended to a specific concern about insulating state religious establishments from being eliminated or replaced by the Congress, such that the final version can be read as being essentially jurisdictional.

The Antifederalists said very little about religion, and even less about establishments. Muñoz cites three writers whose essays were not widely reprinted; they did not explicitly say that the states' decisions about religious establishments needed special protection; and it is difficult to locate any Antifederalist who does so. And while there were, in fact, jurisdictional proposals on the subject of religion, they did not deal with establishments. Virginia's ratification declaration, for example, said "that among other essential rights, the liberty of conscience . . . cannot be cancelled, abridged, restrained or modified by any authority of the United States."[85]

New Hampshire's proposal that "Congress shall make no laws touching religion" is the only one that might be susceptible to an interpretation of this kind of federalism-enhancing way. Yet, because of the dearth of materials from that convention, the Granite State's ambiguous language has been interpreted by some scholars as expressing an especially strong anti-establishment principle,[86] and by others, such as Muñoz, as primarily seeking to promote local religious choices. Meanwhile, the two other New England states that were taxing their citizens to support churches did not propose any sort of jurisdictional or federalism-enhancing language. Connecticut recommended no amendments at all, and Massachusetts' proposals had nothing to do with religion. Eventually, when the First Congress discussed the establishment clause, two amendments were offered by Massachusetts' representatives, and neither of them included "no touching" language: archetypical Antifederalist Gerry ("no religious doctrine shall be established by law") and Federalist Fisher Ames, who submitted the version adopted by the House ("Congress shall make no law establishing religion").[87]

To bolster his focus on the Antifederalists' concerns about religious uniformity, Muñoz argues that "[m]ost Anti-Federalists did not object to religious establishments per se," citing Storing to the effect that "Anti-Federalists never championed a right or principle of 'no establishment.'"[88] Yet these arguments tend not to be based on Antifederalist writings about the federal government. Rather, they rely primarily on the views of some

Antifederalists-to-be when they had previously addressed church-state issues in their states. This use of older materials involving local issues to interpret the new national Constitution raises the key question of whether the Antifederalists, in fact, held consistent positions about church-state principles irrespective of whether they were speaking of the federal or the state governments.

There were certainly Antifederalists, such as Virginia's Richard Henry Lee and Patrick Henry, who had favored tax support for religion in their states. There were others—the Virginia Baptists, for example—who did not, and who strongly believed that religious taxes violated the liberty of conscience.[89] Similarly, prominent Federalists also split on this issue: Madison and Isaac Backus had each been leaders in state-level fights against religious taxes, while some of the most eloquent statements about the importance of religion to civic virtue can be found in the writings of George Washington and Massachusetts Federalist leader Theophilus Parsons.[90]

In writing about the Constitution, most Antifederalists expressed no view whatsoever about questions of establishment. Yet Antifederalist sentiment was strong enough that several states proposed an amendment to the effect that "no particular sect or society ought to be favored or established by law in preference to others," and the widely reprinted Maryland minority report said: "There shall be no National Religion established by law." From these statements, it seems reasonable to conclude that a substantial number of Antifederalists opposed the idea of a nationally established church along the lines of the Church of England. Unfortunately, there is no clearly articulated set of reasons for why Antifederalists took that position, nor is it evident that they would have applied these nonestablishment views to their state governments.

In short, there is very limited information from which to identify an Antifederalist church-state principle, and the best reading of the evidence is likely to be that the Antifederalists either favored, or at least went along with, a constitutional nonestablishment amendment, even if they believed in governmental support for religion at the state level. This apparent contradiction could be attributed to a number of causes, including the possibility that some Antifederalists supported amendments primarily in a strategic effort to derail the entire Constitution through an overwhelming number of proposed changes.

Perhaps the best explanation is suggested by Stephen Botein, who pointed out that even those who devoutly believed in the importance of religion to the success of a political community did not see the new national government as enough of a "state" to require the aid of religion. A considerable number of framers, Federalists and Antifederalists alike, saw their own states as the kinds of governments that needed "a religious dimension," and it was not until the 1830s that "many people [thought that] the federal government was ... beginning to reveal enough attributes to warrant some semblance of [an] official religious identity."[91] Such a limited view of the federal government at the time of the founding would certainly have appealed to the Antifederalists, who were united on one basic point, which was that the new government should do as little as possible. And so, they could quite consistently support religious establishments in their states, where civic virtue should be inculcated, but, at the same time, oppose them at the federal level. Meanwhile, Antifederalists opposing establishments in principle (e.g., the Virginia Baptists) as well as Federalists sharing the same view (e.g., Madison) could also support a federal nonestablishment amendment.

While most of the scholarly discussion has focused on issues of establishment, which were rarely mentioned by the framers, the Antifederalists' appeals for protecting religious liberty appeared considerably more frequently. Their comments do not, however, provide a clear picture of what they meant by "liberty of conscience." Scholars have sought to explain the apparent contradiction in the Antifederalist calls for amendments guaranteeing religious freedom with the support of a few vocal Antifederalists in favor of a religious test for federal office. For the most part, this effort has led to one being emphasized and the other downplayed. Cecelia Kenyon, for example, discounts the appeals for religious liberty, and focuses on the "prejudiced views against non-Protestants [that] 'would not have been expressed so vigorously ... had they not represented a sizeable segment of constituent opinion.'"[92] Morton Borden, in contrast, observes that "not a single important Antifederalist writer or orator ... attacked" the no religious test provision.[93] Moreover, looking at the Federalists' support for religious tests for those holding office in their states, he points out that many "Federalists were not only anti-Catholic, but anti-secular, and their understanding of religious freedom was severely limited."[94] He thus concludes that "no philosophic difference separated Federalists and Antifederalists on the question of religious freedom; [and] that the contemporary definition of religious freedom was quite narrow," despite some scholars' desire to take the "liberal words" of certain Federalists "at face value, neglecting to consider their actions," while overstating the degree of intolerance among Antifederalists.[95]

Borden's point is a useful reminder that it is unreasonable to assume that all—or even most—Federalists subscribed to James Madison's or Thomas Jefferson's beliefs about religion and government, much as this chapter has struggled to identify clear and consistent positions that can be broadly attributed to "The Antifederalists." Most of the time, Antifederalists said nothing about religion, and when they did, it was generally to include liberty of conscience in a list of fundamental rights. Exactly what they meant by religious freedom is not clearly stated, and, at least for some of them, religious tests and liberty of conscience were fully compatible. Other comments about ecclesiastical establishments, military exemptions, or the need to acknowledge God appear even less frequently, and do not provide an especially clear view of what the "forgotten purposes" of the Bill of Rights might be.

Conclusion

Modern Americans' desire to find clear answers to constitutional questions tends to oversimplify the views of the framers. There is no reason to believe that they were all as religiously narrow-minded as some were, nor as liberal as others. As to the relationship of church and state, most Antifederalists said nothing about it at all, not necessarily because they rejected the view that religion plays an important role in fostering civic virtue, but, quite possibly, because they believed that the states, not the federal government, were the governments that, in Botein's words, needed a "religious dimension." Antifederalists' widely expressed fear of the power of a national government undoubtedly meant that they would have opposed any interference in state religious activities, but there is little evidence to support the idea that the proposed nonestablishment amendments were meant solely (or even partially) to add yet another layer to the fundamental principle of federalism.[96]

In sum, the various interpretations of the Antifederalists advanced by scholars addressing contemporary constitutional issues may be plausible, but these scholars tend to overinterpret the very few existing references to religion by assuming that they are a representative sampling of Antifederalist thinking. This wrong-end-of-the-telescope perspective has distorted our view of the founding. Because church-state issues are important to us, it is hard to imagine that they were unimportant to those involved in framing the Constitution, especially since there were heated debates over religion when the states had adopted new constitutions just a few years before.[97] In debating the Constitution, the founders did not need to resolve their sharp disagreements over how church and state should relate to each other. Rather, they simply answered three straightforward questions over which there was remarkably little disagreement: Would there be a religious test for federal office? Would there be a national religion? And would religious freedom be mentioned, along with various other individual rights, in a federal declaration of rights? The lack of contentious debate demonstrates how much the Federalists and Antifederalists agreed on these issues at the national level, even if they vehemently disagreed about those same issues within their own states.

Perhaps Elbridge Gerry's comments during the First Congress can provide a useful window on Antifederalist thinking about matters of religion and the new nation. He was much more agitated by the word "national" than he was concerned about a nonestablishment principle, which was a concept that he seemed to support. And the entire discussion was sufficiently unimportant that he was willing to distract his congressional colleagues from their remarkably brief debate about religion with a weak pun about rats. Church-state issues were simply not seen by the framers as contentious federal issues; all of the various areas of continuing disagreement were being left for the states to work out.[98] As his Antifederalist colleague Thomas Tudor Tucker said in response to Federalist Elias Boudinot's proposal to have a national day of prayer and thanksgiving to celebrate the new Constitution, "it is a religious matter, and, as such is proscribed to us. If [such a] day must take place, let it be done by the authority of the several States."[99]

Notes

Donald L. Drakeman would like to thank Michael Breidenbach for his outstanding research assistance, and Joel Alicea, Zachary Calo, Brad Wilson, and John F. Wilson for their insightful comments.

1. See Neil H. Cogan, ed., *The Complete Bill of Rights: The Drafts, Debates, Sources, and Origins* (New York: Oxford University Press, 1997), 59–61.
2. Ibid.
3. James H. Hutson, "Country, Court, and Constitution: Antifederalism and the Historians," *William and Mary Quarterly*, 3rd ser., 38 (July 1981): 337–368, 337.
4. Cecelia M. Kenyon, "Men of Little Faith: The Anti–Federalists on the Nature of Representative Government," *William and Mary Quarterly*, 3rd ser., 12 (Jan. 1955): 3–43.

5. See, for example, Saul A. Cornell, "The Changing Historical Fortunes of the Anti-Federalists," *Northwestern University Law Review* LXXXIV (1989): 39–74.
6. See, for example, *Everson v. Board of Education*, 330 U.S. 1 (1947); Mark David Hall, "Jeffersonian Walls and Madisonian Lines: The Supreme Court's Use of History in Religion Clause Cases," *Oregon Law Review* 85 (2006): 563–614.
7. See Stephen A. Marini, "Religion, Politics, and Ratification," in Ronald Hoffman and Peter J. Albert, eds., *Religion in a Revolutionary Age* (Charlottesville, VA: US Capitol Historical Society, 1994); Whitman H. Ridgway, "Popular Sentiment and the Bill of Rights Controversy," in Ronald Hoffman and Peter J. Albert, eds., *The Bill of Rights: Government Proscribed* (Charlottesville, VA: US Capitol Historical Society, 1997); and Jackson Turner Main, *The Anti-Federalists: Critics of the Constitution, 1781–1788* (Chapel Hill, NC: University of North Carolina Press, 1961), 260–261.
8. Main, *Anti-Federalists*, 260.
9. Ibid., 260–261.
10. Main, *Anti-Federalists*, 261. Ridgway notes that Backus "was identified as an Antifederalist when he was elected to the Massachusetts ratifying convention," although he "voted for ratification along with twelve Congregational ministers, while two–thirds of the twenty Baptists [at] the convention voted against. . . ." Ridgway, "Popular Sentiment," 218–219.
11. Main, *Anti-Federalists*, 261.
12. Ibid., 261.
13. Stephen Marini has pointed out that there is a "rough correlation" between "the Federalist–Antifederalist political contest and the liberal and evangelical religious constituencies of the 1780s. . . ." Marini,"Religion, Politics, Ratification," 200. Similarly, there may have been a higher proportion of Antifederalists in the interior or "backcountry" regions, although some of the most prominent essays opposing ratification were written by leading citizens of the major coastal regions.
14. John F. Wilson, "The Founding Era (1774–1797) and the Constitutional Provision for Religion," in Derek H. Davis, ed., *The Oxford Handbook of Church and State in the United States* (New York: Oxford University Press, 2010), 30. See also Herbert J. Storing, *What the Anti-Federalists Were For* (Chicago: University of Chicago Press, 1981).
15. Compare Saul Cornell, *The Other Founders: Anti-Federalism & the Dissenting Tradition in America, 1788–1828* (Chapel Hill, NC: University of North Carolina Press, 1999) (hereinafter "OF"), 10: "Weighting texts according to their influence in their time . . . reveals a clear, consistent Anti-Federalist critique . . ." with Herbert J. Storing, *What the Anti-Federalists Were For*, 6: "In searching for the underlying unity in the Anti–Federal position we are not tabulating the frequency of different arguments. We are looking not for what is *common* so much as for what is *fundamental*." See also Herbert Storing, *The Complete Anti-Federalist* (Chicago: University of Chicago Press, 1981) (hereinafter "CAF"). A more complete collection of Antifederalist writings can be found in Merrill

Jensen et al., *The Documentary History of the Ratification of the Constitution* (Madison, WI: University of Wisconsin Press, 1976) (hereinafter "DHRC").

16. This is true for Federalists as well. As Marini has observed, "By any measure the delegates to the ratifying conventions were religious. Literally hundreds of them were Anglican vestrymen, Congregationalist deacons, and Presbyterian ruling elders. . . . [A] hundred or so were ordained ministers and priests." Marini, "Religion, Politics, Ratification," 190–191.
17. OF, 29. Gerry's essay, first published on November 3, 1787, was reprinted forty-three times, far more than any other Antifederalist essay. DHRC, XIII: 595. It is the first essay in Storing's compilation. CAF, 2: 4–8.
18. CAF, 2: 6–7. For an analysis of how these concerns led Gerry and other Antifederalists in the First Congress to adopt "originalist" arguments, see David J. Siemers, *Ratifying the Republic: Antifederalists and Federalists in Constitutional Time* (Stanford, CA: Stanford University Press, 2002), Chapter 3.
19. CAF, 2: 7.
20. CAF, 2: 13. Mason's "Objections" were reprinted 30 times. DHRC, XIV: 532.
21. Robert Yates and John Lansing, "Reasons of Dissent," published in the *New York Journal* (January 14, 1788). CAF, 2: 15–18. It was reprinted 20 times. DHRC, XV: 578.
22. Letter from Edmund Randolph, Giving His Reasons for Refusing His Signature to the Proposed Federal Constitution (October 10, 1787). CAF, 2: 83–98. It was reprinted twenty-two times. DHRC, XV: 576.
23. William Pierce, as quoted in CAF, 2: 19.
24. Luther Martin, *The Genuine Information Delivered to the Legislature of the State of Maryland Relative to the Proceedings of the General Convention Lately Held at Philadelphia* (1788). CAF, 2: 19–82. The portion of the document relating to the no-religious-test provision was reprinted less often than some other sections of Martin's essay. DHRC, XV: 146–150.
25. CAF, 2: 23.
26. CAF, 2: 75. For a discussion of this provision, see Daniel L. Dreisbach, "The Constitution's Forgotten Religion Clause: Reflections on the Article VI Religious Test Ban," *Journal of Church and State* 38 (1996): 261–295, and Gerard V. Bradley, "The No Religious Test Clause and the Constitution of Religious Liberty: A Machine that has Gone of Itself," *Case Western Law Review* 37 (1986–87): 674–747.
27. CAF, 2: 75.
28. Ibid.
29. Ibid.
30. "Letter of Richard Henry Lee" (October 16, 1787). CAF, 5: 111–118. For reprintings, see DHRC, XIV: 533.
31. OF, 309–316.
32. For a history of the ratification process, see Pauline Maier, *Ratification: The People Debate the Constitution, 1787–1788* (New York, NY: Simon & Schuster,

2010); for Pennsylvania, see chapter 4. For a state-by-state review of ratification, see Michael Allan Gillespie and Michael Lienesch, eds., *Ratifying the Constitution* (Lawrence, KS: University Press of Kansas, 1989).
33. George J. Graham, Jr., "Pennsylvania: Representation and the Meaning of Republicanism," in Gillespie and Lienesch, *Ratifying the Constitution*, 66–67.
34. "The Address and Reasons of Dissent of the Minority of the Convention of Pennsylvania to their Constituents" (December 18, 1787). CAF, 3: 145–166, 157. It was reprinted twenty times. DHRC, XV: 575.
35. Ibid., 151.
36. Ibid., 164.
37. "To the People of Pennsylvania" [Centinel essay no. 2] (October 24, 1787). CAF, 2: 152. DHRC, XIII: 594.
38. "Essays of Philadelphiensis" (November 1787–April 1788), CAF, 3: 107; Essays of An Old Whig (October 1787–February 1788), ibid., 36–37. The various letters of Philadelphiensis and Old Whig were each reprinted between two and seven times. OF, 312–313.
39. Centinel went on to emphasize "that no authority . . . shall in any case interfere with . . . the right of conscience in the free exercise of religious worship." CAF, 2: 152.
40. CAF, 3: 36–37.
41. Essay by Deliberator (February 20, 1788), CAF, 3: 179. It does not appear to have been reprinted. OF, 309–317. There is also a long, satirical, and sometimes confusing 1788 essay by Aristocrotis, "The Government of Nature Delineated," that appears to argue against the no-religious-test provision. CAF, 3: 205–207. It was reprinted only once. DHRC, XVII: 418. See also "Letter from a Customer" (March 1788), published in Maine, which appears to support religious tests as well. CAF, 4: 202.
42. See Maier, *Ratification*, Chapters 4 and 5. Storing includes very few documents from these states, none of which are enlightening on the subject of religion.
43. Letter from William Williams to the Landholder (February 11, 1788). Daniel L. Dreisbach and Mark David Hall, eds., *The Sacred Rights of Conscience: Selected Readings on Religious Liberty and Church-State Relations in the American Founding* (Indianapolis, IN: Liberty Fund, 2009), 351–352. Another prominent founder, Benjamin Rush, expressed similar sentiments. Ibid., 353–355.
44. CAF 4: 232. A Watchman was reprinted three times. DHRC, XVI: 533, n.1. For the debate about religious tests, see Dreisbach and Hall, *Sacred Rights of Conscience*, 388–391.
45. CAF, 4: 196. It appears not to have been reprinted.
46. Ibid., 195.
47. Charles Turner's Speeches in the Massachusetts Ratifying Convention (January 17 and February 6, 1788), CAF, 4: 221.
48. See Maier, *Ratification*, 166. All quotations from the states' ratification resolutions are found in The Avalon Project, Documents in Law, History and Diplomacy, http://www.avalon.law.yale.edu.

49. See Maier, *Ratification*, 244–245.
50. William Paca et al., "Address of a Minority of the Maryland Ratifying Convention" (May 1788). CAF, 5: 92–100.
51. See DHRC, XVII: 240–246. It was reprinted forty-three times. DHRC, XIII: 595.
52. Maier, *Ratification*, 251. See also Dreisbach, "Constitution's Forgotten Religion Clause," 292.
53. CAF, 4: 242.
54. Ibid. See also the New Hampshire Senate President's Letter of February 26, 1788, which said, "The want of a religious test was [an issue] but even if that was given up in all other cases, the president at least ought to be compelled to submit to it for otherwise says one 'a Turk, a Jew, a Roman Catholic, and what is worse than all a universalist may be president. . . .'" Otis G. Hammond, *Letters and Papers of Major-General John Sullivan*, 3 vols. (Concord: New Hampshire Historical Society, 1939), 3: 567–568.
55. See Maier, *Ratification*, Chapter 8.
56. Cogan, *Complete Bill of Rights*, 69–70.
57. Patrick Henry, Virginia Ratifying Convention (June 12, 1788), CAF, 5: 240.
58. Ibid., 264.
59. "Address by Denatus" (June 11, 1788), CAF, 5: 263.
60. "Letters from the Federal Farmer IV" (October 12, 1787), CAF, 2: 249. Unlike many commentators who complain about the lack of a bill of rights, Federal Farmer (probably Melancton Smith) points out that "the 9th and 10th sections in Art. I . . . are no more nor less, than a partial bill of rights." Ibid., 248. This essay was reprinted five times. OF, 311.
61. "Essays by Cincinnatus III" (November 15, 1787), CAF, 6: 14. It was reprinted twice. DHRC, XIV: 531.
62. "A Countryman V" (January 17, 1788), CAF, 6: 87. It was reprinted three times. DHRC, XV: 575.
63. Ibid.
64. "Address of the Albany Antifederal Committee" (April 26, 1788), CAF, 6: 123–124.
65. Quoted in Dreisbach, "Constitution's Forgotten Religion Clause," 282. Henry Abbot, a Baptist minister representing a Federalist constituency, also worried that the government "might make a treaty with foreign powers to adopt the Roman Catholic religion in the United States." Cogan, *Complete Bill of Rights*, 62–63.
66. Quoted in Ellis M. West, *The Religion Clauses of the First Amendment: Guarantees of States' Rights?* (Lanham, MD: Lexington Books, 2011), 72. See also Dreisbach and Hall, *Sacred Rights of Conscience*, 394–400.
67. Main, *Antifederalists*, 159. While Main notes that "[t]hree 'rights' were especially emphasized: freedom of religion, or conscience; the right to trial by jury; and freedom of the press," he points out that the "first of these was least mentioned." Ibid.
68. Gary D. Glenn, "Forgotten Purposes of the First Amendment Religion Clauses," *Review of Politics* 49, no. 3 (Summer, 1987): 340–367. Glenn cites as the

"conventional view" the Supreme Court's analysis in *Reynolds v. United States* (1878) and *Everson v. Board of Education* (1947), and scholars such as Leonard Levy, *The Establishment Clause: Religion and the First Amendment* (New York: Macmillan, 1986). Ibid., 363, n. 4.

69. Glenn, "Forgotten Purposes," 341. Glenn notes that "[w]hile this seems obvious, it has never been done at least in any systematic way." Ibid. See also Daniel L. Dreisbach, Mark David Hall, and Jeffry H. Morrison., *The Forgotten Founders on Religion and Public Life* (Notre Dame, IN: University of Notre Dame Press, 2009), xiii–xix.
70. Glenn, "Forgotten Purposes," 342.
71. Ibid.
72. Ibid. He notes that this concept of religion is not "limited to Christianity or to Protestantism." Ibid.
73. Ibid. 344–345.
74. CAF, 1: 22.
75. Ibid., 64.
76. "A Proposal for Reviving Christian Conviction" (October 31, 1787). CAF, 5: 125; "Letter by David" (March 7, 1788), CAF, 4: 246.
77. CAF, 1: 22–23. See also Dreisbach, who argues that "Antifederalists, in particular, feared the new Constitution failed to safeguard religion adequately and recognize religion's beneficial influence on social order and civic virtue." Dreisbach, "Constitution's Forgotten Religion Clause," 281.
78. Note also that Turner does not propose a federal solution. His "hope . . . [is that] the Continental Legislature will . . . recommend to the several States" to educate children in "those pious and moral principles, which are the . . . life and soul of the republican government. . . ." CAF, 4: 221.
79. As discussed above, the only amendment relating to the no-religious-test language was the South Carolina proposal to add "other."
80. CAF, 1: 64.
81. See, for example, Vincent Phillip Muñoz, *God and the Founders: Madison, Washington, and Jefferson* (Cambridge: Cambridge University Press, 2009), and Donald L. Drakeman, *Church, State, and Original Intent* (Cambridge: Cambridge University Press, 2010).
82. Vincent Phillip Muñoz, "The Original Meaning of the Establishment Clause and the Impossibility of its Incorporation," *University of Pennsylvania Journal of Constitutional Law* 8 (2006): 585–639.
83. Ibid., 616.
84. See also Akhil Reed Amar, *The Bill of Rights: Creation and Reconstruction* (New Haven, CT: Yale University Press, 1998), 33–42; Steven D. Smith, "The Jurisdictional Establishment Clause: A Reappraisal," *Notre Dame Law Review* 81 (2005–06): 1843–1893.
85. Similarly, the Pennsylvania minority report was quite clear on this jurisdictional issue as it related to liberty of conscience. See above at note 35.

86. See Philip Hamburger, *Separation of Church and State* (Cambridge, MA: Harvard University Press, 2002), 101.
87. Cogan, *Complete Bill of Rights*, 59–62.
88. Muñoz, "The Original Meaning of the Establishment Clause," 615, 617, citing CAF, 1: 23, where Storing says, "[m]any Anti–Federalists supported and would even have strengthened the mild religious establishments that existed in some states."
89. While Virginia's Baptists opposed tax support for religion, their own churches often took on civil functions, especially in the backcountry. See Monica Najar, *Evangelizing the South: A Social History of Church and State in Early America* (New York: Oxford University Press, 2008).
90. Vincent Phillip Muñoz, "Religion and the Common Good: George Washington on Church and State," in Daniel L. Dreisbach, Mark D. Hall, and Jeffry H. Morrison, *The Founders on God and Government* (Lanham, MD: Rowman & Littlefield, 2004): 1–22; and Theophilus Parson's opinion in *Barnes v. Falmouth*, 6 Mass. 401 (1810).
91. Stephen Botein, "Religious Dimensions of the Early American State," in Richard Beeman, Stephen Botein, and Edward L. Carter, eds., *Beyond Confederation: Origins of the Constitution and American National Identity* (Chapel Hill: University of North Carolina Press, 1987), 315–330.
92. Morton Borden, "Federalists, Antifederalists, and Religious Freedom," *Journal of Church and State* 21 (1979): 469–482, 470, quoting Cecelia M. Kenyon, ed., *The Antifederalists* (Indianapolis, IN: Bobbs-Merrill, 1966), lxix.
93. Borden, "Federalists, Antifederalists," 476. He does not say why he omits Luther Martin, who did.
94. Ibid., 482.
95. Ibid., 470, 482.
96. For a much lengthier discussion, see Drakeman, *Church, State, and Original Intent*, Chapters 5 and 6.
97. See, for example, Thomas J. Curry, *The First Freedoms: Church and State in America to the Passage of the First Amendment* (New York: Oxford University Press, 1986).
98. See also Wilson, who has noted, "Had the framers of the draft Constitution chosen to stipulate more fully the role(s) to be accorded to religion, it is altogether likely that their entire effort to supersede the Articles of Confederation would have collapsed." Wilson, "Founding Era," 33.
99. Joseph Gales, Jr., *The Debates and Proceedings in the Congress of the United States*, 42 vols. (Washington, DC, 1834–1856), 1: 949–950. This day of prayer proposal should baffle supporters both of the conventional view that Federalists wanted strict separation, and the revisionist argument that Antifederalists would look for ways to link government with religion.

7

The Bible and the Political Culture of the American Founding[1]

Daniel L. Dreisbach

THE GENERATION OF Americans who fought for and secured independence from Great Britain and then crafted the constitutions and institutions of the new nation were, according to leading scholars of the era, greatly influenced by the English common law and constitutional tradition, as well as republican and European Enlightenment political thought. The shelves of a small library could be filled with all the scholarship written on John Locke's intellectual contributions to the American founding. Similar scholarly attention has been devoted to the influence of the Baron de Montesquieu. Largely missing from the literature on the American founding is a serious discussion of the Bible's influence on the founders' political ideas and rhetoric. The omission is striking given the Bible's expansive influence on the wider culture. The Bible's influence is not merely ignored in the scholarship; rather, some scholars contend that the leading founders, informed by rationalism, rejected biblical ideas.

Many students of the founding era have described it as an age of Enlightenment and rationalism in which "the founding generation," according to political theorist Wilson Carey McWilliams, "rejected or deemphasized the Bible and biblical rhetoric."[2] Writing more specifically of the arguments and rhetoric Americans used as they contemplated resistance to British tyranny and, eventually, independence, historian John Fea asserted that, "when one examines the specific arguments made by colonial political leaders in the years leading up to 1776, one is hard-pressed to find any Christian or biblical language apart from a few passing references to God."

Rather, the "most important documents" produced by Americans "focused more on Enlightenment political theory about the constitutional and natural rights of British subjects than on any Christian or biblical reason why resistance to the Crown was necessary."[3] Historian Mark A. Noll observed "that the nation's founders were conversant with scripture," which "should not be surprising . . . for they lived at a time when to be an educated member of the Atlantic community was to know the Bible." He further contended, however, that explicit references to Scripture or Christian themes "are conspicuously absent in the political discussions of the nation's early history. . . . In short," Noll concluded, "the political figures who read the Bible in private rarely, if ever, betrayed that acquaintance in public. . . . [T]he Bible's direct political influence was extremely limited, the occasions when leaders turned to it for assistance in political reasoning extremely rare."[4]

Did the founders avoid or repudiate biblical influences on their politics? Reports of the Bible's demise in the founding era are controverted by the written record the founders left to posterity. The Bible permeated both the private expressions and public pronouncements of those who shaped the new nation and its civic institutions. Compared to an earlier age dominated by Puritan divines, biblical language in the founding generation's political rhetoric may seem muted. Nonetheless, late-eighteenth-century Americans remained biblically literate, and, contrary to the claims of modern scholarship, the Bible informed public culture. Biblical language pervaded the rhetoric of not only pious founders, such as Samuel Adams, Patrick Henry, John Jay, Roger Sherman, and John Witherspoon, but also those figures most influenced by the Enlightenment, including Benjamin Franklin and Thomas Paine.

The founders read the Bible. Their many quotations from and allusions to both familiar and obscure scriptural passages confirm that they knew the Bible from cover to cover. Biblical language and themes liberally seasoned their rhetoric. The phrases and cadences of the King James Bible, especially, informed their written and spoken words. Its ideas shaped their habits of mind. The founders' frequent use of the Bible is no surprise because they lived in an overwhelmingly Protestant culture and in a biblically literate society.[5] Protestant theology reveres the Bible as the revealed word of God and emphasizes its role as authority in all matters of faith and practice (this is encapsulated in the popular phrase of the Reformation, *sola scriptura*—"Scripture alone"). One would expect the Bible to occupy a place of prominence in such a culture.

Many founders were students of the Bible, and a few even wrote Bible commentaries and learned discourses on theology and Christian doctrine and practice.⁶ In addition, several prominent founders were involved in Bible projects designed to make the Bible more accessible and improve the moral conditions of their fellow men. Charles Thomson, who for fifteen years served as secretary to the Continental (1774–1781) and Confederation (1781–1789) congresses, retired from public life to devote nearly two decades to preparing a four-volume English translation of the Bible from the Greek. John Witherspoon, a signer of the Declaration of Independence, as well as a Presbyterian clergyman and educator, apparently provided scholarly assistance to publisher Isaac Collins in preparing a popular 1791 American edition of the Holy Bible. He penned a brief preface for Collins's Bible, replacing the Authorized Version's flowery dedication to King James I of England, which Witherspoon thought "wholly unnecessary for the purposes of edification" and, perhaps, "improper" for a republican audience.⁷ Most famously, Thomas Jefferson, with the aid of scissors and paste pot, prepared two abridgements of the life of Jesus extracted from the New Testament: "The Philosophy of Jesus of Nazareth" (1804) and "The Life and Morals of Jesus of Nazareth" (1819–1820?). Jefferson believed these digests of Christ's moral teachings contained the essence of true Christianity, uncorrupted by Christ's followers. Finally, in their declining years, some notable founders were involved in organizing Bible societies. Benjamin Rush, another signer of the Declaration of Independence and a respected polymath, served as the first vice-president of the Bible Society of Philadelphia, the first Bible society in America, founded in 1808.⁸ Elias Boudinot, a past president of the Continental Congress, was elected the American Bible Society's first president in 1816. He was succeeded in 1821 by John Jay, also a president of the Continental Congress and the first chief justice of the US Supreme Court. The society counted numerous other prominent public figures among its leaders.

Following an extensive survey of American political literature from 1760 to 1805, political scientist Donald S. Lutz reported that the Bible was cited more frequently than any European writer or even any European school of thought, such as the Enlightenment or Whig intellectual traditions.⁹ Indeed, the Bible accounted for about a third of all citations.¹⁰ According to Lutz, "Deuteronomy is the most frequently cited book, followed by Montesquieu's *The Spirit of the Laws*."¹¹ Biblical sources figured prominently in this study even though Lutz excluded from his sample most political sermons that made no mention of secular sources.¹² This significantly undercounted biblical sources because reprinted sermons accounted for about eighty percent of the political pamphlets of the 1770s and 1780s and, yet, Lutz included only about one-tenth of this literature in his sample (by contrast, the sample included "about one-third of all significant secular publications"). If Lutz had not excluded so many political sermons and had surveyed religious sources in equivalent proportion to secular sources, then the percentage of biblical citations would have been markedly greater. Again, even though Lutz significantly undersurveyed religious sources, the Bible still "accounted for roughly one-third of the citations in the sample. . . . Saint Paul is cited about as frequently as Montesquieu and Blackstone, the two most-cited secular authors, and Deuteronomy is cited almost twice as often as all of Locke's writings put together." About three-fourths of all references to the Bible in Lutz's survey came from political sermons; however, had he surveyed only secular works, the Bible would still have accounted for 9 percent of all citations— "about equal to the percentage for classical writers."[13] The point is that, despite rational and secular influences of the age, the Bible continued to figure prominently in the political discourse of the founding era.

The Bible was the most accessible book in late-eighteenth-century America.[14] It was among the most important sources of cultural influence in the colonial and early national periods. It shaped the language. It also informed education, letters, law, and politics. The founding generation wove biblical language, often without quotation marks or explicit references, into their ordinances, official proclamations, judicial opinions, political discourses, private correspondence, and last wills and testaments. Quotation marks and citations were unnecessary to identify the source of words so familiar to a biblically literate people. In 1781, Benjamin Franklin, then serving as the American Minister to France, wrote a letter to his old friend the Reverend Doctor Samuel Cooper, pastor of Boston's influential Brattle Street Church. Some months before, the prominent Congregationalist clergyman had sent Franklin a copy of the sermon he had delivered on the commencement of the government under a new state constitution.[15] The sermon, Franklin responded, gave him an "abundance of Pleasure," and he said he intended to translate and print the sermon for a European audience. He explained, however, that he would need to insert biblical references for European readers even though such references were unnecessary for Cooper's American audience: "It was not necessary in New England where every body reads the Bible, and is acquainted with Scripture Phrases, that you should note the Texts from which you took them; but I have observed in England as well as in France, that Verses and Expressions taken from the sacred Writings, and not known to be such, appear very strange and awkward to some Readers; and I shall therefore in my Edition take the Liberty of marking the quoted Texts in the Margin."[16]

The mere fact that an individual founder referenced the Bible tells us little about whether or not this figure revered Scripture or, even, was a Christian. Christians and skeptics alike incorporated the Bible into their rhetoric. Some polemicists have made the error of assuming that selected founders were committed Christians based principally on the number of quotations from and allusions to the Bible in that founder's political rhetoric. Pamphleteer Thomas Paine illustrates the error. He made frequent allusions to the Bible, yet no figure of the founding era was more famously dismissive of orthodox Christianity and its view of Scripture than Paine.

Noting that Thomas Paine or Benjamin Franklin made extensive use of the Bible does not mean that they abandoned their rationalist perspectives. It simply acknowledges that they added biblical notions to their arsenal of ideas and arguments. The claim that some founders were influenced by the Bible does not suggest that they were theocrats intent on imposing a biblical order on the polity. It no more follows that the founding generation was entirely orthodox Christian merely because it was influenced by the Bible than it is to assume that the founders were all rationalists because some prominent founding figures were influenced by Enlightenment rationalism. Acknowledging and studying the Bible's influence enriches an understanding of the political themes and theories that informed the American founding.

Reading the Bible with the Founders

The Bible was the most prominent literary text in late-eighteenth-century America, and few aspects of early American culture escaped the influence of Christianity and its sacred text. According to historian Joyce Appleby, the Bible was "[t]he most important source of meaning for eighteenth-century Americans."[17] It was integral to the founders' education—both formal and informal. It was indispensable to literacy education in the colonial and early national periods. Oral and written expressions were influenced by religious culture in general and the Bible in particular. The cadences and phrases of the King James Bible informed the rhetoric of the age, and some founders were tutored from the pulpit in oratorical arts. Not surprisingly, politicians and polemicists of the age frequently invoked the text sacred to the American people.

Many founders expressed reverence for the Bible and commended its role in fostering the civic virtues required of a self-governing people. The Bible was, thus, honored and revered above all other literature. It "is a book worth more than all the other books that were ever printed," Patrick Henry reportedly remarked.[18] John Dickinson of Delaware and Pennsylvania (serving both states as the elected chief executive), a member of the First and Second Continental Congresses and one of Delaware's delegates to the Constitutional Convention of 1787, opined in a tract written to encourage ratification of the proposed national Constitution: "the book [Bible] has done more good than all the books in the world; would do much more, if duly regarded; and might lead the objectors against it to happiness, if they would value it as they should."[19] "I maintain," declared Benjamin Rush, "that there is no book of its size in the whole world, that contains half so much useful knowledge for the government of states, or the direction of the affairs of individuals as the bible."[20] John Jay, a president of the Continental Congress and co-author of *The Federalist Papers*, similarly opined: "The Bible is the best of all Books, for it is the word of God, and teaches us the way to be happy in this world and in the next. Continue therefore to read it, and to regulate your Life by its precepts."[21] One of only two men who signed the three great expressions of American organic law—the Declaration of Independence, the Articles of Confederation, and the US Constitution—Roger Sherman of Connecticut was among the most influential founders. Also a devout Congregationalist, Sherman revealed his view of the Bible in a Confession of Faith, a copy of which in Sherman's handwriting survives, he or a committee apparently drafted for his church, White Haven Church, in 1788: "I believe that ... the scriptures of the old and new testaments are a revelation from God, and a complete rule to direct us how we may glorify and enjoy him." Whether the Confession was the product of Sherman's pen alone or the work of a committee, it doubtless reflects his belief at the time.[22] Robert Treat Paine of Massachusetts, a signer of the Declaration of Independence, served as a military chaplain before embarking on a career in the law and entering politics. In a statement of his creed, he confessed: "I Believe the Bible to be the written word of God & to Contain in it the whole Rule of Faith & manners."[23] In his 1801 rebuttal of Thomas Paine's *The Age of Reason*, Elias Boudinot, a former president of the Continental Congress, said of the Bible:

> For near half a century, have I anxiously and critically studied that invaluable treasure [the Bible]; and I still scarcely ever take it up, that

I do not find something new—that I do not receive some valuable addition to my stock of knowledge; or perceive some instructive fact, never observed before. In short, were you to ask me to recommend the most valuable book in the world, I should fix on the Bible as the most instructive, both to the wise and ignorant. Were you to ask me for one, affording the most rational and pleasing entertainment to the inquiring mind, I should repeat, it is the Bible: and should you renew the inquiry, for the best philosophy, or the most interesting history, I should still urge you to look into your Bible. I would make it, in short, the Alpha and Omega of knowledge; and be assured, that it is for want of understanding the scriptures, both of the Old and New Testament, that so little value is set upon them by the world at large. The time, however, is not far off, when they will command a very different reception, among the sons of men.[24]

John Adams similarly testified, "I have examined all [religions], as well as my narrow Sphere, my streightened means and my busy Life would allow me; and the result is, that the Bible is the best book in the World. It contains more of my little Phylosophy than all the Libraries I have seen."[25] His son John Quincy Adams proclaimed: "The first and almost the only Book deserving of universal attention is the Bible."[26]

In a June 1783 Circular Letter to the States, written in anticipation of his resignation as commander in chief of the Continental Army, George Washington offered his disinterested political advice and "final blessing" to the country. The missive poignantly expressed his sentiments on important subjects respecting the political "tranquility of the United States" and their "mutual felicitation" or happiness. Washington asserted that the foundation of the American "Empire" was laid at a near-perfect moment in human history, not in some "gloomy age of Ignorance and Superstition." It was an "Epocha," he said,

> when the rights of mankind were better understood and more clearly defined, than at any former period, the researches of the human mind, after social happiness, have been carried to a great extent, the Treasures of knowledge, acquired by the labours of Philosophers, Sages and Legislatures, through a long succession of years, are laid open for our use, and their collected wisdom may be happily applied in the Establishment of our forms of Government; the free cultivation of Letters, the unbounded extension of Commerce, the progressive

refinement of Manners, the growing liberality of sentiment, and above all, [Washington continued,] the pure and benign light of Revelation, have had a meliorating influence on mankind and increased the blessings of Society.

Significantly, Washington identified "Revelation"—by which he meant the Bible—as having had "a meliorating influence on mankind" *greater* than an understanding of "the rights of mankind," the "researches of the human mind," knowledge and wisdom in the science of politics, an "extension of Commerce," or "liberality of sentiment."[27] In essence, Jeffry H. Morrison said of this passage, Washington "claimed that the revelation of the Bible was the most important boon to society in history."[28]

Not all the founders acknowledged the Bible as the revealed word of God. A few prominent figures of this generation, especially those most influenced by Enlightenment rationalism, rejected an orthodox Christian view of the Bible. These critics of revealed religion renounced the Bible not only for its irrational accounts of the supernatural (i.e., virgin birth, resurrection, and other miracles) but also for its lack of textual authenticity and reliability, perpetuation of superstition, and cruel and brutal narratives, especially the Gospel's central claim that God sacrificed His only Son to atone for the sins of others. Thomas Jefferson, for example, while professing great admiration for Christ's moral teachings, described the Gospel accounts as containing "a groundwork of vulgar ignorance, of things impossible, of superstitions, fanaticisms, and fabrications." Employing an earthy metaphor revealing of his sentiments on the Bible, Jefferson likened the task of the discerning reader of Scripture to distinguishing "diamonds in a dunghill."[29] From an early age, Benjamin Franklin similarly "began to doubt of Revelation it self,"[30] although he acknowledged the existence of the Deity, the Creator of the world.[31] Ethan Allen, a leader of Vermont's Green Mountain Boys and a celebrated hero of the capture of Fort Ticonderoga, renounced Christianity and embraced a religion of reason. His treatise, *Reason the Only Oracle of Man, or A Compenduous [sic] System of Natural Religion* (1784), identified reason as the "standard, by which we determine the respective claims of revelation."[32] Allen ultimately rejected the Bible as God's word. Questions about the authenticity of texts and accuracy of translations, the incompatibility of reason and biblical accounts of miracles, and characterizations of God as cruel, brutal, and jealous shaped Allen's critique of the Bible.

No assault on the Bible was more vociferous than Thomas Paine's, especially in his infamous *The Age of Reason* (1794/1795). Paine was one of the few figures of the founding era openly contemptuous of the idea that the Bible was the revealed word of God:

> People in general know not what wickedness there is in this pretended word of God. Brought up in habits of superstition, they take it for granted, that the bible is true, and that it is good. They permit themselves not to doubt of it; and they carry the ideas they form of the benevolence of the Almighty to the book which they have been taught to believe was written by his authority. Good heavens, it is quite another thing! It is a book of lies, wickedness, and blasphemy; for what can be greater blasphemy than to ascribe the wickedness of man to the orders of the Almighty.[33]

Removing all doubt about his position, Paine affirmed unequivocally his belief that "the Bible is not the word of God, that it is a falsehood."[34]

Among those who rejected the Bible's divine origin, most, it would seem, respected the Bible for its literary qualities or for its ethical and moral instruction. Jefferson, for example, admired the language of selected Psalms,[35] and he prized Christ's moral teachings recorded in the Gospels as "the most benevolent and sublime probably that has been ever taught."[36] "As to Jesus of Nazareth," Franklin said, ". . . I think his system of morals and his religion, as he left them to us, the best the world ever saw or is like to see."[37] Even Paine referenced extensively and approvingly portions of the Scriptures in his writings and expressed admiration for the benevolent "morality that [Jesus Christ] preached and practised," as recorded in the Gospels.[38] This suggests that these skeptical founders perceived a utilitarian value in Christ's ethical teachings as an instrument for social control, even though they rejected Jesus Christ as God's Son and denied that the Bible was God's word.

How the Founders Used the Bible

A study of the Bible's place and role in the political culture of the age must be attentive to the purposes for which biblical texts were invoked and the contexts in which this generation appealed to the Bible. Scripture was employed for literary, rhetorical, and political purposes, in addition to its theological uses. These distinctions are important insofar as it is misleading to read spiritual meaning into purely literary, rhetorical, or political uses of the Bible or vice versa. The Bible was used then, as it is sometimes used today, to enrich a common language and cultural vocabulary through distinctively biblical allusions, expressions, figures of speech, proverbs, aphorisms, and the like; to enhance the power and weight of rhetoric; to identify and define normative standards and transcendent rules for ordering and judging public life; and to gain insights on the character and designs of God, especially as they pertain to His dealings with humanity. There are, perhaps, other uses one could add to this list.

A ubiquitous literary text, the Bible provided a distinct and familiar language recognized and respected by virtually all Americans in the founding era. The founders frequently quoted from and made allusions to the Bible because it was the most authoritative, accessible, and familiar literary text in America. It was the source of a common cultural vocabulary and served as a shared reference point for civil discourse. Historian Gordon S. Wood said of Thomas Paine, the most successful polemicist of his age, that, in an effort to connect with the common man, "he counted on his audience being familiar with only one literary source—the Bible."[39] Simply put, Paine appealed to Scripture so frequently because he knew the Bible-reading proclivities of his audience.[40] In a sense, the English of the King James Bible was the lingua franca of late-eighteenth-century America, and effective mass communicators, especially politicians and polemicists, adeptly used this language to reach their audiences.

The two most familiar and accessible sources of literary allusions available to late-eighteenth-century Americans were the Bible and classical literature. Like classical mythology, the Bible is a bountiful storehouse of literary resources. It is a rich source of history, prophecy, poetry, proverbs, parables, and metaphors. It would have been extraordinary, indeed, if the founding generation had not drawn on this familiar literary source. A few examples will illustrate this use of the Bible. In recommending a patient rather than intemperate approach to the crisis confronting the colonies, John Adams wrote to James Warren in April 1776: "The Management of so complicated and mighty a Machine, as the United Colonies, requires the Meekness of Moses, the Patience of Job and the Wisdom of Solomon, added to the Valour of Daniel."[41] In his infamous 1796 Mazzei letter, which was widely interpreted as denigrating the aging President George Washington, Thomas Jefferson similarly alluded to two Old Testament characters: "In place of that noble love of liberty, & republican government which carried us triumphantly thro' the war, an Anglican monarchical, & aristocratical party has sprung up, whose avowed object is to draw over us the substance, as they have already done the forms, of the British government. . . . It would give you a fever were I to name to you the apostates who have gone over to these heresies, men who were Samsons in the field & Solomons in the council, but who have had their heads shorn by the harlot England."[42] Jefferson, whose sympathies for the revolution in France were well publicized, was the target of an allusion to Samson a couple years later. In 1798, after the French Revolution had turned bloody and anti-Christian, an anonymous Federalist purportedly toasted the incumbent president: "JOHN ADAMS. May he, like *Samson*, slay thousands of Frenchmen with the *jawbone* of JEFFERSON."[43] The Old Testament book of Judges records that Samson, a Nazarite of great strength (Numbers 6:1–21), "slew a thousand" Philistines with a "jawbone of an ass" (Judges 15:15). Such recurrence to biblical expressions, figures of speech, proverbs, allegories, and allusions to communicate, explicate, or illustrate important principles or concepts was typical of the public discourse and literature of the age. Moreover, the source and meaning of such references would have been immediately apparent to a biblically literate audience.

Biblical expressions and figures of speech were ubiquitous in the founders' rhetoric. The language of the English Bible so permeated the vernacular that some speakers and writers may not always have been conscious of the fact that a popular phrase or allusion had biblical origins. Volumes could be filled illustrating the founders' appropriation of biblical language, but a handful of examples from the papers of George Washington will exemplify the Bible's place in the literature of the age. Washington is a useful subject for examination because his frequent recurrence to biblical language is typical of many leading political figures in the founding era. Washington, by most accounts, was a pious man but not an evangelical or religious enthusiast who would have been expected to invoke the Bible more than other gentlemen of his time or social standing. In any case, he routinely incorporated into his working vocabulary familiar biblical language such as "forbidden fruit" (Genesis 3),[44] "fat of the land" (Genesis 45:18),[45] "seven times seven years" (Leviticus 25:8),[46] "thorn in our side" (Numbers 33:55; Judges 2:3; see also 2 Corinthians 12:7),[47] "first fruit" (Deuteronomy 26:2),[48] "sleep with my Fathers" (Deuteronomy 31:16; 2 Samuel 7:12; 1 Kings 1:21),[49] "neither sleep nor slumber" (Psalm 121:4; Isaiah 5:27),[50] "like sheep, to the Slaughter" (Psalm 44:22; Acts 8:32; Romans 8:36),[51] "engraved on every man's heart" (see Jeremiah 17:1; Jeremiah 31:33; Romans 2:15),[52] "seperating [sic] the Wheat from the Tares" (Matthew 13:25ff),[53] "a millstone hung to your neck" (Matthew 18:6; Mark

9:42; Luke 17:2);⁵⁴ "wars and rumors of wars" (Matthew 24:6; Mark 13:7),⁵⁵ "good and faithful servant" (Matthew 25:21, 23),⁵⁶ "take up my bed and walk" (Mark 2:9; John 5:8–12),⁵⁷ "widow's mite" (Mark 12:42; Luke 21:2–3),⁵⁸ *"the scales are ready to drop from the eyes"* (Acts 9:18),⁵⁹ and "Throne of Grace" (Hebrews 4:16).⁶⁰ A sentence in a 1785 letter Washington wrote to his friend the Marquis de Lafayette is replete with biblical expressions: ". . . I wish to see the sons and daughters of the world in Peace and busily employed in the more agreeable amusement of fulfilling the first and great commandment [Matthew 22:38], *Increase and Multiply* [Genesis 1:22, 28; see also Genesis 8:17, 9:1,7, 35:11, Leviticus 26:9]: as an encouragement to which we have opened the fertile plains of the Ohio to the poor, the needy [cf. Deuteronomy 15:11; Deuteronomy 24:14; Psalm 35:10] and the oppressed of the Earth; any one therefore who is heavy laden [Matthew 11:28], or who wants land to cultivate, may repair thither and abound, as in the Land of promise [promised land; Exodus 12:25; Deuteronomy 9:28, 19:8], with milk and honey [a phrase descriptive of the promised land ubiquitous in the Pentateuch; see, for example, Exodus, 3:8, 13:5, 33:3, Leviticus 20:24, Numbers 13:27, 14:8, 16:13, 14, Deuteronomy 6:3, 11:9, 26:9, 15, 27:3, 31:20, Joshua 5:6]: the ways are preparing, and the roads will be made easy [Isaiah 40:3], thro' the channels of Potomac and James river."⁶¹ A biblical phrase familiar in Washington's papers and in the wider literature of the era is the "vine and fig tree" motif found throughout the Hebrew Scriptures (see, for example, 1 Kings 4:25; Micah 4:4; Zechariah 3:10; and 1 Maccabees 14:12). This was a metaphor for not only freedom from want and fear but also freedom of religion and the right to private property. Washington alone invoked this image on nearly four dozen occasions during the last half of his life.⁶²

Washington and his contemporaries also made frequent use of biblical proverbs and aphorisms. Quoting Solomon, Washington informed his stepgrandson that "The wise man, you know, has told us (and a more useful lesson never was taught) that there is a *time for all things* (Ecclesiastes 3:1, 17)."⁶³ In correspondence with a Mount Vernon overseer, Washington counseled, "The habit of postponing things is among the worst in the world[,] doing things in season is always beneficial; but out of season [cf. 2 Timothy 4:2], it frequently happens that so far from being beneficial, that oftentimes, it proves a real injury. It was one of the sayings of the wise man you know, that there is a season for all things [Ecclesiastes 3:1], and nothing is more true; apply it to any occurrence or transaction in life."⁶⁴ In another missive, he borrowed the words not only of Solomon but also the psalmist: "I have been occupied from the 'rising of the sun to the setting of the same,'

[Psalm 113:3, 50:1; Malachi 1:11] and which as the wise man has said 'may be all vanity and vexation of spirit'" (Ecclesiastes 1:14, 2:11, 17, 26, 4:4, 16, 6:9).[65]

Again, Washington's frequent recurrence to biblical language is typical of many in the founding generation.[66] Biblical allusions, expressions, images, metaphors, and proverbs were used by believers and nonbelievers alike. These phrases and motifs resonated with late-eighteenth-century Americans, and many such expressions became a part of the political vernacular.

The founders employed biblical language because, as a venerated and authoritative text, its mere invocation, it was believed, enhanced the persuasive power of, or lent rhetorical weight to, an argument. The evocative use of biblical language stirs an audience's "religious imagination," often appealing as much to emotion as to reason.[67] Such uses of Scripture, which often mimic pulpit oratory, are calculated to persuade by capturing an audience's attention (with, perhaps, the fear of God), arousing a righteous passion, solemnifying a discourse, projecting an aura of transcendence and truth, emphasizing the gravity of an idea or argument, and/or underscoring an argument's moral implications or sacred connotations. Therefore, the founders deployed biblical language (such as was illustrated above) to enhance the power and weight of their rhetoric. There are even examples of orators who, "in order to increase the gravity of their words," employed "a phraseology, cadence, or tone" that imitates or "parallels the classic phrasing of the King James Version."[68] A mere resemblance to the mellifluous language of the King James Bible, in other words, added gravitas to rhetoric.

Few late-eighteenth-century political figures were more fluent in biblical language or adept in appropriating the distinct cadences and vernacular of the King James Bible in political prose than Patrick Henry. Consider, for example, arguably the most famous lines of revolutionary rhetoric, Henry's "give me liberty or give me death" declamation delivered before the Virginia Convention on March 23, 1775.[69] Familiar biblical images and phrases are integral to this revolutionary prose. Henry adroitly tapped the righteous indignation of the Old Testament prophets and, in a stirring political jeremiad, warned "Virginia of impending doom."[70] The oration's dramatic climax is punctuated by the unmistakable words of the Prophet Jeremiah. Henry, like Jeremiah two and a half millennia before, ridiculed the idea of peace when "there is no peace" (Jeremiah 6:14, 8:11) and boldly called on his fellow citizens to prepare for war:[71]

> Sir, we are not weak if we make a proper use of those means which the God of nature hath placed in our power. The millions of people,

armed in the holy cause of liberty, and in such a country as that which we possess [cf. Deuteronomy 3:12], are invincible by any force which our enemy can send against us. Besides, sir, we shall not fight our battles alone. There is a just God [Isaiah 45:21] who presides over the destinies of nations, and who will raise up friends to fight our battles for us [2 Chronicles 32:8]. The battle, sir, is not to the strong alone [Ecclesiastes 9:11]; it is to the vigilant, the active, the brave. Besides, sir, we have no election. If we were base enough to desire it, it is now too late to retire from the contest. There is no retreat but in submission and slavery! Our chains are forged! Their clanking may be heard on the plains of Boston! The war is inevitable—and let it come! I repeat it, sir, let it come. It is in vain, sir, to extenuate the matter. Gentlemen may cry, Peace, Peace—but there is no peace [Jeremiah 6:14, 8:11]. The war is actually begun! The next gale that sweeps from the north will bring to our ears [cf. Acts 17:20] the clash of resounding arms! Our brethren are already in the field! Why stand we here idle [Matthew 20:6]? What is it that gentlemen wish? What would they have? Is life so dear [Acts 20:24], or peace so sweet, as to be purchased at the price of chains and slavery? Forbid it, Almighty God! I know not what course others may take; but as for me [cf. Genesis 17:4; Joshua 24:15], give me liberty or give me death![72]

Biblical language so permeates the text that it reads like a lay sermon.[73] Henry deployed biblical phrases and Bible-like language to great rhetorical effect, communicating the gravity of the moment, the righteousness of the Patriots' cause, and the promise of God's sustaining aid.

Americans of the era were drawn to Scripture to discern and explicate the divine character, especially as it pertains to His dealings with humanity and involvement in the material world. This is not surprising for a nation of theists who believed that God intervenes in the affairs of men and nations. An often recounted episode at the Constitutional Convention of 1787 illustrates a use of the Bible for this end. At a particularly difficult moment, as deliberations reached an apparent impasse and tempers frayed, the elder statesman Benjamin Franklin made a poignant appeal for harmony and divine intervention:

In this Situation of this Assembly, groping, as it were, in the dark [Job 12:25] to find Political Truth, and scarce able to distinguish it when presented to us, how has it happened, Sir, that we have not hitherto once thought of humbly applying to the Father of Lights [James 1:17] to illuminate our Understandings? In the Beginning of the Contest with Britain, when we were sensible of Danger, we had daily Prayers in this Room for the Divine Protection. Our Prayers, Sir, were heard;—and they were graciously answered. All of us, who were engag'd in the Struggle, must have observed frequent Instances of a superintending Providence in our Favour. To that kind Providence we owe this happy Opportunity of Consulting in Peace on the Means of establishing our future national Felicity. And have we now forgotten that powerful Friend? or do we imagine we no longer need its assistance? I have lived, Sir, a long time; and the longer I live, the more convincing proofs I see of this Truth, *that* GOD *governs in the Affairs of Men* [cf. Daniel 4:17]. And if a Sparrow cannot fall to the Ground without his Notice [Matthew 10:29; Luke 12:6], is it probable that an Empire can rise without his Aid? We have been assured, Sir, in the Sacred Writings, that "except the Lord build the House, they labour in vain that build it" [Psalm 127:1]. I firmly believe this; and I also believe, that, without his concurring Aid, we shall succeed in this political Building no better than the Builders of Babel [Genesis 11:1–9]; we shall be divided by our little, partial, local Interests, our Projects will be confounded, and we ourselves shall become a Reproach and a Bye-word [see Deuteronomy 28:37; 1 Kings 9:7; 2 Chronicles 7:20; Psalm 44:14] down to future Ages. And, what is worse, Mankind may hereafter, from this unfortunate Instance, despair of establishing Government by human Wisdom, and leave it to Chance, War, and Conquest.[74]

If we take his words at face value, this solemn plea reveals that Franklin believed in a God—an omniscient God who orders the affairs of men and nations and who is cognizant of the minute details of the material world. Moreover, the wisdom of Franklin's God far surpasses that of humankind, and this God's concurrence is vital to the success of human endeavors. And most pertinent to the speech, Franklin's God responds to a people's supplications for divine blessing and assistance. "Our Prayers," said Franklin of an earlier occasion, "were heard; and they were graciously answered."

Franklin delivered this speech in a closed, secret proceeding. This suggests that he was not merely appealing to popular religious sentiments beyond the Convention's chambers, and he may have been expressing his true beliefs at the time. As a younger man, it should be noted, Franklin expressed a different view of God—one removed and disengaged from the concerns of humankind. Even if one concedes that he was appealing to popular religious prejudices to gain some immediate political benefit, then that suggests there was considerable sentiment within the Convention for the view of God expressed in Franklin's speech.

A familiar analogy of the founding era compared the Children of Israel escaping Egyptian bondage with the American colonies seeking relief from tyrannical British rule. The president of Yale College, Ezra Stiles, delivered a 1783 election sermon before Connecticut's highest officials in which he called the United States "God's American Israel,"[75] a commonplace description of the American states in the founding era. On July 4, 1776, the Continental Congress appointed John Adams, Thomas Jefferson, and Benjamin Franklin to a committee to design "a seal for the United States of America."[76] Franklin, playing on this biblical theme, proposed an image of Moses extending his hand in anticipation of God's supernatural parting of the Red Sea, allowing the Children of Israel to escape Pharaoh's army (Exodus 14). Jefferson similarly recommended a portrayal of the "Children of Israel in the Wilderness, led by a Cloud by Day, and a Pillar of Fire by night" (Exodus 13:21–22).[77] Remarkably, both men, sons of the Enlightenment, drew on familiar Old Testament images of the Children of Israel, who were miraculously delivered from Pharaoh's bondage by the guiding hand of Divine Providence just as Americans believed they would be providentially delivered from the tyranny of George III, as fitting allegorical portrayals of the new nation's plight.

Did the Bible Influence Political Ideas and Institutions?

There are scholars of the founding who acknowledge that Christianity and its sacred text exerted immense influence on the American people, and, given its influence on the culture, politicians and polemicists of the era incorporated biblical language and themes into their public rhetoric and private communications. Yet some of these scholars contend that the founders did not rely on the Bible in ways that informed their political theory or shaped the public institutions of the new nation. In a book dedicated to debunking the notion of a "Christian America," Baptist pastor and academic Mark Weldon Whitten stated emphatically: "No theological or biblical arguments and no prayers for divine guidance or approval were offered during the Constitutional Convention of 1787."[78] Political theorist Gregg Frazer similarly asserted: "In the hundreds of pages comprising Madison's notes on the constitutional convention (and those of the others who kept notes), there is no mention of biblical passages/verses in the debates/discussions on the various parts and principles of the Constitution. They mention Rome, Sparta, German confederacies, Montesquieu, and a number of other sources—but no Scripture verses."[79]

These sweeping, unequivocal assertions do not stand up to scrutiny. The Bible was cited at the Constitutional Convention as authority in support of a specific provision. In the waning days of the Convention during debate on a proposal to require the ownership of property as a qualification for public office under the Constitution, Benjamin Franklin spoke in opposition to any proposal "that tended to debase the spirit of the common people. . . . We should remember the character which the Scripture requires in Rulers," Doctor Franklin said, invoking Jethro's qualifications for prospective Israelite rulers, "that they should be men hating covetousness [Exodus 18:21]."[80] Franklin was engaged in a substantive debate about a specific constitutional provision. Significantly, he appealed to a biblical standard ("the character which the Scripture requires in Rulers"), informed his audience in unambiguous language that his source was "Scripture," and then quoted a specific biblical text.

More generally, but no less significant to their political vision, influential founders believed the Bible provided an indispensable aid to and worthy model of republican government. In a republican government, the founders believed, the people must be sufficiently virtuous that their personal responsibility and discipline would facilitate the social order and stability necessary for a regime of self-government. A free, self-governing people, in other words, had to be a virtuous people who were controlled from within by an internal moral compass. Believing that "without national morality a republican government cannot be maintained" and that "[t]he Bible contains the most profound philosophy, the most perfect morality, and the most refined policy, that ever was conceived upon earth," John Adams described the Bible as "the most republican book in the world."[81] Recognizing Christianity's vital contributions to social virtues, John Dickinson of Delaware and Pennsylvania also wrote: "The Bible is the most republican Book in the World."[82] The Bible, in short, fosters the civic virtues that give free citizens in a republic the capacity for self-government. Such sentiments were commonplace in the political discourse of the founding.

In his Circular Letter, written to the state governors, George Washington referenced the words of an Old Testament prophet in similarly affirming the need for civic virtue in securing the nation's political happiness: "I now make it my earnest prayer, that God would . . . most graciously be pleased to dispose us all, to do Justice, to love mercy, and to demean ourselves with that Charity, humility and pacific temper of mind, which were the Characteristicks of the Divine Author of our blessed Religion, and without an humble imitation of whose example in these things, we can never hope to be a happy Nation."[83] Significantly, Washington Christianized the Hebraic text, Micah 6:8, emphasizing the second person of the Trinity in the place of Micah's "God," to express his hope that God would help Americans to imitate Christ for the political objective of securing national happiness. He did not say, it should be emphasized, that *belief* in Christ is a necessary condition for national happiness, only the *imitation* of Christ.

Influential Americans in the founding era believed the model of political leadership and civil government established by God through Moses and practically developed under Joshua and his successors for the Hebrew nation was worthy of imitation in their own polities. They thought the Hebrew Commonwealth, which endured for approximately a half millennium of Jewish history from the exodus until Saul was anointed king, was a perfect model of and divine precedent for a form of republican government best suited to promote political prosperity.[84] Late-eighteenth-century Americans were well aware that republicanism found expression in traditions apart from the Hebrew model, and, indeed, they studied these traditions both ancient and modern. They were students, for example, of both classical and civic republican thinkers. The republican model found in the Hebrew Scriptures, however, reassured pious Americans that republicanism was an idea that enjoyed a divine imprimatur. A growing body of scholarship identifies Hebraic republicanism as among the ideas that informed the political thought of the founders.[85]

This notion that the newly independent American states should emulate the Hebrew Commonwealth's "republican" form of government was expressed in political tracts and sermons and even in various deliberative bodies. "A volume," one scholar observed, "would not contain all the politico-theological discourses delivered during the decade prior to the restoration of peace, wherein the Hebrew Commonwealth was held up as a model, and its history as a guide for the American people."[86] And most of what the founding generation knew about the Hebrew republic they learned from the Bible. In an influential 1775 election sermon preached to Massachusetts' highest public officials, the president of Harvard College, Samuel Langdon, opined: "The Jewish government, according to the original constitution which was divinely established, if considered merely in a civil view, was a perfect Republic.... Every nation, when able and agreed," Langdon continued, "has a right to set up over themselves any form of government which to them may appear most conducive to their common welfare. The civil Polity of Israel is doubtless an excellent general model, allowing for some peculiarities; at least some principal laws and orders of it may be copied, to great advantage, in more modern establishments."[87] Thomas Paine, in *Common Sense* (1776), similarly drew on the history of the Hebrew Commonwealth to repudiate monarchy and hereditary succession. Such appeals to the Hebrew experience were commonplace in the literature of the era.

Once Americans, against remarkable odds, had secured independence and turned their attention to the difficult task of framing a plan of civil government, they again looked to the Hebrew Commonwealth as a guide and model for establishing their own polities. In the heated debate of the mid-1780s on the need for constitutional reform, the influential founder Roger Sherman of Connecticut responded to an ardent critic of the Articles of Confederation, proposing in a 1784 tract that "the civil polity of the Hebrews" was a commendable exemplar of civil government:

> And in truth and reality, the framing a perfect and complete system of government for a rising empire, is a most arduous and very important subject; and as he seems desirous of Divine Aid, I would recommend it to him once more to consult his bible, and duly weigh and consider the civil polity of the Hebrews, which was planned by Divine Wisdom, for the government of that people although their territory was small; . . . their laws were few and simple—their judges and elders of their cities, well acquainted with the credibility of the parties and their evidences—they held their courts in the places of greater concourse, the gates of the city, and their processes were neither lengthy nor expensive.[88]

In state conventions called to ratify the Constitution, delegates referenced political lessons learned from the nation Israel.[89] These "references, parallels, and analogies to the children of Israel in their struggle for political liberty would not have been made again and again" in the political rhetoric of the era had they not resonated with the Bible-reading American audience to whom they were addressed.[90]

Among the biblical texts that Americans thought offered useful guidance on republican government and political leadership were Exodus 18:13–27, Deuteronomy 1:9–18, and Deuteronomy 16:18–20. In a 1788 New Hampshire election sermon, for example, the Congregationalist minister, former president of Harvard College (1774–1780), and delegate to New Hampshire's convention that ratified the US Constitution, the Reverend Samuel Langdon, specifically cited Deuteronomy 16:18–19 in arguing that the Hebrew Republic was a laudable model of republican government.[91] Among the simple, but important, lessons Americans thought this and related passages taught were that civil government is ordained by God and under His authority. Moreover, God ordained the office of civil magistrate and instructed His people to select their civil magistrates.[92] God, they believed, had identified specific qualifications for civil magistrates. Those qualifications are expressed most concisely in Exodus 18:21: "able men, such as fear God, men of truth, hating covetousness."[93] Civil magistrates are accountable to the people to exercise good judgment in the performance of their official duties, and they must rule justly and wisely in conformity with God's standards.[94] Civil magistrates must pursue justice and respect the rule of law and due process of law.[95] Some commentators saw in the separation of powers between magistrates in "thy gates" and "throughout thy tribes" (Deuteronomy 16:18) a rudimentary form of federalism. In the Hebrew republic, Americans saw models and lessons for their own experiment in building republican institutions.[96]

Why Is the Bible's Influence Discounted?

The influence of Locke, Montesquieu, and other European Enlightenment figures on the American founding has been exhaustively examined;[97] virtually ignored is the Bible's influence in thought and expression. Why has modern scholarship missed or dismissed the Bible's place in the founding? Often the most important things in life, like the air we breathe, are overlooked because they are so pervasive and so much a part of our very existence that we take them for granted. This may account for the inattention of scholars to the Bible's place in the political culture of the founding. A biblical illiteracy, especially a lack of familiarity with the distinct phrases and cadences of the King James Bible, may explain the failure of many scholars to recognize biblical language in the founders' political discourse. The founders often quoted the Bible without the use of quotation marks or citations, which were not necessary for a biblically literate society but the absence of which fail to alert a biblically illiterate modern audience to the Bible's invocation. Also, scholars trained in the modern academy with its emphasis on the rational and the secular may discount biblical themes because they find them less noteworthy or sophisticated than the intellectual contributions of the Enlightenment. There may even be a discomfort with explicitly religious material and themes. Moreover, some commentators find a focus on the God of the Bible and religion divisive or even offensive to twenty-first-century, secular sensibilities. In an admonition seldom mentioned in the scholarly literature, for example, George Washington warned that one who labors to subvert a public role for religion and morality cannot call oneself a Patriot.[98] Such rhetoric, unexceptional in its time, is discordant with the secular ethos of our time. Other founders held views similarly out of step with secular academic and popular sentiments of the twentieth and twenty-first centuries, such as advocating state support for Protestant denominations and restricting the civil and religious rights of Catholics, Unitarians, atheists, and Jews. In any case, the notion that the founding generation rejected biblical language and themes in their political discourse is unfounded.

The Bible was a prodigious source of ideas and expressions in the political culture of the founding era. It was an extraordinarily accessible, familiar, and authoritative text for most Americans. Not surprisingly, both influential and ordinary citizens drew on biblical language, ideas, and themes in thinking about and talking about the political challenges that confronted them. The use of biblical language was not always deliberate. Certain phrases and images from the King James Bible, especially, permeated the vernacular so thoroughly that speakers made use of them without regard to their biblical origins. This underscores the Bible's historical and expansive influence on the culture. The Bible's influence, it must be emphasized, did not necessarily supersede or crowd out all other influences on the founders' political thought and rhetoric. The founding generation drew on multiple sources, one of which was the Bible. Biblical influences coexisted with other—even seemingly competing—influences, such as Enlightenment, republican, and English constitutional and common law sources. Also, an individual founder's invocation of biblical ideas or phrases does not necessarily indicate whether or not that figure was a Christian or sought to promote a Christian polity. Believers and skeptics alike made use of the Bible. Along with Christianity in general, the Bible informed their views of human nature, social order, political authority, civic obligations, and other ideas essential to organizing a stable and prosperous civil polity.

Notes

1. Portions of this chapter are adapted from Daniel L. Dreisbach, "The Bible in the Political Rhetoric of the American Founding," *Politics and Religion* 4, no. 3 (2011): 401–427, and are reprinted here with permission.
2. Wilson Carey McWilliams, "The Bible in the American Political Tradition," in *Religion and Politics*, ed. Myron J. Aronoff (New Brunswick, NJ: Transaction Books, 1984), 21. McWilliams goes so far as to say: "[Thomas] Paine's *Common Sense* is almost alone among the great works of the founders in making an explicit appeal to the Bible." Ibid, 22.
3. John Fea, *Was America Founded as a Christian Nation?: A Historical Introduction* (Louisville, KY: Westminster John Knox Press, 2011), 93, 106. Fea acknowledged that the Bible and biblical themes can be found in the founders' private writings and in the political sermons of Patriot preachers. Ibid, 107.
4. Mark A. Noll, "The Bible in Revolutionary America," in James Turner Johnson, ed., *The Bible in American Law, Politics, and Political Rhetoric* (Philadelphia: Fortress Press; Chico, California: Scholars Press, 1985), 39–40, 43, 52. Noll acknowledged that "Scripture exerted a greater influence among the secondary ranks of the United States' early political leaders than among the Revolution's most important leaders. Many of these lesser lights were devoted students of Scripture and tried to apply its teachings to a wide range of spiritual concerns." Examples of these "lesser lights" include Elias Boudinot, Patrick Henry, John Jay, Roger Sherman, and John Witherspoon. Mark A. Noll et al. *The Search for Christian America* (Westchester, IL: Crossway Books, 1983), 74.
5. Historians estimate that around the time of independence, 98 percent or more of Americans of European descent identified with Protestantism. See Barry A. Kosmin and Seymour P. Lachman, *One Nation Under God: Religion in Contemporary American Society* (New York: Harmony Books, 1993), 28–29. Furthermore, the population was primarily of the Reformed theological tradition. See Sydney E. Ahlstrom, *A Religious History of the American People* (New Haven, CT: Yale University Press, 1972), 350 (the Reformed theological tradition was "the religious heritage of three-fourths of the American people in 1776"). Adherents of the Reformed theological tradition included the New England Puritans and later the Congregationalists, the Scottish Covenanters, the French Huguenots, the Dutch and German Reformed communities, and the Scotch and Irish Presbyterians.
6. Among the influential founders who wrote about Christian theology and doctrines are Elias Boudinot, John Dickinson, Oliver Ellsworth, John Jay, Benjamin Rush, Roger Sherman, and John Witherspoon.
7. John Wright, *Early Bibles of America*, 3rd ed. (New York: Thomas Whittaker, 1894), 95.
8. Wright, *Early Bibles of America*, 260; "Part of Bible Society History," *Pennsylvania Bible Society* (Summer 2008), 1.

9. Donald S. Lutz, *A Preface to American Political Theory* (Lawrence: University Press of Kansas, 1992), 136. For a description of Lutz's method of analysis and sample, see Donald S. Lutz, "The Relative Influence of European Writers on Late Eighteenth–Century American Political Thought," *American Political Science Review* 78 (March 1984): 189–197.
10. For purposes of his study, Lutz defined a citation "as any footnote, direct quote, attributed paraphrasing, or use of a name in exemplifying a concept or position." Lutz, "The Relative Influence of European Writers on Late Eighteenth-Century American Political Thought," 191. Not all of the citations counted in his study are to direct quotations. Moreover, the study does not capture unattributed direct quotations, paraphrases, or allusions to the Bible, which students of the era know are found frequently in this literature. This generation of Americans was sufficiently biblically literate that many would have known a quote, paraphrase, or allusion was biblical in origin even without quotation marks or explicit attribution. Lutz's study counts citations. It does not reveal whether the Bible or any other source was cited approvingly or disapprovingly, accredited or discredited in an examined text. It simply identifies the sources and reports the frequency with which sources were consulted. Lutz, "The Relative Influence of European Writers on Late Eighteenth-Century American Political Thought," 191.
11. Lutz, *A Preface to American Political Theory*, 136.
12. Lutz reported that his study excluded "the majority of sermons that had no references to secular thinkers." Lutz, *A Preface to American Political Theory*, 136.
13. Donald S. Lutz, *The Origins of American Constitutionalism* (Baton Rouge: Louisiana State University Press, 1988), 140.

   Those who see expanding Enlightenment or rationalist influence and diminishing Christian or biblical influence on American constitutional thought in the late eighteenth century highlight Lutz's finding that, although in the decade of the 1780s 34 percent of citations were to the Bible (which is the same percentage as the entire founding period [1760–1805]), in the years 1787 and 1788—the crucial years in which the US Constitution was drafted and ratified—the percentage of citations to the Bible in Lutz's sample declined sharply. He reports no citations to the Bible in Federalist writings, and only 9 percent of Antifederalist references are to the Bible. Lutz, "The Relative Influence of European Writers on Late Eighteenth-Century American Political Thought," 194, Table 4. This is offered as evidence that the Bible and a biblical culture were much less influential on the Constitution than Lutz's overall findings might suggest. Lutz commented briefly on this finding: "The Bible's prominence disappears, which is not surprising since the debate centered upon specific institutions about which the Bible had little to say. The Anti-Federalists do drag it in with respect to basic principles of government, but the Federalists' inclination to Enlightenment rationalism is most evident here in their failure to consider the Bible relevant." Lutz, "The Relative Influence of European Writers on Late Eighteenth-Century American Political Thought," 194–195.

14. This claim is supported by probate records, which reveal that the Bible was the book most frequently inventoried in the property of the deceased.
15. Samuel Cooper, *A Sermon Preached before His Excellency John Hancock, Esq; Governour, the Honourable the Senate, and House of Representatives of the Commonwealth of Massachusetts, October 25, 1780. Being the Day of the Commencement of the Constitution, and Inauguration of the New Government* (Boston, 1780).
16. Benjamin Franklin to Samuel Cooper, May 15, 1781, in Barbara B. Oberg, ed., *The Papers of Benjamin Franklin* (New Haven, CT: Yale University Press, 1999), 35:70.
17. Joyce Appleby, *Liberalism and Republicanism in the Historical Imagination* (Cambridge, MA: Harvard University Press, 1992), 225.
18. William Wirt, *Sketches of the Life and Character of Patrick Henry* (Philadelphia: James Webster, 1817), 402.
19. [John Dickinson], *The Letters of Fabius, in 1788, on the Federal Constitution; and in 1797, on the Present Situation of Public Affairs* (Wilmington, DE: W. C. Smyth, 1797), 36.
20. Benjamin Rush, *A Plan for the Establishment of Public Schools and the Diffusion of Knowledge in Pennsylvania; to Which are Added, Thoughts upon the Mode of Education, Proper in a Republic* (Philadelphia, 1786), 19. In another essay, Rush stated: "the bible contains more knowledge necessary to man in his present state, than any other book in the world." Benjamin Rush, "A Defence of the Use of the Bible as a School Book," in *Essays, Literary, Moral & Philosophical* (Philadelphia: Thomas and Samuel F. Bradford, 1798), 93.
21. John Jay to Peter Augustus Jay, April 8, 1784, in Richard B. Morris, ed., *John Jay: The Winning of the Peace: Unpublished Papers, 1780–1784* (New York: Harper & Row, 1980), 709.
22. Lewis Henry Boutell, *The Life of Roger Sherman* (Chicago: A. C. McClurg & Co., 1896), 272–273. See also Roger Sherman Boardman, *Roger Sherman Signer and Statesman* (Philadelphia: University of Pennsylvania Press, 1938), 318–319. This confessional statement accords with other things Sherman said about the Bible. He wrote to Samuel Hopkins, for example, "The revealed law of God is the rule of our duty. . . . That the word of God is the only rule of faith in matters of religion." Roger Sherman to Samuel Hopkins, June 28, 1790, in Andrew P. Peabody, ed., *Correspondence Between Roger Sherman and Samuel Hopkins* (Worcester: Press of Charles Hamilton, 1889), 10. Sherman's language here is similar to that of the answer to Question 3 of the Westminster Larger Catechism, which refers to the Old and New Testaments as "the only rule of faith and obedience." See also Roger Sherman to Simeon Baldwin, November 26, 1791, in The Roger Sherman Collection, Box 1, folder 14, Yale University ("what was written (aforetime) in the holy Scriptures was written for our learning. . . . Rom 15.4").
23. "Robert Treat Paine's Confession of Faith" [March or April 1749], in Stephen T. Riley and Edward W. Hanson, eds., *The Papers of Robert Treat Paine*, 3 vols. to date (Boston: Massachusetts Historical Society, 1992–), 1:xviii, xx, 49.

24. Elias Boudinot, *The Age of Revelation: or the Age of Reason Shown to be An Age of Infidelity* (Philadelphia: Hugh Maxwell for Asbury Dickens, 1801), xv–xvi.
25. John Adams to Thomas Jefferson, December 25, 1813, in Charles Francis Adams, ed., *The Works of John Adams, Second President of the United States*, 10 vols. (Boston: Little, Brown and Company, 1850–1856), 10:85.
26. Letter from Ex-President [John Quincy] Adams [to Mssrs Lewis Audoun, H.D. McCulloch, and C.L.L. Leary, a Committee of the Franklin Association of Baltimore], June 22, 1838, reprinted in *Niles' National Register* (Washington City), December 1, 1838, vol. 5 (14), 219. See also John Quincy Adams, *Letters of John Quincy Adams, to His Son, on the Bible and Its Teachings* (Auburn: James M. Alden, 1850), 9–10 ("[the Bible] is of all books in the world, that which contributes most to make men good, wise, and happy—that the earlier my children begin to read it, the more steadily they pursue the practice of reading it throughout their lives, the more lively and confident will be my hopes that they will prove useful citizens to their country, respectable members of society, and a real blessing to their parents").
27. George Washington, Circular to the States, June 8, 1783, in John C. Fitzpatrick, ed., *The Writings of George Washington*, 37 vols. (Washington, DC: Government Printing Office, 1931–1940), 26:484–485 [hereinafter WGW].
28. Jeffry H. Morrison, *The Political Philosophy of George Washington* (Baltimore, MD: Johns Hopkins University Press, 2009), 171.
29. Thomas Jefferson to William Short, August 4, 1820, in Andrew A. Lipscomb and Albert Ellery Bergh, eds., *The Writings of Thomas Jefferson*, 20 vols. (Washington, DC: The Thomas Jefferson Memorial Association, 1903–1904), 15:259 [hereinafter *Writings of Jefferson*]; Thomas Jefferson to John Adams, October 13, 1813, in *Writings of Jefferson*, 13:390.
30. Benjamin Franklin, *The Autobiography*, in J. A. Leo Lemay, ed., *Benjamin Franklin: Writings* (New York: Library of America, 1987), 1359.
31. Franklin, *The Autobiography*, in *Benjamin Franklin: Writings*, 1382; Benjamin Franklin to Ezra Stiles, March 9, 1790, in *The Works of Benjamin Franklin*, ed. John Bigelow, Federal Edition, 12 vols. (New York: G.P. Putnam's Sons, 1904), 12:185.
32. Ethan Allen, *Reason the Only Oracle of Man, or A Compenduous* [sic] *System of Natural Religion* (Bennington, VT: printed by Haswell and Russell, 1784), 475.
33. Thomas Paine, *The Age of Reason Part the Second* (1795), in Eric Foner, ed., *Collected Writings* (New York: Library of America, 1995), 747.
34. Thomas Paine, Letter, May 12, 1797, in Moncure Daniel Conway, ed., *The Writings of Thomas Paine*, 4 vols. (New York: G.P. Putnam's Sons, 1896), 4:199.
35. See Jefferson to John Adams, October 13, 1813, in *Writings of Jefferson*, 13:392–393
36. Jefferson to Dr. Joseph Priestley, April 9, 1803, in *Writings of Jefferson*, 10:375. Jefferson often expressed admiration for Christ's morals. See Jefferson to Edward Dowse, April 19, 1803, in *Writings of Jefferson*, 10:377; Jefferson to John Adams, October 13, 1813, in *Writings of Jefferson*, 13:390; Jefferson to Charles

Clay, January 29, 1815, in *Writings of Jefferson*, 14:233; Jefferson to William Short, October 31, 1819, in *Writings of Jefferson*, 15:220; Jefferson to Jared Sparks, November 4, 1820, in *Writings of Jefferson*, 15:288.

37. Franklin to Ezra Stiles, March 9, 1790, in *Works of Franklin*, 12:185.
38. Paine, *The Age of Reason* (1794), in *Collected Writings*, 669–670.
39. Gordon S. Wood, "The Democratization of Mind in the American Revolution," in Robert H. Horwitz, ed., *The Moral Foundations of the American Republic* (Charlottesville: University Press of Virginia, 1977), 111. See also McWilliams, "The Bible in the American Political Tradition," 22 ("Paine invoked Scripture because he aimed to reach a wider public that revered the Bible and knew virtually no other book").
40. David Ramsay, Paine's contemporary and the first major historian of the American Revolution, observed of Paine's rhetoric and arguments in *Common Sense*: "With the view of operating on the sentiments of a religious people, scripture was pressed into [Paine's] service. . . ." David Ramsay, *The History of the American Revolution*, 2 vols. (London, 1790), 1:338.
41. John Adams to James Warren, April 22, 1776, in Robert J. Taylor, ed., *Papers of John Adams* (Cambridge, MA: The Belknap Press of Harvard University Press, 1979), 4:135. See also speech of William Phillips (Massachusetts Ratifying Convention), in Jonathan Elliot, ed., *The Debates in the Several State Conventions, on the Adoption of the Federal Constitution*, 2nd ed., 4 vols. (Washington, DC: printed for the editor, 1836), 2:67–68 [hereinafter Elliot's *Debates*] (January 22, 1788) ("My concern is for the majesty of the people. If there is no virtue among them, what will the Congress do? If they had the meekness of Moses, the patience of Job, and the wisdom of Solomon, and the people were determined to be slaves, sir, could the Congress prevent them? If they set Heaven at defiance, no arm of flesh can save them").
42. Thomas Jefferson to Philip Mazzei, April 24, 1796, in *Thomas Jefferson: Writings*, ed. Merrill D. Peterson (New York: The Library of America, 1984), 1036–1037.
43. "Toasts," *Columbian Centinel* (Boston), July 14, 1798, 3 (emphasis in the original).
44. GW to Mrs. Annis Boudinot Stockton, September 2, 1783, in WGW, 27:128.
45. GW to Robert Dinwiddie, April 22, 1756, in WGW, 1:326.
46. GW to Mrs. Martha Washington, June 18, 1775, in WGW, 3:294.
47. GW to Samuel Purviance, March 10, 1786, in WGW, 28:393; GW to James Madison, March 31, 1787, in WGW, 29:192.
48. See GW to Brigadier General Thomas Nelson, Junior, February 8, 1778, in WGW, 10:433; GW to Daniel Bowers, May 28, 1779, in WGW, 15:176; GW to Barbe Marbois, July 9, 1783, in WGW, 27:56; GW to Richard Sprigg, June 28, 1786, in WGW, 28:471; GW to The Secretary of State, April 11, 1794, in WGW, 33:321.
49. GW to Marquis de Lafayette, February 1, 1784, in WGW, 27:317–318.
50. For the biblical phrase "neither sleep nor slumber" (Psalm 121:4; Isaiah 5:27) or some variation thereof, see GW to John Augustine Washington, June 6 [July 6] 1799, in WGW, 19:136; GW to Henry Knox, December 26, 1786, in WGW, 29:124; GW to John Sullivan, February 4, 1781, in WGW, 21:181; GW to Benjamin

Harrison, May 5–7, 1779, in WGW, 15:6; GW to John Augustine Washington, May 12, 1779, in WGW, 15:59; GW to James Warren, March 31, 1779, in WGW 14:313; GW to Benjamin Harrison, December 18 [–30] 1778, in WGW, 13:466.
51. GW to the Officers of the Army, March 15, 1783, in WGW, 26:225.
52. GW to Earl of Buchan, May 26, 1794, in WGW, 33:382.
53. GW to John Augustine Washington, May 31, 1776, in WGW, 5:92.
54. GW to George Washington Parke Custis, November 28, 1796, in WGW, 35:295–296
55. See GW to Catherine Macaulay Graham, July 19, 1791, in WGW, 31:317 ("while you, in Europe, are troubled with war and rumors of war, every one here may sit under his own vine and none to molest or make him afraid"); GW to Marquis de la Luzerne, April 29, 1790, in WGW, 31:40; GW to Marquis de Chastellux, April 25 [–May 1] 1788, in WGW, 29:485.
56. GW to Tobias Lear, June 15, 1791, in WGW, 31:297; see also GW to the Clergy of Different Denominations Residing in and near the City of Philadelphia, [March 3, 1797], in WGW, 35:416–417.
57. GW to the Marquis De Lafayette, July 4, 1779, in WGW, 15:370; GW to The Secretary of War, March 25, 1799, in WGW, 37:159.
58. GW to Bushrod Washington, January 15, 1783, in WGW, 26:40; GW to George Washington Parke Custis, November 15, 1796, in WGW, 35:283.
59. GW to Charles Cotesworth Pinckney, June 28, 1788, in WGW, 30:10.
60. GW to the German Lutherans of Philadelphia, April 1789, in *The Papers of George Washington*, Presidential Series, ed. W. W. Abbot et al. (Charlottesville: University Press of Virginia, 1987), 2:180 ("that righteousness which exalteth a nation" [Proverbs 14:34] and "Throne of Grace" [Hebrews 4:16]).
61. GW to Marquis de Lafayette, July 25, 1785, in WGW, 28:206–207.
62. See Daniel L. Dreisbach, "The 'Vine and Fig Tree' in George Washington's Letters: Reflections on a Biblical Motif in the Literature of the American Founding Era," *Anglican and Episcopal History* 76, no. 3 (September 2007): 299–326.
63. GW to George Washington Parke Custis, March 19, 1798, in WGW, 36:187. See also GW to George Washington Parke Custis, June 13, 1798, in WGW, 36:288 ("Recollect again the saying of the wise man, 'There is a time for all things'" [Ecclesiastes 3:1, 17]).
64. GW to Howell Lewis, November 3, 1793, in WGW, 33:148.
65. GW to William Vans Murray, December 3, 1797, in WGW, 36:88.
66. Washington's papers contain many additional examples of his uses of biblical language. One study identifies "over two hundred different biblical allusions and expressions," used in many more instances, in Washington's writings. Peter A. Lillback, with Jerry Newcombe, *George Washington's Sacred Fire* (Bryn Mawr, Penn.: Providence Forum Press, 2006), 305; see generally, 305–333, 739–760. This should put to rest the frequently repeated, but erroneous, assertion that Washington rarely quoted or referred to the Bible in his writings. See Paul F. Boller, Jr., *George Washington and Religion* (Dallas: Southern Methodist University Press, 1963), 40 ("there are astonishingly few references to the Bible in his

letters and public statements"); Gregg L. Frazer, *The Religious Beliefs of America's Founders: Reason, Revelation, and Revolution* (Lawrence: University Press of Kansas, 2012), 201 ("Yet most of Washington's few references to the Bible were humorous. Occasionally, he referred to biblical passages without humor. . ."); Paul K. Longmore, *The Invention of George Washington* (Berkeley: University of California Press, 1988), 217 ("He rarely alluded to or quoted the Scriptures."); Samuel Eliot Morison, *The Young Man Washington* (Cambridge, MA: Harvard University Press, 1932), 37 ("I have found no trace of Biblical phraseology" in Washington's letters); Martin Marty, "America's Iconic Book," in Gene M. Tucker and Douglas A. Knight, eds., *Humanizing America's Iconic Book: Society of Biblical Literature Centennial Addresses 1980* (Chico, CA: Scholars Press, 1982), 7 ("There are few biblical allusions in his writings, and they are in settings as near to the jocular as Washington ever came."); Kenneth L. Woodward and David Gates, "How the Bible Made America," *Newsweek*, December 27, 1982, 47 ("George Washington rarely referred to the Scriptures in his voluminous private letters").

67. Joseph R. Fornieri, *Abraham Lincoln's Political Faith* (DeKalb: Northern Illinois University Press, 2003), 46. I am indebted to Fornieri's insightful discussion of Abraham Lincoln's uses of the Bible.

68. Mark Noll, "The Bible in American Public Life, 1860–2005," *Books & Culture* 11, no. 5 (September/October 2005): 7.

69. The speech was reconstructed many years after it was given, not from Henry's text, notes, or memory, but from an auditor's recollections. Thus, the accuracy of this text has been questioned. Defenders of the text observe that its content is no less documented than many of the great speeches of antiquity.

70. Charles L. Cohen, "The 'Liberty or Death' Speech: A Note on Religion and Revolutionary Rhetoric," *William and Mary Quarterly* 38, no. 4 (3rd ser., 1981): 706.

71. Cohen, "The 'Liberty or Death' Speech," 713–714. See also George Washington's references to this passage in GW to Marquis De Lafayette, December 25, 1798, in WGW, 37:67 ("crying peace, Peace"); GW to Jonathan Trumbull, August 30, 1799, in WGW, 37:348 ("there will be 'no peace in Israel'").

72. William Wirt Henry, *Patrick Henry: Life, Correspondence and Speeches*, 3 vols. (New York, 1891), 1:262–266; Wirt, *Sketches of the Life and Character of Patrick Henry*, 120–123.

73. For an interpretation of this speech as "a sermon in the evangelical tradition," see David A. McCants, *Patrick Henry, The Orator* (New York and Westport, CT: Greenwood Press, 1990), 57–63.

74. Franklin's speech in the Constitutional Convention, June 28, 1787, in Franklin, *Benjamin Franklin: Writings*, 1138–1139; *The Records of the Federal Convention of 1787*, Max Farrand, ed., 3 vols. (New Haven, CT: Yale University Press, 1911), 1:451–452. After a brief discussion of Franklin's motion to commence business each morning with prayer, the Convention adjourned without adopting the motion.

75. Ezra Stiles, *The United States Elevated to Glory and Honor. A Sermon, Preached before His Excellency Jonathan Trumbull, Esq L.L.D., Governor and Commander in Chief, and the Honorable the General Assembly of the State of Connecticut, Convened at Hartford, at the Anniversary Election, May 8, 1783* (New Haven, CT: Thomas and Samuel Green, 1783), 7.
76. *Journals of the Continental Congress, 1774–1789*, Worthington C. Ford et al., eds., 34 vols. (Washington, DC: Government Printing Office, 1904–1937), 5:517–518 (July 4, 1776).
77. Proposal for the Great Seal of the United States, [Before August 14, 1776], in *The Papers of Benjamin Franklin*, ed. William B. Willcox (New Haven, CT: Yale University Press, 1982), 22:562–563; Report on a Seal for the United States, with Related Papers, [August 20, 1776], in *The Papers of Thomas Jefferson*, ed. Julian P. Boyd et al., 38 vols. to date (Princeton, NJ: Princeton University Press, 1950–), 1:494–495; John Adams to Abigail Adams, August 14, 1776, in L. H. Butterfield, ed., *The Adams Papers*, series II, *Adams Family Correspondence* (New York: Atheneum, 1965), 2:96.
78. Mark Weldon Whitten, *The Myth of Christian America: What You Need to Know About the Separation of Church and State* (Macon, GA: Smyth & Helwys, 1999), 20.
79. Gregg Frazer, as quoted by Jonathan Rowe, "The Bible as a Source for Founding Documents," American Creation, first posted June 26, 2008, http://americancreation.blogspot.com/2008/06/bible-as-source-for-founding-documents.html, retrieved September 17, 2012. See also Ed Brayton of *The Michigan Messenger*, as quoted in Jeremy Binckes, "Backstory: How the Texas Textbook Revision Came to Be," HuffPost Social News, first posted May 14, 2010, http://www.huffingtonpost.com/2010/03/14/backstory-how-the-texas-t_n_496831.html, retrieved September 17, 2012 ("not once, according to the notes of those in attendance, was the Bible ever referenced at the constitutional convention in Philadelphia to justify a concept or provision" in the US Constitution).
80. Benjamin Franklin, August 10, 1787, as quoted in James Madison's *Notes of Debates in the Federal Convention of 1787*, in Max Farrand, ed., *The Records of the Federal Convention of 1787*, 2:249.
81. John Adams to Benjamin Rush, February 2, 1807, in John A. Schutz and Douglass Adair, eds., *The Spur of Fame: Dialogues of John Adams and Benjamin Rush, 1805–1813* (San Marino, CA: The Huntington Library, 1966), 75–76.
82. John Dickinson, notes [n.d.]. Copy provided courtesy of The John Dickinson Writings Project, University of Kentucky.
83. GW, Circular to the States, June 8, 1783, in WGW, 26:496.
84. Oscar S. Straus, *The Origin of Republican Form of Government in the United States of America* (New York: G. P. Putnam's Sons, 1887), 70.
85. See, for example, Daniel J. Elazar, *The Covenant Tradition in Politics*, 4 vols. (New Brunswick, NJ: Transaction, 1995–1998); Nathan R. Perl-Rosenthal, "The 'divine right of republics': Hebraic Republicanism and the Debate over Kingless

Government in Revolutionary America," *William and Mary Quarterly* 66, no. 3 (3rd ser., 2009): 535–564; Eran Shalev, "'A Perfect Republic': The Mosaic Constitution in Revolutionary New England, 1775–1788," *New England Quarterly* 82, no. 2 (2009): 235–263.

86. Straus, *The Origin of Republican Form of Government in the United States of America*, 131.
87. Samuel Langdon, *Government Corrupted by Vice, and Recovered by Righteousness. A Sermon Preached before the Honorable Congress of the Colony of the Massachusetts-Bay in New England, assembled at Watertown, on Wednesday the 31st Day of May, 1775* (Watertown, MA: Benjamin Edes, 1775), 11, 12.
88. Connecticut Farmer [Roger Sherman], *Remarks on a Pamphlet, Entituled "A Dissertation on the political Union and Constitution of the Thirteen United States of NORTH–AMERICA"* (New Haven, CT, 1784), 25–26.
89. See, for example, speech of John Lansing (NY), in Elliot's *Debates*, 2:218 (June 20, 1788); speech of Robert R. Livingston, Chancellor of New York, in Elliot's *Debates*, 2:210 (June 19, 1788); speech of John Smith (NY), in Elliot's *Debates*, 2:225–226 (June 20, 1788).
90. Straus, *The Origin of Republican Form of Government in the United States of America*, 131.
91. See Samuel Langdon, *The Republic of the Israelites an Example to the American States, A Sermon, Preached at Concord, in the State of New-Hampshire; Before the Honorable General Court at the Annual Election. June 5, 1788* (Exeter, 1788), 10.
92. Deuteronomy 16:18 ("Judges and officers shalt thou make thee").
93. See also Deuteronomy 1:13 ("Take you wise men, and understanding, and known among your tribes").
94. Deuteronomy 16:18 ("Judges and officers . . . shall judge the people with just judgment").
95. Deuteronomy 16:20 ("That which is altogether just shalt thou follow"); Deuteronomy 16:19 ("Thou shalt not wrest judgment; thou shalt not respect persons, neither take a gift [bribe]").
96. See Lutz, *A Preface to American Political Theory*, 116.
97. For an introduction to and survey of the scholarship examining the diverse schools of political thought that influenced the American founding, see Alan Gibson, *Interpreting the Founding: Guide to the Enduring Debates over the Origins and Foundations of the American Republic* (Lawrence: University Press of Kansas, 2006). Significantly, Gibson neglects distinctly religious influences on the American founding, including Hebraic republicanism and Protestant Reformation thought.
98. George Washington, Farewell Address, September 19, 1796, in WGW, 35:229.

8

Religion, Race, and the Founders

Jonathan D. Sassi

IN NOTES ON *the State of Virginia,* Thomas Jefferson commented on many subjects, not the least of which were religion and race. He categorized inhabitants among three "races" according to a rudimentary color scheme, namely as "white, red, and black." Native Americans compared favorably with whites, in Jefferson's estimation, but about blacks he thought very differently. Responding to French critics who had posited that New World creatures, including humans, were smaller and weaker than their Old World counterparts, Jefferson defended Native Americans. He praised them for several virtues and talents, including bravery, oratorical eloquence, and "vivacity and activity of mind." Were a proper scientific inquiry carried out, Jefferson averred, "we shall probably find that they are formed in mind as well as in body, on the same module with the 'Homo sapiens Europæus.'" Natives displayed artistic creativity, Jefferson noted, and uttered "strokes of the most sublime oratory; such as prove their reason and sentiment strong, their imagination glowing and elevated. But never yet," he continued, "could I find that a black had uttered a thought above the level of plain narration; never see even an elementary trait of painting or sculpture." Nor had African Americans produced any worthwhile poetry. Phillis Wheatley's work he pronounced "below the dignity of criticism" and chalked it up merely to an effusion of "religion." Jefferson opined that blacks were physically not as attractive as whites and intellectually wanting too; in his estimation, blacks and whites possessed similar powers of memory, but blacks were "in reason much inferior . . . [and] in imagination they are dull, tasteless, and anomalous." He summarized, albeit as "a suspicion only, that the blacks, whether originally a distinct race, or made distinct by time and circumstances, are inferior to the whites in the endowments both of body and mind."[1]

Jefferson's pronouncements about religion manifested his Enlightenment beliefs in reason and liberty. "It is error alone which needs the support of government," he argued. "Truth can stand by itself." In a famous turn of phrase that his critics would later seize upon to prove his religious "infidelity," Jefferson remarked that "it does me no injury for my neighbour to say there are twenty gods, or no god. It neither picks my pocket nor breaks my leg." But not everything that Jefferson had to say about religion was so sanguine. When he considered that Virginia was a slave society, he wrote, "I tremble for my country when I reflect that God is just: that his justice cannot sleep for ever." Masters in every slave society feared uprisings, and Jefferson admitted that "[t]he Almighty has no attribute which can take side with us in such a contest." He voiced the hope that "under the auspices of heaven" there would be "a total emancipation."[2] Were that eventually to occur, the former slaves would have to be colonized somewhere far away, "beyond the reach of mixture." Abandoning his characteristic optimism, Jefferson reasoned that "[d]eep rooted prejudices entertained by the whites; ten thousand recollections, by the blacks, of the injuries they have sustained; new provocations; the real distinctions which nature has made; and many other circumstances, will divide us into parties, and produce convulsions which will probably never end but in the extermination of the one or the other race."[3]

Jefferson's remarks, while representing only one man's views, open a range of issues that were debated broadly in the era of the founding of the United States. Given the demographics of the new nation, Americans generally framed discussion in terms of three races as Jefferson had, and like him they grappled with the morality of slavery and the fundamental question of the unity versus the diversity of mankind. Where one stood on the unity versus diversity question helped determine whether one thought that racial coexistence would be the way forward or that racial separation, if not "extermination," would be the best long-term solution. In seeking answers, some members of the intellectual elite, such as Jefferson, turned to transatlantic science, but even more Americans—white, red, and black alike—turned to religion. The era of the Revolution and early republic was one of religious liberty, which Jefferson did much to advance, but in a trend that he observed with disdain, as in his disparaging remark about Phillis Wheatley, the most flourishing religious movement was Protestant evangelicalism. Like Jefferson, Americans invoked God's providence and divine wrath when speaking about the subject of race; unlike him, they also harkened to preachers and prophets and interpreted their scriptures and dreams for answers.

The United States emerged as a nation amid a debate over religion and race that was already generations old by 1776, and much continuity extended across the Revolutionary era. The numerical and geographical expansion of slavery continued into the nineteenth century, for example, and in an extension of a colonial-era trend, racial identities became more reified. The American Revolution, however, also interrupted the status quo. It cast into sharper relief the issue of slavery's injustice, which led to the first emancipation, the growth of free black communities, and a new dividing line between the free North and the slave South. It also split Native Americans between Christian and nativist factions over the question of how to respond to the new nation. By the late 1810s, as leadership passed from the founders to a new generation shaped by the War of 1812, much of the groundwork had already been laid for the antebellum era's "racial modernity" of essentialism and white supremacy, but so, too, would abolitionists and opponents of Indian removal draw inspiration from the founding era's arguments over religion and race.[4]

Before proceeding, a few brief definitions are in order. First, by "race" I refer to socially constructed categories. While racial types make reference to physical attributes such as skin color, hair, or facial features, race is not biologically determined. Rather, people make use of race in forming their own identities and labeling others perceived as different. During the period under examination in this essay, ideas of race were in flux. Just emerging from the context of the Enlightenment in Europe was an attempt to ground racial categories within schemes of scientific classification, which would become more prominent in the nineteenth century.[5] Most Americans, like Jefferson, thought in terms of three races, and during the eighteenth and into the nineteenth century these three categories became more rigid. Individuals of mixed race were usually grouped with one of the two nonwhite categories and sometimes played leading roles in those communities. Second, by "religion" I refer broadly to beliefs and practices that seek to connect mankind to the supernatural. In Revolutionary America and the early republic this usually involved Christianity, more specifically some variation of Protestantism that was by far the predominant expression in the United States, but the essay also takes into view Native and African religions that either opposed or blended with Christianity in some of the period's most dynamic movements.[6]

Finally, in terms of "founders," the essay goes far beyond just "founding fathers" like Thomas Jefferson and includes a host of lesser known, but seminal figures who shaped the American discourses of religion and race, such as Neolin, Daniel Coker, and the essayist who signed himself "A Lover of true Justice."

Questions of religion and race had been mooted in the Americas for over two and a half centuries prior to the era of the American Revolution, and colonial precedents would frame the thoughts and actions of the founding generation. Indeed, historians have unearthed even deeper patterns of Europeans' interactions with peoples of different religion and ethnicity that preceded and shaped colonization in the New World, such as in the Spanish reconquest of the Iberian peninsula or the English colonization of Ireland.[7] Nevertheless, this essay begins briefly with the Spanish, who as the first European colonizers to the Americas poured molds for dealing with religion and race that the English would also use. Over time, conflict spoiled initial English efforts toward converting Native Americans to Christianity, while African American slaves showed little interest in their masters' faith until the middle of the eighteenth century. The long-term trend across the colonial period was a shift from distinctions made between Christians and "heathens" or between "civilization" and "savagery" to more explicitly racial lines, although the former by no means disappeared and remained a prominent mode of thought. Notions of a universal humanity vied with racial separatism for everyone concerned.

The Spanish experience in the New World during the sixteenth century laid down a number of patterns that later English colonizers would replicate. While some writers asserted the inferiority of the peoples of the Americas, whom Columbus enduringly misidentified as "Indians," the prevailing view accepted their basic humanity. Their religion, however, the Spanish rejected as heathenish and sought its overthrow. Conquistadores and clergymen engaged in a campaign of iconoclasm and supplanted the temples they found with churches. The pope authorized Spanish claims to New World territories provided "that they assumed responsibility for protecting and evangelizing the indigenous inhabitants." Friars of the Franciscan, Dominican, and other religious orders arrived to convert the Natives to Roman Catholicism, believing their mission to be nothing less than a prelude to Christ's second coming. They succeeded in making Native converts, but as historian J. H. Elliott writes, "the whole programme of conversion carried with it an inexorable subtext of hispanicization, as spiritual and social pressures alike pushed the Indians into the orbit of the

Europeans, and notions of Christianity and civility became hopelessly entangled." Moreover, during the course of the sixteenth century, he adds, "the image of the Indian changed, and changed for the worse," as the Spanish generally came to regard the Natives as lazy, addicted to vice, and unsuited for the priesthood.[8] The English experience with Native Americans would follow the same basic trajectory of trying to replace indigenous religious beliefs with Christianity and English cultural norms followed by growing disillusionment. Sixteenth-century Spanish colonists set one other momentous precedent that the English would later follow: as the Native American population imploded following the introduction of Old World diseases like smallpox, measles, and pneumonia, the Spanish turned to imported African slaves to meet their labor needs.[9]

When the English began to think about establishing New World colonies of their own in the late sixteenth century, they listed converting the Indians to true (that is, Protestant) Christianity as a major goal. One early proponent of the colonization of Virginia described as its primary purpose "to preach and baptize into *Christian Religion*, and by propagation of the *Gospell*, to recover out of the Armes of the Divell, a number of poore and miserable soules, wrapt up unto death, in almost *invincible ignorance*." Initial reports used the words "tanned or tawny" rather than "red" to describe Native Americans' coloring, which these English writers speculated had been darkened by exposure to the sun or the application of various dyes.[10] Members of a shared human family, in other words, differed due to environmental and cultural factors, not inherent characteristics, and thus could all potentially join Christ's church.

Over the span of the seventeenth century, English ideas about Native Americans shifted between attempts at coexistence and conversion and a belief in their irredeemable savagery. At Jamestown, the first permanent English colony, the baptism of Pocahontas and her famous marriage to John Rolfe symbolically expressed England's best hopes. It is impossible to know to what extent Pocahontas embraced Anglicanism, but the marriage clearly had diplomatic implications that were evident to all. Indeed, as Daniel K. Richter has argued, "When Pocahontas took the name Rebecca and went to live among Europeans, she did so not to abandon her culture but to incorporate the English into her Native world, to make it possible for them to live in Indian country by Indian rules."[11] However, when Pocahontas's kinsmen of the Powhatan Confederation rose up against the English colonists in 1622 and killed 347 of them, English authorities quickly changed their outlook. Reflecting on the events of that year, one writer opined that "these miscreants," the Native Americans, "who have thus despised God[']s great mercies so freely offered to them, must needs in time therefore be corrected by his justice," and he meant for the English to administer the punishment. Following a final war between English colonists and the remnants of the Powhatan Confederation in the mid 1640s, the victorious English expelled the Natives from the peninsula between the James and York rivers and consigned them to a reservation.[12]

A similar tension between desires for conversion and conquest characterized the English Puritan colonization of New England. The "Apostle to the Indians," the Reverend John Eliot, translated the Bible into the Massachusett language, and he led the way in the establishment of "praying towns" where Native converts could live together and practice the ways of English culture. The Puritans welcomed their Native American brethren, in other words, but only on the condition that they completely adopt English ways of life. For the Natives of southern New England, whose tribes had been decimated by diseases and outnumbered by the prolific English colonists, the praying towns offered a chance to rebuild community amid Christian fellowship.[13] As in Virginia, however, warfare brought the processes of conversion and civilization to a grinding halt. During King Philip's War in 1675–1676, many English colonists lashed out at the praying Indians as a fifth column in their midst, and few denounced their treachery as bitterly as Mary Rowlandson, the author of a famous narrative of her captivity among the Indians. Many shared her view in the war's aftermath "that the Indians were, and always had been, degenerate barbarians."[14]

In sum, the typical encounter between English colonists and Native Americans during the seventeenth century resulted in violent conflict, as the ever-expanding settler population clashed repeatedly with Natives over land and cultural misunderstanding, but the colony of Pennsylvania provided an exception that proved the rule. Founded by pacifist Quakers in the 1680s, Pennsylvania enjoyed peaceful Indian relations for its first three-quarters of a century. By the end of the seventeenth century, the English had little to show for their attempts to convert Native Americans to Christianity, in contrast to the more successful efforts of Roman Catholic missionaries in French Canada, who did not demand of the natives a wholesale rejection of indigenous ways.[15]

The English similarly had scant success in bringing their African slaves to Christianity—and made even less of an effort. Europeans' problems in dealing with Native Americans prompted the initial importation of African slave labor to the Americas, which raised another set of thorny issues about race and religion. The slave trade jumbled together disparate peoples from a long stretch of the West African coast, and they brought with them a diversity of religious backgrounds. Most had practiced an indigenous African religion, but those caught up by the trade also included Muslims, particularly from Senegambia, and a few who had been exposed to Roman Catholicism, especially those from the Kingdom of Kongo where Portuguese missionaries had been active. Whatever their slaves' backgrounds, the English tended to view their religious practices as they viewed Native Americans,' as idolatry, witchcraft, or superstition. While the English professed, at least initially, a desire to evangelize the Natives, they were largely disinterested in sharing the gospel with people whom they viewed as drudges. Planters feared that conversion and baptism would mean freedom for their slaves, so when Virginia, for example, took steps to codify its slave code during the last third of the seventeenth century, it passed a law in 1667 that clarified that "the conferring of baptisme doth not alter the condition of the person as to his bondage or Freedome." The Church of England in North America was chronically undersupplied with clergymen during the seventeenth century, and those who bothered to minister to the slaves generally preached submission. At best, someone like the Quaker founder George Fox called for the evangelization and kind treatment of slaves when he visited Barbados in 1671, but the planter class found even this message too subversive and subsequently drove the Quakers out. Not surprisingly, African slaves showed little interest in what the English were offering in the name of Christianity.[16]

Between the late seventeenth century and the first half of the eighteenth, a number of changes transformed the demographics of British North America's colonists, Natives, and slaves alike. The settler population grew rapidly and became more diverse; whereas in the seventeenth century most had come from England, in the eighteenth they included large numbers of Scots-Irish and Germans especially. For example, by 1760 the English made up less than 50 percent of Middle Colony residents. This growing ethnic diversity also carried with it a corresponding pluralism of Protestant denominations as Presbyterians and various German sects added to the prior mix of Anglicans, Puritans, and Quakers. The number of Africans and African Americans surged as well as colonists invested heavily in slaves to meet their labor needs; by 1760 they constituted 40 percent of Virginia's total population and over half of South Carolina's. And slavery was not confined to the South, but was legal and present everywhere from Georgia to New Hampshire.[17] For Native Americans, the growing numbers of British colonists and slaves meant that those who remained east of the Appalachians found themselves increasingly pushed to the margins. Many more moved westward to "Indian country," where they joined others in powerful, conglomerate tribes that dominated the trans-Appalachian region. The Cherokees in the Southeast, the Shawnees in the Ohio River Valley, and the Iroquois in present-day upstate New York are just three examples of Native peoples who skillfully played the British, French, and/or Spanish against one another during the first half of the eighteenth century and in so doing leveraged their power and maintained their independence.[18]

Amid these changes in population, ideas about race took on a harder edge, and religion could accentuate people's sense of differences. During the middle of the eighteenth century, a number of prophets emerged in Indian country and advocated a separation from European trade goods and values such as manufactured items and alcohol, acquisitiveness, and Christianity. In the words of historian Gregory Evans Dowd, there occurred "an awakening to the notion that Indians shared a conflict with Anglo-America, and that they, as Indians, could and must take hold of their destiny by regaining sacred power." The most important of the prophets was Neolin, "the Delaware Prophet," who provided inspiration for the Ottawa chief Pontiac's 1763 uprising against the British outposts in the Ohio Valley and Great Lakes region. Neolin espoused the theory of polygenesis, or that Europeans, Africans, and Natives had been created separately and were not descendents of a single human race, which also carried with it an emphasis on pan-Native racial identity. "In this way," two historians have concluded, "a new red people was called into existence."[19]

Among Euro-American settlers, meanwhile, an equally separatist mentality took hold during the mid-century wars that racked the frontier. As British General Thomas Gage observed, "all the people of the frontiers, from Pennsylvania to Virginia inclusive, openly avow[ed], that they [would] never find a man guilty of murder, for killing an Indian."[20] Pennsylvania's Paxton Boys typified the sentiment. In December 1763, the group of Scots-Irish frontiersmen attacked a Native settlement at Conestoga and murdered everyone they could get their hands on, and they subsequently marched on Philadelphia in search of more Native victims who had sought refuge there. Only the intervention of Benjamin Franklin and other Philadelphia leaders halted them on the city's outskirts, but gone for good was Pennsylvania's peaceful relations with the Natives that Quakers had cultivated. "In parallel ways," concludes Daniel K. Richter, "Pontiac and the Paxton Boys preached the novel idea that all Native people were 'Indians,' that all Euro-Americans were 'Whites,' and that all on one side must unite to destroy the other."[21]

Two other developments of the eighteenth century, however, Enlightenment environmentalism and Protestant evangelicalism, ran counter to this sanguinary racial separatism. The concept of environmentalism posited that an individual's or group's surroundings, natural as well as cultural, exercised a determinative influence, as opposed to the idea that characteristics were innate. Rooted in the Lockean theory that people entered the world as tabula rasa, environmentalism had implications for many dimensions of human experience. When applied to ideas about race, environmentalism cast doubt upon notions of inherent inferiority or fixed characteristics. Rather, in this understanding everything was the product of environment, from societal customs to skin color, and hence subject to manipulation and amelioration. Writers during the Revolutionary era, who were fashioning new institutions and seemingly recasting the entire basis of their society, would sometimes invoke environmentalist logic in their theorizing about race.[22] It should be noted, however, that the Enlightenment also gave birth to the racial classifications of Carl Linnaeus and Johann Friedrich Blumenbach, which Jefferson referenced in his remark about Native Americans being roughly equivalent to "Homo sapiens Europæus."[23]

The evangelical revivals of the mid-eighteenth century, commonly known as the Great Awakening, went beyond theory and brought people together across racial lines in locations as diverse as lowcountry South Carolina, urban New England, and frontier Pennsylvania. For the first time, African Americans came to Christianity in significant numbers, including Phillis Wheatley, who penned a poem in tribute to the English evangelist, George Whitefield. In part, African Americans accepted the gospel message because evangelicals sought them out and preached a message of radical spiritual equality: all were sinners in need of a savior. Equally important, evangelicals encouraged black leadership in prayer and exhortation, and their worship style made room for emotion and participation, in contrast to the Anglicans' more formal liturgy. "Never have I been so much struck with the appearance of an assembly," remarked the Virginia Presbyterian Samuel Davies, "as when I have glanced my eyes to one part of the Meeting-house adorned (so it has appeared to me) with so many black countenances, especially attentive to every word they heard, and some of them washed with tears." For all these reasons, as well as the stirring oral performance of itinerant preachers, the awakening roused blacks and whites throughout the colonies and yielded converts.[24]

For many of the same reasons, the Great Awakening reached small but important pockets of Native Americans. The Moravians, a German pietistic sect, sent missionaries to the Pennsylvania frontier, where they made converts among the Delawares, while in New England the Awakening inspired New Light preachers to undertake a renewed outreach to nearby Natives. As one celebrated result of the latter, Samson Occom, a Mohegan, experienced conversion, studied with the Reverend Eleazar Wheelock, and became an evangelist to Native communities in New York and New England.[25] In addition to spiritual benefits, Christianity offered to the Natives of eastern Long Island and southern New England both a way to reconstitute community and an enhanced standing when dealing with colonial and imperial officialdom. As a result, writes David J. Silverman, "the Indians' shared struggles with colonialism followed by their common Christianity led them to identify with each other as a race of people and to express that solidarity in the language of Protestantism."[26] In other words, evangelicalism blazed an alternate path toward a pan-Native racial identity, while it also provided a firewall against the idea of polygenesis, which contradicted the biblical account of creation.

Parallel to the spread of the evangelical revivals, an awakening of a different sort—not boisterous, but prompted by the Spirit's "still small voice" (1 Kings 19:12)—was taking place among Quakers. Quakers had prospered in their Delaware Valley settlements, and by the middle of the eighteenth century the founders' zeal had waned. As John Woolman wrote at the outset of his journal, "From what I had read and heard, I believed there had been in past ages people who walked in the uprightness before God in a degree exceeding any that I knew, or heard of, now living." A generation of young reformers undertook to revive the Quakers' earlier purity and simplicity and to reassert prohibitions against marrying outside the meeting, unethical business dealings, or drunkenness, to name just a few of their targets.[27] One iniquity that the reformers sought to extirpate among Friends was slavery. Slavery was legal and fairly prevalent in colonial Pennsylvania with slaves constituting an estimated 8.5 percent of Philadelphia's population during the 1740s, for example, and Quakers employed slaves in the home, workshop, and farm.[28] John Woolman, however, felt the first pangs of conscience over slavery when as a young store clerk in New Jersey he had written for his employer a bill of sale for a slave woman. A trip through the slave societies of Maryland, Virginia, and North

Carolina in 1746 confirmed his antislavery convictions, and after returning home he drafted the manuscript that would be published in 1754 as *Some Considerations on the Keeping of Negroes*. That same year the Philadelphia Yearly Meeting issued an epistle that discouraged Friends from buying slaves. Thus began a two decades-long process of purging the Society of Friends of slavery until in 1776 the Philadelphia Yearly Meeting declared that any member still holding slaves would be disowned. Furthermore, Quakers like Anthony Benezet did not confine their antislavery efforts to the Friends alone but sought to change opinions and laws throughout the Atlantic world.[29] The Quakers' turn against slavery would have profound implications for thinking about race in the founding era.

The founders of the United States, therefore, inherited a complex legacy about religion and race from the colonial era. Initial English hopes to convert Native Americans to Christianity and civilization had born little fruit and largely given way in the face of violent conflicts to a desire simply to be rid of them, while the Natives developed their own ideas of separatism and polygenesis. Yet hopes died hard, and renewed missionary outreach during the Great Awakening led to small but significant breakthroughs. The English had a similarly futile experience in trying to convert their African slaves to Christianity until the middle of the eighteenth century when a new style of evangelical Protestantism suddenly appeared to African Americans to be more germane to their experience and genuinely proffered. While slavery remained the context that defined white-black interactions, a few outspoken critics began to question the status quo. In one way or another, the American Revolution would accentuate all of these themes of civilization and separation, slavery and abolition.

In many ways, the American Revolution served to deepen the racial fault lines that had emerged by the early 1760s. One person who immediately realized the Revolution's potential for racial division was the British governor of Virginia, John Murray, Earl of Dunmore, who in 1775 promised freedom to slaves who abandoned their rebel masters and joined him in arms. Virginia's Patriot militia quickly crushed Dunmore's force, but whites were terrified at the prospect of a general slave uprising. When representatives of the thirteen colonies declared independence in 1776, they included in their list of charges against the king that he "has excited domestic insurrections amongst us," a reference to Dunmore's proclamation. The Revolution provided slaves with an unprecedented chance to gain their freedom, which thousands seized either by enlisting in one of the armies or simply running away. When the victorious Americans framed a new national government in 1787, they made sure to fasten the slaves' shackles more securely.[30]

The Declaration also charged that George III "had endeavoured to bring on the inhabitants of our frontiers, the merciless Indian Savages, whose known rule of warfare, is an undistinguished destruction of all ages, sexes and conditions." During the ensuing War for Independence, the Christian Natives of southern New England fought on the Patriot side, but many other Natives sided with the British. As a consequence of the latter, Patriot forces launched devastating raids into Indian country, punishing the Cherokees and some of the Iroquois nations. "[T]he endemic warfare of the Revolution threw many traditional religious practices and sacred observances into disarray," notes one scholar, and the 1782 massacre of Native Christians at the Moravian settlement of Gnadenhutten again showed that conversion offered little protection from frontier vigilantes.[31] In the Treaty of Paris, the British ceded to the new United States all the territory to the Mississippi River between Florida and the Great Lakes, which flabbergasted their Native allies who lived there. "It was an act of cruelty and injustice that Christians *only* were capable of doing, that the Indians were incapable of acting so," they deplored.[32]

At the same time, however, the American Revolution fundamentally challenged the racial order of the colonial period. The broad discussion of the colonists' rights and liberties along with fears that British tyranny portended their political enslavement led to questioning of the chattel slavery that was all around them. As early as 1766, for example, Anthony Benezet took advantage of the Stamp Act Crisis to point out that while "the general rights and liberties of mankind, and the preservation of those valuable privileges transmitted to us from our ancestors" were much debated, "many of those who distinguish themselves as the Advocates of Liberty, remain insensible and inattentive to the treatment of thousands and tens of thousands of our fellow men, who, from motives of avarice, and the inexorable degree of tyrant custom, are at this very time kept in the most deplorable state of Slavery." As Douglas R. Egerton summarizes, "quickly ideological freedom for white men became associated with literal freedom for black men."[33] Christians ranging from Quakers to Calvinists to Wesleyans combined their faith with Revolutionary rhetoric in speaking out against slavery. Such "clerical founding fathers," observes David Brion Davis, "established a prophetic tradition that later American abolitionists, both black and white, revived and reformulated to suit their needs." Beginning with Pennsylvania in 1780, all of the states north of Maryland would respond over the next twenty-four years by either abolishing slavery or, more typically, adopting gradual emancipation laws that granted freedom to the children born to slaves once they reached their twenties. For the first time, a large population of free blacks grew as a result of such laws and a wave of private manumissions.[34] To the south of Pennsylvania, a similar debate over slavery and emancipation took place but with an outcome that preserved slavery intact. Meanwhile, the new federal government launched its own program that combined missionary hopes with Enlightenment optimism in a renewed push to "civilize" the Natives, who divided among themselves in their responses. In short, religion would serve as a major point of reference in Revolutionary America as people sought to erase old racial lines or draw new ones.

What follows are brief analyses of the Revolutionary-era contest over religion and race as it played out in four contexts: the New Jersey newspaper debate over emancipation in 1780–1781; the Virginia debate over the same that Methodists precipitated with their petitioning in 1785; the response of the free black community in the urban Mid-Atlantic to spreading racism in the 1790s and early 1800s; and the contemporaneous federal policy of civilizing Native Americans and their responses. In each context, the Bible occupied a central place in the debate. What did it have to say about slavery and race, and what authority did it carry compared with secular philosophy or prophetic visions? Participants continued to ground their arguments for racial similarities or differences, for coexistence or separation, in religious beliefs. At bottom was the question, could Americans accept a multiracial society? For many, like Jefferson, the answer was no.

An extraordinary series of essays about slavery and abolition published in the (Trenton) *New-Jersey Gazette* between September 1780 and June 1781 demonstrated clearly how the American Revolution could bring to the surface fundamental and intertwined issues of liberty, justice, religion, and race. The nine essays proved to be particularly revealing, in part because the extended back-and-forth of debate allowed for principles to be challenged, elaborated, and refined.[35] Advocates for emancipation found their biblically grounded arguments matched at every turn by Christians who were just as steeped in Scripture, if more fearful or dubious about black freedom. The debate in the *New-Jersey Gazette* foreshadowed how during the next quarter century religion would facilitate both the gradual dismantling of slavery throughout the Northern states and a continuing contest over the meaning of race.

The first four essays, two opposed to slavery and two written in its defense, showed that the Bible would offer no easy solutions, because seemingly self-explanatory texts were subject to divergent interpretations and both sides could find passages that supported their positions. An essay by the New Jersey Quaker John Cooper, the only one to carry its author's name, commenced the exchange. Cooper began by pointing out the contradiction between chattel slavery and the words of the Declaration of Independence, and he drew an analogy between the United States and biblical Israel based upon Deuteronomy 7:26, arguing that victory would elude the Americans in the War of Independence as long as they had "the accursed thing" of slavery among them. Expressing ideas about divine providence and justice that Jefferson would similarly invoke in *Notes on the State of Virginia*, Cooper asked, "Can we imagine our prayers to Almighty God will meet with his approbation . . . whilst the groans of our slaves are continually ascending mingled with them?" He concluded, "let the dread of divine retribution—of national calamities—induce us" to proclaim an immediate emancipation.[36]

Two weeks later, however, an essay signed by "A Whig" attacked "the fancifulness and enthusiastick turn" of Cooper's argument, dismissing his interpretation of "the accursed thing" as far-fetched. Moreover, this writer cited Leviticus 25:45–46 to say that *"perpetual slavery* seems rather more than permitted" under the Mosaic law. In return, "A Friend to Justice" came to Cooper's defense the next month, arguing that the example from Leviticus of the Israelites' holding slaves was no longer applicable, but rather a command that pertained to them alone. In closing, this writer invoked the Golden Rule of Matthew 7:12 and stated, "We are now at liberty to do them [the slaves] justice—to do to them as we would they should do to us were we in their situation." The fourth essay, by "Impartial," focused primarily on the property rights of slaveholders and the inexpediency of emancipation during wartime, but the author also denied that the Golden Rule implied liberation for slaves; rather, it meant only that slaves should be treated well and exposed to the gospel. "Impartial" also revealed that a racist fear of black freedom fueled the defenses of slavery when he asked, "is it reasonable to suppose that our slaves, naturally indolent; unaccustomed to self-government; destitute of mechanical knowledge; unacquainted with letters; with a peculiar propensity to spirituous liquors; destitute of property, and without credit, would pay their taxes and provide for themselves, in the path of integrity, the necessaries and comforts of life?"[37] In these first four essays, the opponents and defenders of slavery had fought to a draw on Scriptural grounds, and the Revolutionary principles of liberty and property were at loggerheads.

The fifth essay sought a decisive breakthrough of the impasse by providing a more extensive exposition of the biblical grounds for slaveholding. Its author, who signed himself "A Lover of true Justice," was probably a Reformed clergyman as indicated by his Hebrew exegesis and references to the Synod of Dort and the German Calvinist theologian Johannes Crocius. In addition to the aforementioned Leviticus 25:44–46, which permitted the Israelites to own "bondmen" and "bondmaids" from among the "heathen" in perpetuity, "A Lover of true Justice" also cited the example in Genesis 17:23 of Abraham's servants who were "bought with his money" and the directive in Exodus 21:6 and Deuteronomy 15:17 that servants for life should be marked by having their ears bored with an awl. Responding to the claim of "A Friend to Justice," he argued that these Old Testament examples could not be waved off as particular to the Israelites, because that would still implicate God in evil if slavery were wrong. Turning to the New Testament, "A Lover of true Justice" pointed to texts that urged obedience under slavery such as 1 Corinthians 7:20–21 and Ephesians 6:5–8, and he also cited Philemon 15 for its suggestion that Onesimus would remain a slave "forever." Upon this foundation, he concluded that slavery could not be considered sinful; rather, what was "an heinous sin" was "the keeping of slaves among christians, in stupid ignorance, neglect of the gospel and its ordinances, permitting them the profanation of the Lord's day, and indulging them in all kinds of wickedness, if the owners get but their labour."[38] Southern evangelicals would similarly seek during the early republic to defend slavery by rendering it compatible with Christianity.

While certain that slavery was not sinful, "A Lover of true Justice" at least granted that freedom was a status to be preferred. He therefore endorsed the goal of eventually emancipating slaves, but only under strictly qualified conditions. First and foremost, property rights had to be respected, so uncompensated emancipation he dismissed as unjust. He cited various biblical texts that supported the chattel principles that slaves were as good as money (Exodus 21:21) and inheritable (Leviticus 25:45–46). "Note here," he underscored, "*the special care God took of property.*" His other two reasons for being opposed to immediate abolition, however, had nothing to do with the Bible and everything to do with racism. "The preservation and interest of civil society" had to be taken into consideration, because he predicted that immediate emancipation would dump on society an ill-prepared class of innate dependents, who were "[s]low, sluggish, and stupid by nature, unaccustomed to prudent care, without any thing in hand, or trades to begin with, numerous families of children to take care of and to be provided for." In addition, like Jefferson he feared the specter of miscegenation, and he called for either a long period of apprenticeship to prepare slaves for freedom or, again like Jefferson, their removal.[39]

The final four essays served as a denouement to the forceful case put forward by "A Lover of true Justice." A writer who signed himself only as "E" replied that the biblical term "servant" did not correspond to modern slavery, while "Homo Sum" noted that immediate emancipation was not the issue under debate but a gradual plan. (That actually signaled a retreat from John Cooper's initial position in the face of the race-baiting of "A Lover of true Justice.") "Homo Sum" repeated the argument that the war should be seen as a providential punishment for slavery, writing that "The danger we have been in of losing our *own* liberty, may be a wise dispensation of Providence to awaken in us a juster sense of *theirs*." He also called readers' attention back to the racial underpinnings of this debate over slavery and abolition, admonishing that "it behoves us seriously to consider whether the just and merciful maker and father of all mankind is not now contending with us for the insult offered to his image and the workmanship of his hands, in depriving our fellow men of that liberty with which Christ has made them free [Galatians 5:1], and insolently and impiously arrogating this privilege, as peculiar to ourselves alone, for no better reason but because our skins are white, when it has pleased the all-wise God to make much the greater part of mankind of a different complexion."[40] In reply, "Truth et Justice" fell back on the sanctity of property argument, asking "If the Almighty is offended with us for keeping slaves, would he be pleased with an act which should liberate them at the expence of fraud and injustice?" Finally, "A Lover of true Justice" wrote the ninth essay in response to "E" and piled up more biblical texts to show that lifetime slavery was permitted and not condemned in either the Old or New Testament. He concluded, "qualified slavery is not repugnant to scripture, but plainly allowed of, and therefore is no sin, and deserves no judgments of God."[41]

The *New-Jersey Gazette*'s debate over slavery and abolition illuminates much about religion, race, and the founders. In the first place, it epitomizes how Quakers and their allies led the attack on slavery as sinful and contradictory to the principles of the American Revolution. They emphasized biblical themes of justice, equality, and, where those were lacking, divine wrath and stressed the basic unity of mankind as in the references by "Homo Sum" to the "father of all mankind" and "our fellow men." Arguments such as these undergirded the Revolutionary era push to eradicate slavery that led to the first emancipation in every state from Pennsylvania northward.

The debate in the *New-Jersey Gazette*, however, also reveals why that first emancipation took the gradualist path that it did in the northern states. The founding generation held property rights in high regard, and slaveholders could easily enlist the Old and New Testaments in defense of their human chattel. This debate also showed how the prospect of black freedom drew forth racist arguments about innate inferiority; put another way, apologists for slavery stressed the basic diversity of mankind.

A similar debate took place later in the same decade in Virginia, the state with the largest population of slaves, but produced different results. In response to both Revolutionary principles of liberty and persistent Quaker lobbying, the legislature passed a law in 1782 that made it easier for individual owners to manumit their slaves. As a result, the population of free blacks in the state soared from around two thousand in 1782 to more than thirty thousand by 1810, which produced a tectonic shift in Virginians' concept of race.[42] "Virginians understood that the language colonials had used to describe the two basic categories of Virginians, free and negro, no longer sufficed," explains Eva Sheppard Wolf, because "the main social division in Virginia was no longer between a negro/slave and a white/freeperson but between all people of color and whites. Race, not slave status, was the dividing line." Accordingly, Virginia whites coined a new label, "person of color," that lumped enslaved and free blacks together.[43] Throughout the nation a similar dynamic operated during the early republic: the growth of the free black population accentuated race where slavery had formerly defined social relations.

The rising Methodist denomination, an evangelical offshoot of the Church of England that would become the nation's largest Protestant denomination by the Civil War, precipitated a further crystallization of Southern beliefs about slavery, religion, and race. On the heels of Virginia's 1782 manumission act, Methodists followed the example of the Quakers and ruled at a conference in Baltimore in December 1784 that members who did not free their slaves would be expelled. The decision caused an immediate uproar, however, and was "suspended" the following June. Nevertheless, Methodist leaders Francis Asbury and Thomas Coke launched a petition campaign in 1785 to urge the Virginia legislature to pass an emancipation law. The Methodists' agitation provoked a counter-campaign of proslavery petitioning that garnered hundreds of signatures. Just like "A Lover of true Justice" had done in the *New-Jersey Gazette* a few years earlier, slavery's defenders cited passages such as Leviticus 25:44–46 and 1 Corinthians 7:20–24 as validation for their human property. The

Methodists' emancipation proposal failed to advance in the legislature, and the denomination reconciled itself to slavery along with Southern Baptists and Presbyterians. "Methodism was a people's movement," concludes Donald G. Mathews, "and the people either wanted slavery or feared emancipation." Better to be able to evangelize masters and slaves alike, evangelicals reasoned, than adopt a strict antislavery testimony and consign themselves to the margins of southern society as the Quakers had chosen to do. The Christianization of slavery, rather than its abolition, became the standard policy of southern evangelicals in the early republic.[44]

African American Methodists, not surprisingly, had a different take on these issues, which they did not keep to themselves; rather, they used the platform of their new community organizations and the medium of print to engage the debate. For instance, in 1794, Absalom Jones and Richard Allen, both ex-slaves from Delaware who had been converted to Methodism and had settled in Philadelphia, published a pamphlet to rebut an accusation that the city's blacks had taken advantage of a yellow fever outbreak the previous year to loot from whites. At the end of their text they included "An Address To Those Who Keep Slaves and Uphold the Practice." Taking an environmentalist tack, they turned the tables on those like Jefferson who asserted black inferiority. "We believe if you would try the experiment of taking a few black children, and cultivate their minds with the same care, and let them have the same prospect in view, as to living in the world, as you would wish for your own children, you would find them upon the trial, they were not inferior in mental endowments." Allen's insistence on black equality extended to the church. "[W]hile he was loyal to the faith that had freed him from slavery as well as from sin," observes Dee E. Andrews, "he was simultaneously eager to escape the official dictates of the church that bound him to second-class citizenship." In 1794, Allen was one of the leading figures behind the formation of a separate African Methodist Episcopal Church. Similar African churches soon appeared in other locations such as New York and Baltimore. "It was no accident that blacks called their churches African churches, their schools African schools, and their benevolent societies African benevolent societies," notes Ira Berlin, because it represented a proud assertion of identity. Separate but equal was the strategy of the post-Revolutionary free black community in the face of white charges of inferiority and subordinate status.[45]

Daniel Coker's 1810 pamphlet, *A Dialogue Between a Virginian and an African Minister*, well articulated the African American response to white Christian defenses of slavery. Coker served as a minister of the African

Methodist Episcopal Church in Baltimore, and his pamphlet took the form of an imagined conversation between a minister such as himself and a white Virginia slaveholder, in which the former rebutted all of the latter's arguments against emancipation. When the Virginian brought up conventional biblical justifications for slavery such as from Genesis 17, Leviticus 25, and 1 Corinthians 7, the minister explained how they had been taken out of context and erroneously employed in support of American slavery. Rather than get bogged down in a tit-for-tat of competing verses, Coker argued that "the unreasonableness of perpetual unconditional slavery, may be easily inferred from the righteous and benevolent doctrines and duties, taught in the New Testament. . . . [S]lavery is contrary to the spirit and nature of the Christian religion." He appealed to the ultimate Christian principle of the Golden Rule and stated simply, "No man, when he views the hardships and misery, the boundless labours, the unreasonable punishments, the separation between loving husbands and wives, between affectionate parents and children, can say, in truth, were I in their place, I should be contented." Coker also tackled the argument that emancipation would create a dangerous and dependent underclass of free blacks by pointing out that it was slavery that habituated people to "such vicious habits as lying, pilfering, and stealing." "But," Coker asked, "are these evils confined to a people of a sable countenance?" In other words, blacks were not innately depraved but the victims of slavery, so the solution was to abolish the institution. Coker invoked the words of Isaiah 1:4 in threatening divine wrath for America's sin of slavery, and in an interesting cross-fertilization with Quaker antislavery he closed by quoting John Parrish's *Remarks on the Slavery of the Black People* (1806), which called for a gradual emancipation plan like Jefferson had sketched in *Notes on the State of Virginia*.[46] While his *Dialogue* failed to produce a gradual emancipation in either Virginia or Maryland, it revealed themes that would become staples for later black abolitionists, such as an appeal to the transcendent justice expressed in the Old and New Testaments against the harsh realities of racism and slavery in America.

Questions of religion and race were similarly intertwined for Native Americans and those whites who interacted with them. For many Natives in the Ohio Valley, war did not end with their sellout by the British in 1783, and a unified identity coalesced amid the dislocated tribes that reestablished themselves there. At a meeting in present-day Ohio in 1792, for example, one Shawnee speaker, Painted Pole, declared that "the great Spirit" had brought together for "the good of all nations of our colour" the more than one dozen tribes assembled there. However, the United States' decisive victory at the Battle of Fallen Timbers in 1794 ended Native resistance in the Old Northwest for over a decade.[47] Also during the 1780s, many of southern New England's Christian Natives decided to relocate to the Oneida country of upstate New York and founded the settlements of Brothertown and New Stockbridge. They were attracted by the prospect of sizeable tracts of land and the opportunity, they hoped, to establish communities of Christian fellowship away from white encroachment. They also decided to bar non-Natives from these settlements, particularly African Americans with whom had intermarried, and thereby cultivated a unified racial identity.[48] In these different ways, Natives once again had to choose between coexistence or separatism, and religious beliefs shaped their decisions.

In the early 1790s, Henry Knox and Timothy Pickering, President George Washington's first Secretary of War and his successor, advocated a plan with a lineage that reached back to sixteenth-century Spanish America: they proposed to instruct Native Americans in Christianity and civilization. They envisioned a comprehensive program that would transform Natives into American yeomen through training in agriculture, crafts, and literacy, and resident Protestant missionaries were an integral part of their vision. Anticipating criticism that the Natives were irredeemable savages, Pickering wrote in 1792 that he refused to "admit the idea that their minds are cast in a mould so different from that of the rest of their species as to be incapable of cultivation." When Jefferson became president, he maintained the Native American policies of his Federalist predecessors and, in contrast to his professed repugnance toward black-white miscegenation, he even advocated intermarriage between whites and Natives. "You will unite yourselves with us, and we shall all be Americans. You will mix with us by marriage," Jefferson said to a visiting group of Natives in 1808. Federal policies aimed to assimilate Natives to the values of the United States and also make land available to settlers. "I feel it consistent with pure morality," Jefferson wrote in 1803, "to familiarize them to the idea that it is for their interest to cede lands at times to the US, and for us thus to procure gratifications to our citizens, from time to time, by new acquisitions of land."[49]

Faced with such policies, Native Americans divided over the best way to respond. One response accepted the power of the United States and made a series of accommodations. In exchange for federal payments, some Native leaders signed away land in treaties with the government. Black Hoof of the Shawnees also encouraged the setting up of a "demonstration farm" where his people could learn agricultural and household production techniques from Quaker missionaries. In the South, some

Creeks and Cherokees not only welcomed Moravian and Presbyterian missionaries, but also they adopted the ways of white society by acquiring African American slaves to work their land. Mixed-race individuals often provided the leadership for such assimilative strategies.[50] Such strategies of accommodation, however, met strong resistance from those Natives who emphasized their distinctiveness from whites. In the late 1790s and early 1800s, several Native prophets emerged and reiterated Neolin's message of polygenesis, purification through rituals, rejection of Christianity, and separation from Euro-American ways. "You yourselves can see that the white people are entirely different beings from us;" stated a Cherokee prophet in 1811, "we are made of red clay; they, out of white sand." Furthermore, Tenskwatawa, "the Shawnee Prophet" and brother of Tecumseh, accused some of those who cooperated, including Black Hoof, with witchcraft. Thus, as the War of 1812 approached, Native Americans found themselves divided, and differences over religious and racial identity were at the heart of the matter.[51]

That war exacerbated racial divisions in the United States. When the British invaded the Chesapeake, they found that slaves again fled to them by the thousands as had occurred during the Revolution. In the West, prophetic religious figures such as Tenskwatawa inspired the armed resistance of Tecumseh and the Creek Red Stick faction, but Native Americans suffered crushing defeats against United States forces led by Generals William Henry Harrison and Andrew Jackson. Jackson embodied the frontiersmen's outlook that "did not want Indians, assimilated or not, to remain on the lands they coveted."[52] After the war, Natives faced growing pressure to forfeit their remaining lands. One Western governor remarked in 1816 that if the Cherokees would relocate to territory promised them across the Mississippi River, then any remaining individuals "could have 'all the rights of a free citizen of color of the United States,'" which, of course, meant inferior status. It was a far cry from Jefferson's dreams of intermarriage. The year 1816 also witnessed the founding of a national organization, the American Colonization Society, with the goals of transporting African Americans to Africa and thereby evangelizing that continent. Religion and racial separatism would go hand in hand in the society's vision.[53]

Yet there remained many who resisted such a vision and found in their religious beliefs tools to counteract the racism of nineteenth-century America. Such was the mixed legacy of the founding era of United States history for the interconnected histories of religion and race. For example, in 1810 the president of the College of New Jersey, Samuel Stanhope

Smith, published a second edition of *An Essay on the Causes of the Variety of Complexion and Figure in the Human Species.* Contrary to Jefferson's "suspicion" that blacks and whites belonged to different and unequal races, Smith sought "to establish the unity of the human species." For Smith such an enquiry had "an obvious and intimate relation with religion, by bringing in science to confirm the verity of the Mosaic history" of a unified creation. Almost two decades later, it was Protestant missionaries and their northeastern supporters who led the protest against Jackson's Indian removal policies, and that campaign helped to precipitate Garrisonian abolitionism by making people see the similarities between removal and African colonization. Like the Quakers and African Methodists who preceded them in the founding era, antebellum abolitionists would attack slavery with the message of the unity of mankind, proclaiming the words of Acts 17:26 that God "hath made of one blood all nations of men for to dwell on all the face of the earth."[54]

Notes

1. Thomas Jefferson, *Notes on the State of Virginia*, William Peden, ed. (London, 1787; Chapel Hill: University of North Carolina Press, 1954), 59–62, 139–143.
2. Ibid., 159–60, 163.
3. Ibid., 143, 138.
4. James Brewer Stewart, "The Emergence of Racial Modernity and the Rise of the White North, 1790–1840," *Journal of the Early Republic* 18, no. 2 (Summer 1998): 181–217.
5. John Barnshaw, "Race," in *Encyclopedia of Race, Ethnicity, and Society*, ed. Richard T. Schaefer, 3 vols. (Thousand Oaks, CA: Sage Publications, 2008), 3:1091; Pierre H. Boulle, "Race," in Alan Charles Kors, ed., *Encyclopedia of the Enlightenment*, 4 vols. (New York: Oxford University Press, 2003), 3: 384–387.
6. Here I follow Jon Butler, *Awash in a Sea of Faith: Christianizing the American People* (Cambridge, MA: Harvard University Press, 1990), 3.
7. J. H. Elliott, *Empires of the Atlantic World: Britain and Spain in America, 1492–1830* (New Haven, CT: Yale University Press, 2006), 17.
8. Ibid., quotes from 11 and 71.
9. David Brion Davis, *Inhuman Bondage: The Rise and Fall of Slavery in the New World* (New York: Oxford University Press, 2006), 98–99.
10. *A True and Sincere declaration of the purpose and ends of the Plantation begun in Virginia . . .* (London, 1610), in Warren M. Billings, ed., *The Old Dominion in the Seventeenth Century: A Documentary History of Virginia, 1606–1689* (Chapel Hill: University of North Carolina Press, 1975), 14; Karen Ordahl Kupperman,

"Presentment of Civility: English Reading of American Self-Presentation in the Early Years of Colonization," *William and Mary Quarterly*, 3rd ser., 54, no. 1 (Jan. 1997): 193–228, quote from 207.

11. Daniel K. Richter, *Facing East from Indian Country: A Native History of Early America* (Cambridge, MA: Harvard University Press, 2001), 69–78, quote from 78.

12. Edward Waterhouse, "A Declaration of the state of the Colonie and Affaires in Virginia. With a Relation of the barbarous Massacre . . ." (1622), in Billings, *Old Dominion in the Seventeenth Century*, 208 (number killed), 222 (quote); Elliott, *Empires of the Atlantic World*, 62.

13. Richter, *Facing East from Indian Country*, 95–105, 111–129.

14. Mary Rowlandson, *The Sovereignty and Goodness of God, Together with the Faithfulness of His Promises Displayed*, ed. Neal Salisbury (Cambridge, MA, 1682; Boston: Bedford Books, 1997), 98; Elliott, *Empires of the Atlantic World*, 78 (quote).

15. Alan Taylor, *American Colonies* (New York: Penguin, 2001), 268–269; James Axtell, *The Invasion Within: The Contest of Cultures in Colonial North America* (New York: Oxford University Press, 1985).

16. Sylvia R. Frey and Betty Wood, *Come Shouting to Zion: African American Protestantism in the American South and British Caribbean to 1830* (Chapel Hill: University of North Carolina Press, 1998), 1–79; "An Act Declaring that Baptism Does Not Bring Freedom, September 1667," in Billings, *Old Dominion in the Seventeenth Century*, 172; Thomas E. Drake, *Quakers and Slavery in America* (New Haven, CT: Yale University Press, 1950; reprint, Gloucester, MA: Peter Smith, 1965), 5–8.

17. Jon Butler, *Becoming America: The Revolution before 1776* (Cambridge, MA: Harvard University Press, 2000), 10, 40.

18. Richter, *Facing East from Indian Country*, 164–173.

19. Gregory Evans Dowd, *A Spirited Resistance: The North American Indian Struggle for Unity, 1745–1815* (Baltimore, MD: Johns Hopkins University Press, 1992), 27–36, quote from 27; Richter, *Facing East from Indian Country*, 180–181; James Sidbury and Jorge Cañizares-Esguerra, "Mapping Ethnogenesis in the Early Modern Atlantic," *William and Mary Quarterly*, 3rd ser., 68, no. 2 (April 2011): 194.

20. Quoted in Richter, *Facing East from Indian Country*, 213.

21. Ibid., 201–208, quotes from 206 and 208. See also Krista Camenzind, "Violence, Race, and the Paxton Boys," in William A. Pencak and Daniel K. Richter, eds., *Friends and Enemies in Penn's Woods: Indians, Colonists, and the Racial Construction of Pennsylvania* (University Park: Pennsylvania State University Press, 2004): 201–220; and Kevin Kenny, *Peaceable Kingdom Lost: The Paxton Boys and the Destruction of William Penn's Holy Experiment* (New York: Oxford University Press, 2009).

22. Winthrop D. Jordan, *White over Black: American Attitudes toward the Negro, 1550–1812* (Chapel Hill: University of North Carolina Press, 1968), 287–289.

23. George M. Fredrickson, *Racism: A Short History* (Princeton, NJ: Princeton University Press, 2002), 56–57.
24. Harvey H. Jackson, "Hugh Bryan and the Evangelical Movement in Colonial South Carolina," *William and Mary Quarterly*, 3rd ser., 43, no. 4 (October 1986): 594–614; Frey and Wood, *Come Shouting to Zion*, 81–111, Davies quoted from 97.
25. Dowd, *A Spirited Resistance*, 64; Jane T. Merritt, "Dreaming of the Savior's Blood: Moravians and the Indian Great Awakening in Pennsylvania," *William and Mary Quarterly*, 3rd ser., 54, no. 4 (October 1997): 723–746; William S. Simmons, "The Great Awakening and Indian Conversion in Southern New England," in William Cowan, ed., *Papers of the Tenth Algonquian Conference* (Ottawa, ON: Carleton University, 1979): 25–36; Linford D. Fisher, *The Indian Great Awakening: Religion and the Shaping of Native Cultures in Early America* (New York: Oxford University Press, 2012).
26. David J. Silverman, *Red Brethren: The Brothertown and Stockbridge Indians and the Problem of Race in Early America* (Ithaca, NY: Cornell University Press, 2010), 32–69, quote from 32.
27. Phillips P. Moulton, ed., *The Journal and Major Essays of John Woolman* (New York: Oxford University Press, 1971), 24; Jack D. Marietta, *The Reformation of American Quakerism, 1748–1783* (Philadelphia: University of Pennsylvania Press, 1984).
28. Gary B. Nash and Jean R. Soderlund, *Freedom by Degrees: Emancipation in Pennsylvania and Its Aftermath* (New York: Oxford University Press, 1991), 3–40, statistic on 15.
29. Moulton, ed., *Journal and Major Essays of John Woolman*, 32–33, 36–38, 44–45; Thomas P. Slaughter, *The Beautiful Soul of John Woolman, Apostle of Abolition* (New York: Hill and Wang, 2008); Geoffrey Plank, *John Woolman's Path to the Peaceable Kingdom: A Quaker in the British Empire* (Philadelphia: University of Pennsylvania Press, 2012), 97–120; Drake, *Quakers and Slavery in America*, 51–73; Maurice Jackson, *Let This Voice Be Heard: Anthony Benezet, Father of Atlantic Abolitionism* (Philadelphia: University of Pennsylvania Press, 2009).
30. Benjamin Quarles, *The Negro in the American Revolution* (1961; Chapel Hill: University of North Carolina Press, 1996); "Declaration of Independence," in *Colonies to Nation, 1763–1789: A Documentary History of the American Revolution*, ed. Jack P. Greene (New York: Norton, 1975), 300; David Waldstreicher, *Slavery's Constitution: From Revolution to Ratification* (New York: Hill and Wang, 2009).
31. Silverman, *Red Brethren*, 108–120; Richter, *Facing East from Indian Country*, 216–223; Colin G. Calloway, "The Continuing Revolution in Indian Country," in Frederick E. Hoxie, Ronald Hoffman, and Peter J. Albert, eds., *Native Americans and the Early Republic* (Charlottesville: University Press of Virginia, 1999), quote from 22.
32. Dowd, *A Spirited Resistance*, 93.
33. Bernard Bailyn, *The Ideological Origins of the American Revolution*, enl. ed. (Cambridge, MA: Harvard University Press, Belknap Press, 1992), 232–246; Anthony

Benezet, *A Caution and Warning to Great Britain and Her Colonies, in a Short Representation of the Calamitous State of the Enslaved Negroes in the British Dominions* . . . (Philadelphia, 1766), 3; Douglas R. Egerton, *Death or Liberty: African Americans and Revolutionary America* (New York: Oxford University Press, 2009), 46.

34. James D. Essig, *The Bonds of Wickedness: American Evangelicals against Slavery, 1770–1808* (Philadelphia: Temple University Press, 1982); David Brion Davis, "American Slavery and the American Revolution," in Ira Berlin and Ronald Hoffman, eds., *Slavery and Freedom in the Age of the American Revolution* (Charlottesville: University Press of Virginia, 1983), 277; Arthur Zilversmit, *The First Emancipation: The Abolition of Slavery in the North* (Chicago: University of Chicago Press, 1967).

35. For more on this New Jersey abolition debate, see Zilversmit, *First Emancipation*, 141–146, who deemed it "perhaps the most extensive newspaper debate on the subject before the 1830's" (141). I differ from Zilversmit's account, however, since he paid little attention to the profoundly religious basis of many of the arguments.

36. *New-Jersey Gazette* [hereafter *NJG*], Sept. 20, 1780, 2.

37. "A Whig," *NJG*, October 4, 1780, 1; "A Friend to Justice," *NJG*, November 8, 1780, 1; "Impartial," *NJG*, January 10, 1781, 1.

38. *NJG*, February 14, 1781, 1.

39. Ibid.

40. "E," *NJG*, March 14, 1781, 1; "Homo Sum," *NJG*, March 21, 1781, 1.

41. "Truth et Justice," *NJG*, April 11, 1781, 2; "A Lover of true Justice," *NJG*, June 27, 1781, 1.

42. Eva Sheppard Wolf, *Race and Liberty in the New Nation: Emancipation in Virginia from the Revolution to Nat Turner's Rebellion* (Baton Rouge: Louisiana State University Press, 2006), 7–16, 28–35; Ira Berlin, "The Revolution in Black Life," in Alfred F. Young, ed., *The American Revolution: Explorations in the History of American Radicalism* (DeKalb: Northern Illinois University Press, 1976), 359–360.

43. Wolf, *Race and Liberty in the New Nation*, 158.

44. Donald G. Mathews, *Slavery and Methodism: A Chapter in American Morality, 1780–1845* (Princeton, NJ: Princeton University Press, 1965), 10–29, quotes from 12 and 23; Fredrika Teute Schmidt and Barbara Ripel Wilhelm, "Early Proslavery Petitions in Virginia," *William and Mary Quarterly*, 3rd ser., 30, no. 1 (Jan. 1973): 133–146; Wolf, *Race and Liberty in the New Nation*, 88–101. As historian Monica Najar has shown, Virginia Baptists followed "a similar trajectory" as the Methodists in deciding that emancipation was too divisive an issue for their churches and should be left to the legislature; see Najar, *Evangelizing the South: A Social History of Church and State in Early America* (New York: Oxford University Press, 2008), 138–150, quote from 139. On the larger theme of evangelicals' accommodations with Southern society, see also Christine Leigh Heyrman, *Southern Cross: The Beginnings of the Bible Belt* (New York: Knopf, 1997).

45. Absalom Jones and Richard Allen, "A Narrative of the Proceedings of the Black People During the Late Awful Calamity in Philadelphia" (1794), in Richard Newman, Patrick Rael, and Phillip Lapsansky, eds., *Pamphlets of Protest: An Anthology of Early African-American Protest Literature, 1790–1860* (New York: Routledge, 2001), 41–42; Dee E. Andrews, *The Methodists and Revolutionary America, 1760–1800: The Shaping of an Evangelical Culture* (Princeton, NJ: Princeton University Press, 2000), 139–154, quote from 140; Berlin, "The Revolution in Black Life," 376; Richard S. Newman, "Liberation Technology: Black Printed Protest in the Age of Franklin," *Early American Studies* 8, no. 1 (Winter 2010): 173–198.
46. Daniel Coker, "A Dialogue Between a Virginian and an African Minister" (1810), in *Pamphlets of Protest*, 52–65, quotes on 59–60. On Parrish's work, see Drake, *Quakers and Slavery in America*, 113.
47. Calloway, "The Continuing Revolution in Indian Country," 3–33; Dowd, *A Spirited Resistance*, 59–60, 103–115, quote from 103.
48. Silverman, *Red Brethren*, 101–105, 121–124.
49. Bernard W. Sheehan, "The Indian Problem in the Northwest: From Conquest to Philanthropy," in Ronald Hoffman and Peter J. Albert, eds., *Launching the "Extended Republic": The Federalist Era* (Charlottesville: University Press of Virginia, 1996), 212–221, Pickering quote from 216; Dowd, *A Spirited Resistance*, 116–117; Richter, *Facing East from Indian Country*, 226; Reginald Horsman, "The Indian Policy of an 'Empire for Liberty,'" in *Native Americans and the Early Republic*, 37–61, quotes from 50–51.
50. Dowd, *A Spirited Resistance*, 134–139, 152–153, 159, quote on 134; Joel W. Martin, "Cultural Contact and Crises in the Early Republic: Native American Religious Renewal, Resistance, and Accommodation," in *Native Americans and the Early Republic*, 232–234.
51. Dowd, *A Spirited Resistance*, 123–129, 136–141; Martin, "Cultural Contact and Crises in the Early Republic," 232 (quote from Cherokee prophet).
52. Wolf, *Race and Liberty in the New Nation*, 133–134; Dowd, *A Spirited Resistance*, 181–190; Horsman, "The Indian Policy of an 'Empire for Liberty,'" quote from 55.
53. Horsman, "The Indian Policy of an 'Empire for Liberty,'" quote from 59; P. J. Staudenraus, *The African Colonization Movement, 1816–1865* (New York: Columbia University Press, 1961).
54. Samuel Stanhope Smith, *An Essay on the Causes of the Variety of Complexion and Figure in the Human Species*, Winthrop D. Jordan, ed. (Cambridge, MA: Harvard University Press, Belknap Press, 1965), 3; Mary Hershberger, "Mobilizing Women, Anticipating Abolition: The Struggle against Indian Removal in the 1830s," *Journal of American History* 86, no. 1 (June 1999): 15–40; Paul Goodman, *Of One Blood: Abolitionism and the Origins of Racial Equality* (Berkeley and Los Angeles: University of California Press, 1998).

PART II
Faith and the Founders

9

Gouverneur Morris and Theistic Rationalism in the Founding Era

Gregg Frazer

GOUVERNEUR MORRIS DESERVES as much remembrance and recognition as any "forgotten founder." From 1775 to 1777, he was first an influential member of New York's Provincial Congress and later its constitutional convention. The Provincial Convention (as the Provincial Congress had been renamed) appointed him to the Continental Congress in 1778, and he signed the Articles of Confederation that same year. In the 1790s, Morris served as America's ambassador to France and was the only foreign minister to stay in the country during the Reign of Terror, giving America a signal foreign policy advantage. At the turn of the century, he served in the United States Senate for three years. But he most deserves to be remembered for his work on the United States Constitution.

Morris spoke more often than anyone at the Constitutional Convention, and he was an influential member of the important Committee of Style. In fact, he wrote the Preamble to the Constitution, which "provides, as does the Declaration, a set of dynamic principles by which citizens could measure the actions of their government."[1] As James Madison, known as the "Father of the Constitution," testified, Morris's contribution to the writing of the Constitution did not end with the Preamble:

> The *finish* given to the style and arrangement of the Constitution fairly belongs to the pen of Mr. Morris. . . . A better choice could not have been made, as the performance of the task proved. . . . [T]here was sufficient room for the talents and taste stamped by the author on the

face of it. The alterations made by the Committee are not recollected. They were not such, as to impair the merit of the composition."[2]

In an 1814 letter, Morris himself says of the Constitution: "That instrument was written by the fingers, which write this letter."[3] Given his credentials and accomplishments, it is surprising that he is not better known to the average American today. Things might have been different if he had not "declined" when "warmly pressed by Hamilton to assist in writing the Federalist."[4] As demonstrated in a recent survey, scholars are more familiar with Morris than average Americans; he was ranked the third most important "forgotten" founder.[5]

Morris's accomplishments are known among academics, but his religious beliefs remain a puzzle even for students of the era. There are at least two reasons for this. First, while Morris was not at all hesitant to speak out on political or social issues, he did not often speak about his religious beliefs in public or in private. John Adams, Thomas Jefferson, and Benjamin Franklin wrote extensively—even systematically at times—about their religious beliefs, but Morris left only scattered clues and isolated comments. Second, Morris's expressed beliefs do not fit conveniently into either of the two categories generally recognized by scholars of the period: Christianity and Deism. Rather, what we can glean of Morris's beliefs indicates that he was a *theistic rationalist* (a term I define below).

Biographers and Morris's Religion

Biographers of Gouverneur Morris do not expend much effort trying to figure out his religious beliefs. Their somewhat minimal efforts appear to be designed to quickly place Morris into one of the two accepted niches and then to move on to other matters. Consequently, some simply mention that Morris "belonged to the ruling Episcopal Church,"[6] while another finds great significance in his studies with a Huguenot preacher between the ages of six and eight and concludes that he was a Christian;[7] yet another finds his "religious feelings" to be "thoroughly Deist" and substantively "not far" from those of Thomas Paine.[8] Two scholars mention the fact that Morris was not a Calvinist and was not influenced by Calvinism or Puritanism.[9] Several note the required religious practices at King's College during Morris's time there, but say nothing about Morris's participation or level of enthusiasm.[10] Finally, brief hints from two biographers point in the right direction. Max Mintz notes that, as a law clerk, Morris studied Pufendorf, who "sought to reconcile rationalism with Christianity;"[11] and James Kirschke concludes that "[l]ike Jefferson, Morris was of no special religious opinion."[12] As we will see below, such attempts at reconciliation may lead to belief in theistic rationalism; and theistic rationalists, who disdain doctrine, reflect no "special" religious opinion.

Biographers and Morris's View of Church and State

While biographers have not labored over Morris's religious beliefs, they discuss at some length his views and actions regarding the relationship between church and state. Scholars agree that Morris was "always a firm believer in religious liberty" and that he "consistently argued for the broadest possible religious freedom." The consensus among his biographers seems to be that "Gouverneur Morris was, along with Franklin and Jefferson, among the most religiously tolerant of the Founders."[13] The evidence most commonly presented concerns his opposition to an anti-Catholic article in the plan of reconciliation adopted by the Provincial Congress of New York in 1775 and his opposition to anti-Catholic amendments proposed by John Jay for the New York Constitution.[14] His efforts, including counterresolutions and reports, are all the more significant given Morris's personal disdain for Catholicism. In private, he often employed his keen sardonic wit to ridicule Catholics and Catholicism,[15] but publicly he was adamant about ensuring their religious freedom. Rarely one to mince words, Morris referred to the anti-Catholic article adopted by the Provincial Congress as "that foolish religious business" and as "most arrant nonsense."[16] In a 1778 letter cited by two biographers, Morris summed up his position concerning religious freedom: "It was always my opinion, that matters of conscience and faith, whether political or religious, are as much out of the province, as they are beyond the ken of human legislatures."[17]

Two other examples of Morris's position concerning church and state are covered by various biographers. The first is his "characteristically complex" attitude toward pacifist sects. According to Kirschke, the "religious beliefs of the Quakers were of no moment to him," and he suggested to Robert Livingston the advantages of trying to bring them to the revolutionary cause.[18] William Howard Adams adds that Morris held the Pennsylvania government in contempt because they harassed Quakers for refusing to take up arms.[19] On the other hand, Kirschke says, Morris was "impatient with pacifism" and wrote a "long essay" for *The Pennsylvania Packet* in 1779 urging Quakers to take up arms against the British.[20] Morris's approach was consistent: he did not allow his personal views to interfere with what he saw as the proper public position, which was to grant religious freedom.

The second example cited is Morris's opposition to religious tests for office. At the Constitutional Convention, Morris spoke against religious tests and supported the "no religious test" clause. Morris worked to add a clause in New York that declared "the free exercise and enjoyment of religious profession and worship, without discrimination or preference, shall forever hereafter be allowed, within this State, to all mankind." Kirschke concludes that Morris "strongly opposed the union of church and state" and offers as final evidence a dinner party conversation in which Morris proudly asserted that there is no establishment of religion in America, telling a guest "that God is sufficiently powerful to do his own business without human Aid."[21]

There are two events—each mentioned by one biographer—which might call into question Morris's opposition to the union of church and state and even his commitment to religious freedom. In 1778, Morris drafted an *Address to the Inhabitants of North America*, which was "written to be read from every church pulpit in America" and argued for the "significance of the alliance with France" and contained "a plea for sustained American patriotism."[22] Apparently, Morris did not think it was a problem for churches to make specific political pronouncements or to support a particular political position. Furthermore, as indicated by this address, he thought it appropriate for a political figure to use churches to spread political views. The second event concerns what Jared Sparks calls a "curious clause" in a resolution "drafted by Gouverneur Morris" and sent by the New York Constitutional Convention to the Continental Congress a week after the Declaration of Independence was signed.[23] According to Theodore Roosevelt's biography of Morris, the resolution urged "some measures for expunging from the Book of Common Prayer such parts, and discontinuing in the congregations of all other denominations all such prayers, as interfere with the interests of the American cause."[24] Sparks points out the problematic nature of this suggestion when he says: "what power, despotic or liberal, in a country where every individual is allowed to worship in his own way, could expect to take cognizance of the extemporaneous prayers of all the congregations, and prescribe the words which should be used or omitted?" Sparks concludes that "[s]uch an attempt . . . would have been a greater bar to union and independence, than all the deep plots of tories, combined with the power of the English fleets and armies."[25]

What is to be made of this astonishing resolution written by Morris? Roosevelt ignores the larger question and simply says that the resolution indicates that "the Church of England men were standing by the mother country."[26] One is tempted to dismiss the resolution as a hasty, ill-conceived suggestion made in the heat of conflict; but this was an official request from a state convention to the Continental Congress. Surely it would not have been taken lightly. This resolution is mysterious, given every other indication of Morris's views on religious freedom. There is one possible explanation consistent with Morris's views. Roosevelt omits what may be a key phrase. The resolution actually suggested that the Congress consider "the propriety of" taking the measures mentioned above and then says "[i]t is a subject we are afraid to meddle with."[27] Perhaps the intent was to warn the Congress against such measures—that, in fact, makes more sense in light of the sentences which follow in Sparks's account. Perhaps Sparks said it best: it is a "curious clause."

Finally, biographers sprinkle in a few quotes here and there from Morris's diary kept while in France. He frequently made observations about the religious condition and practices of the French and, especially, reveled in criticisms of the Catholic Church. Writing to a nineteenth-century audience, Roosevelt makes greater mention of religion than Morris's other biographers. He includes several of Morris's anti-Catholic comments as well as examples of his concern over the irreligion of the French people and its debilitating effects on society. In general, the biographers of Gouverneur Morris include more coverage of religious material than would be expected in studies of the life of a man who was not overtly particularly religious.

Categorizing Morris's Religion

Scholars who study the religion of the American Founders are generally prone to error when categorizing the religious beliefs of their subjects because they adhere to a kind of false dichotomy. They try to make the key Founders fit into one of two accepted niches: Christianity or Deism. Gouverneur Morris is a classic example of a key Founder who does not fit nicely into either camp. This explains why some biographers list him as a Christian and others as a Deist. Morris exhibited some of the characteristics and beliefs of a Christian and some of a Deist. So a casual observer exposed to incomplete or convenient evidence can find support for whichever claim fits his or her preconception. Careful, in-depth study which is not bound by the assumption that there are only two possibilities leads to the discovery of a third belief system held by Morris and several key Founders: *theistic rationalism*.[28]

Theistic Rationalism vs. Deism and Christianity

Theistic rationalism was a hybrid belief system mixing elements of natural religion, Protestant Christianity, and rationalism. Theistic rationalists believed that these three elements would generally be in accord and lead to the same end, but that reason was determinative on those relatively rare occasions in which there was disagreement. Rationalism as used here is the philosophical view that regards reason as the chief source and test of knowledge. Educated in Enlightenment thought, theistic rationalists were at root rationalists, but their Christian—or loosely Christian—upbringing combined with reason to convince them that a creator God would not abandon his creation. Consequently, they rejected the absentee god of Deism and embraced a theist God of, to a significant extent, their own construction. Hence the term theistic rationalism.

An emphasis on reason had long been accepted in the Christian community, but in Christian thought, reason was a supplement to revelation, which was supreme. Theistic rationalism turned this on its head and made revelation a supplement to reason. In fact, for theistic rationalists, reason determined what should be accepted as revelation from God. Unlike Deists, theistic rationalists accepted the notion of revelation from God; unlike Christians, they felt free to pick apart the Bible and to consider only the parts that they determined to be rational as legitimate divine revelation. They similarly felt free to define God according to the dictates of their own reason and to reject Christian doctrines that to them did not seem rational.

The God of the theistic rationalists was a unitary, personal God whose controlling attribute was benevolence. Theistic rationalists believed that God was present and active in the world and in the lives of men. Consequently, they believed in the efficacy of prayer—that someone was listening and might intervene on their behalf. Theistic rationalism was not a devotional or inward-looking belief system; it was centered on public morality. God was served by living and promoting a good, moral life. The primary value of religion was the promotion of morality, and the morality generated by religion was indispensable to a free society. Since all of the religions with which they were familiar promoted morality, they held that virtually all religions were more or less equally valid and led to the same God who is called by many names. Theistic rationalists generally disdained doctrines or dogmas. They found them to be divisive, speculative, and ultimately unimportant since many roads lead to God.

Natural religion was a system of thought centered on the belief that reliable information about God is best discovered and understood by examining the evidence of nature and the laws of nature. Deism was the primary expression of natural religion in the eighteenth century. The critical elements of eighteenth-century Deist belief were the effective absence of God from the material world and the denial of any written revelation from God.[29] These two elements clearly separated theistic rationalists from Deists. In addition, Deism was in many ways as much a critique of Christianity as a religion of its own. Deist thought rejected virtually every tenet of orthodox Christianity, and Deists were generally critical of Christianity's central figure: Jesus.[30] In short, Deists wanted nothing to do with Christianity or its Christ. While theistic rationalists shared some ideas with Deists, they had a much greater regard for Christianity and for Jesus than did most Deists.

In the eighteenth century, all of the major Christian sects in America officially espoused a certain set of beliefs. Various sects added to this core of fundamental beliefs, but none subtracted from it. So, in eighteenth-century America, those who did not hold these core beliefs were not considered Christians. The fundamentals of Christianity were common knowledge to contemporaries of the period. Despite disputes over church polity and sacramental issues that resulted in a number of sects, the period saw remarkable unanimity regarding central doctrines. According to the creeds, confessions, catechisms, and articles of faith of the major denominations in America during the period, all of them shared common belief in: the Trinity, the deity of Jesus, a God active in human affairs, original sin, the Virgin Birth, the atoning work of Christ in satisfaction for man's sins, the bodily resurrection of Jesus, eternal punishment for sin, justification by faith, and the authority of the Scriptures.[31] Even the Catholic Church, though irreconcilably separated from the Protestant churches, embraced all of these fundamental doctrines, which is further evidence of the consensus concerning the substance of Christianity. Theistic rationalists shared some beliefs with Christians, but only those that seemed to them to be reasonable.

Morris's Theistic Rationalism

Theistic rationalism was a kind of mean between Christianity and Deism, and its adherents shared beliefs in common with both of those belief systems. In concert with Christians and in stark contrast to Deists, Gouverneur Morris believed in a present God who was interested and active in the affairs of nations and the lives of men. I have uncovered more than 40 references by Morris to God's activity in the world, the nation, and the lives of individuals. Although he thought the decrees of Heaven and the ways of Providence "inscrutable by man," Morris was confident that the "Almighty will work out his wise ends by the means of human folly." In fact, Morris maintained: "I know that in the order of his providence, the wisest ends frequently result from the most foolish measures. It is our duty to submit ourselves to his high dispensations." Furthermore: "In the great course of events, which divine Providence may have marked out, human wisdom can do but little."[32] On the large scale, Morris's God actively ruled over this world and the universe: "My trust is not in a President, Senate, and House of Representatives, but in Him who governs empires, the world, the universe." He concluded that "when you take occasion to pity the infirmity of human nature . . . you assail the wisdom of Providence in his moral government of the world." He urged a correspondent: "Be persuaded, that, in spite of our feeble efforts and empty vows, events in this world, and in the thousands of worlds, which roll through the regions of space, will pursue the course marked out by Omnipotence. Every inferior intelligence, the greatest as well as the least, is but an instrument in his hand."[33]

Unlike the Deists, Morris believed that God's superintendence extended beyond the mere operation of general natural laws. In 1776, he declared to the New York Congress: "Providence has kindly interfered so far for our preservation." In the midst of a warning of "distress" and "affliction" to come, Morris cautioned that "divine providence exalts or depresses states and kingdoms . . . in proportion to their obedience or disobedience of his just and holy laws." Upon observing the behavior of Europeans, he suggested "the Almighty had prepared a scourge for the abominations, which prevailed among the people" of Europe, and he acknowledged the "wisdom," "hand," and "mercy" of God on behalf of refugees.[34] In unofficial commentary on European events, Morris concluded that France had not become too powerful because "Providence had otherwise ordained"; and that two nations had suffered because "divine justice has brought disaster, distress, and disgrace" upon them. Similarly, speaking of a piece of land acquired by the United States, Morris stated that "it is joined to us by the hand of the Almighty."[35]

Morris saw the active hand of God on a national scale and on an individual scale in relation to national issues. Speaking years later of the Constitution, Morris wondered when "the period shall arrive, which Providence may have designated for the change of our organization." Ten years later, apparently believing that the "period" may have arrived, Morris said of the controversial Hartford Convention: "May the blessing of God be upon them, to inspire their councils and prosper their resolutions."[36] Whatever one thinks of the propriety of Hartford, Morris apparently believed in a God who might "inspire" men. Indeed, Morris testified that his own belief in God's presence had political significance for him. He spoke of his "reliance on the Almighty" as "an active principle of political conduct."[37] Morris also saw God's hand in national issues on the battlefield. He referred to "the God of battles" and said that victories "demand our thanks to Almighty God, by whose Providence they are ordered."[38] For him, "superior force and skill" and the power of national armies combined with "Divine direction" and "the will of God" to determine military results. But the end ultimately came down to God's providence: "I always consider Princes, and Generals, and Statesmen, as mere instruments, and generally blind instruments, in the hands of the Almighty to work out his ends."[39] God's active role in war extended to the personal level, as well. Morris believed that unjust wars were in opposition to God and that it was "impious" to support an unjust war. Speaking of the War of 1812, which he considered to be unjust, Morris said: "I firmly believe the Almighty will punish those, who voluntarily participate in its prosecution."[40]

Morris also believed that God intervenes in and, to some extent, controls individual human lives. When he decided to remain in France despite the dangers of the Reign of Terror, Morris told Jefferson that "as to Consequences they are in the Hand of God." Regarding those committing the horrors in France, Morris assured the Duchess of Orleans: "The vengeance of Heaven will, sooner or later, strike the wretches, who have escaped from human justice; and the God of peace and mercy, will, I hope, have pity on this people, pardon them, and give them at last repose and tranquillity [sic]." Indeed, Morris expected justice from God in this life. Commenting on a wife being presented with the head of her husband on a pole, Morris wrote: "Surely it is not in the usual Order of divine Providence to leave such Abominations unpunished."[41] Speaking of refugees fleeing French violence, Morris affirmed: "Oh God! it is thy wisdom which hath ordained, and thy hand which heavily hath inflicted this blow, consistent most surely with those just decrees, which we may not presume to measure, nor even dare to know, but yet we know, for we feel, that thy mercy will season to those, who suffer them, the sharpness of these afflictions."[42] Morris testified that his belief in a present, active, and benevolent God gave him a peace and confidence in difficult times. He told his mother that he looked "forward serenely to the course of events, confident that the Fountain of supreme wisdom and virtue will provide for the happiness of his creatures."[43] In a discussion of establishment of religion, Morris expressed belief that God might invade men's thoughts, as he favored "leaving to the supreme Being to influence the Thoughts as he may think proper." In a discussion of laborers in various occupations, he said that each was "in that state of life to which it has pleased God to call them."[44]

It is in matters of protection, life, death, and consolation that Morris's belief in a God present in individual lives is most apparent. He committed correspondents to "the protection of God" and petitioned God to "bless" and to "keep" and to "preserve" them. He suggested that Washington would die "when it shall please God" and couched his plans for his son with the condition "if God shall spare his life." Just before his own death, Morris said: "Sixty-four years ago it pleased the Almighty to call me into existence—here, on this spot, in this very room; and now shall I complain that he is pleased to call me hence?" Again concerning his son, a clause in Morris's will began: "If it should please God to take him away, before he arrives at full age . . ."[45] Morris mentioned several times God's role in giving and taking away. In particular, he did so in letters of consolation to mothers who lost their children. In such a letter to his mother on the death of his sister Catherine, Morris declared: "There is one Comforter, who weighs our Minutes, and numbers out our Days. It is He, who has inflicted upon us the Weight of public and private Calamities, and He best knows when to remove the Burthen." He encouraged his grieving sister to "submit with something more than patience to the high hand of heaven." He reminded her that God's will cannot be resisted, but that "His bounty is as unbounded as His power." He then identified God's will as the source of happiness "both here and hereafter" and instructed her in the proper attitude in response to God's giving and taking away. Finally, in a letter to another grieving mother, Morris assured her that God could "mitigate" her anguish and encouraged her with the belief that "his divine providence acts only according to the designs of his paternal love, both when he grants a favor and when he takes it away."[46] Morris, then, expressed belief in an active and intervening God who *loves* His children. Such an expression was completely foreign to Deist thinking.

There are a few other factors separating the beliefs and practices of Gouverneur Morris from Deism. One was his church attendance, which was regular when he was in America, though quite irregular in Europe.[47] Of course, for one who was not Catholic, church attendance options in eighteenth-century France were quite limited. Another factor distinguishing Morris from Deists was his reliance upon God for his destiny after death. As was noted above, Morris expressed belief that the will of God would be done and declared: "It is on that will, which nothing can resist, that must depend our happiness both here and hereafter." Later in life, as Morris spoke of "descend[ing] gradually towards the grave," he affirmed: "I rely on providence as well for what remains here, as for what may happen hereafter."[48] The Deist conception of the afterlife was less personal and depended not at all on any supernatural power or will, but entirely on one's own works.

Morris also had a greater appreciation for organized religion and its positive effect on society than did a Deist. Deists believed that traditional religion was superstition and that man would be better off if he could separate himself from it. Morris and the theistic rationalists, on the other hand, saw great value in the moralizing effect of religion, regardless of specifics. Despite his own disdain for Catholicism, Morris was greatly concerned by "the dismission of all the bishops and curates" in France and by the "degree of ferment [which] may be excited by the disbanding of those ecclesiastical regiments." He expressed doubts as to "whether, in crying down and even ridiculing religion, they will be able on the tottering and uncertain base of metaphysical philosophy to establish a solid edifice of morals." The "tottering and uncertain base" remark was a reference to the Deism promoted in place of Catholicism in France. Morris was scathing and sarcastic in his criticism of Deism: "I have lived to see a new religion arise. It consists in a denial of all religion, and its votaries have the superstition of not being superstitious." He further complained that the "open contempt of religion, also, cannot but be offensive to all sober minded men." Finally, in his plan for a new constitution for France, he gave culture-forming government positions to bishops and rectors.[49] As a theistic rationalist, Morris preferred significant influence by a religion he detested to a lack of religious influence.

Finally, Morris had greater respect for, and familiarity with, the Bible than did the Deists. While he never mentioned chapter and verse or that he was referencing the Bible, his writings contain about a dozen clear references to passages of Scripture. A few are humorous,[50] but most are for purposes of illustration or exhortation. For example, he used Luke 16:31 to argue that "those who will not trust the experience of history are incapable of political knowledge." He twice referred to the principle in Psalm 118:22 to suggest that someone or something that was suffering criticism could recover a good reputation or be considered successful. At various times and for various purposes, he promoted the Golden Rule (Matt. 7:12), referred to the "christian maxim" of not returning evil for good (Rom. 12:17), and affirmed "the text, that 'the wisdom of man is foolishness with God' [1 Cor. 1:25]." In order to make a point, he used 2 Kings 8:13 as an illustration, changing the text to fit his argument. Finally, he referred to a hopeful event as "a star in the east," a clear reference to Matthew 2:2.[51] Morris had respect for the Bible and took it more seriously than did Deists, but he did not go so far as to attribute infallibility to the Scriptures. According to him, only experience could "pretend to Infallibility."[52] Most people in eighteenth-century America were familiar with the Bible, but Deists typically held it up to ridicule and rarely, if ever, employed it in a favorable way. Theistic rationalists held a higher view of the Bible than did Deists, but not as high a view as was typical of Christians. Gouverneur Morris's use of the Bible reflects a theistic rationalist perspective.

Because theistic rationalism was a sort of mean between Deism and Christianity, Morris shared some beliefs with Deism, as well. Like the Deists, Morris "detested Calvinism."[53] Like the Deists, Morris and other theistic rationalists used generic "God-words" rather than specifically Christian terms for God and studiously avoided references to "Jesus" or to "Jesus Christ." As can be seen in the quotations above, Morris's favorite terms for God were "Providence" and "the Almighty."[54] Most of the other "God-words" that Morris employed emphasize the Deist triad of divine attributes: wisdom, goodness, and power. His third favorite term for God was "the Omnipotent" or "Omnipotence,"[55] which, like Almighty, focuses on power. Morris regularly emphasized God's wisdom, as well, including a reference to God as "the Fountain of supreme wisdom."[56] He also used a number of terms to emphasize God's goodness. He called God "the great Parent," "indulgent father," "Comforter," "the Giver of all good," and "Creator" and spoke of "the kindness of that Being" and of His "paternal love."[57] Morris twice used the specifically biblical (though not necessarily Christian) term "Lord of Hosts,"[58] but he also once used the classic Deist term "architect."[59] Morris used specifically Christian terminology twice, once referring to "our

Saviour" and once, in a poem, to "Christ."⁶⁰ The reference to Christ occurred when Morris was 18 and had just left King's College and its religious influence. So, Morris's terms for God reflect a Deist influence with a little fence-straddling to be expected in a theistic rationalist.

Concerning references to God, some of Morris's statements reflect a level of ambiguity concerning the personality of Providence. Generally, as can be seen above, Morris's references indicate the personal nature of Providence, including the use of personal pronouns such as "him," "his," or "whose."⁶¹ Occasionally, however, Morris suggested that Providence is not a personal being. He wrote to one correspondent that "Providence has reserved to **it**self the knowledge of what we call events" and, to another, of those "to whom Providence in **its** bounty has imparted a sincere affection for their fellow men."⁶² [Bold mine.] At times, Morris's references to Providence seem to reflect the influence of stoicism. He equated "fortune" with Providence or Heaven on at least three occasions,⁶³ equated "Circumstances" with Providence,⁶⁴ and spoke more than once of "fate" in the context of Providence.⁶⁵ Theistic rationalists were not wedded to any particular set of doctrines or dogma and, consequently, were open to numerous influences. One scholar suggests that "Morris seems not to have bestowed enough thought on religion to have worked out a consistent position" on Providence, while another concludes that he "never quite swept together" his views concerning Providence.⁶⁶ Although he may not have worked out all of the details, the frequency of personal references to God's intervention indicate that Morris did believe in the personal and particular intervention of God in human affairs.

Morris also straddled the fence, in a sense, concerning miracles. Some theistic rationalists believed in miracles and some did not, but the standard was the same: if they thought it rational that God would perform miracles, then they believed in them. If not, they did not. Morris seemed to indicate that he thought miracles to be possible, but he did not expect to see any: "The strong arm of Omnipotence can indeed upheave and overturn the foundations of empires, but we cannot prudently expect miraculous interference, and if it were not presumptuous almost to impiety, I would say it is easier to prepare the human instrument than perform the miracle." Similarly, in an essay written to convince Quakers to take up arms against the British, Morris asked: "How then can you expect that he should *miraculously* destroy our enemies, merely to convince you that he favors our cause?"⁶⁷ Morris was incredulous concerning miracles promulgated by the Catholic Church, however—he disbelieved them and found them to be foolish, deceptive mythology. He summarily declared that mythology "absurd" and "degrading to the Omnipotent." Upon being shown the site of a supposedly miraculous event by his Catholic guide in Antwerp, Morris noted that alternatives entered his "unbelieving Noddle" and that he could "very easily have explained this Miracle," but thought it unwise in the circumstances. Morris found a silver lining in the otherwise despicable and blasphemous acts done by some of the French in Notre Dame Cathedral: "The burning of legs, and arms, and grinders of saints, male and female, with relics from the wood of the original cross, must have the good effect of undeceiving those, who imagined there were miraculous qualities inherent in those crumbling materials."[68] Deists denied the possibility of miracles; while all Christians affirmed their existence and some expected them. Morris took something of a middle position, appropriate for a theistic rationalist.

Morris also shared with the Deists the priority of reason in religious matters. Like the Deists, he advocated reason as a means of understanding God and our obligations to Him. One example is that reason, using religion, "impresses a love of country upon the heart of every social being." In another case, he contended that "real Piety" suffers when a passion "gets . . . the better of Reason."[69] It is significant that, as a law clerk, Morris studied Pufendorf, who "sought to reconcile rationalism with Christianity."[70] That was the step beyond natural religion that the Deists did not take, but theistic rationalists did.

One other view that Morris shared with the Deists was support for religious toleration rooted in disdain for sects and the doctrines which distinguish them. Morris was rightly identified above as a champion of toleration. He argued that "each one has a right to entire liberty as to religious opinions, for religion is the relation between God and man; therefore it is not within the reach of human authority."[71] I contend that it was his theistic rationalist beliefs that paved the way for Morris—and for the other key Founders—to support a robust understanding of religious liberty. They could afford to grant religious freedom since they did not support the advancement of specific doctrines, they believed that the primary purpose of religion was to promote morality, and they believed that virtually all religions promote morality. Having no attachment to a particular set of doctrines, they essentially had no horse in the race. Morris's scorn for sects is evident in the following: "Each preacher holds fast to his sect, and nine out of ten . . . will insinuate, if not insist, that unless he deliver over to Satan all but their own adherents, it will require his omniscience to show that he has not broken his word." He expressed concern about "the enmities and prejudices of particular sects of religion" and feared their tendency to desire to "lay Waste the World in order to make Proselytes." This idea that religious sects cause division and, frequently, violence and war, was a standard view among theistic rationalists. Morris also expressed opposition to religious "bigotry," which, in eighteenth-century parlance, simply meant holding to particular and exclusive doctrines. Morris warned that when a country is "too bigoted, . . . Truths almost universally acknowledged appear almost like Atheism" because each sect believes their own doctrines to be necessary. Morris indicated another of his criticisms of doctrine when he distinguished between an "active principle" of conduct and "a barren tenet of religious creed."[72] Finally, Morris and the theistic rationalists believed that many or all religions lead to the same God, so each sect's unique or particular image of God is too limited or restricted. For example, upon watching a religious procession, Morris commented:

> These good Folks seem to be of Opinion that the Omnipotent can be coaxed and flattered into their Measures, but in this Idea I fear they are not singular. Voltaire's Observation is very just: *"Si le bon Dieu a fait l'homme d'apres son Image, l'homme le lui a bien rendu."* ["If the good God made man after his own image, the man has returned it well to him."][73]

Morris suggested that these worshipers were "not singular" because each sect tries to make God after their own image. It is for these reasons that Kirschke, commenting on Morris's brief sojourn in Pennsylvania, mentions that Philadelphia was religiously "particulary diverse and comparatively tolerant, qualities Gouverneur Morris no doubt appreciated."[74]

Turning to Morris's relationship to Christianity, we know that he belonged to an Episcopalian church and that he attended it regularly when in New York. Beyond that, however, there is little evidence connecting him to belief in Christianity. Of the ten fundamental doctrines of Christianity listed above, Morris only identified clearly with one of them: belief in a present, active Creator God; which is the least definitive of the doctrines. Referring to Christianity, Thomas Jefferson testified: "I know that Gouverneur Morris, who pretended to be in his secrets & believed himself to be so, has often told me that Genl. Washington believed no more of that system than he himself did."[75] It is instructive to note that, at least in his writings, Morris never claimed to be a Christian and never put forward

Christianity as a superior belief system—or even Protestant Christianity as a better religion than the Catholicism he detested. In fact, upon being told that many Dutch were converting to the Catholic faith and that, therefore, religion should not be a problem in uniting Flanders with Holland, Morris responded: "I express my Joy at this happy Circumstance and add my Opinion that the Dutch believe in God, but this is expressed with an Air of Doubt which requires farther [sic] Information." What was important to Morris was the public effect of religion, not advancement of Christian faith. On another occasion, Morris said of a Catholic: "if I should convince him of the Folly of the Faith he has held for above sixty Years, 'tis ten to one if he could now find a better and therefore it is best to leave him in Possession of his present Property."[76] Although Morris thought Catholicism to be foolishness, it served the purpose of religion in the life of this man as well as any other might.

There is another factor separating Morris from Christianity, or at least highly inconsistent with Christian faith—Morris's immoral conduct. As to reputation, when he was nominated to be minister to France, Roger Sherman is reported to have said of Morris that "with regard to moral character I consider him an irreligious and profane man." James Monroe observed: "Upon the grounds of character he was twice refused as a member of the Treasury Board." Though he publicly defended his appointment of Morris, George Washington wrote to Morris about his "imprudence of conversation and conduct" and asked him to display "more caution and prudence" and "more circumspection." A few years later, Monroe referred to Morris as "a man without morality."[77] Of course, this could have simply been a matter of political partisanship or personality conflict, but, in Morris's case, the reputation was well-earned. Morris once threatened to kill a man if he spoke disrespectfully of him, and he frequently got "very drunk" while in France.[78] His most conspicuous moral problems, however, concerned women.

Morris had numerous illicit affairs with married and unmarried women and, by his own admission, was constantly trying to initiate new ones right up to his marriage years after leaving public office. One of his earliest dalliances may have cost him one of his legs. One account of the loss of the leg, which is reported as fact by most biographers, is that it happened as a result of a cart accident. Yet there is a good chance that this was merely a cover story. There is reason to believe that Morris lost his leg jumping from a window to escape a jealous husband. John Jay joked about it in a letter of consolation to Morris, and Lord Palmerston testified that

Morris told him the whole story at breakfast a decade later. There is also circumstantial evidence surrounding the woman involved which lends credence. Morris denied the story in a letter to Jay, but not very convincingly.[79] If true, the unfortunate event did not dissuade Morris from similar activity in the future. In fact, he used the curiosity afforded by his one-legged status to attract and seduce other women.[80]

Morris's diary entries during his time in France are filled with sexual escapades. He had an ongoing affair with Madame de Flahaut for more than three years. She and Morris were eventually so "wanton and flagrant" that they engaged in intercourse "in the passage . . . at the harpsichord . . . downstairs . . . the doors are all open," and in a coach with the coachman staring straight ahead.[81] They became so shameless that they engaged in intercourse inside a convent and even tried to conceive a child while she denied her husband conjugal rights. Morris's diary contains at least eighteen references to their sexual liaisons, but Morris claimed that they had made love "several hundred" times.[82] In addition to Madame de Flahaut, Morris reported having affairs with Madame Simon, an unnamed "damsel," Madame de Lita, Madame de Crayen, Miss Matthiesen and her "young sister," Miss Gehrt, and Mrs. Perez Morton.[83] According to the diary entries, he tried to seduce—or thought of doing so—Madame de Flahaut's niece, Lady Webster, the "daughter of a Frenchman," Madame Foucault, the daughter of his landlord, Madame de Nadaillac, Madame de Fontana, and even Dolley Madison![84] Even granting the Christian belief that all men, except Jesus, sin, the extent, duration, and brazenness of Morris's immoral conduct must call into serious question the idea that he was a Christian. As the Founder of Christianity observed, a tree is known by its fruit (Matthew 7:16).

Like all theistic rationalists and most Deists, Morris believed that the primary purpose of religion is promotion of morality, and that it is therefore indispensable in a free society. Morris did not share the view of some modern jurists and scholars that there should be a high wall of separation between church and state. In an address to the New York Historical Society, Morris maintained: "There must be something more to hope than pleasure, wealth, and power. Something more to fear than poverty and pain. Something after death more terrible than death. There must be religion. When that ligament is torn, society is disjointed and its members perish." Kirschke rightly says of Morris: "national independence, he believed, required a grounding principle that religion might very well provide."[85] Speaking of such a grounding principle, Morris told Lord George Gordon: "I believe that Religion is the only solid Base of Morals and that

Morals are the only possible Support of free governments." When he constructed his own constitution for France, he built on that premise: "Religion is the only solid basis of good morals; therefore education should teach the precepts of religion, and the duties of man towards God. . . . [T]herefore provision should be made for maintaining divine worship as well as education."[86] In order to put that principle into practice, Morris's proposed system included a "first minister, a Chancellor" whose "duty is to superintend distributive justice, education, and morals." Furthermore: "In each department there shall be a Council of Education and Worship, which shall be formed by the Bishop and the Professor of the department and six Rectors . . ." in addition to a tithe collected to pay for worship.[87]

Morris had serious doubts as to whether the French would be able to "establish a solid edifice of morals" upon "the tottering and uncertain base" of Deistic philosophy. After having denounced the "utter prostration of morals" in France and the "extreme rottenness of every member" of the French body politic, he observed with incredulity that it was "from such crumbling matter that the great edifice of freedom is to be erected here." He even told the Swedish Ambassador to France that it was the "prostration of morals which unfits them [the French] for good government." For Morris and the theistic rationalists, there was a strong and direct connection between good government and maintenance of morality, with religion providing the necessary bridge. Consequently, he largely blamed the French Assembly for the immorality of the French people, saying that the Assembly had "taken from this fierce ferocious people every restraint of religion."[88] "And what end are we to look for as the result of unbridled licentiousness? History tells us of but one. Reason can discover but one. Experience proclaims that it is despotism." For free government to work, a good constitution and morality generated by religion must work together:

> I consider the Establishment of a good Constitution here as the principal Means, under divine Providence, of extending the Blessings of Freedom to the many millions of my fellow Men who groan in Bondage on the Continent of Europe. But I do not greatly indulge the flattering Illusions of Hope, because I do not yet perceive that Reformation of Morals without which Liberty is but an empty Sound.[89]

Morris applied this principle beyond France and its desperate circumstance, as well. Speaking of Prussia, he explained one reason that morality is important to government: "The destruction of religion has loosened the bonds of duty, and those of allegiance must ever be weak, where there is a defect both of piety and morality." His observations of America in the early 1800s prompted him to denounce "corruption," lack of virtue, "baseness," "relaxation of morals," and "vice." In his criticism of corruption in the Jefferson Administration, Morris offered another explanation of the negative effect that immorality has upon government: "It is to be noted that sound heads are rarely found in the company of rotten hearts. Vice corrupts alike the judgment and the will; whereby it happens that bad projects are seldom well matured." We employ religion to protect against vice and corruption, for "the object of religion is to regulate our conduct" and good men "consider themselves as moral agents accountable to God."[90]

One might wonder whether Morris considered himself a good man, given the immorality in which he indulged—particularly in France. While Morris's apparent hypocrisy lessens his credibility, his inconsistent morality might, in a sense, be consistent with his theistic rationalism. For theistic rationalists, it was public morality, or morality which impacts society, which matters. Morris may have seen his escapades as a personal matter with no societal effects, particularly in decadent France. What is clear is that Gouverneur Morris was a dynamic, but severely flawed individual. His expressed beliefs put him at odds with Deism and Christianity, but in line with theistic rationalism. The flaws in his character indicate that he relied heavily on the benevolence of the God that he recognized as being present and having great power and mercy. What is most certain is that Gouverneur Morris should not be a "forgotten" Founder. As Theodore Roosevelt concluded: "He took a most prominent part in bringing about the independence of the colonies, and afterwards in welding them into a single powerful nation. . . . With all his faults, there are few men of his generation to whom the country owes more than to Gouverneur Morris."[91]

Notes

1. Some material revised and adapted from chapters 1 and 6 of Gregg L. Frazer, *The Religious Beliefs of America's Founders: Reason, Revelation, and Revolution* (Lawrence: University Press of Kansas, 2012) with the permission of the University Press of Kansas. John E. Semonche, *Keeping the Faith: A Cultural History of the U.S. Supreme Court* (New York: Rowman & Littlefield Publishers, Inc., 1998), 27.
2. Morris to Jared Sparks, April 8, 1831, in Max Farrand, ed., *The Records of the Federal Convention of 1787* (New Haven, CT: Yale University Press, 1966), III:499.

3. Morris to Timothy Pickering, December 22, 1814, in Jared Sparks, ed., *The Life of Gouverneur Morris, With Selections From His Correspondence and Miscellaneous Papers* (Boston: Gray & Bowen, 1832), III:323.
4. Morris to William Hill Wells, February 24, 1815, in Sparks, *Life of Gouverneur Morris*, III: 339.
5. Gary L. Gregg II and Mark David Hall, eds., *America's Forgotten Founders* (Wilmington, DE: ISI Books, 2008), 5.
6. Theodore Roosevelt, *Gouverneur Morris* (Boston: Houghton, Mifflin and Co., 1898), 26; Beatrix Cary Davenport, ed., *A Diary of the French Revolution* (Boston: Houghton Mifflin Company, 1939), I: xvii.
7. James J. Kirschke, *Gouverneur Morris: Author, Statesman, and Man of the World* (New York: Thomas Dunn Books, 2005), 5, 164.
8. Richard Brookhiser, *Gentleman Revolutionary: Gouverneur Morris, the Rake Who Wrote the Constitution* (New York: Free Press, 2003), 33, 139.
9. William Howard Adams, *Gouverneur Morris: An Independent Life* (New Haven, CT: Yale University Press, 2003), 17; Howard Swiggett, *The Extraordinary Mr. Morris* (Garden City, NY: Doubleday & Co., 1952), 3.
10. Kirschke, *Gouverneur Morris*, 8–9; Adams, *Gouverneur Morris*, 17–19; Max M. Mintz, *Gouverneur Morris and the American Revolution* (Norman: University of Oklahoma Press, 1970), 16.
11. Mintz, *Gouverneur Morris*. 29.
12. Kirschke, *Gouverneur Morris*, 222.
13. See, for example, Mintz, *Gouverneur Morris*, 75; Kirschke, *Gouverneur Morris*, 28, 334 n10.
14. For examples, see Roosevelt, *Gouverneur Morris*, 34–37, 52–57; Kirschke, *Gouverneur Morris*, 22, 32–33, 61; Brookhiser, *Gentleman Revolutionary*, 32–33; Adams, *Gouverneur Morris*, 51–52; Mintz, *Gouverneur Morris*, 49–50, 75–76.
15. See, for examples, October 2, 1790 diary entry in Davenport, *Diary*, II: 9; October 7, 1790 diary entry in Davenport, *Diary*, II: 14; March 29, 1791 diary entry in Davenport, *Diary*, II: 150; October 18, 1789 diary entry in Davenport, *Diary*, I: 264.
16. Roosevelt, *Gouverneur Morris*, 35–36.
17. Morris to Peter Van Schaak, September 8, 1778, in Henry C. Van Schaak, *The Life of Peter Van Schaak* (Appleton & Company, 1842), 131; Brookhiser, *Gentleman Revolutionary*, 3; Adams, *Gouverneur Morris*, 83.
18. Kirschke, *Gouverneur Morris*, 106.
19. Adams, *Gouverneur Morris*, 148.
20. Kirschke, *Gouverneur Morris*, 06.
21. Mintz, *Gouverneur Morris*, 198; Adams, Gouverneur Morris, xii; Kirschke, *Gouverneur Morris*, 196; quoted in Kirschke, *Gouverneur Morris*, 222.
22. Kirschke, *Gouverneur Morris*, 85.
23. Sparks, *The Life of Gouverneur Morris*, I: 117.
24. Roosevelt, *Gouverneur Morris*, 52.

25. Sparks, *The Life of Gouverneur Morris*, I: 118.
26. Roosevelt, *Gouverneur Morris*, 52.
27. Sparks, *The Life of Gouverneur Morris*, I: 118.
28. In addition to Morris, other founders holding to this belief system include John Adams, Thomas Jefferson, Benjamin Franklin, George Washington, Alexander Hamilton, James Madison, and James Wilson. For a complete presentation of this concept, see Frazer, *The Religious Beliefs of America's Founders*.
29. See Kerry S. Walters, *The American Deists: Voices of Reason and Dissent in the Early Republic* (Lawrence: University Press of Kansas, 1992), 41; Harold R. Hutcheson, ed., *Lord Herbert of Cherbury's De Religione Laici* (New Haven, CT: Yale University Press, 1944), 55; E. Graham Waring, ed., *Deism and Natural Religion: A Source Book* (New York: Frederick Ungar Publishing Co., 1967), x; and especially Peter Gay, *Deism: An Anthology* (Princeton, NJ: D. Van Nostrand Co., 1968), 11–12, 42, 167–168, 176.
30. Walters, *The American Deists*, 26–33; JohnLeland, *A View of the Principal Deistical Writers* (London: W. Richardson and S. Clark, 1764), II: 360; Elihu Palmer, *Principles of Nature*, quoted in Kerry S. Walters, *Elihu Palmer's "Principles of Nature"* (Wolfeboro, NH: Longwood Academic, 1990), 35, 114–115, 231–232.
31. The major denominations and the relevant creeds or confessions were: Congregational & Presbyterian (Westminster Creed); Baptist (Philadelphia Confession); Anglican & Episcopalian (Apostles' Creed, Nicene Creed, Athanasius' Creed, 39 Articles); Lutherans & Reformed (Augsburg Confession); and Catholic (Decrees passed by the Council of Trent). While Catholics disagreed with Protestants about the sufficiency of faith for justification and the relative authority of the Bible, they agreed that justification required faith and that the Bible was God's Word.
32. Morris to William Short, 1790, in Anne Cary Morris, ed., *The Diary and Letters of Gouverneur Morris* (New York: Charles Scribner's Sons, 1888), I: 344; Morris to Joseph Kingsberry, June 22, 1815, in Sparks, *The Life of Gouverneur Morris*, III: 340; Morris to Timothy Pickering, October 17, 1814, in Sparks, *The Life of Gouverneur Morris*, III: 313; *Speech on the Free Navigation of the Mississippi River, and the Right of Deposit Within the Spanish Territories* (February 24, 1803), in Sparks, *The Life of Gouverneur Morris*, III: 434; Morris to George Washington, November 22, 1790, in Sparks, *The Life of Gouverneur Morris*, II: 51.
33. Morris to Lewis B. Sturges, February 12, 1814, in Sparks, *The Life of Gouverneur Morris*, III: 302; Morris to John Parish, February 18, 1806, in Sparks, *The Life of Gouverneur Morris*, III: 232; Morris to Madame de Damas, December 1, 1809, in Sparks, *The Life of Gouverneur Morris*, I: 494.
34. *Speech to New York Congress* (1776), in Sparks, *The Life of Gouverneur Morris*, I: 106; *An Address on the Bank of North America* (1785), in Sparks, *The Life of Gouverneur Morris*, III: 465; Morris to John Parish, July 22, 1806, in Sparks, *The Life of Gouverneur Morris*, III: 236; August 19, 1796 diary entry in Sparks, *The Life of Gouverneur Morris*, I: 435.

35. Morris to John Parish, November 12, 1806; Morris to William Meredith, January 27, 1810; *Speech on Free Navigation*, in Sparks, *The Life of Gouverneur Morris*, III: 239, 253, 432.
36. Morris to Jonathan Mason, February 20, 1804, and Morris to Timothy Pickering, December 22, 1814, in Sparks, *The Life of Gouverneur Morris*, III: 206, 324.
37. Morris to Lewis B. Sturges, February 12, 1814, in Sparks, *The Life of Gouverneur Morris*, III: 303.
38. *Speech on Free Navigation*, and Morris to Harrison Gray Otis, April 29, 1813, in Sparks, *The Life of Gouverneur Morris*, III: 433, 288.
39. Morris to David Ogden, February 11, 1814, in Anne Morris, *Diary and Letters of Gouverneur Morris*, II: 559; Morris to Rufus King, December 27, 1813, in Sparks, The Life of Gouverneur Morris, III: 299; Morris to George Washington, October 23, 1792, in Sparks, *The Life of Gouverneur Morris*, II: 229; Morris to Thomas Jefferson, October 23, 1792, in Sparks, *The Life of Gouverneur Morris*, II: 237.
40. Morris to Lewis B. Sturges, December 5, 1812; Morris to David Ogden, April 5, 1813; Morris to Egbert Benson, June 23, 1813, in Sparks, *The Life of Gouverneur Morris*, III: 275, 286, 294.
41. Morris to Jefferson, August 22, 1792, in Davenport, *Diary*, II: 533; Morris to the Duchess of Orleans, Sep. 7, (1795?), in Sparks, *The Life of Gouverneur Morris*, I: 386; October 21, 1789 diary entry in Davenport, *Diary*, I: 265–266.
42. August 19, 1796 diary entry in Sparks, *The Life of Gouverneur Morris*, I: 435.
43. Morris to his mother, April 17, 1778, in Sparks, *The Life of Gouverneur Morris*, I:158.
44. February 28, 1790 diary entry in Davenport, *Diary*, I: 430; Morris to De Witt Clinton, February 19, 1815, in Sparks, *The Life of Gouverneur Morris*, III: 336.
45. Morris to James Donatus Leray, February 22, 1794, in Sparks, *The Life of Gouverneur Morris*, II: 405; Morris to Washington, February 14, 1793, in Sparks, *The Life of Gouverneur Morris*, II:286; Morris to Washington, June 25, 1793, in Sparks, *The Life of Gouverneur Morris*, II: 335; Morris to John Parish, July 6, 1816, in Sparks, *The Life of Gouverneur Morris*, I: 495; quoted in Anne Morris, *Diary and Letters of Gouverneur Morris*, II: 602; Morris's will in Sparks, *The Life of Gouverneur Morris*, I: 505.
46. Morris to his mother, December 19, 1776, in Mintz, *Gouverneur Morris*, 127; Morris to Euphemia Ogden, June 23, 1793, in Sparks, *The Life of Gouverneur Morris*, III: 44; Morris to the Countess of Hohenthal, November 1, 1801, in Sparks, *The Life of Gouverneur Morris*, III: 155.
47. Robert C. Hartnett, "The Religion of the Founding Fathers," in R. Ernest Johnson, ed., *Wellsprings of the American Spirit*, (New York: Harper & Brothers, 1948), 59; Swiggett, *Extraordinary Mr. Morris*, 336–337; Morris to Dr. John Jones, April 18, 1789, in Sparks, *The Life of Gouverneur Morris*, II: 65.
48. Morris to Euphemia Ogden, June 23, 1793, and Morris to Madame de Damas, December 1, 1809, in Sparks, *The Life of Gouverneur Morris*, III: 44, I:494.

49. Morris to Jefferson, November 16, 1793, in Sparks, *The Life of Gouverneur Morris*, II: 381; Morris to Jefferson, October 23, 1792, in Sparks, *The Life of Gouverneur Morris*, II: 240; Morris to Lord George Gordon, June 28, 1792, in Sparks, *The Life of Gouverneur Morris*, III: 32; Morris to Jefferson, December 21, 1792, in Sparks, *The Life of Gouverneur Morris*, II: 255; *Notes On the Form of a Constitution For France* (1791?), in Sparks, *The Life of Gouverneur Morris*, III: 488.

50. See, for example, Morris to John Parish, January 14, 1803, in Sparks, *The Life of Gouverneur Morris*, III: 176–177, for the use of three biblical passages used sarcastically to make fun of Jefferson, and his June 5, 1789 diary entry in Sparks, *The Life of Gouverneur Morris*, I: 311.

51. Morris to Aaron Ogden, December 28, 1805, in Anne Morris, *Diary and Letters of Gouverneur Morris*, II: 471; Morris to John Parish, January 14, 1803, in Sparks, *The Life of Gouverneur Morris*, III: 177; Morris to John Jay, February 1, 1778, in Sparks, *The Life of Gouverneur Morris*, I: 154; *Bank of North America* address, in Sparks, *The Life of Gouverneur Morris*, III: 465; Morris to James Lovell, April 30, 1793, in Sparks, *The Life of Gouverneur Morris*, III: 43; Morris to Washington, November 12, 1788, in Sparks, *The Life of Gouverneur Morris*, I: 292; Morris to Aaron Ogden, December 28, 1805, in Anne Morris, *Diary and Letters of Gouverneur Morris*, II: 475; Morris to Timothy Pickering, December 22, 1814, in Sparks, *The Life of Gouverneur Morris*, III: 324.

52. See Anne Morris, *Diary and Letters of Gouverneur Morris*, I: 134.

53. Henry F. May, *The Enlightenment in America* (New York: Oxford University Press, 1976), 125.

54. Two other examples of his use of "the Almighty" include: October 11, 1790 diary entry in Davenport, *Diary*, II: 15, and *Observations on Government, Applicable to the Political State of France* (July, 1789), in Sparks, *The Life of Gouverneur Morris*, II: 463.

55. See, for example, October 2, 1790 diary entry in Davenport, *Diary*, II: 8; October 3, 1790 diary entry in Davenport, *Diary*, II: 12; Morris to Madame de Damas, December 1, 1809, in Sparks, *The Life of Gouverneur Morris*, I: 494; Morris to John Parish, July 22, 1806, in Sparks, *The Life of Gouverneur Morris*, III: 235; Morris to William Hill Wells, March 3, 1814, in Sparks, *The Life of Gouverneur Morris*, III: 305.

56. Morris to his mother, April 17, 1778, in Sparks, *The Life of Gouverneur Morris*, I: 158; *Observations on Government*, in Sparks, *The Life of Gouverneur Morris*, II: 463; Morris to John Parish, February 18, 1806, in Sparks, *The Life of Gouverneur Morris*, III: 232; Morris to Timothy Pickering, October 17, 1814, in Sparks, *The Life of Gouverneur Morris*, III: 313.

57. Morris to Kitty Livingston, May 24, 1772, quoted in Swiggett, *Extraordinary Mr. Morris*, 17; August 19, 1796 diary entry in Sparks, *The Life of Gouverneur Morris*, I: 435; Morris to his mother, December 19, 1776, quoted in Mintz, *Gouverneur Morris*, 127; Morris to Madame de Damas, December 1, 1809, in Sparks, *The Life*

of Gouverneur Morris, I: 494; *Observations on Government*, in Sparks, *The Life of Gouverneur Morris*, II: 469; Morris to the Countess of Hohenthal, November 1, 1801, in Sparks, *The Life of Gouverneur Morris*, III: 155.

58. Morris to Robert Morris, November 16, 1790, in Davenport, *Diary*, II: 48, and *Observations on Government*, in Sparks, *The Life of Gouverneur Morris*, II: 464.
59. Morris to John Jay, February 1, 1778, in Sparks, *The Life of Gouverneur Morris*, I: 154.
60. Morris to Washington, May 21, 1778, in Sparks, *The Life of Gouverneur Morris*, I: 167; poem quoted in Swiggett, *Extraordinary Mr. Morris*, 15.
61. Morris to Lewis Sturges, February 12, 1814, in Sparks, *The Life of Gouverneur Morris*, III: 302; essay for *The Pennsylvania Packet* (1779), quoted in Kirschke, *Gouverneur Morris*, 106; Morris to the Countess of Hohenthal, November 1, 1801, in Sparks, *The Life of Gouverneur Morris*, III: 155; Morris to Joseph Kingsberry, June 22, 1815, in Sparks, *The Life of Gouverneur Morris*, III: 340.
62. Morris to Madame de Stael, April 27, 1805, in Sparks, *The Life of Gouverneur Morris*, III: 219; Morris to Washington, September 30, 1791, in Sparks, *The Life of Gouverneur Morris*, II: 142.
63. Morris to Jefferson, October 23, 1792, in Sparks, *The Life of Gouverneur Morris*, II: 236; Morris to Robert Morris, March 27, 1794, in Sparks, *The Life of Gouverneur Morris*, III: 49; quoted in Swiggett, *Extraordinary Mr. Morris*, 232.
64. Morris to Joseph Kingsberry, December 19, 1815, in Sparks, *The Life of Gouverneur Morris*, III: 342.
65. Morris to the Countess of Hohenthal, November 1, 1801, in Sparks, *The Life of Gouverneur Morris*, III: 155; Morris to William Hill Wells, March 3, 1814, in Sparks, *The Life of Gouverneur Morris*, III: 305; *Speech on Free Navigation*, in Sparks, *The Life of Gouverneur Morris*, III: 433.
66. Hartnett, "The Religion of the Founding Fathers," 59; Brookhiser, *Gentleman Revolutionary*, 213.
67. Morris to John Parish, July 22, 1806, in Sparks, *The Life of Gouverneur Morris*, III: 235; essay for *The Pennsylvania Packet* (1779), quoted in Kirschke, *Gouverneur Morris*, 106.
68. October 2, 1790 diary entry in Davenport, *Diary*, II: 8; October 2, 1790 diary entry in Davenport, *Diary*, II: 11; Morris to Jefferson, November 16, 1793, in Sparks, *The Life of Gouverneur Morris*, II: 381.
69. Morris to Euphemia Ogden, June 23, 1793, in Sparks, *The Life of Gouverneur Morris*, III: 44; Morris to William Hill Wells, March 3, 1814, in Sparks, *The Life of Gouverneur Morris*, III: 304–305; Morris to Robert Morris, undated letter, in Davenport, *Diary*, I: xvii.
70. Mintz, *Gouverneur Morris*, 29.
71. *Notes On the Form of a Constitution For France* (1791?), in Sparks, *The Life of Gouverneur Morris*, III: 483.
72. Morris to William Hill Wells, March 3, 1814, in Sparks, *The Life of Gouverneur Morris*, III: 305; Morris to Jefferson, September 27, 1792, in Sparks, *The Life of*

Gouverneur Morris, II: 224; Morris to Lord George Gordon, June 28, 1792, in Davenport, *Diary*, II: 452; October 2, 1790 diary entry in Davenport, *Diary*, II: 9; February 28, 1790 diary entry in Davenport, *Diary*, I: 430; Morris to Lewis Sturges, February 12, 1814, in Sparks, *The Life of Gouverneur Morris*, III: 303

73. October 3, 1790 diary entry in Davenport, *Diary*, II: 12.
74. Kirschke, *Gouverneur Morris*, 115.
75. Thomas Jefferson, "The Anas," (February 1, 1800), in Paul Leicester Ford, ed., *The Works of Thomas Jefferson* (New York: G.P. Putnman's Sons, 1904), I: 353.
76. February 21, 1790 diary entry in Davenport, *Diary*, I: 418; October 2, 1790 diary entry in Davenport, *Diary*, II: 11.
77. Quoted in Swiggett, *Extraordinary Mr. Morris*, 225, 226, 331.
78. Swiggett, *Extraordinary Mr. Morris*, 192, 162, 179, 190.
79. Mintz, *Gouverneur Morris*, 235; Swiggett, *Extraordinary Mr. Morris*, 80, 220; Mintz, *Gouverneur Morris*, 141.
80. Swiggett, *Extraordinary Mr. Morris*, 182.
81. Quoted in Swiggett, *Extraordinary Mr. Morris*, 238, 179, 218.
82. Ibid., 209, 181, 183, 220, 238.
83. Ibid., 290, 297, 317, 320–323, 362.
84. Ibid., 211, 216, 222, 314, 315, 356.
85. Kirschke, *Gouverneur Morris*, 259.
86. Morris to Lord George Gordon, June 28, 1792, in Davenport, *Diary*, II: 452; *Notes On the Form of a Constitution For France* (1791?), in Sparks, *The Life of Gouverneur Morris*, III: 483.
87. *Notes* in Sparks, *The Life of Gouverneur Morris*, III: 486, 488, 489.
88. Morris to Washington, April 29, 1789, in Sparks, *The Life of Gouverneur Morris*, II: 68; quoted in Swiggett, *Extraordinary Mr. Morris*, 192; Morris to Washington, November 22, 1790, in Sparks, *The Life of Gouverneur Morris*, II: 117.
89. *Observations on Government*, in Sparks, *The Life of Gouverneur Morris*, II: 466; Morris to Thomas Pinckney, December 3, 1792, in Davenport, *Diary*, II: 581.
90. Morris to John Parish, October 25, 1804, in Sparks, *The Life of Gouverneur Morris*, III: 214; Morris to Aaron Ogden, December 28, 1805, in Anne Morris, *Diary and Letters of Gouverneur Morris*, II: 472–473; Morris to Samuel Hunt, October 3, 1806, in Anne Morris, *Diary and Letters of Gouverneur Morris*, II: 486; Morris to William Hill Wells, March 3, 1814, in Sparks, *The Life of Gouverneur Morris*, II: 305; Morris to David B. Ogden, April 5, 1813, in Sparks, *The Life of Gouverneur Morris*, III: 286.
91. Roosevelt, *Gouverneur Morris*, 317.

10

John Hancock: Congregationalist Revolutionary

Gary Scott Smith

DESPITE HIS SUBSTANTIAL contributions to American independence, John Hancock is one of the lesser-known and appreciated founders. Although he served as the first president of the Continental Congress (1775–1777), did more than any other man except Robert Morris to finance the American Revolution, presided over the Massachusetts convention that ratified the Constitution, and played a major role in the state's politics for two decades, Hancock has been overshadowed by Benjamin Franklin, George Washington, John Adams, Thomas Jefferson, James Madison, and others. As a Boston selectman, the president of the Massachusetts Provincial Congress (1774–1775), a key member of the Committee of Safety, a delegate to the Continental Congress (1775–1780, 1785–1786), the first governor of Massachusetts (serving from 1780 to 1785 and 1787 to 1793), and one of the richest merchants in the colonies, Hancock had tremendous influence. Hancock paid a large price for his support of the Revolution. He lost much of his fortune and put his life at risk, but the Patriot victory gave him great political power, international acclaim, the gratitude of many Americans, and the deep affection of most residents of Massachusetts.[1]

Today a Boston-based insurance company uses Hancock's name and occupies the most prominent building in the city, and a World War II aircraft carrier and dozens of streets bear his name, but most Americans at best know that his signature is by far the largest on the Declaration of Independence. He had no connections to the company founded in 1862 and named for him—today called John Hancock Financial Services, Inc. The enterprise chose his name because he was a famous founder, Massachusetts' first governor, and a very generous philanthropist who assisted many whose houses and businesses were destroyed by Boston's numerous fires and helped rebuild the city after the devastation of the Revolutionary War.[2]

Hancock has also usually remained on the sidelines in the debate over how to classify the religious beliefs of the founders. He has not been identified as either a devout Christian as have John Jay, Patrick Henry, John Witherspoon, Elias Boudinot, Roger Sherman, Samuel Adams, John Dickinson, Benjamin Rush, Charles Carroll, and Oliver Ellsworth or as a Deist as have Washington, John Adams, Jefferson, Franklin, Thomas Paine, and Gouverneur Morris. Neither scholars nor popularizers have paid much attention to Hancock's faith even though it strongly shaped his view of the world and his actions.[3] A lifelong member of the Brattle Street (Congregationalist) Church in Boston, Hancock was one of the nation's major founders, along with John Adams, Samuel Adams, Roger Sherman, John Witherspoon, and James Wilson, who either belonged to or pastored a Congregationalist or Presbyterian church or had a Reformed theological background. As Mark David Hall explains in Chapter 2, during the second half of the eighteenth century a sizable portion of Americans shared this religious heritage and Calvinism was a powerful force in American society and life. Like other Reformed Christians, Hancock frequently used biblical arguments to justify America's revolt against England and providentialist language to describe its battle to obtain independence. As did other Calvinist founders, Hancock also emphasized God's sovereignty, human depravity, basing government on the consent of the people, and separating and limiting governmental powers. He shared Reformed convictions that magistrates should promote the public good and the Christian faith; they should create a society grounded on biblical norms that fostered orthodox Christianity. In addition, while serving as Massachusetts' governor, he repeatedly thanked God for blessing its residents, exhorted them to repent of their sins, and strove to base his policies on his understanding of the biblical norms of justice and fairness. Convinced that moral conduct depended on Christian commitment, he supported the establishment of Congregationalism in Massachusetts and the strict observance of the Sabbath.

Hancock's Early Life

The first Hancock to migrate to America was Nathaniel, an English Puritan farmer, who arrived in Massachusetts in 1634. The future merchant's grandfather and father, both named John, were Congregationalist ministers. His grandfather, who pastored in Lexington, near Boston, was dubbed the town's "bishop" because he ruled his congregation with an iron fist. During his fifty-four–year tenure there, he baptized about one thousand individuals and added three hundred members to the church. John's father graduated from Harvard and served the Congregationalist church in North Braintree, south of Boston.[4] One of Hancock's biographers labeled his father "a modest man of laudable intentions but mediocre attainments."[5] His eulogist, by contrast, described him as a "faithful and prudent" pastor who supplied his flock with a "bright and engaging Example" of "Hospitality," "Uprightness," and "Works of Mercy."[6]

John Hancock was born in Braintree, Massachusetts, on January 23, 1737. Family members expected him to follow his grandfather and father into the ministry.[7] However, his father's death when he was seven and his adoption by his uncle Thomas Hancock, Boston's most affluent merchant, and his wife Lydia changed the course of young John's life. His uncle and aunt participated actively in and contributed generously to Brattle Street Church, where they owned a pew, and John grew up attending this church.[8]

In addition to his heritage as the grandson and son of Congregationalist ministers, Hancock received a biblically based education at Harvard. Although it included the study of rhetoric, mathematics, the natural sciences, and Greek and Enlightenment philosophers, the core of Harvard's curriculum was metaphysics, theology, and ethics. Its president during Hancock's years there was Edward Holyoke, an Old Light Congregationalist clergyman who opposed the First Great Awakening because he thought it excessively emotional and divisive. Needing the support of orthodox Calvinists who supplied much of the institution's funding, he kept the study of the Bible central to the school's educational program. As a result, Hancock gained a solid understanding of God's sovereignty, predestination, and providence from his study at Harvard.[9]

After graduating in 1754, Hancock worked as a clerk in his uncle's office. He spent 1760 in London as the representative of his uncle's firm. In 1763 Thomas made John a partner in his flourishing business, and the next year when his uncle died, Hancock inherited his company and most of his fortune. Like many other influential eighteenth-century merchants, Hancock engaged in a wide variety of enterprises: importing, exporting, warehousing, wholesaling, shipbuilding, operating ships and wharfs, managing real estate, and investment banking.[10]

Hancock's Faith and Brattle Street Church

Hancock was a long-time member and major benefactor of Brattle Street Church, Boston's most prominent congregation. Pastored from 1747 to 1783 by Samuel Cooper, its other parishioners included Samuel Adams, John and Abigail Adams, Joseph Warren, federal judge John Lowell, wealthy merchant Richard Clarke, Benjamin Franklin's sister, Jane Mecom, and James Bowdoin, governor of Massachusetts from 1785 to 1787. One-third of Boston's residents who commissioned John Singleton Copley to paint their portraits attended this church. No other Boston church could begin to match the affluence and prominence of Brattle Street's members or the status and renown of its pastor. After a conflagration destroyed a section of the city in 1760, Brattle Street parishioners contributed one-fourth of the amount Boston's seventeen churches raised to help the victims. Despite the political unrest of the early 1770s and his own financial problems, Hancock helped convince its members to build a new church and donated £1,000 to the project. Moreover, he personally selected the church's pulpit, deacons' pew, and communion table. The new building's impressive sanctuary befitted the wealth of its members and Cooper's reputation for eloquence. The names of its pastor and chief patron were inscribed on the church's cornerstone.[11]

Disagreeing with the early Puritans, Cooper preached that the common welfare was not always superior to individual interests. Self-interest and true virtue, he asserted, were not necessarily opposed. "The Glory of God and our own Happiness," Cooper argued in a frequently repeated sermon, "ought never to be set in opposition to one another." His claim that God called Christians "to pursue our own Welfare" by following the path He designated was more in tune with Adam Smith's economic theory than with John Calvin's theology.[12] Cooper insisted that merchants did not have to choose between profits and piety; they could complement one another.[13] While never repudiating the basic tenets of Calvinism, Cooper emphasized attaining peace with God and achieving personal comfort. He described Christian service as "Sweet and delightful" and declared that Christ's "Yoke is easy." Devout followers of Jesus would gain "the truest and most substantial Happiness" and attain "all the best in life." However, because New England Patriots also had to cope with natural disasters, epidemics, the French and Indian War, and revolt against England, Cooper also urged his parishioners to accept God's control of events even when it involved hardship and suffering.[14]

Charles Akers explains that in contrast to some of Boston's fiery Patriot preachers, Cooper avoided taking a political stance in the pulpit, while covertly helping to lead residents' opposition to various British measures. His "reassuring, warm spirituality," "pragmatic Calvinism," and linking of Christianity and prosperity managed to keep both Whigs and Tories satisfied and worshipping together at Brattle Street until 1775. After the small cadre of committed Loyalists left the congregation that year, Cooper openly supported the Revolution.[15] Moreover, Akers argues, Cooper assured Patriots of substantial means that in defending their material interests they were battling "for the Lord in a holy cause against a hellish foe."[16] The political gospel Cooper preached and Hancock promoted as his "chief disciple aimed to unite people of all classes and political views by a spiritual bond of mutual respect and assistance." Not surprisingly, Hancock and other wealthy Bostonians strongly approved of a minister who supplied a religious justification for their prosperity and strove to convince all social groups to support the Revolution.[17]

While defending the ethical pursuit of wealth, Cooper also urged the rich to be generous. He exhorted affluent Christians to act benevolently, to deny themselves "the Delicacies of Life" to help furnish the poor "with the Means of Subsistence."[18] More than any other Boston resident, Hancock modeled Cooper's ideal Christian benefactor. John Adams testified that before the Revolution, a thousand families depended on Hancock for "their daily bread" every day of the year.[19] As will be discussed later, the merchant assisted hundreds of Bostonians who suffered from fires, unemployment, and financial problems caused by the Revolution.

Brattle Street members played a major role in Massachusetts politics. James Bowdoin chaired the convention that in 1780 framed the state's constitution and seven of Boston's twelve delegates belonged to this congregation. After Hancock was elected Massachusetts' first governor and Samuel Adams its first lieutenant governor that year, Cooper preached the inaugural election sermon. Cooper justified America's revolt, lauded Hancock's and Adams' contribution to their nation, thanked God for France's aid, and declared that God had chosen the United States to bring "knowledge and liberty, of agriculture, commerce, and arts," and most importantly, "christian piety and virtue" to a large part of the world.[20]

Hancock's Christian commitment is evident in his frequent church attendance, practice of prayer, regular reading of the Bible, forgiveness of individuals who wronged him, and belief in an afterlife. Hancock asserted that God created people to worship Him individually and corporately, and that giving praise and thanks to the Lord were essential aspects of worship. The merchant rejoiced that "God has blest us with his glorious Light of the Gospel," which provided "Peace and Joy."[21] The merchant promised his wife and numerous friends and fellow Patriots in letters that he was praying for them. Immediately after being inaugurated as governor of Massachusetts, Hancock and his associates and friends held a service of worship at Brattle Street Church to thank God for His goodness and invoke His guidance of and assistance in their work.[22] Hancock frequently read the Bible to his son, John George Washington Hancock, and his letters and public statements testify to his familiarity with Scripture.[23] For example, he counseled his brother in 1771 "to be Steadfast & immoveable, always abounding in the Work of the Lord & then you may be assured that your Labour shall not be in vain for Time & Eternity."[24] His son was baptized at Brattle Street three days after his birth in 1778, and when he died tragically from a fall while ice skating at age nine, Hancock's faith helped sustain him.[25] The statesman forgave Samuel Adams for his many verbal attacks and efforts to thwart Hancock from obtaining political positions and even chose Adams to be his lieutenant governor. The Bostonian also forgave other merchants, such as William Bowes, who cheated him or failed to pay their bills. Hancock frequently expressed his belief in heaven. He declared, "I wish him [Bowes] no ill in the other world."[26] In resigning as governor in 1785, Hancock told members of the legislature that he hoped that they would appear in the "hereafter with characters of honor."[27] In a 1789 sermon he expressed his belief in a "higher Life beyond the Grave" and of a perfect society where the saints' "Glory and Felicity" would "never be interrupted & can never decay." Piety and "true Goodness," he promised, "will triumph at last." They should be practiced in "both Worlds": "the Life that now is, and of that which is to come."[28]

Hancock and the American Revolution

Scholars disagree about Hancock's motives for supporting American independence. While financial, political, religious, and social reasons all influenced his decision, most scholars emphasize pecuniary factors. Harlow G. Unger, for example, contends that Hancock embraced the Patriot cause to "preserve his life and property." To achieve these ends, he accepted financial losses and assumed "the role of martyr and symbol of patriot resistance."[29] Most historians or political scientists have paid little attention to

Hancock's religious arguments for why the colonists needed to separate from England.

Hancock's support of the Revolution was very likely influenced by Samuel Cooper's sermons. Like the earlier Puritans and most other Congregationalists in the second half of the eighteenth century, Cooper interpreted all events in light of God's providence. Proponents of this perspective insisted that only those who had "just motives and methods" received divine aid. The revolution could be considered righteous, Cooper asserted, only if colonies could supply "historical analogies, political theories, and religious assumptions" to justify it. This "documentation also had to prove that the conflict was unavoidable, that victory was possible, that the methods were just, and that the Patriots were morally and religiously superior combatants."[30] This was precisely the case that Hancock, Samuel Adams, John Witherspoon, Samuel Langdon, and many other Patriot leaders strove to make.

Hancock's Reformed religious and political convictions were closely intertwined and strongly influenced his decision to side with the Patriots. Like other Calvinists, he insisted that unrestrained political power greatly threatened individual liberty. This led him to insist that power must be limited, which was best achieved through creating a representative government and motivating citizens to be vigilant.[31]

In his 1774 Boston Massacre Oration, Hancock declared that government existed to provide security for citizens and their property. Therefore, it was neither virtuous nor honorable to support a government which did not make this its "principal basis." "I am a friend," he continued, of a "righteous government . . . founded upon the principles of reason and justice," but an enemy of despotism. He denounced the British government as tyrannical because it did not respect "the security of the persons or properties of the inhabitants of the Colonies." The British had imposed taxes on the colonists without their consent and sent fleets and armies to enforce their unjust policies. Troops had crossed the Atlantic "not to engage an enemy, but to assist a band of traitors in trampling on the rights and liberties" of George III's "loyal subjects in America," "to enforce obedience to acts of the British Parliament, which neither God nor man ever empowered them to make."[32]

Accepting the Patriot version of the Boston "massacre," Hancock urged Americans to pray together to God that "the inhuman, unprovoked murders of the fifth of March, 1770" had no parallel in history. While he blamed British soldiers for planning and executing this horrific act, he attributed ultimate responsibility to the Devil. For "a dreadful moment," God permitted Satan "to take the reins" and to "sacrilegiously" pollute "our land with the dead bodies" of New England's "guiltless sons." Not only did these troops "violate our civil rights," Hancock protested, they tried to prevent colonists from enjoying their "religious privileges" and to pervert their morals. Their noisy clamor disrupted the "solemn devotions" in churches on the Sabbath, the "day hallowed by heaven, and set apart by God himself for his peculiar worship." British troops promoted "idleness and luxury," leading youth into "extravagance and effeminacy," and "infamy and ruin" and causing reverence for religion to decline. Hancock expected "the same kind Providence which has watched over this country from her infant state" to "enable us to defeat our enemies."[33]

Like many other Reformed Christians who supported the American Revolution, Hancock contended that Americans' opposition to and defeat of one of the world's "most potent Kingdoms" was "the Lord's Doing." The British were so determined to force the colonists into "an absolute & unlimited Subjection" that colonists "were obliged to draw the Sword in our own Defense, and appeal to Heaven." Americans did not "ambitiously aspire" to be "a distinct Nation"; they were driven to declaring independence by Britain's "haughty and relentless Power." The Patriots were forced to do so to attain their "valuable Rights" as both human beings and "Members of civil Society."[34]

As did numerous other members of Congress with substantial wealth, Hancock contributed large sums of money to help finance the Revolution. He spent thousands of pounds on arms and ammunition, and he loaned money to the Patriot cause to help purchase other essential supplies. In addition, two of Hancock's houses and one of his ships were destroyed, his seven tenement buildings near Mill Creek were reduced to rubble, and several of his stores at his wharf were burned to the ground. Strapped for cash and preoccupied with his political roles, he did not invest in privateers or confiscate Loyalists' property despite amble opportunity to do so. While some other wealthy Patriots profited greatly from the war, Hancock lost much of his personal fortune, one of the largest any colonial American possessed.[35] Therefore, if Hancock's principal motive for supporting the Revolution was economic gain, he failed miserably as he had far fewer assets after the war than before it.[36] Hancock sacrificed a significant part of his fortune to support the Revolution. While many other affluent Americans used "their influence to make money in shady schemes," Hancock refused to do so.[37]

Hancock's Providentialism

As previously discussed, Hancock, like many other founders, especially Reformed Christians, repeatedly acknowledged and celebrated God's sovereignty and providential control of history. In both personal letters and public proclamations, he affirmed his belief that God controlled all events. Hancock thanked God for healing illnesses and providing safe travel, and often invoked God's blessing on family, friends, and associates.[38] In 1771 he wrote his brother, "that God may bless your future endeavors is . . . [my] sincerest wish."[39] He ended a 1779 letter to George Washington: "May God Almighty shield you in every Danger."[40] Over and over, he declared that God ruled over nations and determined events. Hancock warned in a 1765 letter that unless God caused the Stamp Act to be repealed "we are a gone people."[41] In calling for *"A Day of Fasting, Humiliation and Prayer"* in April 1775, he asserted that God ruled the universe and without His "blessing, the best human counsels are but foolishness." He entreated Americans to "humble themselves before God," confess their sins that had evoked God's "heavy judgments," and implore His forgiveness. He also urged them to pray that the rulers and residents of Great Britain would discern what they needed to do to re-establish peace in the colonies, redress American grievances, and restore all their "invaded liberties."[42]

Hancock's Reformed convictions led him to insist that God ruled the universe and that His justice would ultimately triumph. The soldiers who murdered Boston civilians in March 1770 and received either no or only minor punishment would someday have to answer for their actions "at the tremendous bar of God!"[43] Hancock counseled colonists to "humbly commit" their "righteous cause to the great Lord of the Universe" who loved righteousness and hated iniquity. They should faithfully do their duty and trust the One "who raiseth up and pulleth down the empires and kingdoms of the world as he pleases." They should cheerfully submit to "his sovereign will and devoutly say": "'Although the fig tree shall not blossom, neither shall fruit be in the vines; the labor of the olive shall fail, and the field shall yield no meat; the flock shall be cut off from the fold, and there shall be no herd in the stalls; yet we will rejoice in the Lord, we will joy in the God of our salvation'" (Hab. 3: 17).[44]

In numerous statements as president of the Congress and governor of Massachusetts, Hancock reminded Americans that God was sovereign over earthly affairs and sought to reassure them of His blessings. Writing to the leaders of the Continental Army in March 1776, Hancock asserted that the same God who had baffled the British attempt to conquer

Massachusetts would defeat their "deep-laid scheme" against other colonies.[45] In an appeal to all the states in September 1776, he declared that members of Congress relied firmly "on Heaven for the justice of our cause." "I am persuaded," he added, that "under the gracious smiles of Providence, assisted by our own most strenuous endeavors, we shall finally succeed...."[46] In his inaugural address as governor in 1780, Hancock praised God for "the peaceable and auspicious" adoption of a state constitution. "May the Supreme Ruler of the world," he continued, "establish and perpetuate these new foundations of liberty and glory" and complete the "deliverance of our country."[47] In 1782, Hancock assured members of the Massachusetts legislature that "the favor of Heaven" would eventually establish America's righteous claims.[48] Shortly after members of Congress signed the Treaty of Paris with Britain the next year, Hancock praised God for His "uncommon favour" to the United States. "Divine Providence," he rejoiced, "has most kindly put into the hands of these States the means of our political happiness."[49] Hancock's Thanksgiving proclamation that fall celebrated God's gracious intervention on behalf of the Patriot cause. He exhorted citizens to express their gratitude for God's numerous blessings and to recognize their "entire Dependence" on "His Goodness and Bounty."[50] In 1785, Hancock contended that God's favor had exalted the United States above other nations. He beseeched "the Supreme Ruler of Nations" to take America "under his Holy Protection" and "direct and prosper" its federal and state governments.[51] Speaking to the Massachusetts legislature in 1788, Hancock proclaimed that God raised up and pulled down earthly governments "according to his Sovereign Pleasure." He praised God for giving Americans "a rich & extensive Country," "a name & a standing among the Nations of the World," and "external peace, & internal tranquility."[52] In 1790, Hancock exhorted the residents of Massachusetts to work diligently to "possess this good land which God" gave "our forefathers." He urged them to remember that God had supported them in many trials and delivered them from many dangers. They should celebrate His goodness in giving Americans "success & victory," making them "an Independent & prosperous Nation," and enabling them to establish smoothly functioning "Political & Civil institutions." Because "obedience to the divine will is the best expression of gratitude," he called for "a true spirit of piety & virtue [to] be every where seen & encouraged."[53] In another Thanksgiving Proclamation, the governor declared, "we ... offer up fervent Supplications [to God] ... to cause pure Religion and Virtue to flourish ... and to fill the World with his Glory."[54]

In his 1787 Thanksgiving Proclamation, Hancock declared that the "manifold Bounties" Americans were "constantly receiving at the Hands of Almighty GOD, ought ever to remind us of our dependence upon, and obligations to Him." He urged people to pray fervently "to the Great Governour of the World" that "He would continue His gracious Providence over us," that He would direct the state government, insure civil and religious liberties, guide the delegates who would be selected to the convention to consider the newly framed national constitution, and cause "Peace and Concord, Truth and Justice, Benevolence and undefiled Religion" to "universally prevail."[55]

Unlike those of presidents, Hancock's proclamations as governor of Massachusetts not only thanked God for His blessings and implored Him to guide the government; they also acknowledged the Lordship of Jesus Christ and rejoiced that His gospel was advancing on earth. In his 1790 Thanksgiving Proclamation, for example, Hancock expressed his hope that the "benign Religion of our Lord and Savior Jesus Christ" would "be known, understood, and practiced among all the Inhabitants of the Earth."[56] His 1791 proclamation praised God for the greatest and "most important Blessing" Americans enjoyed—"the Gospel of Jesus Christ." Moreover, it urged citizens to "bow to the Scepter of our LORD JESUS CHRIST" so that "the whole Earth [would] be filled with his Glory."[57] In other proclamations, Hancock beseeched residents of the state "to confess their Sins before God and implore His forgiveness through the Merits and Mediation of Jesus Christ, our Lord and Savior."[58] He expressed his hope that "the *spiritual* Kingdom of our Lord and Savior Jesus Christ" would continually increase, that God would overrule all the obstacles that hindered the spread of "the true Religion of our Lord Jesus Christ in its Purity and Power among all the People of the Earth," and that "the Kingdom of our Lord and Savior Jesus Christ" would "be established in Peace and Righteousness among all the Nations of the Earth."[59]

Hancock and Public Support for Christianity and Policies as Governor

Like almost all the founders, Hancock believed that religion was indispensable to morality, and like many of them, including most fellow Reformed Christians, he favored public support of Christianity. The existence of republics and the happiness of their citizens, he avowed, depended on their "public institutions of religion."⁶⁰ Because "Christian piety and virtue" were essential to the stability and success of a state, Governor Hancock urged the Massachusetts legislature to support every measure that did not infringe on individuals' rights of conscience.⁶¹ He repeatedly asked representatives to fund "teachers of religion and morality."⁶² Children who did not have "a regular gospel Ministry" and proper Christian schools were in danger of not possessing the "Ideas, habits and abilities" they needed to be "good and useful Citizens."⁶³ Hancock also exhorted legislators to pass laws that promoted "truth, integrity & every moral virtue," encouraged citizens to revere Christianity and respect virtue, and helped guard people's hearts against corruption and depravity (including laws prohibiting "lewdness, intemperance, gambling, idleness, levity & dissipation of manners").⁶⁴

Hancock emphasized that "Righteousness ... exalteth a Nation" (Prov. 14: 34). Recognizing their "Dependence upon him who builds or destroys the Nations of the Earth according to his sovereign Pleasure," Americans must strive to act righteously.⁶⁵ He rejoiced that Harvard's graduates who entered politics, the military, and commerce, "by their precepts and example," honored "our holy religion" and laid "a foundation for the practice of the purest morals and patriotism."⁶⁶ As did John Winthrop, Hancock claimed that because "the Eyes of all the World are upon us" Americans must "establish a fair & honourable National Character."⁶⁷ Hancock strongly supported republicanism and insisted that government must insure justice in society. "All citizens," he declared, "have an equal right to elect, & to be elected to office."⁶⁸ "It is our duty to Enact wise Laws, & to make ample provision for an equal & regular distribution of Justice."⁶⁹

Like his fellow Reformed Christians, Hancock also supported state laws that mandated strict observance of the Sabbath. Proper "observation of the Lord's Day," he argued, was not only important to religion, "but greatly conducive to the order and benefit of civil society." The cessation of business, politics, and other daily activities reminded people that they were accountable "to the great Lord of all." The civil government should support all measures consistent with "reasonable personal liberty" to promote worship, rest, and meditation on the Sabbath.⁷⁰ The Massachusetts legislature responded to Hancock's request for stringent observance of the Sabbath by passing a law that fined residents who did not attend church for three consecutive months.⁷¹

As governor, Hancock displayed compassion and concern for ordinary citizens by convincing the state's General Court to grant full pardons to all those who had participated in Shay's Rebellion, an armed rebellion of mostly poor farmers in central and western Massachusetts in 1786–1787. Angered by high taxes and their large debts, several thousand men tried to prevent the courts from seizing their property by forcing them to close. Hancock pushed bills through the state legislature that prohibited "creditors from seizing clothing, household goods, or tools of trade as security for debt." He also denounced seizing men's tools and putting them in jail for failure to pay their debts as self-defeating practices. Finally, he cut government spending to reduce taxes, and to set a good example he decreased his own salary by £300.[72]

Hancock's Christian convictions also influenced his opposition as governor to slavery, state lotteries, and brutal punishments of criminals. In 1783 South Carolina demanded that Massachusetts return nine slaves who had been captured by a Boston-based privateer and spent four years in Massachusetts after a British ship had taken them from South Carolina in 1779. Hancock refused to do so, and Massachusetts courts ruled in his favor and released them from jail where they had recently been confined pending the outcome of South Carolina's plea because they had committed no crime in the state.[73]

In 1791, Governor Hancock informed the Massachusetts Assembly that he would veto any bills to use a lottery to raise revenue. Sadly, Massachusetts had frequently employed this "pernicious practice" instead of collecting taxes to fund its activities. Lotteries, Hancock protested, were "a very unequal tax upon the People at large" because the poor were the most likely to squander their money trying to get rich through such enterprises.[74] Two years later he urged the legislature to end "cropping and branding, as well as . . . the Public Whipping Post," which he denounced as "an indignity to human nature." Sentencing offenders to "hard labour" was likely to "have a more salutary effect than mutilating or lacerating the human body." Hancock also implored the state to end capital punishment for burglary. "Degrees of guilt," he asserted, "demand degrees of Punishment in order to maintain the equity of the Government."[75]

Business Ethics, Lavish Living, and Philanthropy

In addition to disagreeing about Hancock's motives for supporting American independence, scholars also differ about whether Hancock and his uncle Thomas followed ethical practices in their business. Unger argues that like colonial merchants they "mercilessly manipulated markets," "extracted every penny they could" from suppliers and customers, and "smuggled and bribed customs inspectors to avoid paying import duties." The Hancocks made more money than other merchants because they were "more daring, more willing to take risks, and sometimes more clever at analyzing market conditions and minimizing those risks."[76] William Baxter also accuses Thomas and John Hancock of smuggling.[77] On the other hand, O. M. Dickerson claims that charges that Hancock was a smuggler rest upon accepting the false charges of British officials. In reality, the British persecuted and mistreated Hancock more than any other American. He simply "stood his ground" and "insisted upon his legal rights." Hancock was "a tested patriot" who made great sacrifices for the "common cause, not a smuggler who used the popular agitation to make personal profits."[78] The case for whether Hancock smuggled is complex and depends on how smuggling is defined and whose testimony is accepted as valid. Dickerson admitted that Hancock's sloop Liberty, which was seized by the British in 1768, had technically violated the provisions of the Navigation Acts, but he argued that so had every other ship in Boston harbor at the time. Dickerson claimed that the testimony of Thomas Kirk, an employee of the custom service, which many historians have used to indict Hancock for smuggling, was unreliable and motivated by personal interest. Moreover, the charges against Hancock were eventually dropped. On the other hand, Baxter maintained that Hancock shrewdly evaded various British taxes on trade. While admitting that smuggling typically required "bribery, perjury and other unsavory means," Baxter contended that smuggling improved the welfare of Bostonians and other Americans and was a form of civil disobedience against misguided laws that inhibited economic development and prosperity.[79]

Hancock has also been greatly criticized both in his own era and by later biographers for his luxurious lifestyle, which exceeded that of any other founder. Unger contends that Hancock relished and reveled in wealth.[80] He lived in a lavishly furnished Boston mansion, ate sumptuous meals, wore elegant clothes, hosted expensive parties, loved pomp and circumstances, and rode around the city and from Boston to Philadelphia for meetings of the Continental Congress in a golden coach pulled by four white horses. While most leaders lived more modestly during the Revolutionary era and downplayed their differences with other Americans, Hancock continued to live as extravagantly as circumstances permitted. One critic complained in 1778 that Hancock appeared in public "with all the state and pageantry of an Oriental prince" riding "in an elegant chariot."[81] A commitment to republican virtue and simplicity led some other leaders, most notably Samuel Adams and James Warren, to denounce the merchant's lifestyle as profligate and his entertainments as excessive.[82]

While Hancock's lifestyle was more luxurious than any other American, he was one of the colonies' and nation's greatest philanthropists. Influenced by his uncle, who gave liberally to Boston's residents and taught his younger partner the importance of civic responsibility, and his pastor's sermons, Hancock greatly aided the city's needy.[83] Many of his speeches while he was governor exhorted the wealthy to assist widows and orphans. In a 1789 sermon, for example, Hancock proclaimed that God's goodness should inspire Christians to promote justice and provide charity for their fellow citizens and those who belonged to the "Household of Faith." While enjoying their abundance, which was God's undeserved gift, the rich must never forget the poor. Those who were warm, well fed, and comfortable must assist others who lived in deplorable conditions, especially "the Widow [who] weeps; the Orphan [who] cries for Bread; and the whole Family [which] pines with hunger, & shivers with Cold." He prayed that God would inspire Americans to act justly and charitably to lessen the inequalities the Revolution had produced and to soften "Distress where it falls heavy."[84] As governor, he argued that the Bible required magistrates to protect widows and orphans and continually implored the state legislature to supply relief to these groups.[85]

While urging the state and private citizens to help the needy, Hancock set a very positive example. He financially assisted his brother Ebenezer, his mother, and his sister.[86] The merchant helped numerous people to establish their own businesses; during Boston's harsh winters he furnished the destitute with food and firewood; he helped rebuild neighborhoods destroyed by fires; he took care of many widows and orphans and enabled some indigent youth to attend college; he purchased the city's first fire engine; he paid for a concert hall; and at his own expense he maintained Boston's marvelous Common.[87] Hancock often rode throughout the city looking for underprivileged people who needed assistance. In addition to giving food, firewood, and free rent to the impoverished, he contributed substantially to many of Boston's churches, providing free seats, Bibles, and money for poor parishioners and paying for window glass, pulpits, and Communion tables. Ministers frequently lauded his generosity in their sermons, and he developed a reputation as Boston's principal patron who cared deeply for his community and its residents. He supported the children of Joseph Warren, who died at the Battle of Bunker Hill, and frequently loaned money to friends and even political adversaries, including Samuel Adams. Hancock also assisted the families of numerous men who fought in the Revolutionary War.[88] Furthermore, he gave generously to the needy who lived in Jamaica Plains, south of Boston, where he vacationed in the summers.[89] While critics accuse him of political paternalism and point out that such acts brought Hancock substantial applause and many votes, he appeared to be motivated in large part by his Christian convictions and his genuine concern for the welfare of others.[90]

In his funeral sermon, Peter Thacher, Samuel Cooper's successor at Brattle Street Church, declared that no person in America had "done more generous and noble actions" or "contributed more liberally to public institutions" than Hancock. Moreover, "his acts of [private] charity ... were numerous and constant." "The poor, the widow, the fatherless, the unhappy debtor, the prisoner, [and] the decayed gentleman, all experienced his bounty." He gave away "astonishing" sums and "his generosity was proverbial."[91]

A Final Assessment

Hancock was widely lauded in his own era. In November 1790 the *Boston Gazette* proclaimed:

> *Seraphs his brows around with laurels grace,*
> *At God's Right Hand he'll take the sacred place,*
> *For Deeds so Generous and deserv'd Renown,*
> *Thy Worth Oh Hancock claims a heav'nly Crown.*[92]

In his 1790 election sermon, Daniel Foster, the pastor of a Congregationalist church near Boston, praised the governor for his "ardent love" of his country, "indefatigable labor" on its behalf, and the many alms he had "distributed to the poor and needy." Although God had deprived Hancock of a son to continue his name, He had given him a name that was "better than that of many sons," which virtuous Republicans would always remember. Foster extolled the merchant's service to America and his state as well as his "good disposition, and uncommon abilities."[93] Akers maintains that the vast majority of Massachusetts voters repeatedly elected Hancock to office because of their "deep sense of gratitude" for his decisive role in the Revolution and his personification of "republican ideals."[94]

After Hancock died in 1793, more than twenty thousand people from the Boston area participated in America's "largest, most glorious, most sumptuous funeral procession" to date, testifying to their affection for Hancock and gratitude for his many political and financial contributions to their welfare.[95] Although John Adams had long been a political adversary of Hancock, in an 1812 letter he declared, "I could melt into tears when I hear his name. . . . If benevolence, charity, generosity were ever personified in North America, they were in John Hancock." He acknowledged the merchant's "sufferings and sacrifices" and praised his military, civil, and political services to his nation.[96]

John Hancock's contributions to American independence and the political foundation and success of the new nation were monumental. As the president of the Continental Congress for two-and-a-half grueling years, he fairly and winsomely mediated between various factions and helped convince them to work together for the good of the cause. When competing interests threatened to tear the fledgling country apart, Hancock supplied a symbol of stability, moderation, and compromise that helped Americans elevate their mutual goals above their selfish desires.[97] In both Congress and the state of Massachusetts, he served as "the centre of union" around which a majority of citizens were able to coalesce.[98] His effective leadership as president of the Continental Congress kept many delegates from deserting and shattering the unity essential to winning the war against Britain.[99] Moreover, during the war his "desk was the central command post for the entire Continental Army," and he functioned as a liaison between Washington, other military leaders, and Congress. Hancock oversaw the purchase, assembly, and shipment of the money, weapons, and ammunition that Congress approved for the army.[100] He guided delegates through numerous crises, including resolving their fifteen-month debate over the Articles of Confederation. As governor, Hancock helped persuade the Massachusetts constitutional convention to support the Bill of Rights, contributing to its passage.[101] Although John Adams opposed his election as president of the Congress, he later testified that Hancock "was radically generous and benevolent" and that his talents "were far superior to many who have been much more celebrated."[102]

While Hancock did not possess Washington's character, John Adams' intellect, or Jefferson's eloquence, he played the principal role in Massachusetts politics for almost a quarter of a century and did much to attain and preserve American independence.[103] Although the merchant prince wrote little about the philosophy of government, his flexible, adaptable style enabled him to govern effectively.[104] Contemporary scholars have both effusively praised and sharply criticized Hancock's character and actions. Speaking for most of them, Unger argues that the merchant was both "haughty and humble, vain and meek, petulant and composed, selfish and generous, garish and modest, pompous and retiring, aloof and deeply loving and caring."[105] Paul Brandes contends that even most of Hancock's admirers were usually troubled by the fact that "he almost always won" and "did not seem to be damaged by actions that would have subjected others to ridicule."[106] Although Hancock's vanity, lavish lifestyle, some of his business practices, and some of his motives for supporting the Revolution conflicted with Christian principles, his faith appeared to be genuine and helped motivate his sacrifices for his nation, his political philosophy and service, and his concern for the poor and needy and generous gifts to individuals and Boston. Many of his letters, speeches, relationships, and actions testify to his commitment to Reformed Christianity. Despite his flaws, Charles Akers' assessment rings true, "For many of his countrymen he personified American virtue as a man of great wealth but of greater public spirit and Christian patriotism."[107]

Notes

1. Harlow Giles Unger, *John Hancock: Merchant King and American Patriot* (New York: John Wiley & Sons, 2000), 3.
2. Unger, *John Hancock*, 337.
3. David Holmes does not mention Hancock in *The Faiths of the Founding Fathers* (New York: Oxford University Press, 2006). Both Frank Lambert, *The Founding Fathers and the Place of Religion in America* (Princeton, NJ: Princeton University Press, 2003), 167, and Brooke Allen, *Moral Minority: Our Skeptical Founding Fathers* (Chicago: Ivan R. Dee, 2006), 179, only state that Hancock, along with several other founders, graduated from Harvard. James H. Hutson, *Forgotten Features of the Founding: The Recovery of Religious Themes in the Early American Republic* (Lanham, MD: Lexington Books, 2003), makes only two incidental references to Hancock. Hancock is also not included in Alf J. Mapp, Jr., *The Faiths of Our Founders: What America's Founders Really Believed* (Lanham, MD: Rowman and Littlefield, 2003) or profiled in MichaelNovak, *On Two Wings: Humble Faith and Common Sense at the American Founding* (San Francisco: Encounter books, 2002). Steven Waldman, *Founding Faith: Providence, Politics, and the Birth of Religious Freedom in America* (New York: Random House, 2008), is one of the few scholars who labels Hancock an "orthodox Christian" (192). Tim LaHaye, *Faith*

of Our Founding Fathers (Brentwood, TN: Wolgemuth and Hyatt, 1987), does not discuss Hancock, and his chapter titled "Outstanding Christians among the Founding Fathers" includes sixteen men. David Barton, *Original Intent: The Courts, the Constitution, and Religion* (Aledo, TX: WallBuilder Press, 1997), does not mention Hancock in his chapter titled "The Religious Nature of the Founding Fathers" in which he discusses more than 60 founders. Nor does he refer to Hancock in *America's Godly Heritage* (Aledo, TX: WallBuilder Press, 1993). John Eidsmoe, *Christianity and the Constitution: The Faith of Our Founding Fathers* (Grand Rapids, MI: Baker Book House, 1987), lists such luminaries as George Washington and Alexander Hamilton as "strongly Christian" and Gouveneur Morris and John Adams as "probably Christian," while ignoring Hancock altogether. While several biographers note Hancock's religious background and Christian commitments and quote speeches with religious themes and biblical allusions, no one has written about his faith at any length.

4. Herbert S. Allan, *John Hancock: Patriot in Purple* (New York: MacMillan, 1948), 20.
5. Allan, *John Hancock*, 22.
6. Ebenezer Gay, *The Untimely Death of a Man of God Lamented. In a Sermon Preach'd at the Funeral of the Reverend Mr. John Hancock, Pastor of the First Church of Christ in Braintree; Who Died May 7, 1744* (Boston 1744), 18, 19, 24, 25.
7. Unger, *John Hancock*, 9–10.
8. Unger, *John Hancock*, 49. In addition, Hancock left £700 in his will to the Society for Propagating Christianity to help fund its missions to Indians (67).
9. Unger, *John Hancock*, 42; Lorenzo Sears, *John Hancock, The Picturesque Patriot* (1912; reprint, Boston: Gregg Press, 1972), 37; Allan, *John Hancock*, 39.
10. Unger, *John Hancock*, 2, 16.
11. Charles W. Akers, *The Divine Politician: Samuel Cooper and the American Revolution in Boston* (Boston: Northeastern University Press, 1982), 128–131, 26. See also William Fowler, *The Baron of Beacon Hill: A Biography of John Hancock* (Boston: Houghton Mifflin, 1980), 143; Sears, *John Hancock*, 333. Akers adds that by 1763 a quarter of Boston's merchants attended Brattle Street. Of the one hundred residents of the city "with the highest real estate assessments, twenty-seven attended Brattle Street, as did twenty-four of the one hundred merchants with the highest assessments on their trading stocks." See Charles W. Akers, "Religion and the American Revolution: Samuel Cooper and the Brattle Street Church," *The William and Mary Quarterly*, 3rd series, 35: 3 (July 1978), 481.
12. Akers, *The Divine Politician*, 27 (first quotation); Akers, "Religion and the American Revolution," 483 (second quotation). See, for example, Cooper's Sermon on Psalm 40:8, March 22, 1759, Samuel Cooper Papers, Henry E. Huntington Library, San Marino, CA.
13. Cooper, Sermon on Psalm 40:8, March 22, 1759, as cited in Akers, *The Divine Politician*, 27–28.

14. Akers, "Religion and the American Revolution," 483; Akers, *The Divine Politician*, 22. Akers notes that "these conclusions are based on a study of Cooper's manuscript sermons. The Cooper Papers contains [sic] 146 sermons, and the New York Public Library, New York City, has 32." See particularly these sermons: Mt. 3: 12 (December 1756), and 1 John 5: 4 (January 1768), at the N.Y. Pub. Lib.; Heb. 3: 12 (September 1758), Mt. 11: 30 (February 1746), Rev. 14: 13 (April 1749), Ps. 18: 46 (February 1750), 1 Pet. 5: 8 (February 1762), Mt. 26: 42 (January 22, 1764), Ps. 26: 3 (January 29, 1749), 2 Pet.1: 10 (October 1765), and Col. 1: 21–22 (n. d.), Cooper Papers. Akers does not identify the specific sources of the quotations.

15. Akers, "Religion and the American Revolution," 478.

16. Ibid., 487.

17. Ibid., 498. John Buchanan argues that "to substantiate the justice of the American cause and its potential for success, Cooper combined the strands of politics and religion. He wove a pattern from Whig theory and Puritan theology which was designed to explain the course of contemporary history and to direct the conduct of men." See John G. Buchanan, "The Justice of America's Cause: Revolutionary Rhetoric in the Sermons of Samuel Cooper," *The New England Quarterly* 50: 1 (March 1977), 124.

18. Samuel Cooper, *A Sermon Preached in Boston, New-England, Before the Society for Encouraging Industry, and Employing the Poor*, August 8, 1753 (Boston, 1753), 3–8; Cooper, Sermon on Mt. 11: March 5, 1754, Cooper Papers as quoted in Akers, "Religion and the American Revolution," 484.

19. Akers, "Religion and the American Revolution," 484; Charles Francis Adams, ed., *The Works of John Adams, Second President of the United States. With a Life of the Author*, 10 vols. (Boston: Little, Brown, and Co., 1856), 10: 260.

20. Akers, "Religion and the American Revolution," 494–495; Samuel Cooper, *A Sermon Preached before His Excellency John Hancock, Esq, Governour* . . . (Boston, 1780), 52.

21. John Hancock, sermon, November 26, 1789, in Paul D. Brandes, *John Hancock's Life and Speeches: A Personalized Vision of the American Revolution, 1763–1793* (Lanham, MD: Scarecrow Press, 1996), 346, 353; quotation from 353. Scholars have been unable to determine where Hancock preached this sermon. It is one of the few extant speeches in his own handwriting. It may have been delivered at Brattle Street Church. It is housed in the J. Pierpont Morgan Library in New York (347).

22. Worthington Chauncey Ford, ed., *Journals of the Continental Congress, 1774–1789*, 34 vols. (Washington, DC: US GPO, 1904–1937), 9: 839.

23. Unger, *John Hancock*, 306; Brandes, *Hancock's Life and Speeches*, 180.

24. JH to Ebenezer Hancock, January 11, 1771, Boston Public Library, quoted in Unger, *John Hancock*, 152.

25. *Records of the Church in Brattle Square* (Boston: The Benevolent Fraternity of Churches, 1902), 190; Fowler, *The Baron of Beacon Hill*, 229; Unger, *John Hancock*, 267, 309–310.

26. Frederick Wagner, *Patriot's Choice: The Story of John Hancock* (New York: Dodd, Mead & Co., 1964), 162; JH to Captain James Scott, November 14, 1783, in Abram English Brown, *John Hancock, His Book* (Boston: Lee & Shepherd, 1898), 235.
27. *Journal of the House*, MA, 5, February 24, 1785 (February 18, 1785, resignation address as MA governor), in Brandes, *Hancock's Life and Speeches*, 294.
28. Hancock, Sermon, in Brandes, *Hancock's Life and Speeches*, 353–354; first three quotations from 353, remainder from 354.
29. Unger, *John Hancock*, 104, 122; quotations in that order.
30. Buchanan, "The Justice of America's Cause," 103.
31. Fowler, *Baron of Beacon Hill*, 52.
32. John Hancock, "Boston Massacre Oration," March 5, 1774, in Hezikiah Niles, ed., *Republication of the Principle Acts of the Revolution in America* (1822; reprint, New York: A.S. Barnes & Co., 1876), 38–40.
33. Ibid.
34. Hancock, Sermon, in Brandes, *Hancock's Life and Speeches*, 350–351; first four quotations from 350, the remainder from 351.
35. Fowler, *Baron of Beacon Hill*, 206, 223–24; Unger, *John Hancock*, 4, 4, 216, 335; Allan, *John Hancock*, 4; Brandes, *Hancock's Life and Speeches*, 23, 184; Akers, *Divine Politician*, 311.
36. Brandes, *Hancock's Life and Speeches*, 23. See also JH to James Scott, November 14, 1783, in Massachusetts Historical Society. Unger contends that Hancock spent about £100,000 during the Revolution for arms and ammunition. When he died, his estate amounted to less than £40,000 (*John Hancock*, 335).
37. Fowler, *Baron of Beacon Hill*, 281. Fowler claims that when Hancock died his cash was only half what his uncle had at his death, and the land he owned was only a small fraction of his uncle's.
38. For example, JH to Thomas Pownal, March 27, 1766, in Brown, *John Hancock*,123; JH to Haley and Hopkins, November 14, 1771, in ibid., 172; JH to Dolly Hancock, March 11, 1776, in ibid., 218; JH to William Palfrey, October 19, 1777, Houghton Library, Harvard University in Unger, *John Hancock*, 260; JH to Dorothy Hancock, August 19, 1778, Boston Public Library in ibid., 272; JH to George Washington, October 15, 1783, Massachusetts Historical Society in ibid., 300; JH to the Gentlemen of the Committee of Safety, April 24, 1775, in Sears, *John Hancock*, 170; JH to Dolly Hancock, March 11, 1777, in ibid., 218; JH to Dolly Hancock, November 8, 1777, in ibid., 228; JH to Henry Quincy, August 30, 1778, in ibid., 260.
39. JH to Ebenezer Hancock, January 11, 1771, as quoted in Unger, *John Hancock*, 152.
40. JH to George Washington, November 19, 1779 in George Washington Papers at the Library of Congress, http://memory.loc.gov/cgi-bin/query/P?mgw:1:./temp/~ammem_BeOe::
41. JH to Barnards and Harrison, December 21, 1765, in Brown, *John Hancock*, 99.
42. John Hancock, "A Day of Fasting, Humiliation and Prayer, with a total abstinence from labor and recreation. Proclamation on April 15, 1775," in *The Journal of Each*

Provincial Congress of Massachusetts in 1744 and 1775 (Boston: Dutton and Wentworth, 1838), 144–145. Hancock's proclamation also asserted that "when the Powers of Earth and Hell" combined against the church, God's "Throne of Grace" could most easily be accessed. Moreover, "the Father of Mercies" had assured his Children that when they asked for "Bread he will not give them a Stone" (144).

43. Hancock, "Boston Massacre Oration," 40.
44. Ibid., 38–42. This address contains many biblical allusions, including the mark of Cain, "a den of thieves," "the prosperity of our [New] Jerusalem," and dissolving the bonds with which the Philistines have bound us.
45. JH to George Washington, March 25, 1776, in Brown, *John Hancock*, 207.
46. JohnHancock, "Appeal to the Thirteen United States," September 24, 1776, in Brown, *John Hancock*, 212.
47. John Hancock, "Inaugural address as Governor of Massachusetts, 1780," in Brown, *John Hancock*, 267–268; all quotations but the last one from 267.
48. John Hancock, "Address to the MA Legislature," January 24, 1782, in *Journal of the House*, 2, 470–472, MA, in Brandes, *Hancock's Life and Speeches*, 265. Cf. Hancock's June 6, 1792 speech in Boston *Gazette*, June 11, 1792, 2, in Brandes, *Hancock's Life and Speeches*, 398.
49. John Hancock, "Address to the MA Legislature," Sept. 25, 1783, in *Journal of the House*, 4, 178–181, MA, in Brandes, *Hancock's Life and Speeches*, 269.
50. John Hancock, *A Proclamation for a Day of Thanksgiving*, November 8, 1783.
51. John Hancock, "Resignation address as governor of MA," February 18, 1785, in *Journal of the House*, MA, 5, February 24, 1785, in Brandes, *Hancock's Life and Speeches*, 293–294; quotations from 294.
52. John Hancock, "Adoption of the MA Constitution Address," February 27, 1788, in Brandes, *Hancock's Life and Speeches*, 332. Cf. his address on February 6, 1788, in *Debates and Proceedings of the Convention of the Commonwealth of Massachusetts . . .* (Boston, 1856), 279–280, in Brandes, *Hancock's Life and Speeches*, 329.
53. John Hancock, "Address to the MA Legislature," January 19, 1790, *Boston Gazette*, January 25, 1790, 2–3, in Brandes, *Hancock's Life and Speeches*, 361. Cf. Hancock's January 27, 1791, address, in Brandes, *Hancock's Life and Speeches*, 381.
54. John Hancock, November 8, 1783, *A Proclamation for a Day of Thanksgiving—signed by Governor John Hancock from Boston, Massachusetts*. From an original in the Evans collection, #18025, by the American Antiquarian Society.
55. John Hancock, *A Proclamation for a Day of Public Thanksgiving*, Boston, October 25, 1787, http://www.wisconsinhistory.org/ratification/digital/resource/0146.pdf
56. John Hancock, *A Proclamation for a Day of Public Thanksgiving* (Boston, 1790).
57. John Hancock, *A Proclamation for a Day of Public Thanksgiving* (Boston, 1791). http://www.classicapologetics.com/h/hauthor.html.
58. John Hancock, *Proclamation for a Day of Fasting and Prayer*, February 11, 1791. Cf. John Hancock, *Proclamation For a Day of Fasting and Prayer*, March 16, 1789.

59. John Hancock, *Proclamation for a Day of Public Thanksgiving*, October 29, 1788; John Hancock, *Proclamation for Day of Public Fasting, Humiliation and Prayer*, March 4, 1793; John Hancock, *Proclamation for a Day of Public Thanksgiving*, October 25, 1792; quotations in that order. Cf. John Hancock, *Proclamation for a Day of Fasting, Prayer and Humiliation*, February 24, 1792.
60. Hancock, "Inaugural Address," in Brown, *John Hancock*, 269.
61. Hancock, "Inaugural Address," in Brown, *John Hancock*, 269. Cf. Hancock's January 27, 1791, address, in Brandes, *Hancock's Life and Speeches*, 380.
62. For example, Hancock, "Inaugural Address," in Brown, *John Hancock*, 269; Hancock, "Address to the MA Legislature," June 6, 1792, Boston *Gazette*, June 11, 1792, in Brandes, *Hancock's Life and Speeches*, 398; Hancock, "Address to the MA Legislature," January 30, 1793, Boston *Gazette*, February 4, 1793, 3, in ibid., 415.
63. John Hancock, "Address to the MA Legislature," June 1, 1790, in Brandes, *Hancock's Life and Speeches*, 372.
64. Hancock, "Address to the MA Legislature," June 6, 1792, 2, in Brandes, *Hancock's Life and Speeches*, 398 (first quotation); Hancock, "Address to the MA Legislature," January 30, 1793, *Boston Gazette*, February 4, 1793, 3, in Brandes, *Hancock's Life and Speeches*, 415–416 (second quotation).
65. Hancock, "Sermon," in Brandes, *Hancock's Life and Speeches*, 351.
66. John Hancock, "Harvard Commencement Address," July 19, 1788, *Boston Gazette*, July 21, 1788, 2–3, in Brandes, *Hancock's Life and Speeches*, 341. Cf. Hancock, "Adoption of the MA Constitution Address," February 27, 1788, in Brandes, *Hancock's Life and Speeches*, 333; Hancock, "Address to the MA Legislature," May 26, 1791, in Brandes, *Hancock's Life and Speeches*, 390; Hancock, "Address at Harvard," *Boston Gazette*, July 25, 1791, in Brandes, *Hancock's Life and Speeches*, 395.
67. Hancock, Sermon, in Brandes, *Hancock's Life and Speeches*, 351.
68. John Hancock, "Address to the MA Legislature," January 27, 1791, in Brandes, *Hancock's Life and Speeches*, 381.
69. Hancock, "Address to the MA Legislature," May 26, 1791, in Brandes, *Hancock's Life and Speeches*, 389.
70. Hancock, "Inaugural Address," in Brown, *John Hancock*, 269.
71. Unger, *John Hancock*, 289.
72. Ibid., 311.
73. George William Van Cleve, *Slavery, Politics, and the Constitution in the Early American Republic* (Chicago: University of Chicago Press, 2010), 56; Unger, *John Hancock*, 299.
74. Allan, *John Hancock*, 351 (first quotation); John Hancock, *Acts and Resolves of the State of Massachusetts*, 1791, May session, 567–579, as quoted in Unger, *John Hancock*, 326 (second quotation).
75. Hancock, "Address to the MA legislature," January 30, 1793, in Brandes, *Hancock's Life and Speeches*, 417.
76. Unger, *John Hancock*, 2.

77. William T. Baxter, *The House of Hancock: Business in Boston, 1724–1775* (Cambridge, MA: Harvard University Press, 1945), xxi.
78. O. M. Dickerson, "John Hancock: Notorious Smuggler or Near Victim of British Revenue Racketeers?" *Mississippi Valley Historical Review* 32: 4 (Mar. 1946), 517–540; quotation from 540.
79. Dickerson, "John Hancock," 517–530; Baxter, *House of Hancock*, 259–260, 305–307, quotation from 306.
80. Unger, *John Hancock*, 1.
81. *Pennsylvania Ledger*, March 11, 1778; cited in Allan, *John Hancock*, 275. Cf. Unger, *John Hancock*, 264.
82. Fowler, *Baron of Beacon Hill*, 207, 224. Cf. Unger, *John Hancock*, 5, 56; Brandes, *Hancock's Life and Speeches*, 185; Gregory H. Nobles, "'Yet the Old Republicans Persevere': Samuel Adams, John Hancock, and the Crisis of Popular Leadership in Revolutionary Massachusetts, 1775–1790," in Ronald Hoffman and Peter J. Albert, eds., *The Transforming Hand of Revolution: Reconsidering the American Revolution as a Social Movement* (Charlottesville: University Press of Virginia, 1996), 268, 272.
83. Unger, *John Hancock*, 49.
84. Hancock, Sermon, in Brandes, *Hancock's Life and Speeches*, 354; Hancock, "Inaugural Address," in Brown, *John Hancock*, 269.
85. Unger, *John Hancock*, 288.
86. Brandes, *Hancock's Life and Speeches*, 168; Allan, *John Hancock*, 122–123.
87. Unger, *John Hancock*, 6, 110. Hancock "helped at least four of his own clerks . . . set up their own shops, with innovative, fifty-fifty profit-sharing arrangements" (103).
88. Fowler, *Baron of Beacon Hill*, 225.
89. Sears, *John Hancock*, 334.
90. Nobles, "The Old Republicans," 277; Stephen E. Patterson, *Political Parties in Revolutionary Massachusetts* (Madison: University of Wisconsin Press, 1973), 186–187.
91. Peter Thacher, *A Sermon, Preached to the Society in Brattle Street, Boston, October 20, 1793, and Occasioned by the Death of His Excellency John Hancock, Boston, October 2, 1793* (Boston: Young, 1793), 23. Thacher focuses on Hancock's generosity and reverence for religion but says nothing about his personal faith, relationship with God, or hope of heaven, despite his exhortation to mourners to prepare for heaven.
92. *Boston Gazette*, November 29, 1790, 4.
93. Daniel Foster, *A Sermon Preached Before His Excellency John Hancock, Esq. Governor . . . May 26, 1790* (Boston: Thomas Adams, 1790), first three quotations from 28, fourth and fifth from 29. Foster urged Hancock to remember that his authority came "from Christ, though by the mediation of the people." He exhorted him to imbibe Christ's teachings in his heart and support them in his government so that citizens would recognize that he had "been with Him" by the way he ruled.

94. Akers, *Divine Politician*, 311.
95. Unger, *John Hancock*, 331. See also "Biographical Sketch of the Life and Character of His Late Excellency Governor John Hancock," *Independent Chronicle*, October 1793, Boston Public Library.
96. John Adams to Richard Rush, July 31, 1812, quoted in Allan, *John Hancock*, 364.
97. Unger, *John Hancock*, 219; Wagner, *Patriot's Choice*, 163.
98. See James Sullivan to Elbridge Gerry, August 13, 1789, Sullivan Papers, Massachusetts Historical Society, as quoted by Fowler, *Baron of Beacon Hill*, 280
99. Unger, *John Hancock*, 258.
100. Ibid., 220.
101. Brandes, *Hancock's Life and Speeches*, xi; Unger, *John Hancock*, 258. Unger calls Hancock's January 31, 1788, speech at the convention "perhaps the crowning achievement of his life. It resolved all the bitter conflicts of the convention by recommending nine so-called Conciliatory Amendments—essentially the articles that would later evolve into the Bill of Rights" (314).
102. Adams, ed., *The Works of John Adams* 10: 259, 261. Brandes, *Hancock's Life and Speeches*, 17, called my attention to this point.
103. Fowler, *Baron of Beacon Hill*, 280.
104. Brandes, *Hancock's Life and Speeches*, 166.
105. Unger, *John Hancock*, 7. Cf. Allan, *John Hancock*, 232; Patterson, *Political Parties in Revolutionary Massachusetts*, 195, 216. Gregory Nobles notes that many of Hancock's contemporary critics and some modern historians have denounced Hancock as "a shallow charlatan" and a "professional politician" who "pandered to a gullible public" ("The Old Republicans," 274). Nobles concludes that "Hancock was hardly a paragon of character or a profile in courage" (271).
106. Brandes, *Hancock's Life and Speeches*, 17.
107. Akers, "Religion and the American Revolution," 488. For another very positive assessment of Hancock, see Donald J. Proctor, "John Hancock: New Soundings on an Old Barrel," *Journal of American History* 64:3 (December 1977), 652–677. Proctor especially praises Hancock's "adroitness as a politician," "rapport with the masses," and "conviction that government rested upon the consent of the governed" (677).

11

Elias Boudinot, Presbyterians, and the Quest for a "Righteous Republic"

Jonathan Den Hartog

IN 1793, ELIAS Boudinot (1740–1821), a lawyer and member of the US House of Representatives, was invited to address the New Jersey Society of the Cincinnati for their Fourth of July celebration. At this point, independence had been gained, the new Constitution (which Boudinot had supported) had gone into effect several years previously, and the government seemed to be functioning successfully. Boudinot delivered a striking oration to the society which revealed his positive vision for a close alignment of republican ideals with evangelical Christianity.[1] In particular, Boudinot expressed the complementary arrangement which characterized the outlook of Presbyterians in the Mid-Atlantic region during and after the Revolution.

In the address, Boudinot offered an optimistic interpretation of the Revolution by focusing on political equality, the nature of representation, and the duties of citizenship. He quickly moved from honoring the occasion and eulogizing the fallen to describing the political principles which he believed justified their sacrifice. "The first great principle" to Boudinot was *"the rational equality and rights of man, as men and citizens."* In describing equality, Boudinot was speaking about the rights which he considered *"natural, essential,* and *unalienable;* such as the security of *life, liberty,* and *property."* He was quick to assert that he did not mean men were equal in acquired position, since "Men must and do continually differ in their genius, knowledge, industry, integrity, and activity." Boudinot's second principle was the right of the people to govern themselves. His discussion of this allowed him to speak about the proper place of representatives in such government. Because representatives had a high calling, Boudinot believed they should be largely left alone to fulfill their duties and allowed "a fair and candid experiment of the plans they form, and the laws they enact for the public weal."[2] Because they were men, though, they would be imperfect; a little suspicion was thus also warranted. In short, Boudinot was expressing the Federalist notion of representation, that the people should vote and then leave their chosen representatives alone to govern. Boudinot believed that by repeating these principles regularly the nation could act as a model for the whole world.

Because of this high opportunity, a commensurate duty fell on Americans. They could not be "careless, indolent, or inattentive in the exercise of any right of citizenship." To Boudinot, morality was necessary to support the republic, because "if the moral character of a people once degenerate, their political character must soon follow." That morality, in Boudinot's mind, was best produced by the religion of Christianity. The political endeavor, then, was ultimately tied to a religious vision. America, "the country for which we have fought and bled," had the possibility of becoming "a theatre of greater events than yet have been known to mankind," the possible fulfillment of both Old and New Testament prophecies. Thus, Boudinot concluded his peroration with a vision of how the political principles he had described might help bring about "that happy state of the world, when, from every human breast, joined by the grand chorus of the skies, shall arise with the profoundest reverence, that divinely celestial anthem of universal praise—'*Glory to God in the highest,—Peace on earth—Good will towards men.*'"[3] In short, America had an immediately positive role to play, which, if fulfilled, carried even greater spiritual promise. From the Revolution to the early 1790s, Boudinot acted under an optimistic belief about the destiny of America, that the nation could be the instrument to bring about the Kingdom of God. Through performances such as an address to the Society of the Cincinnati, civil religion might be used to point his hearers to full religion and their millennial destiny.

For Boudinot, Presbyterian Christianity inspired his quest for a "righteous republic," a religiously inflected government that pursued justice. Boudinot desired a political arrangement in which church and state, although separate, would informally support each other. A strong national government would promote peace and safety for its citizens, which would allow the Church to advance its mission of caring for the spiritual well-being of everyone in the nation and engender the virtues necessary for a republican government. In his pursuit of "public righteousness"—a similar term Boudinot also used—he found himself a Patriot during the Revolution, a Federalist during the disputes over the Constitution, and a Federalist (still) in the party struggles of the 1790s–1810s. Later in life, he pioneered voluntarist strategies to preserve the republic apart from politics. In his career, then, Boudinot pursued a "righteous republic" through political involvement, standing against slavery, writing and publishing, and organizing the American Bible Society.

Brief Biography

Boudinot's contribution to the entire Revolutionary Era makes him a figure whose life deserves more attention. His public service spanned the period from the Revolution to the 1820s. Born in 1740 in Philadelphia, he was baptized by George Whitefield. When a boy, his parents moved to Princeton, New Jersey, at a time when the Presbyterian college at Princeton was headed successively by Aaron Burr, Sr. and Jonathan Edwards. Boudinot was admitted to the New Jersey bar in 1760, and he established an office in Elizabethtown, New Jersey. His practice was successful, earning him enough to marry Hannah Stockton in 1762. Hannah was the sister of Richard Stockton, a future signer of the Declaration of Independence.[4]

In the face of increasing conflict with Great Britain, Boudinot defended American rights. He opposed the Stamp Act and became an advocate of the Patriot position. His moderate approach to politics, however, precluded his advocating any rash political moves. For instance, he actively opposed John Witherspoon's attempt to get New Jersey to declare independence before the Continental Congress.[5] By 1775, he had been elected a member of New Jersey's provisional Congress.

Against the backdrop of the Continental Army's presence in New Jersey, Boudinot worked to supply the army as a private citizen. Those services led George Washington to appoint Boudinot as Commissary of Prisoners, a post he accepted with reluctance. In this capacity, Boudinot had to visit American prisoners of war held by the British and insure that they were being properly supplied. When supplies from Congress ran low, Boudinot even provided for the prisoners from his own pocket.[6] Boudinot filled this position from 1777 until 1778, leaving only upon his election as a New Jersey delegate to the Continental Congress. Despite encountering difficulties—including Philadelphia's summertime heat—Boudinot persevered, seeing his position as a Christian duty to serve others and as part of God's providential plan. Because he believed that God was working through the American Revolution to bring about republican government, his duty was to be involved in the process, even if it meant personal sacrifices.[7]

Boudinot remained in Congress, and in November 1782 he was elected to be its president the following year. Although the post had few powers, it was the highest national office, invested with the duties of running Congress and corresponding with American ambassadors overseas. As such, Boudinot received both the preliminary articles of peace and the final peace treaty from Paris.[8] Even with peace, Boudinot still had to confront the daunting problems of a lack of finances and a still-mobilized army. Financially, Boudinot found Congress in a "most Deplorable situation," but he could only request funds from the states while urging the American diplomats in Europe to continue seeking loans.[9] Boudinot also faced an immediate danger, when in June 1783 several hundred Pennsylvania militiamen mutinied and marched to Philadelphia to demand their back wages. The danger of military coercion loomed, and so Boudinot acted quickly, moving Congress from Philadelphia to Princeton, where they could conduct their business in peace.[10] Boudinot left Congress after his term expired at the end of 1783, hoping to return to private life.

Boudinot was not involved in drafting the new national constitution, but he supported it.[11] Upon the establishment of the new federal government, Boudinot's district elected him to the House of Representatives. In honoring his service, the House appointed Boudinot to the delegation that welcomed president-elect Washington to New York City. Washington even breakfasted at Boudinot's home in Elizabethtown before Boudinot accompanied him into the city by ferry.[12]

Serving in the first three Congresses, Boudinot emerged as a "friend of government." He supported the administration in assuming state debts, funding the national debt, establishing the Bank of the United States, and putting a tariff in place, in the process siding with Fisher Ames, Theodore Sedgwick, and other Federalists.[13] As a Federalist "friend of government," Boudinot sided with the Washington administration but watched with dismay as partisanship grew over the next several years.

A major impetus to sharpening Boudinot's political vision came from developments in foreign affairs and the consequent political polarization. European events—especially the French Revolution and the clash of

England and France on land and sea—increasingly crowded into Americans' political consciousness and actions. Varying domestic reactions to these foreign conflicts fueled the growth of political parties and partisan animosities. Boudinot witnessed and contributed to the party struggles between Federalists and Democratic-Republicans of the 1790s.

During the third Congress, Boudinot supported the president's policy of neutrality toward Britain. He applauded Washington's strategy of sending John Jay to negotiate with Britain, which produced the Jay Treaty. While Federalists welcomed the Treaty, the Democratic-Republicans lambasted it as a surrender of American independence. Boudinot railed against "The disorganizing Democrats," who, "no sooner heard of the arrival of the Treaty, than they began without knowing its Contents, to rouse the lower People into a flame agt. it." Boudinot reserved special hostility for Benjamin Franklin Bache of the *Aurora*, who Boudinot believed was behind much of the Democratic activity.[14] Instead of standing unified during a time of national danger, the Democrats (to Boudinot's mind) were threatening to tear the nation apart by "disorganizing" it and creating factions. For Boudinot, the ratification of the Jay Treaty was a positive event.[15] Despite its faults, the treaty was going to benefit the country as a whole. It would bring "Pleasure" to the Friends of Government (not just of the administration, but of the entire Constitutional order), because of the good it would do. Its opponents clearly could not be interested in the good of the country.

The party conflicts wore on Boudinot. By the end of his third term, he was ready to leave Congress and again return to private life. Despite such sentiments, Washington prevailed on Boudinot to become the director of the US Mint, a position which had opened in 1795. Serving until 1805, Boudinot proved to be an efficient administrator, and the post allowed him time to read, write, and keep in contact with other Federalists.[16]

After 1800, Boudinot wrote several books on Christian themes. He seemed to sense the importance of contributing to the emerging print culture of the new nation.[17] The most striking was his *The Age of Revelation*, a rebuttal of Tom Paine's work *The Age of Reason* (discussed below). His most popular work was a *Memoir of the Rev. William Tennent*. Boudinot had known Tennent, attended his church, and been married by him. This *Memoir* transmitted Tennent's colorful personality and recounted several miraculous stories, such as Tennent's falling into such a powerful religious trance that he was assumed dead—only to have him awaken. After its initial publication in 1806, the work would be reprinted at least eleven separate times throughout the country in the coming twenty years.[18] Finally, Boudinot shared his interpretation of biblical prophecy in *The Second Advent*, published 1815. Among other things, he used the forum to call Americans back to Christianity and to rededicate the country to righteous behavior.[19]

In the last years of his life, Boudinot contributed to the growth of religious voluntary societies, with the most important being the American Bible Society. Beginning at the state level, Boudinot helped form the New Jersey Bible Society in 1809. After several successful years, in 1814 Boudinot and the New Jersey Society issued a call for a convention of Bible societies to form a national organization, largely following a Federalist plan of organizing local branches for national and international ends. The organizing convention met in New York City in May 1816, although Boudinot was unable to attend because of illness. The delegates formed the American Bible Society (ABS) and elected Boudinot its first president.[20] Boudinot would serve in that role until his death in 1821, when he would be succeeded by the former chief justice of the Supreme Court, John Jay.[21]

Religious Beliefs

Boudinot's life showed extended connections to New Side (Evangelical) Presbyterianism.

Although his family was of Huguenot origin, when he was born in 1740 he was baptized by George Whitefield—an immediate connection to Reformed revivalism. Three years later, when the debates over the Great Awakening caused a church split, Boudinot's father led his family into the New Side Second Presbyterian Church. There he grew up under the preaching of the revivalist Gilbert Tennent (father of William).[22] After the family moved to Princeton, they were closely connected with the college and its circle. From Aaron Burr, Sr., Elias would have heard a great deal of millennial preaching. The Boudinots were also in town when Jonathan Edwards assumed his short-lived presidency of the college in 1757.[23] Boudinot thus grew up around key figures in the Great Awakening, and he seems to have listened attentively to their messages, even adopting their warm, hortatory style in his earliest correspondence, where he called on friends to be converted.[24] This warm evangelicalism was no mere youthful enthusiasm; Boudinot would make similar exhortations to various groups for the rest of his life. He joined the local Presbyterian church in Elizabethtown, and as early as 1765 was serving as the president of the church's board of trustees.[25]

Boudinot's religious vision cohered around three central elements—belief, Providence, and action. For Boudinot, belief in a Presbyterian version of Christianity ran throughout his life and endeavors. Belief was entered by a definitive process of conversion—a new birth. Boudinot acted passionately to see others converted, because he believed the stakes were high—the destiny of individual souls in this world and the world to come. He also believed that Providence was actively working in the world. Providence, for Boudinot, was no mere code for a deistical clockmaker-God. Instead, to him a personal deity actively watched over, engaged with, and affected events in the world. Boudinot believed that God's sovereignty embraced specific plans for both individuals and nations. These plans, tied to divine foreknowledge and even predestination, informed how God acts providentially in the world. Because of Boudinot's belief in Providence, he could participate in the affairs of the world, assured that this-worldly matters were not products of chance but of a divine plan. Believing himself to be within that plan (even if not able to comprehend it completely), Boudinot felt motivated to active service, which he often expressed in terms of duty. If divine Providence had acted to save his soul, then a zealous activity was incumbent upon him as a response to the grace he had received. Boudinot's Christianity was practiced within the context of the larger Reformed tradition, which also stressed Providence as part of God's plan for the world, which He both foreknew and predestined. As a Presbyterian, Boudinot shared these attitudes with other Reformed churches, such as New England's Congregationalists, and was part of a broad stream which might also be characterized as Edwardsean (though Jonathan Edwards was not the only articulator of it) and evangelical.[26] Shared beliefs allowed for cross-denominational activities, while individuals remained within their own denominations.[27] As a Presbyterian, Boudinot participated in the dominant Reformed expression in the Mid-Atlantic states. He was thus positioned as a leader in a significant region of the new nation, among a strong body of opinionated and active individuals. Boudinot's involvement in Reformed churches both shaped his individual religiosity and positioned him to influence how Reformed Christians dealt with the new nation.[28]

Scholarly Treatment

Knowledge of Boudinot's contribution to the Revolutionary era, even apart from his religious beliefs or their bearing on his politics, has truly been insufficient. Treatment of Boudinot has ranged from misguided, to trivial, to outdated, to passing. A first, misguided step often occurs when Boudinot is confused or conflated with the Cherokee printer Elias Boudinot (1804?-1839). That Cherokee met Boudinot (then president of the American Bible Society) on a trip from Georgia to a mission school in Connecticut and took his name in his honor.[29] A second wrong-headed approach comes in reducing Boudinot to trivia. Several "gotcha" websites exist on the Internet, claiming that Boudinot should be regarded as a US president—and sometimes the first president—because he was president of Congress when the Articles of Peace arrived from Paris. This minimizes Boudinot's contribution to no more than a chip in a debate over semantics.[30]

The major printed works on Boudinot are older, and although they contain much factual information, they falter in providing analysis—especially of Boudinot's concern for religion and politics. The standard work on Boudinot's life is by George Adams Boyd, published in 1952. Boyd wrote at a time when consensus political history was mainstream. Hence he produced a biography of Boudinot as a politician and "founding father." Boyd relegated Boudinot's religious beliefs to the background and limited his consideration of Boudinot's voluntarist activities to a consideration of his philanthropy. Unable to acknowledge Boudinot's strong disagreement with Tom Paine's religious skepticism, Boyd sniffed, "The spirit of the age was against it [Boudinot's book *The Age of Revelation*]. Tom Paine is still read; Boudinot's volume has become a curiosity." With such an outlook, Boyd clearly lacked the sympathy to articulate Boudinot's complex thinking about religion and politics.[31] Several decades later, during the bicentennial celebration, Barbara Clark penned an adulatory biography of Boudinot. Although fine in narrative, the biography lacked any critical analysis of Boudinot—hardly a presentation that would prompt deeper study.[32]

One more recent notice of Boudinot—and one that finally noticed the significance of Boudinot's beliefs—came in David Holmes's study on *The Faiths of the Founding Fathers*. Holmes discussed Boudinot as one of "Three Orthodox Christians" who were active in the Founding Era. Holmes only devoted five pages to Boudinot and spent most of them surveying Boudinot's writing projects, with no attempt to connect Boudinot's beliefs with his politics.³³ As a result, the field is wide open for a serious consideration of Boudinot's views and practices of religion and politics in the Revolution and Early Republic.³⁴

Religion and Politics in Action

Boudinot's vision of a "Righteous Republic" was more than just an ideal; he actively worked to bring it about. In so doing, he demonstrated strong salient connections between religious belief and political action. Boudinot adopted a number of strategies to further the righteous republic, including organizing political expressions of thanksgiving to God, monitoring political developments and interpreting them through a religious lens, standing for antislavery, writing and contributing to the print culture of the period, and developing voluntarism through Bible Societies.

Giving Thanks in the Revolution and New Nation

Boudinot clearly believed that a formal recognition of God's providential blessing on the nation was required as an activity which the nation should implement through its legislature. He first engaged in this when president of Congress. Previous Congresses had issued thanksgiving proclamations, and Boudinot continued this practice while giving it a decidedly Protestant tone. The proclamation he produced thanked God "that he hath been pleased to continue to us the light of the blessed gospel, and secured to us in the fullest extent the rights of conscience in faith and worship" and went on to offer the prayer that "it may please him to pardon all our offences" and "to cause pure religion and virtue to flourish, to peace to all nation and to fill the world with his glory." These sentiments showed that Boudinot had no difficulty combining the concerns of Christianity and the republic in the Confederation period—nor did many of the members of Congress.³⁵

Once the new government under the Constitution was underway, Boudinot took the lead in insuring a continuity of practice from the Confederation. Boudinot was the first congressman to advocate a national day of Thanksgiving in the First Congress, and he did so immediately after the House had approved the Bill of Rights and the First Amendment. Rather than creating an "establishment of religion," he believed he was furthering a nonsectarian agenda. Boudinot was recorded as saying that "he could not think of letting the session pass over without offering an opportunity to all the citizens of the United States, of joining, with one voice, in returning to Almighty God their sincere thanks for the many blessings he had poured down upon them." He therefore proposed that Congress wait upon the president to declare "a day of public Thanksgiving and Prayer, to be observed by acknowledging with grateful hearts, the many signal favors of Almighty God, especially by affording them an opportunity peaceably to establish a constitution of government for their safety and happiness." Although the South Carolinians Aedanus Burke and Thomas Tucker opposed the motion, it carried "by a great majority," and Boudinot was later appointed one of the three members to transmit it to the president. Washington agreed and began a tradition which both he and Adams would observe—and which Jefferson would intentionally allow to lapse.[36]

Political and Religious Conflict in Elections

During the late 1790s, Boudinot offered comments and political analysis to friends and Federalist allies. Boudinot interpreted the partisan conflict through the dual lenses of Federalist ideology and Presbyterian Christianity. Thus, in the contested 1796 election, his support for Adams was not surprising. He was genuinely disturbed by the "Anarchy & Confusion" he saw around him. To answer it, he asserted the need for greater activity to counter the Democratic exertions. "There must be more exertions made by the Friends of Order & good Government, or all will be lost at last," he told his brother. Their danger lay in the way they reduced their strategy of fomenting unrest "to a system" and spread it to every state. In the same letter, though, Boudinot expressed hope that "Providence will bring about the designs of his Government, by these very means, tho his Enemies do not mean it."[37] Again, Boudinot cast his opponents, not only as political enemies, but also as adversaries to God's will. Providence, to Boudinot, supported the continuation of Federalist control and would even use the actions of its enemies to secure it.

Boudinot was mostly satisfied with Adams's election, but he remained troubled by Jefferson's appeal despite his heterodox religious beliefs.[38] He wrote a friend, "It is a most remarkable event and one that soon cannot be forgotten, that in the year 1796, on the first disputed election for a President of the United States, the State of Pennsylvania who values herself on her attachment to the christian character should give 13 votes out of 15 for a President [Jefferson] & Vice President who are open & professed

Deists. . . ." To Boudinot, the idea of electing both a president and a vice president who were Deists was too much. Because he drew such a close connection between belief and proper political behavior, dangerous beliefs would necessarily lead to dangerous political actions. To Boudinot, this shocking turn of events was a manifest sign of national declension. "These facts," he continued, "are too remarkable to escape the Pen of our future Historians & I confess they give such substantial evidence of our degenerating from the zeal of our forefathers, who first settled this wilderness, that those who retain any of their spirit have their fears greatly alarmed for the consequences."[39] With his "fears greatly alarmed," Boudinot would seek to avert the threatening collapse by working aggressively to counter the insurgency of unbelief and Democratic politics with a combination of Federalism and politicized Protestantism.

During Adams's administration, Boudinot watched as the French continued their dangerous machinations. He supported Adams's move for a strong defense and welcomed the firm response of his countrymen, which offered a possibility for restoring national unity.[40] Against the backdrop of Quasi-War with France, Boudinot wrote to Samuel Bayard, "When the News [of troubles with France] first was announced, the friends of the Government had very well founded fears, arising from the Body of Jacobins & Democrats. . . ." Boudinot's identification of Democratic-Republicans in America with the Jacobin party in France revealed why the stakes were so high. The Democratic "faction" threatened to strip America of its religion and plunge America into a new revolution, one quite as bloody as the one in France.[41]

Given these dangers and Boudinot's distrust of Jefferson's religion, the upcoming election of 1800 frightened him, and the results caused a great deal of soul searching.[42] After some reflection, Boudinot came to see the moment as an instance of God allowing evil to come to purify his people. He observed to his brother, "This untoward Event of the general Success of the Republicans, may be permitted to try & purify the Friends of government; as they certainly stand in need of it—."[43] The election was thus first a judgment on the Federalist party. Because their own faults had led to this election, perhaps the party would receive correction and thereby be prepared for something greater. Boudinot also saw in the election a token of God's coming judgment on the whole nation, observing that "in the history of God's dealing with his people, when in his providence, he has, what may be called dirty work, to be done, or rather when he intends to punish his people for their follies and wickedness, he does not employ his own

Children, . . . but calls in those who despise his Name. . . ."[44] Boudinot saw God's dealings with Christians in America as parallel to God's dealing with Israel. Jefferson's election was a judgment, but one that could produce a purifying effect. Jefferson's ascent to the presidency strengthened Boudinot's belief in the approach of dangerous times for both the nation and the Church and so motivated him to advance Christianity in the republic.

Antislavery

Boudinot's pursuit of a righteous republic motivated his long-term defense of antislavery policies. In the First Congress, Boudinot had supported reauthorizing the Northwest Ordinance, which had banned slavery in those territories. Then, in 1790, he pressed for the House to receive the original petitions from the Pennsylvania Society for Promoting the Abolition of Slavery. In an address to Congress on the subject, he asserted that, although eliminating the slave trade was prohibited until 1808 by the Constitution, it did not mean that petitions could not be received, especially if the petitions expressed Congress's opposition to slavery. To his mind, defending the African slave trade "indeed was an arduous task in this day of light and knowledge." Boudinot's principled opposition to slavery would continue until the end of his life.[45] In the same speech, Boudinot asserted that it was Congress's "duty of our exalted station to do everything in our power to remove every obstruction to public righteousness."[46] In Boudinot's mind, slavery was an obstacle to "public righteousness," and its removal was necessary for his vision of righteous politics to flourish.

Boudinot's antislavery convictions remained long after he left Congress. When the possibility of the expansion of slavery into the Missouri Territory loomed, Boudinot again roused himself to political action. He gathered likeminded citizens together for a public meeting in Trenton in October 1819. They voiced their opposition to slavery's expansion and urged opposition to any attempt in regard to Missouri. Boudinot saw this as part of a national campaign. As chairman, he sent the meeting's resolutions to his contacts throughout the nation.[47] The campaign tapped popular concern, and Boudinot wrote his nephew, "We have been a good deal agitated here on the dispute relating to once more (and if it should be forever) establishing slavery in the Missouri and of consequence in the United States—It seems to have run like a flaming fire through our middle States and causes great anxiety." Two months later, though, Boudinot was again decrying "the unaccountable Apathy that seemed to have possessed our fellow Citizens...."[48]

The possible spread of slavery alarmed Boudinot, because it would make slavery much more difficult ever to remove from the nation. As he argued, "If it is difficult to get rid of negro slavery now when there are but a little over one million what will it be where there are 10 Millions—" Due to Boudinot's opposition to slavery, such a thought was understandably fearful. Boudinot also realized that the growth of slavery would further strengthen the southern bloc in Congress. In his fear that "the Southern & western States would have the sole Government of the union," Boudinot's fear of the 3/5 compromise run amuck sounded much like the concern of other Federalist leaders such as Timothy Pickering.[49]

By January of 1820, Boudinot had been driven to accept (if necessary) dissolution of the Union over further acceptance of slavery. He wrote to John Pintard, "[T]ho I should devoutly deprecate such a distressing Circumstance, yet on the whole I should prefer a quick & peaceable division of the Union, and let each division enjoy their anxious desires...." Perhaps it was better to let the South go its own way, to let them increase their slaves, rather than to allow their practices to spoil the North. In contrast, Boudinot hoped the North would be allowed to continue their "imperishable Enjoyment of a rational Liberty, with a moderate portion of the good things of this Life, obtained by the sweat of our own Brows, under the inestimable blessings of our national & inherent rights of Life, Liberty, Property & the pursuit of happiness, while there will be none to make us afraid."[50] In a striking combination, Boudinot managed to harmonize John Locke's vision of natural rights, Jefferson's description of them in the Declaration of Independence, and Micah 4:4, a traditional Protestant definition of liberty. The North still retained its desire for "a rational Liberty"— not license, but the freedom to benefit both one's self and one's neighbors, while the selfish southerners were threatening to dissolve the structures which made rational liberty possible. By the time the Missouri question— Jefferson's "firebell in the night"—was settled, Boudinot would have appreciated that the Compromise had not solved anything, merely delayed the final settlement of the question.[51]

Print Culture

Boudinot also viewed his writing endeavors as a contribution to his desire to create a righteous republic. Nowhere is this more clear than in his *Age of Revelation*. In the midst of political struggle in the 1790s, Boudinot encountered Thomas Paine's incendiary salvo against Christianity, *The Age of Reason*. Shortly after he read it, he began working on a manuscript response, which he completed in 1795 and published in 1801. Boudinot's *The Age of Revelation* provides a valuable window into his concern over the spread, influence, and results of religious beliefs he—following the lead of ministers such as Timothy Dwight and Jedidiah Morse—termed as infidelity, the malicious rejection of Christian faith.[52] This infidelity carried both spiritual dangers (as it would lead people away from belief) and political dangers (as it prepared the way for the destruction of self-government). In combating infidelity, good apologetics would help preserve both the religious and the political order.

Boudinot expressed shock at finding that Paine had written for "the youth of America, and her unlearned citizens." He feared Paine's strategy was to find "the best inlet to infidelity," by preying on the uneducated. He did not believe that Paine's arguments were persuasive, but he was concerned that Paine's rhetoric could sway the unstudied. Boudinot responded vigorously because he believed the stakes were so high: Paine's religious ideas could undermine the belief in Christianity, which Boudinot believed served as the foundation of sound republican government. He worried that Paine's arguments would strip his readers of their beliefs, which would then ruin their morals and virtue, making them unfit to be republican citizens. Boudinot wrote, he said, from "an anxious desire that our country should be preserved from the dreadful evil of becoming enemies to the religion of the Gospel, which I have no doubt, but would be introductive of the dissolution of government and the bonds of society." Boudinot's theological work was thus also a practical work meant to defend the republic and preserve it for the next generation. This concern for posterity explains his dedicating the book to his daughter Susan, disturbed as he was by "the melancholy prevalence of a spirit of infidelity."[53] By educating the next generation in the principles of right religion and sound government, Boudinot believed the ideas advanced by Paine could be countered.

Boudinot began by attempting to undermine the trust people had in Paine because of *Common Sense*.[54] He claimed that Paine "has proved himself to be totally ignorant of the subject he has undertaken to elucidate, not only as to the intrinsic merit of the question, but also the ideas and terms, which its advocates have been known always to hold up and use, as expressive of their sense and meaning of it."[55] Boudinot attacked the specific points Paine had raised in sections on Christ's virgin birth, his resurrection and ascension, the trinity, the reliability of the Gospels, and the authenticity of the Pentateuch.[56] In each section, Boudinot described Paine's assertion and then attacked it with references to a number of writers meant to disprove either Paine's logic or his historical assertions.[57]

Voluntarism and the American Bible Society

Finally, Boudinot believed that his work in the American Bible Society would help in creating Christian, republican citizens. By the period after the War of 1812, Federalism was clearly in decline, but many evangelicals were willing to leave politics as they developed voluntarist strategies to influence the nation's development. This effort, led by Boudinot, found many active allies. In planning for the founding convention of the ABS, Boudinot worked closely with William Jay (son of John Jay) in preparing the organization's constitution. Other significant individuals in attendance included minister and geographer Jedidiah Morse, Connecticut Congregationalist minister Lyman Beecher, theologian N. W. Taylor, Eliphalet Nott the president of Union College, Presbyterian Gardiner Spring, and New York minister John Mitchell Mason—many of whom had Federalist ties. The ABS thus spanned sections and denominations, creating a national organization.[58]

In subsequent addresses, Boudinot laid out his ambitious goals for the society. Beginning with a "national superstructure of Heavenly charity [the ABS]," he hoped to "gospelize the world," as he told the New Jersey Society in the year after the formation of the ABS. In going forth, Boudinot reminded them, "Union is our Motto."[59] Just as political union was necessary for the country's survival, so spiritual union would insure the health and strength of the Church in America. Thus unified, evangelical Christians could attempt to "gospelize the world," as the best safeguard against political and social revolution. In Boudinot's mind, the formation of the ABS was important enough to use language that embraced the entire earth. Its success encouraged him so much that he grew increasingly hopeful.[60] Although dangers still remained and vigilance was necessary, the ABS—along with the tract societies, Sunday schools, and other voluntary religious meetings—offered great encouragement. By the time of his death, the ABS had become one of the premier examples of the voluntary societies which would do so much to reorganize America and American Christianity in the first half of the nineteenth century.[61] In its evangelistic success, Boudinot also saw the preservation of the republic.

Boudinot, Presbyterianism, and the New Nation

Boudinot's life reveals much about both religion and politics in the new nation, as well as casting light on the outlook and experience of many American Presbyterians. Already a major denomination, their influence would be strengthened through their cooperation with the Congregationalists after the Act of Union (1801).[62] While a figure of national importance, Boudinot's influence within the denomination largely rose from his participation in the "Princeton Circle," which also included Ashbel Green and Samuel Stanhope Smith. Living in New Jersey, Boudinot had close ties to the institution that would train many significant Presbyterian ministers and statesmen.[63] Although he never attended Princeton himself, Boudinot was named a trustee of the college in 1772, a position he held for the rest of his life. His responsibilities often brought him onto campus. Following a student rebellion in 1807, Boudinot was the official entrusted with regaining control of the college and instructing the students on how to amend their behavior—and why that was necessary for the good of the republic.[64] He made generous contributions both to the college and to the establishment of Princeton Seminary, leaving his personal library to the new institution.[65] Boudinot not only shared the outlook of the other leaders of Princeton but also he contributed to the institution that would train leaders of the coming generation, thereby advancing a righteous republic through education.

As a leading Presbyterian, Boudinot's life and experience provides insights into how British North Americans of a Reformed persuasion could come to support the ideology and activities of the American Revolution. Historian Mark A. Noll has sought to problematize the relationship of evangelicals to the ideology of republicanism, arguing that republicanism emerged from religiously skeptical individuals and challenged biblically legitimate monarchs and so made for an uneasy ally for American Protestants.[66] Yet for Boudinot there appeared to be little problem in adopting a moderate republican position. Accepting the justice of American resistance, Boudinot believed divine providence was guiding the creation of the new nation. Boudinot was not a theologian, but he was a well-read layman who reflected on political matters and responded in a way that he believed would produce a "righteous republic." At a time when John Witherspoon was preaching on *The Dominion of Providence over the Passions of Men*, Boudinot agreed with Witherspoon's assessment—even though he was more circumspect than Witherspoon. It appears that many other Presbyterians agreed with both men.[67]

Boudinot's life further proves important for understanding the politics of the Early Republic. Boudinot provides a window into how Presbyterians—along with other Reformed groups—located themselves in the new nation, defined their vision of citizenship, and participated in early national politics. He demonstrates first the appeal of the Constitution of 1787 and Bill of Rights, with their promise of order, capable government, and religious liberty without any established church. He further helps explain how Presbyterians could see the Federalists as a commendable choice in the 1790s. By portraying themselves as the defenders of orderly government and public religion (particularly nonsectarian Christianity), the Federalists presented a custodial ideal to which Reformed groups could gravitate. As a bulwark against French Revolutionary violence and European religious skepticism, the Federalists were a party with much appeal to Presbyterians. Even after the collapse of the Federalist party, this custodial ideal continued—and would later draw many Presbyterians into the Whig camp.

Finally, Boudinot's later career helps trace the rise of voluntarism as an organizing principle for public expression of religion. With other Federalists, Boudinot sought cultural and religious goals when the political realm was no longer open to them. This was a significant strategy for a country with no religious establishment on either the state or national level. Not surprisingly, this strategy grew out of the Mid-Atlantic states that had never had a strong tradition of establishment. They were thus more flexible than New Englanders, with their long experience of state-sponsored religion. The end result was a continued commitment to the necessity of religious ideals shaping and preserving the state, but doing so without any formal tie to the instruments of civic power. Boudinot's final formulation, then, was to envision a "righteous republic" that was individual and social, rather than structural or corporate. That is, the righteousness of the republic would reside in individual hearts and in the interactions of civil society, apart from and previous to politics. This outlook would prevail for American Christianity through much of the nineteenth century.

Notes

1. The only scholarly biography of Boudinot is George Adams Boyd, *Elias Boudinot: Patriot and Statesman* (Princeton: Princeton University Press, 1952). For the address, see p. 138. For a discussion on the place of public orations in political

culture in the early republic, see David Waldstreicher, *In the Midst of Perpetual Fetes: The Making of American Nationalism, 1776–1820* (Chapel Hill: University of North Carolina Press for Omohundro Institute of Early American History and Culture, 1997) and Simon Newman, *Parades and Politics of the Street: Festive Culture in the Early American Republic* (Philadelphia: University of Pennsylvania Press, 1997).

2. Elias Boudinot, *An Oration, Delivered at Elizabeth-Town, New Jersey, Agreeably to a Resolution of the State Society of Cincinnati, on the Fourth of July, M.DCC.XCIII* (Elizabeth-Town: Sheperd Kollock, 1793), 10, 12–14.

3. Boudinot, *An Oration*, 13, 14, 27.

4. Boyd, *Elias Boudinot*, 15–17.

5. For Boudinot's account of the confrontation, see Elias Boudinot, *Journal or Historical Recollections of the American Events During the Revolutionary War* (Philadelphia: Frederick Bourquin; reprint, New York: Arno Press, 1968), 3–8 [hereafter *Journal*]. Jeffry H. Morrison, *John Witherspoon and the Founding of the American Republic* (Notre Dame, IN: University of Notre Dame Press, 2005), 71–92. Boyd, *Elias Boudinot*, 17.

6. *Journal*, 9–10. Elias Boudinot to Hannah Boudinot, March 11, 1778, Stimson Collection of Elias Boudinot, Box 1, Folder 10, Rare Books and Special Collections, Firestone Memorial Library, Princeton University, Princeton [hereafter RBSC, Princeton]. Boyd, *Elias Boudinot*, 33–67. For New Jersey in the Revolution, see David Hackett Fisher, *Washington's Crossing* (New York: Oxford University Press, 2004) and John Fea, "Revolution and Confederation Period: New Jersey at the Crossroads" in Maxine Lurie and Richard Veit, eds., *New Jersey: A History of the Garden State*, (New Brunswick: Rutgers University Press, 2012), 64–89. For Boudinot's correspondence during this time, see Peter Force Collection, Series 7E, Item 12 (Microfilm reel 3), Library of Congress, Washington, DC; William A. Oldridge Collection of George Washington's Headquarters Staff Writings; Library of Congress, Papers of Elias Boudinot, Library of Congress, Washington, DC.

7. Elias Boudinot to Hannah Boudinot, July 7, 1778, in Paul Smith and Ronald Gephart, eds., *Letters of Delegates to Congress, 1774–1789* (Washington, DC: Library of Congress, 1976–2000), 10: 232. Elias Boudinot to Hannah Boudinot, July 9, 1778, ibid., 241. Elias Boudinot to Hannah Boudinot, August 13, 1778, Stimson Collection of Elias Boudinot, Box 1, Folder 10, RBSC, Princeton.

8. Elias Boudinot to Elisha Boudinot, November 14, 1782, Stimson Collection of Elias Boudinot, Box 1, Folder 8, RBSC, Princeton.

9. Elias Boudinot to George Washington, March 17, 1783, Peter Force Collection, Series 7E, Item 12 (Microfilm reel 3), Manuscripts and Archives Division, Library of Congress, Washington, DC.

10. Boyd, *Elias Boudinot*, 127–137. Elias Boudinot to Elisha Boudinot, June 23, 1783, Thorne Collection of Elias Boudinot, Box 1, Folder 4, RBSC, Princeton; Elias Boudinot to General Livingston, June 23, 1783, *Letters of Delegates to Congress*,

20: 350, 357; and *By His Excellency Elias Boudinot, Esquire, President of the United States in Congress Assembled. A Proclamation* (Philadelphia: David C. Claypoole, 1783); Elias Boudinot to Benjamin Rush, July 25, 1783, Elias Boudinot Papers, Library of Congress, microfilm at Firestone Library, Princeton University. Elias Boudinot to Elisha Boudinot, June 23, 1783, Thorne Collection of Elias Boudinot, Box 1, Folder 4, RBSC, Princeton.

11. Elias Boudinot to Hannah Boudinot, October 27, 1786, Stimson Collection, Box 1, Folder 10, RBSC, Princeton.

12. Elias Boudinot to Hannah Boudinot, April 2, 1789, Stimson Collection, Box 1, Folder 10, RBSC, Princeton. Elias Boudinot to Hannah Boudinot, April 24, 1789, Elias Boudinot Collection, Folder 6, RBSC, Princeton. Boyd, *Elias Boudinot*, 138–167.

13. On Boudinot's election to Congress, see Richard Stockton to Elias Boudinot, February 20, 1789, February 16, 1789, February 26, 1790, December 22, 1790, Boudinot Family Collection, Folder 22, RBSC, Princeton. Cf. Boyd, *Elias Boudinot*, 154–222. Helen E. Veit, Charlene Bangs Bickford, Kenneth R. Bowling, and William C. diGiacomantonio, eds., *Documentary History of the First Federal Congress, 1789–1791, Debates in the House of Representatives, Second Session: January–March 1790* (Baltimore: The Johns Hopkins University Press, 1994), 12: 378–410; 14: 431–441. Stanley Elkins and Eric McKitrick, *The Age of Federalism: The Early American Republic, 1788–1800* (New York: Oxford University Press, 1993), 142, 230–232. Boudinot was also busy as a legislator. He was often named to chair the sessions when the House dissolved itself into the Committee of the Whole, and he served on forty-one different committees. *Documentary History of the First Federal Congress*, 14: 683–687.

14. Elias Boudinot to Samuel Bayard, October 17, 1795, William H. Bradford Princeton Collection, Box 1, Folder 4, RBSC, Princeton. With the reference to newspaper politics, see Jeffrey L. Pasley, *"The Tyranny of Printers": Newspaper Politics in the Early American Republic* (Charlottesville: University Press of Virginia, 2001).

15. Elias Boudinot to Samuel Bayard, November 5, 1795, Berol MS Collection, Folder: Kirkland II, no. 82, Rare Books and Manuscripts Library, Columbia University, New York City. Boudinot's reactions were part of the larger national debate around the treaty, as chronicled by Todd Estes in *The Jay Treaty Debate, Public Opinion, and the Evolution of Early American Political Culture* (Amherst: University of Massachusetts Press, 2006).

16. Elias Boudinot to Elisha Boudinot, May 13, 1796, Thorne Collection of Elias Boudinot, Box 1, folder 4, RBSC, Princeton. For the mint, see Elias Boudinot, *Orders and Directions for Conducting the Mint of the United States, Established by Elias Boudinot, Director of Said Mint. November 2, 1795* (Philadelphia: John Fenno, 1796); Timothy Pickering, *Letter from the Secretary of State, Inclosing a Report of the Director of the Mint, Suggesting the Expediency of Some Alterations in Its Establishment, to Render it Less Expensive to the Public, and More Accommodating*

to Depositors (Philadelphia: published by order of the House of Representatives, 1797); John Adams, *Message from the President of the United States, Transmitting Sundry Statements Relative to the Mint of the United States, Prepared by the Officers Thereof* (Philadelphia: Way & Groff, by order of the House of Representatives of the United States, 1800). Boyd, *Elias Boudinot*, 240–250. Carl Prince, "The Passing of the Aristocracy: Jefferson's Removal of the Federalists, 1801–1805," *Journal of American History* 57 (December 1970): 563–575.

17. On Christian print culture, see Candy Gunther Brown, *The Word in the World: Evangelical Writing, Publishing, and Reading in America, 1789–1880* (Chapel Hill: University of North Carolina Press, 2004); David Paul Nord, *Faith in Reading: Religious Publishing and the Birth of Mass Media in America* (New York: Oxford, 2004).

18. Elias Boudinot, *A Memoir of the Rev. William Tennent, Minister of Freehold, Monmouth County, N.J.* (Morristown, NJ: n.p., 1807). Extant versions exist from Trenton, New Jersey; New York City (multiple printings); Kingston, New York; Salem, New York; Poughkeepsie, New York; Wilmington, Ohio; Philadelphia (multiple printings); Wilmington, Delaware; and Chambersburg, Pennsylvania.

19. Elias Boudinot, *The Second Advent, Or Coming of the Messiah in Glory, Shown to be a Scripture Doctrine, and Taught by Divine Revelation, from the Beginning of the World* (Trenton: D. Fenton and S. Hutchinson, 1815), see esp. pp. iii–iv, 531–532, 551–552.

20. American Bible Society, *Constitution of the American Bible Society, Formed by a Convention of Delegates, Held in the City of New-York, May, 1816. Together with Their Address to the People of the United States; A Notice of Their Proceedings, and a List of Their Officers* (New York: Hopkins, 1816), 3–7.

21. For Jay's journey to the American Bible Society, see Jonathan Den Hartog, "John Jay and the 'Great Plan of Providence,'" in Daniel L. Dreisbach, Mark David Hall, and Jeffry H. Morrison, eds., *The Forgotten Founders on Religion and Public Life* (Notre Dame, IN: University of Notre Dame Press, 2009), 145–170.

22. Boyd, *Elias Boudinot*, 7–8. "New Side" referred to the pro-Great Awakening group within the Presbyterian Church and corresponded to the New Light position in New England. On the First Great Awakening, see Thomas S. Kidd, *The Great Awakening: The Roots of Evangelical Christianity in Colonial America* (New Haven, CT: Yale University Press, 2007). For the political implications of Whitefield's preaching, see Jerome Mahaffey, *Preaching Politics: The Religious Rhetoric of George Whitefield and the Founding of a New Nation* (Waco, TX: Baylor University Press, 2007).

23. George Marsden, *Jonathan Edwards: A Life* (New Haven, CT: Yale University Press, 2003), 490–498.

24. Elias Boudinot to William Tennent III, November 22, 1758, William Tennent III Letter Album, South Caroliniana Library, University of South Carolina, Columbia. Elias Boudinot to Hannah Stockton, August 6, 1758, Stimson Collection of Elias Boudinot, Folder 9, RBSC, Princeton.

25. Boyd, *Elias Boudinot*, 15–17.
26. See Marsden, *Jonathan Edwards*, passim; Mark A. Noll, *The Rise of Evangelicalism: The Age of Edwards, Whitefield, and the Wesleys* (Downers Grove, IL: InterVarsity Press, 2003); David Kling and Douglas Sweeney, *Jonathan Edwards at Home and Abroad: Historical Memories, Cultural Movements, Global Horizons* (Columbia: University of South Carolina Press, 2003); Allen C. Guelzo, *Edwards on the Will: A Century of Theological Debates* (Middletown, CT: Wesleyan University Press, 1989). Defining evangelical belief is notoriously difficult. For the most helpful definition, see David Bebbington, *Evangelicalism in Modern Britain: A History from the 1730s to the 1980s* (Grand Rapids, MI: Baker, 1989), 1–17.
27. See Mark A. Noll, *A History of Christianity in the United States and Canada* (Grand Rapids: William B. Eerdmans, 1992), 114–162; Fred J. Hood, *Reformed America: The Middle and Southern States, 1783–1837* (Tuscaloosa: University of Alabama Press, 1980); Patricia U. Bonomi, *Under the Cope of Heaven: Religion, Society, and Politics in Colonial America* (New York: Oxford University Press, 1986), 87–92, 133–160, 206–222.
28. Mark A. Noll, *America's God: From Jonathan Edwards to Abraham Lincoln* (New York: Oxford University Press, 2002) and Jonathan D. Sassi, *A Republic of Righteousness: The Public Christianity of the Post-Revolutionary New England Clergy* (New York: Oxford University Press, 2001).
29. *Cherokee Editor: The Writings of Elias Boudinot*, ed. Theda Perdue (Athens: University of Georgia Press, 1996); James Parins, *Elias Cornelius Boudinot: A Life on the Cherokee Borders* (Lincoln: University of Nebraska Press, 2006), 3–15.
30. "Elias Boudinot," http://www.eliasboudinot.com (accessed August 1, 2011); "The First American Republic," http://www.firstamericanrepublic.com/elias-boudinot-ninth-american-president.html (accessed August 1, 2011).
31. Boyd, *Elias Boudinot*, 253.
32. Barbara Clark, *EB: The Story of Elias Boudinot IV, His Family, His Friends, and His Country* (Philadelphia: Dorrance, 1977).
33. David L. Holmes, *The Faiths of the Founding Fathers* (New York: Oxford University Press, 2006), 150–154.
34. For an extended discussion of Boudinot's life, beliefs, and politics, see Jonathan Den Hartog, "'Patriotism and Piety': Orthodox Religion and Federalist Political Culture" (PhD Diss., University of Notre Dame, 2006).
35. Thanksgiving Proclamation, October 18, 1783, *Journals of the Continental Congress, 1774–1789* (Washington: Government Printing Office, 1922), 25: 699–701. Clark, *EB: The Story of Elias Boudinot IV*, 286–287. This was in accord with the practice of the Confederation Congress. James H. Hutson, *Church and State in America: The First Two Centuries* (New York: Cambridge, 2008), 95–104.
36. *Documentary History of the First Federal Congress*, 11: 1500–1501. Jane J. Boudinot, ed., *The Life, Public Services, and Addresses and Letters of Elias Boudinot, LL.D.* (Boston: Houghton Mifflin and Company, 1896; reprint edition, New York: Da

Capo Press, 1971), 2: 353–355. Jefferson opposed any religious proclamations from the presidency. See Daniel L. Dreisbach, *Thomas Jefferson and the Wall of Separation between Church and State* (New York: New York University Press, 2002). During the War of 1812, James Madison briefly revived the practice, but after 1815 such proclamations were not used until Abraham Lincoln during the Civil War.

37. Elias Boudinot to Elisha Boudinot, May 13, 1796, Thorne Collection of Elias Boudinot, Box 1, Folder 4, RBSC, Princeton.
38. Elias Boudinot to Elisha Boudinot, November 28, 1796, Thorne Collection of Elias Boudinot, Box 1, Folder 4, RBSC, Princeton.
39. Elias Boudinot to Samuel Bayard, December 14, 1796, quoted in Jane J. Boudinot, II: 119.
40. Elias Boudinot to Elisha Boudinot, June 12, 1798, Thorne Collection of Elias Boudinot, Box 1, Folder 5, RBSC, Princeton.
41. Elias Boudinot to Samuel Bayard, April 22, 1797, Stimson Collection, Box 1, Folder 5, RBSC, Princeton.
42. Elias Boudinot to Jonathan Dayton, December 19, 1800, Elias Boudinot Collection, Folder 18, RBSC, Princeton. On the election of 1800, see James Horn, Jan Ellen Lewis, and Peter S. Onuf, eds., *The Revolution of 1800: Democracy, Race, and the New Republic* (Charlottesville: University of Virginia Press, 2002); John Ferling, *Adams vs. Jefferson: The Tumultuous Election of 1800* (New York: Oxford University Press, 2004); Edward L. Larson, *A Magnificent Catastrophe: The Tumultuous Election of 1800, America's First Presidential Campaign* (Washington, DC: The Free Press, 2007).
43. Elias Boudinot to Elisha Boudinot, January 7, 1801, Thorne Collection of Elias Boudinot, Box 1, Folder 5, RBSC, Princeton.
44. Elias Boudinot to Elisha Boudinot, December 22, 1800, Thorne Collection of Elias Boudinot, Box 1, Folder, 5, RBSC, Princeton.
45. For instance, while serving in Congress, he argued in the New Jersey Supreme Court for the freedom of a slave named Silas and also housed several free blacks. James Pemberton to Elias Boudinot, March 8, 1790, Elias Boudinot Manuscript Collection, vol. 3, p. 47, Historical Society of Pennsylvania, Philadelphia; Joseph Shotwell to Elias Boudinot, June 15, 1792, Elias Boudinot Manuscript Collection, vol. 3, p. 58, Historical Society of Pennsylvania, Philadelphia.
46. Elias Boudinot, in *Documentary History of the First Federal Congress, 1789–1791*, 12: 299. Elias Boudinot, "Subject of Slavery," in Jane J. Boudinot, 218–229, quote is on p. 220. Cf. Boyd, *Elias Boudinot*, 181–182, and Joseph Ellis, *Founding Brothers: The Revolutionary Generation* (New York: Alfred A. Knopf, 2001), 81–119.
47. For instance, Boudinot sent one copy to John Jay. Elias Boudinot to John Jay, November 5, 1819, John Jay Papers, Box 5, Rare Books and Manuscripts Library, Columbia University, New York City.

48. Elias Boudinot to Elias E. Boudinot, November 27, 1819, Stimson Collection, Box 1, Folder 7, RBSC, Princeton; Elias Boudinot to John Pintard, January 9, 1820, Elias Boudinot Papers, Folder 6, American Bible Society, New York City.
49. Elias Boudinot to Elias E. Boudinot, December 15, 1819, Stimson Collection, Box 1, Folder 7, RBSC, Princeton; Elias Boudinot to John Pintard, January 9, 1820, Elias Boudinot Papers, Folder 6, American Bible Society, New York City. Cf. Garry Wills, *Negro President: Jefferson and the Slave Power* (Boston: Houghton Mifflin, 2003).
50. Elias Boudinot to John Pintard, January 9, 1820, Elias Boudinot Papers, Folder 6, American Bible Society, New York City.
51. Thomas Jefferson to John Holmes, April 22, 1820, in Merrill Peterson, ed., *The Portable Thomas Jefferson* (New York: Penguin Books, 1975), 567–569.
52. This significant book has received very little attention. One short and unsatisfactory attempt at understanding it comes in Richard H. Popkin, "*The Age of Reason* versus *The Age of Revelation*: Two Critics of Tom Paine: David Levi and Elias Boudinot," in J. A. Leo Lemay, ed., *Deism, Masonry, and the Enlightenment: Essays Honoring Alfred Owen Aldridge* (Newark, NJ: University of Delaware Press, 1987), 158–170.
53. Elias Boudinot, *The Age of Revelation, Or the Age of Reason Shewn to Be An Age of Infidelity* (Philadelphia: Asbury Dickins, 1801), iv, xii, xx, xxii, 131–132.
54. Ibid., 26.
55. Boudinot, *Age of Revelation*, 27. Boudinot delighted in reporting later that Paine had admitted to not even owning a Bible! Boudinot went so far as to say that Paine had not even learned the alphabet of religious matters. Ibid., 97, 253.
56. See, for example, ibid., 45–60, 71–79, 90–99, 164–177, 221–227, and 249–257.
57. Boudinot's book remained in circulation among orthodox ministers for a number of years. Elias Boudinot to Dr. Edward D. Griffin, October 24, 1809, Miscellaneous MSS—Boudinot, Elias, New York Historical Society, New York City.
58. American Bible Society, *Constitution of the American Bible Society, Formed by a Convention of Delegates, Held in the City of New-York, May, 1816*, passim.
59. "Extracts from the Address of Dr. E. Boudinot[,] President of the American & New Jersey Bible Society, delivered before the Managers & members of the latter Society on Wednesday the 26 August 1817," William H. Bradford Princeton Collection, Box 1, Folder 2, RBSC, Princeton.
60. Elias Boudinot, "Address to the American Bible Society," May 1821, Elias Boudinot Papers, Folder 8, American Bible Society, New York City.
61. See Charles I. Foster, *An Errand of Mercy: The Evangelical United Front, 1790–1837* (Chapel Hill: The University of North Carolina Press, 1960); Donald G. Mathews, "The Second Great Awakening as an Organizing Process, 1780–1830," *American Quarterly* 21 (Spring 1969): 23–43; Lois W. Banner, "The Protestant Crusade: Religious Missions, Benevolence, and Reform in the United States, 1790–1840" (PhD diss., Columbia University, 1970). For a more recent examination of the

political battles surrounding voluntary associations, see Johann N. Neem, *Creating a Nation of Joiners: Democracy and Civil Society in Early National Massachusetts* (Cambridge, MA: Harvard University Press, 2008).

62. The two denominations worked together to found "Union" churches in the West. These churches could later decide to affiliate with either denomination. In the end, the decided majority affiliated with the Presbyterians, thus increasing their national prominence.

63. The "Princeton Circle" refers to the intellectual milieu of Presbyterian leaders with Princeton connections and is used extensively in Mark A. Noll's study *Princeton and the Republic, 1768–1822: The Search for a Christian Enlightenment in the Era of Samuel Stanhope Smith* (Princeton, NJ: Princeton University Press, 1989).

64. For Boudinot's own analysis of events, see Elias Boudinot to Ashbel Green, March 24, 1807, and April 3, 1807, Elias Boudinot Collection, Folders 21–22, RBSC, Princeton. The events are recounted in Mark A. Noll, "The Response of Elias Boudinot to the Student Rebellion of 1807: Visions of Honor, Order, and Morality," *The Princeton University Library Chronicle* 43(1981): 1–22.

65. For Boudinot's involvement, see Princeton Theological Seminary Board of Directors, Reports, 1.43 (May 1822) and 3.6 (May 15–18, 1829), Princeton Theological Seminary Archives, Princeton.

66. Noll, *America's God*, 447–451.

67. John Witherspoon, *The Dominion of Providence over the Passions of Men* (Philadelphia: R. Aitken, 1776). For Witherspoon generally, see Morrison, *John Witherspoon and the Founding of the America Republic*. Another outstanding example of the Presbyterian move to independence comes in John Fea's *The Way of Improvement Leads Home: Philip Vickers Fithian and the Rural Enlightenment in Early America* (Philadelphia: University of Pennsylvania Press, 2008), 126–155, 180–208.

12

The Quaker Contributions of John Dickinson to the Creation of the American Republic

Jane E. Calvert

FEW MEN WORKED harder to establish the American Republic than John Dickinson (1732–1808). His career was distinguished and his contribution to the founding was unique in many ways. He was the only major political figure active in America from the earliest days of the contest with Britain through the early Republic. He probably held more public posts than any other, including, but not limited to, being a member of the Stamp Act Congress (1765), both Continental Congresses (1774–1776), the Confederation Congress (1779), colonel in the Pennsylvania militia (1776), private in the Delaware militia (1777), president of Delaware (1781–1782) and Pennsylvania (1782–1785), president of the Annapolis Convention (1786), member of the Constitutional Convention (1787), and president of the Delaware constitutional convention (1792). He was the most prolific founder, writing pamphlets and broadsides, newspaper articles, military regulations, bills, proclamations, petitions and declarations, constitutions, and more, including most of the official issuances of the congresses he attended and America's first patriotic song. With his eloquent assertions of American rights and liberties, he became the country's first political hero and was seen abroad as the spokesman for the American cause.[1]

Yet despite these contributions, Dickinson is often excluded from the upper echelon of founders. The problem is more historiographical than historical. In his own time, few Americans achieved his name recognition. One contemporary remarked that "[n]o person in Pennsylvania ever approached him as a rival in personal influence."[2] Around the Atlantic world, people saw his name in print and his image in various forms. Admirers viewed with excitement the wax carving of him (along with one of George Whitefield) that was displayed around New England for the benefit of those who could not travel to see him in Philadelphia. They sang his "Liberty Song," dedicated pamphlets to him, wrote poems about him, compared him with classical icons, and toasted his health. Ships bore his pen name, *Pennsylvania Farmer*, as did taverns and a stud horse. Colonial leaders appealed to him for advice on resisting Britain and framing state constitutions. They honored him with academic degrees, society memberships, and other tokens of esteem. In retirement, statesmen at the highest levels sought his counsel.[3]

Complicating factors have influenced the perception of Dickinson, however, causing controversy in his day and historiographical confusion, abuse, and neglect in ours. After vigorous advocacy of the American cause, he refused to vote on or sign the Declaration of Independence. Then, in what seems like yet another reversal, he immediately took up arms to defend the cause, the only Congressman to serve as a private. His strong opposition to the policies of Pennsylvania radicals likely damaged his reputation more than his refusal to sign. Having initially opposed the American Revolution, he seemed to contradict himself as a fervent supporter of the French Revolution. Finally, he was the only major founder deeply and broadly influenced by a little-recognized theologico-political tradition, Quakerism. Any one of these factors alone might have been enough to befuddle historians looking to fit Dickinson into a precast Founding Father mold, one that is usually secular and often based on the modern labels "liberal," "conservative," or "radical."

The historiography on Dickinson is thus a small, confused mixture, short on satisfying analysis but not lacking in assessments of his patriotism and role in the founding, ranging from deep admiration to bitter invective to flippant dismissal. There have been fewer than seventy-five published scholarly works devoted to Dickinson, among them only four monographs and a smattering of graduate theses, articles, book chapters, pamphlets, and speeches. Many try without success to explain his seemingly contradictory behavior in 1776. That Dickinson, who opposed the Revolution, is best known as the "Penman of the Revolution" is ironic and indicative of the confusion.[4] Some sidestep this perplexing topic and focus on more discreet and manageable aspects of his career. Few take seriously the possibility that his religion might hold the key to understanding the essence of his political philosophy, action, and policy.

In Dickinson's day, it was generally known that he was closely affiliated with and influenced by the Society of Friends. Yet, as the more astute studies observe, Dickinson was not a formal member. In 1956, Quaker historian Frederick Tolles noted, "[H]e thought, spoke, and acted like a Friend. Yet no one has ever tried to say with exactness just what that Quaker influence was or just how it expressed itself in Dickinson's thought and action."[5] Nor did Tolles himself, though he made a convincing case that Dickinson "did everything he could to promote Quaker goals by political means."[6] But Tolles' challenge was premature. It would be impossible to describe Dickinson's political Quakerism before Quaker political theory itself had been thoroughly explained. His call thus went unanswered for another half-century. My work in *Quaker Constitutionalism and the Political Thought of John Dickinson* (2009) was a first attempt to explain these related and neglected topics.[7] There is, as yet, no comprehensive study of Dickinson's political and religious thought over his entire career.

What Dickinson's Quaker "contribution" to the creation of the Republic was depends on how we understand the word. If we mean what was *offered*, few contributed more than he with his writings and service. If we mean concrete changes that resulted from his efforts, that is more difficult to gauge. His leadership in the early years of the conflict with Britain gave Americans something invaluable—a sense of their collective rights and liberties and their power and duty to defend them, which fostered a nascent sense of American unity and identity. As the new American republic struggled, he continued to offer real solutions that would secure and perfect American unity. For this, his countrymen celebrated him. But they found his other offerings less acceptable. Quakerism was a "peculiar" religion with correspondingly strange political expressions, many of which were unpalatable to early Americans.

The following pages will recount Dickinson's activities during the founding and early years of the new Republic with special attention to the Quaker ideas he offered for public consumption and implementation. A brief discussion of his religious background and affiliation, will be followed by an overview of the constitutional theory he espoused before independence. Attention will then turn to an examination of some of the Quaker-informed policy decisions he made during the Revolution and so-called Critical Period in an attempt to bring order and justice to Delaware and Pennsylvania. And finally, the discussion will conclude with a glimpse at his religious philosophy and activities during the early Republic.

John Dickinson's Quakerism

John Dickinson was born into a Maryland Quaker family in 1732. His mother was devout, but his father, a wealthy planter and judge, no longer attended meeting. Dickinson's upbringing, which was primarily in Delaware, and his education reflected both maternal and paternal influences. He was raised to be sensitive to Quaker social concerns, but also he was educated in history, languages, and law by the best minds in America and England. After legal training at the Middle Temple in London, Dickinson established his own practice in Philadelphia and shortly thereafter became a leading figure in the Quaker political culture of that city. In 1770 he married Mary Norris, herself a devout Friend and the daughter of the most powerful Quaker politician in the province, Isaac Norris, Jr. His daughters were Friends, and he was related in one way or another to the most prominent Quaker families in the region. In short, Dickinson functioned within a Quaker culture.[8]

Although Dickinson evinced something like ethnic Quakerism throughout his political career, his personal religious views and his attitude towards the relationship of religion and politics evolved dramatically over his fifty-some years in public life. As a young man, he believed that "Religion and Government are certainly very different Things, instituted for different Ends."[9] He personally rejected organized religion and the idea that it possessed a greater moral authority than civil law or secular standards of virtue, morality, and piety. There is no evidence that he attended meeting or the religious services of any denomination. So in 1770, when his Quaker fiancée wanted to get married under the care of the Friends meeting, he objected strenuously. He thought a civil ceremony sufficient and asked, "if an Act is not contrary to the Laws or Virtue or of our Country, can any Rule of a particular Society, however positive it may be, make that act improper or dishonourable?" He urged her "to consider the Reason of any opinions inculcated by Education, and she will distinguish between those essential to Virtue & Piety, and those merely arbitrary & derived from Rules of private Men."[10]

Dickinson's thinking about the relationship between religion and public life would evolve, but not his reservations about formal church membership. Near the end of his life he said, "I am not, and probably never shall be united to any religious Society, because each of them as a Society, hold principles which I cannot adopt."[11] With Quakerism that sticking-point was its strict pacifism. He was rather what we might call a pragmatic pacifist.¹² He explained, "I am on all proper occasions an advocate for defensive war. This principle has prevented me from union with Friends."¹³ But even in this matter, always advocating nonviolence whenever possible, he was closer to Quakerism than any other denomination. Other, smaller concerns also held him apart from Quakers. Most notably, he had little use for the Quaker "guarded" education, which aimed to shield young people from excessive intellectual engagement and thus sinful, worldly influences. Having himself benefited from a broad and rigorous education, he was very serious about the liberal education of youth.

Although Dickinson never joined the Quaker meeting, his religious sentiments became more Quakerly than those of many actual members. He went from rejecting the care of Friends as a young man to, when he was older, attending meeting several times a week, dressing plainly, using the plain speech (thee and thou), and enthusiastically taking up the good Quaker causes as his own—abolitionism, prison reform, limiting the death penalty, education of the poor, and antitheater efforts. And his thinking about the relationship of religion to public life evolved as well. Quakers in turn embraced him. Despite his rejection of strict pacifism (itself a relatively recent development in Pennsylvania Quakerism), Dickinson was the best and most prominent representative of traditional political Quakerism since William Penn.¹⁴ Quakers thus overlooked their disagreements and honored him as one of their own by allowing him to be buried among Friends.

Quaker Constitutionalism before Independence

Dickinson was the most eloquent, if imperfect, spokesman for the theory of Quaker constitutionalism.¹⁵ The core concept of the theory is that a constitution is both perpetual and amendable.¹⁶ This idea of a permanent and flexible constitution is commonplace to us, but when Quakers formulated the idea and the practices it required in the 1650s through the '80s, it was novel, and hardly less so when Dickinson expressed the same ideas in the 1760s and '70s. Only with the 1787 Constitutional Convention did Americans accept this view of a constitution. Dickinson brought this theory with all of its ancillary components to Americans before they were a people and helped make them into one.

The question of constitutional permanence and change was a central issue as Americans confronted the problem of what to do about British oppression. There were two prevailing constitutional theories before 1776, Tory and Whig, each with its own theological basis. Toryism, rooted in Anglicanism, held that the government had authority from God to do what it would, and that the people must submit, or at least not openly disobey.[17] Whiggism, drawing on reformed Calvinism, held that if the government violated the people's rights and broke the contract, revolution—the violent overthrow of the government and abolition of the constitution by the representatives of the people—was sanctioned by God.[18] Most recognized that the British constitution did change over time, but, with no formal mechanisms in place to ensure that it would be peaceful and orderly, all agreed that change was dangerous. They had no theory of peaceful change. None did, except the Quakers, who had a different understanding of a divinely constituted polity and the people's role in it. Dickinson exemplified this theory in word and deed.

Like most Englishmen, Quakers believed the government and constitution were ordained by God. As pacifists, they believed that God "never designed the Injury of one of '*his Offspring*' by another."[19] This included other men, but also the constitution, meaning, ultimately, the unity of the body politic. The government or constitution, Dickinson said, "is founded on the nature of man, that is, on the will of his *Maker*, and is therefore sacred."[20] He specified that "[i]*t is [the people's] duty to watch, and their right to take care, that the constitution be preserved.*"[21] But what can be done if the government should "[fall] into wrong measures"? The question was one that Quakers, the most persecuted dissenters, had to confront often. Then, Dickinson answered, it was "the duty of the governed to endeavour to rectify the mistake."[22] Unlike those who understood *sacred* to mean *untouchable*, Quakers believed that a constitution must also reflect progressive understanding of God's will and what Dickinson called "the living Elasticity within Man."[23] He taught that "[i]f the organization of a constitution be defective, it may be amended."[24] Quakers had invented mechanisms to amend constitutions, both written and unwritten. William Penn wrote the first amendment clause into a constitution, the First Frame of Government for Pennsylvania, in 1681.

Without taking for granted the uniqueness of the Quakers' amendment clause, we must recognize that this was the easy way to change a constitution—having the representatives of the people follow protocol agreed upon at the founding of the polity. The real problem was how to amend an ancient constitution the laws of which were unwritten and in existence from time immemorial, as the British constitution was claimed to be. For that, another approach was needed. It could not be done by representatives, who had no mechanism. Rather, it had to be done directly by the people themselves through active engagement in the public sphere.

First, the people had to become unified into one coherent body. Quakers knew better than most that this was the only way a people could combat oppression. To survive and confront the brutal persecution they suffered under English law was one reason they organized themselves into a formal society. With the same understanding, Dickinson's published his acclaimed *Letters from a Farmer in Pennsylvania* (1767–1768), which clarified the injustices and called for Americans to unify and resist. These letters were neither the first nor the only call for American unity, but they were the call that Americans responded to and the one that set the standard for subsequent resistance.[25] "Let us all be united with one spirit, in one cause," he wrote, because "this opposition can never be effectual, *unless it is the united effort of these provinces.*"[26] It is important to note that Dickinson also emphasized America's connection with Britain, "to which we are united by religion, liberty, laws, affections, relation, language and commerce."[27] America was a part of the British Empire and existed under the British constitution, a relationship Dickinson believed was crucial to preserve. But America was also distinct from Britain. "Let us consider ourselves as MEN---," he wrote, "FREEMEN---CHRISTIAN FREEMEN----*separated from the rest of the world,* and *firmly bound together* by the *same rights, interests* and *dangers.*"[28] He followed the *Letters* with another rousing call in the form of America's first patriotic song, "The Liberty Song" (1768), which was sung in taverns around the colonies. The line "By uniting we stand/, By dividing we fall" became America's reminder to herself. These sentiments were the nascent beginnings of an American identity.

The creation of a sense of unity was only the first step in achieving change. The next was the mobilization and action of individuals. For Quakers, individuals were directed to act by God through the Light in their consciences. They believed that God might speak through any individual—rich, poor, black, white, male, female—and that individual was then obligated to bring this message to the group and perhaps even lead. In order to fulfill this obligation, individuals needed the freedom to find God and then to speak. Religious liberty and freedom of speech thus went hand in hand. They were fundamental to the right functioning of the polity.

From early in his career, Dickinson was a committed supporter of religious and civil liberty for the most despised dissenters, Quakers and Catholics. "[T]hat best and greatest of all rights, *a perfect religious freedom,*" was the most basic political and constitutional principle on which all others depended.[29] He lauded the Quakers' Pennsylvania constitution, the 1701 Charter of Privileges. It was "[t]o *the Honour of the* Friends," he said, that "*the* Charter . . . *establishes* unalterably *an entire Liberty in religious Matters.*"[30] It was to protect this right, which enabled all Quakers' distinctive civil rights—such as no religious test except for a belief in Christ and freedom from swearing oaths, their conscientious objection to which would have prevented them from holding office, voting, and serving on juries or as witnesses—that he fought against the campaign for royal government in Pennsylvania in 1764.[31] And for the same reason, as well as to alert Americans to the dangers of an established church imposed without their consent, he contributed three of the twenty-one "Centinel" letters in the Episcopacy controversy in 1768.[32] When Anglicans petitioned Parliament to install a bishop in the colonies, he argued that "to establish among us any Form of Church-Discipline, deserves to be treated as an Attack upon our civil Liberties."[33] So strongly did Dickinson believe in this principle that he, contrary to most Anglo-Americans' attitudes, defended the rights of French Catholics to enjoy their civil, religious, and economic liberties and objected to the "superstitious Notion of Infidels being our natural Enemies, & deserving no Trials."[34]

With his Quakerly convictions about the importance of individual rights and agency, Dickinson was not neutral on theological disputes. He disagreed with other denominations that did not allow ordinary individuals to preach. He disliked the Anglican doctrine of "*uninterrupted Succession, the Divine Right of Episcopacy.*" In the "Centinel" he wrote with a hint of sarcasm, "I should be glad to see the Edict by which Christ has enjoined the unbroken Succession of Bishops," and followed it with an extensive footnote documenting early Christians choosing their own church leaders.[35] Likewise, he was disappointed that Presbyterians believed in "a succession of ordination" and were not more like Quakers when it came to allowing "Lay-ordinations."[36] The people, Quakers and Dickinson believed, could have immediate access to God through his Light in their consciences and were thereby qualified to speak and lead. This matter of the people's voice—individuals' voices—was a central issue for Dickinson.

Transferring these theological tenets to the civil sphere, as Quakers did, Dickinson believed that every person ought to participate in deliberations on public affairs. He did not go so far as to advocate universal suffrage, as some Quakers had, but his logic headed that direction.[37] "It is," he proclaimed, "not only [the people's] right, but their duty, to declare [their sentiments]."[38] Significantly, the obligation was not simply to speak, but also to disagree, if necessary, with the highest powers, "to testify of [God's] Truth even against those whom he made instruments in preserving them."[39] Dissent was thus a divine injunction and a civic duty. In this case, they must speak out against British oppression.

Dickinson first placed the onus to speak upon himself, and held to it, not simply willing but compelled to express controversial views. "Silence would be guilt," he believed. "I despise its Arts—I detest its Advantages. I must speak, tho I should lose my Life, tho I should lose the Affections of my Country[men]."[40] His rule for personal deportment was "to deliberate on Questions important to [the public] Happiness, distaining all personal advantages to be derived from a Suppression of my real Sentiments, and defying all Dangers to be risked by a Declaration of them, openly to avow them."[41] This was an example he hoped to set for his countrymen.

He extended his call to action to all members of the polity: "WHAT CONCERNS ALL, SHOULD BE CONSIDERED BY ALL."[42] Addressing ordinary Americans in his writings, his aim was "to simplify the subject, so as to facilitate the inquiries of his fellow citizens."[43] He explained the complex political situations to those without the time or education to be able to understand them for themselves, emphasizing their potential contributions. "As a charitable, but poor person does not withhold his *mite*, because he cannot relieve *all* the distresses of the miserable," Dickinson encouraged, "so should not any honest man suppress his sentiments concerning freedom, however small their influence is likely to be. Perhaps he 'may touch some wheel,' that will have an effect greater than he could reasonably expect."[44] The hope of doing good was one thing. But it was more urgent than that. He explained that "individuals may injure a whole society, by not declaring their sentiments."[45]

It was not enough that individuals express themselves; they must do so in a very particular way. Dickinson paired his constant refrain of popular participation with another message, equally strong: the importance of preserving unity. The people must engage so as not to jeopardize the sacred unity of the polity, their constitution. Peace, caution, moderation, prudence, reverence for the constitution were Dickinson's mantra. He said, "[L]et every one freely speak, what he really thinks, but with so sincere a reverence for the cause he ventures to discuss, as to use the utmost caution, lest he should lead any into errors, upon a point of such sacred concern as the public happiness."[46] For his own part, he said, "My Dissent is mingled with Respect."[47] When governmental oppression threatened, his goal was always "to persuade [the people] immediately, vigorously, and unanimously, to exert themselves, in the most firm, but most peaceable manner, for obtaining relief."[48] Eventually, public expression must consist not just of speech, but also action.

Dickinson was not vague either in his own mind or in his public recommendations about what he meant. He had a model to follow. During the contest with Britain, he reminded Pennsylvanians of the history of their own province and urged them to use it as an example:

> there was a certain turbulent Spirit in our [Quaker] Forefathers, which never would suffer them to sit down in Silence and Submission under any Attack upon their Priviledges or Liberties . . . However, tho they had their turbulent Disposition for maintaining their Rights . . . their Turbulence was of such a kind, no other turbulence can be compard with it. It was the Turbulence of Sense, Spirit, Virtue, Meekness, Piety, employed . . . in Defence of publick Happiness. It was cautious: it was firm: it was noble: it was gentle: it was devout:[49] In short, their Policy was like the Religion they profest.[50]

His prescription for resisting Britain was to use the same methods Quakers had been using successfully for one hundred years to resist oppression—peaceful protest, notably, boycotting and civil disobedience. Quakers were the first to originate and practice these two techniques, although the terms would not be coined until centuries later. Boycotting of sugar, indigo, and other goods produced by slave labor had been used by Quakers for decades to protest slavery. Civil disobedience—that is, the public, nonviolent breaking of unjust laws in order to educate the public about the need for reform[51]—had been invented by Friends in the 1660s to defy laws against their religion. During the Revolution, Dickinson advocated the same approach to protest oppressive British laws. He counseled the colonists to go about their "business as usual" ignoring the offending laws.[52] "[T]hus revoked by you," the laws would "soon after [receive] a formal repeal in Parliament."[53] In this way, the "sacred trust" that is the constitution would be preserved and changed peacefully. Dickinson's was the first-ever call for a national program of peaceful protest. It was the same tactic employed two hundred years later in the Civil Rights Movement by Martin Luther King, Jr., himself mentored by Quakers.[54] This sort of protest shows the highest reverence for the existing constitution by attempting to return it to its first principles without doing it harm.

While Dickinson was taking a traditional Quaker approach to resisting Britain, the Quakers as a body were changing course. In the days of the Stamp Act resistance, Friends had answered Dickinson's calls and been among the leaders of peaceful resistance. But as tensions rose, fear for their Charter rights—either under an Anglican establishment if Britain prevailed, or by persecution from their political enemies, the Presbyterians, if independence were declared—caused the body of Quakers first to plead for reconciliation with Britain, and then to turn neutral. In 1775 and '76 they "circumscribe[d] themselves within plain & narrow grounds," which meant restricting their activities to humanitarian efforts and strictly avoiding military and political activity.[55]

Other Americans, including some former Quakers now calling themselves "Free Quakers," were becoming increasingly radical. Before the US Constitution was implemented, they generally still thought with John Locke, who called any resistance with reverence and without the sword "a ridiculous way of resisting."[56] They heeded Dickinson's counsel for a decade—unify, resist peacefully, and try to reconcile—but, thinking of the flawed British constitution as a broken contract to be discarded rather than a trust to be preserved, Americans ultimately opted for revolution. Even as his countrymen rejected Dickinson's peaceful program, they acknowledged that it was "owing to his 'farmer's letters,' and his conduct, that there was a present disposition to dispose the tyranny of Parliament."[57] For Dickinson, there was only one thing to do—join them. For him, there was a sort of hierarchy of constitutions. The British constitution was, he believed, crucial for America's protection. But over the last decade, at his urging, Americans had been gradually unifying until they had begun to constitute themselves as a people. It was this fledgling union that ultimately took priority for Dickinson.

Dickinson's path at this point remained more Quakerly than it might appear at first glance. He spoke openly against the Declaration of Independence. Then, knowing the vote would go against him, he made a principled decision not to vote. America's voice must be unanimous in this moment, "to keep up the appearance of unbroken harmony," and he did not want to obstruct.[58] Quakers call this "standing aside."[59] Naturally, not being in favor of the motion, Dickinson did not sign the Declaration. Then, in what seems like an un-Quakerly move, he joined the cause, serving as a colonel and a private in the Pennsylvania and Delaware militias respectively. Taking up arms went against Quaker pacifism, which Dickinson could do with a clear conscience, not being a Quaker. Indeed, he believed that defense of liberty with a militia was "part of a Freeman's Religion."⁶⁰ But the simple act of supporting the American cause was very much in keeping with traditional Quaker constitutional theory. One who withdraws his objection thereby gives tacit assent and then is morally obligated to preserve the unity of the group by supporting the majority decision.⁶¹ True to this model, Dickinson considered the "public Resolution" to declare independence "as sacred."⁶² He explained his actions thus:

> Although I spoke my sentiments freely,—as an honest man ought to do,—yet when a determination was reached upon the question against my opinion, I regarded that determination as the voice of my country. That voice proclaimed her destiny, in which I was resolved by every impulse of my soul to share, and to stand or fall with her in that scheme of freedom which she had chosen.⁶³

Despite his taking up arms, Quakers generally approved of Dickinson's course of action. Had he been a member of the meeting, he probably would have been formally disowned; had he been less Quakerly, he might have been informally shunned. But Dickinson consistently and eloquently voiced the Quaker priorities of reconciliation, nonviolence, unity, and the protection of liberty of conscience. With such an earnest and influential figure who was also only a "fellow traveler," they could overlook his decision to fight. At the same time, other of his countrymen could not forgive his departure from Whig ideology, a fact that has shaped his legacy. Little attention is given to the notion that, as John Adams—Dickinson's political nemesis—noted, the delay Dickinson caused in the declaring of independence was actually a "great advantage" in that it served to "cement the union."⁶⁴

It might seem that Dickinson's support for the French Revolution in the next decade contradicted his constitutional theory. The French situation, although similar to the American Revolution in some ways, was markedly different in others. Dickinson could not advocate revolution for America because it existed under the British constitution, which offered some protections for rights and liberties. The French had no such protection. Although some sixteenth-century anti-absolutists argued for the existence of an "ancient constitution,"⁶⁵ it was even more of an abstraction in France than in England and none during the Revolution expected any recourse to it. But in spite of Dickinson's assertion that "[w]hen an oppressed nation draws the sword to assert her liberty, all the noblest passions, affections, and faculties are brought into ardent concentration," he still held out hope for Quakerly persuasion, believing that "Truth is a Conqueror without Violence."[66]

Implementing Quaker Policy during the Revolution and "Critical Period"

About mid-career, we can see a change in Dickinson's attitude toward the role of religion in his private life and the public realm. Dickinson himself credited the change to the influence of his daughter. As an elderly man, he recounted the story of how, when she was young and he suggested she take dance lessons, she replied that she would "much rather be a Friend." Her sensibilities "mortified" him, that is, embarrassed him into a closer examination of his own worldliness.[67] This incident might have taken place in the mid-1780s, but evidence suggests a transformation in Dickinson even earlier. And, even as he refused to join the Friends in their new political neutrality, his Quakerism was turning out to be typical in some ways of the "reformed" Quakerism of the late-eighteenth century—strict biblical morality combined with active benevolence for social justice.[68] Dickinson's new religious sensibilities emerged during the chaos of the Revolution and informed his attempt to bring order to his two home states and his country.

Having played a significant role in creating American unity, and knowing that the nation would not survive without a strong written constitution, Dickinson drafted the first version of the Articles of Confederation in June of 1776. It contained several forward-looking provisions that reflected Quaker concerns, all of which were excised from the final version, ratified in 1781. Native Americans, having always had a good relationship with Quakers, received special protections. To preserve the fragile unity of the new nation, there was to be a strong central government to which the states would be subordinate. And there was a provision for protecting the rights of conscience of dissenters that has been called "innovative" and "distinctive."[69] One might have expected Dickinson to add the same language and provisions on religious liberty from the Pennsylvania 1701 Charter, which he valued so highly. Indeed, he noted that for this clause, "such Expressions as are in the Penn[sylvani]a Charter & Laws, to be used—for precision."[70] But his biggest concern was to unite a group of would-be states, most of which had religious establishments and disliked dissenters. A law as liberal as Pennsylvania's would never pass. He therefore sought to enforce the levels of toleration that currently existed according to "the present Laws of the said Colonies" and prohibit any further impositions on the consciences of dissenters.[71] He also added two elements not in the Pennsylvania constitution. The first was gender-inclusive language, so that "No person . . . shall be molested or prejudiced in his or her person or Estate for his or her religious persuasion."[72] Quakers had long recognized men and women as spiritual equals and were the only denomination that allowed women to be ministers. Apparently, Dickinson was merely codifying this recognition. The second was obligatory observance of the Sabbath at some place of worship. Evidence discussed below suggests that this point signaled a shift in Dickinson's thinking about religion in public life.

Dickinson's provisions for religious liberty and a strong central government were not merely concerns resurrected from past Quaker experience. They reflected apprehensions for the welfare of Quakerism in the immediate future. As far as Dickinson was concerned, Pennsylvania was a constitutional disaster in the making.[73] The state was overrun with radicals who had long been contesting with Quakers for control of the government.[74] Once independence was declared and the 1701 Charter abolished, they turned on Friends and other dissenters, denying them the religious and civil rights they had enjoyed since the province's founding.[75] Dickinson's provision in the Articles of Confederation to freeze state laws for the protection of religious dissenters at their colonial levels was clearly written in anticipation of exactly this backlash. But there was no central American constitution in the 1770s to protect civil rights of any kind; and Dickinson found the new 1776 Pennsylvania constitution deeply flawed. He worked tirelessly against it for several years, angering the radicals, in an effort to establish and protect civil rights that Quakers held dear.

Shortly after the Pennsylvania constitution was imposed on the people without their consent, Dickinson spoke against it and suggested improvements. One of his main objections was it had "not settl[ed] some mode for making alterations and amendments" for the first seven years, "if they should be judged expedient, without overturning the government." This, argued Dickinson, "was a high violation of the Rights of the Freemen of this State."[76] He also found "[t]hat in the Constitution . . . the Christian religion is not treated with proper respect."[77] His personal copy of the Declaration of Rights reveals his qualms. There he made extensive edits, including adding a provision against forcing dissenters to swear oaths[78] and one prohibiting tests stipulating anything more than a general belief in Christianity, "exclusive of the articles, disputed between the several Sects thereof."[79] He also published a pamphlet describing how the government should function, including a suggested list of new laws. Several of these laws reflect Quaker priorities, including those for the religious education of youth, strict limitations on the death penalty, protection of trial by jury, and the abolition of slavery.[80] This list was not just idle wishing: for the rest of his life, he did what he could, as a public servant and as a private citizen, to achieve all these things in Delaware and Pennsylvania.

As Delaware's newly elected president in 1781, Dickinson expressed his religiosity in a couple of ways. First, he signaled his increased commitment to Quakerism by choosing to take an affirmation of office instead of an oath.[81] Second, he believed it was his "first and indispensible Duty" to produce a document that blended religion and politics as he had never done before. Concerned about bad public behavior since the beginning of the war, he issued a proclamation for suppressing vice and immorality and promoting religion. Believing that God's "rational Creatures should yield a chearful Submission to his Holy Laws," he revived the provision from the Articles of Confederation and "exhort[ed] all Persons decently and reverently to attend the Worship of god on every *Lord's* Day, at a Service acceptable to him." In Dickinson's vision for the state, everyone would play a role in ensuring that "Religion and good Manners may flourish and increase." He specified "that all well-disposed Persons, and especially all Persons in Place of Authority, will by their own exemplary Conduct encourage and promote Piety and Virtue, guide the young, the weak, and the unexperienced into laudable Courses." Where their example could not be effective, the law would take over. Dickinson recommended legislation reminiscent of Pennsylvania's early morality laws against a litany of bad public behavior, including drunkenness, lewdness, profane swearing, gaming, cursing, blasphemy, or any other "dissolute or immoral Practice" that might profane the Lord's Day. He did not include playing tennis among the crimes against God as earlier Quakers had, but he did enjoin magistrates, judges, justices, and ministers of the Gospel to punish transgression and promote the contents of the proclamation.[82] In contrast to his earlier position, Dickinson had come around to believing that "there is a Relationship between the Principles of Religion and the Principles of Civil Society."[83] Government, he now thought, had a role in promoting religion. His efforts met with approval in Delaware, and the proclamation was reprinted in other states.[84]

Before he had finished his first term as president of Delaware, in 1782 Dickinson was elected president of Pennsylvania. The previous summer he had already taken an affirmation of loyalty to the Commonwealth, again signaling his Quakerly priorities in a state that had recently inflicted persecution on Quakers. Dickinson exemplified Quaker concerns in several notable ways. He again made the publication of a proclamation on religion his inaugural executive act. Much of the content and some of the language was the same as the Delaware proclamation, but this one was more forceful and more detailed. It contained the same admonition to "observe the LORDS DAY," it likewise enlisted public servants and prominent citizens in the cause of promoting piety and virtue, and it called for the passage of similar morality laws.[85] But it also contained a lengthier, more theological meditation on the relation of religion to civil order, as well as more recommendations for promoting piety.

As president, he sought to govern by the precepts in the proclamation, hewing closely to his understanding of piety. For example, in the interest of preserving peace and unity, in the Mutiny of 1783, he defied Congress by refusing to call out the Pennsylvania militia against Continental soldiers who were marching on Philadelphia to demand pay for their services. He instead negotiated with the men, heard their grievances, and thereby averted violence.[86] Seeking to limit the death penalty and preserve basic civil rights, in the famous 1784 case of *Respublica v. Doan*, he defied the Pennsylvania judicial system by refusing to sign a writ of execution for a suspected Loyalist denied benefit of a trial by jury, that "Heaven-taught institution" and one that Quakers had always championed against great odds.[87] His stand was for the right of the people to determine the substantive content of a law.[88]

Dickinson's policy decisions represent an interesting turn in his thinking. In some ways, they appear heavy-handed in a way his younger self might have resented as he admonished against sport and revelry and pressed citizens under his government to greater piety. Whereas before the Revolution, he believed that religion and the state were "instituted for very different ends," by 1786 his views had changed so he thought "it is the duty of government, with the utmost attention and caution, to promote and enforce the sublime and beneficial morality, as well as theology, of Christianity." He mused privately about government "employing men of wisdom, piety, and learning to teach it," suggesting even that "impositions be laid for this purpose." Always most worried about dissenters' rights, however, he specified that those who objected conscientiously would be "permitted to appropriate his share to the use of the poor, or any other public service." Ultimately, however inclined Dickinson was to enforce Christian morality in the public sphere, he was always acutely aware of the dangers. "[A] neglect and contempt of [liberty of conscience]," he warned, "has been the disgrace and curse, and will infallibly be the destruction, of every human institution, however cunningly devised, on this momentous subject."[89] Therefore, although he wrote passionately about the religious instruction of youth, he never publically suggested the institutionalization of public Christian education.

Philosophy and Influence in the Early Republic

In his later years, Dickinson's thinking on religion became expansive, philosophical, and prescriptive.[90] Ultimately, he came to espouse a kind of "nature religion" or "Christian naturalism" that borrowed heavily on Quaker traditions and theology.[91] He agreed in part with thinkers on religion, such as William Bentley, Samuel Miller, Benjamin Rush, and Joseph Priestley, who promoted rationalism in concert with Christianity. Like the Quaker botanist John Bartram, he celebrated God's visible creation and man's relationship with it, emphasizing that if man undertook the scientific study of creation and was true to the sacred laws of nature, he would live happily and help others do the same. He easily combined seemingly contradictory elements in a way that few but Quakers could. Reason was a "divine gift" and an important way to the Truth, but it could not be divorced from revelation.[92] "It is highly improbable," he cautioned, "that God would have left Men to this fallible Guide for finding mistakes and discovering his Duties. All Religion is revealed."[93] The works of great philosophers, jurists, theologians, and historians ancient and modern were crucial, but when these sources reached their limits, to sort out "the discordant sentiments of the good and wise," he said, "I turn with Locke to 'The Holy Scriptures, especially the New Testament.'"[94] Dickinson exalted not just the human spirit, but also the body, with its divinely implanted self-love. Overall, Dickinson evinced a belief in progress and, despite profound worries about current domestic and international affairs, an abiding optimism about human nature and man's capacity for good. By the end of his life, Dickinson was seen by his contemporaries as not just an authority on political matters but on religion as well. The renowned Presbyterian theologian Samuel Miller assured him, "I make it a rule to publish nothing, without submitting it to your inspection."[95]

Even as Dickinson argued strenuously against the Deists, skeptics, and "metaphysical *ballooners*" who sought to undermine the influence of Christianity and, in his view, mislead a vulnerable public, he agreed politically with Jefferson and Paine about the rights of man, the justness of the French Revolution, and a definition of republicanism that countered the Federalist version.[96] Here we can only glimpse the highlights and note the most obvious ways his thinking on religion informed his political engagement and in turn shaped the nation.[97]

As the chairman of the Annapolis Convention in 1786, Dickinson led the national call for a Constitutional Convention to amend the faulty Articles of Confederation. In the 1787 Convention, he deliberated on many issues, but at this point, his religious beliefs came through only subtly. Those unaware of his burgeoning Quakerism might mistake him for an humanitarian when he decried slavery, or a scientific rationalist when he introduced the now-commonplace metaphor for the relationship of the states to the federal government. "Let our Govt. be like that of the solar System," he said. "[L]et the Genl. Govt. be the Sun and the States the Planets repelled yet attracted, and the whole moving regularly and harmoniously in their respective Orbits."[98] This image, which also represented the Quaker meeting structure, was repeated in the Convention, the ratification debates, and beyond.[99] His creative thinking on federalism allowed him to contribute a "crucial conceptual breakthrough" on the matter of representation, that one branch should have equal representation and the other proportional.[100]

In 1788, he published a first set of *Fabius Letters* to encourage ratification of the Constitution. Here his faith is overt. The letters are suffused with admonitions to the public to respect the "sacred law," live according to "divine designs," and be "religiously attentive" in choosing representatives.[101] Dickinson repeated many of his earlier sentiments about the unity of the polity and duty of the individual to deliberate on public matters and voice his opinion. To those looking for guidance, he recommended the Bible, "the most republican book that ever was written."[102] In there is a description of "that *perfect liberty*" that comes from living in society, which is "better described in the Holy Scriptures, than any where else."[103] The *Letters* met with a good reception. "The writer of the pieces signed Fabius," said George Washington, "appears to be master of his subject; he treats it with dignity, and at the same time expresses himself in such manner as to render it intelligible to every capacity." He recommended "an extensive republication" of them.[104]

One significant mystery that remains is why Dickinson did not publicly support a bill of rights or himself propose a clause for religious liberty in the Constitution. Rather, Fabius toed the Federalist line, arguing that a bill was not necessary and that the rights in question were protected by the state constitutions.[105] There is no record of what Dickinson thought of the Bill of Rights once it was proposed and ratified, but it is hard to imagine that he would have found it objectionable.

An issue on which Dickinson tried and failed to exert his influence was abolitionism, despite the fact he took the cause very seriously in his personal life and as a public good. In 1777, a year after advocating the abolition of slavery in Pennsylvania, he manumitted his own slaves, first conditionally, indenturing them to ensure their livelihoods, then unconditionally in 1781 and 1786.[106] Believing that "the recording Angel stood ready to make Record against him in Heaven, had he neglected it," he released about thirty-five inherited from his father and ensured they would not be destitute.[107] Quakers praised him, then worked with him in 1786 to draft an act for the gradual abolition of slavery in Delaware.[108] It did not pass. In 1787, Dickinson was one of the few delegates at the Constitutional Convention to speak out against the slave trade on moral grounds.[109] He tried to abolish slavery in the 1792 Delaware constitutional convention. But, as he explained to a Quaker kinsman, "the effectual remedy for the Evil [of slavery] would have been, to declare all persons born after the establishing of the Constitution, free." When this was attempted and it became clear "that neither this [proposal] nor any like it could succeed," he and others realized that "any Prunings of this Tree of bitter Fruits, would only strengthen it and make it last longer," and mere "[a]lleviation of slavery by the Convention, would have been constitutional sanction of it."[110] Some Quakers hoped that Dickinson would continue to use his influence to promote abolitionism to people such as George Washington; others were disappointed with his efforts, saying those who "came nearest to the truth and were not in it, and profess it, were its greatest enemies."[111] But, even with his considerable influence in Delaware, it is hard to see how Dickinson could have succeeded there, where slavery was so entrenched that the state did not even ratify the Thirteenth Amendment to the US Constitution until 1901.

In retirement, Dickinson continued to contribute to the development of the new Republic in many of the same ways that he always had. His ongoing philanthropy touched hundreds, prompting recognition that "his whole conduct [was] a practical comment upon the divine truths of religion."¹¹² His significant donation "for the relief of those poor who may be 'sick and in prison,' under direction of Friends in Philadelphia" in 1786 was used to found the first modern prison reform society, the Society for Alleviating the Miseries of Public Prisons, which then established America's first penitentiary.¹¹³ He shared Friends' commitment to education—although a more liberal version of it—and, among many donations, especially to aid poor and orphaned children, he provided foundational funding for Dickinson College, established in his name by Benjamin Rush in 1783, and Westtown School, the first Quaker boarding school, founded in 1799.¹¹⁴

His engagement in the public sphere continued, as the leader of citizens' groups protesting or advocating one cause or another, author of pamphlets, and giver of speeches. He was lauded—or denigrated, depending on the source—as a leader of the Democratic-Republicans in Delaware, and he struggled, not always successfully, to keep from being nominated for election to Congress. His last candidacy was in 1807, just months before his death. As an elder statesman of the founding, he retained the ear of politicians at the highest levels, including President Jefferson, Attorney General Caesar Augustus Rodney, Secretary of the Treasury Albert Gallatin, and Pennsylvania Senator George Logan.

Dickinson undoubtedly had the greatest influence on the latter, who, like his mentor, was a Quaker politician. "The personal relations between Dr. Logan and Mr. Dickinson were very close and intimate," wrote Logan's wife, "and their political opinions were evidently formed on the same model." As a Senator, Logan "was in the habit of submitting every measure of importance which came before that body to Mr. Dickinson."¹¹⁵ In some ways, Logan acted as Dickinson's proxy when the latter could no longer be active in politics. The correspondence between the two covers a broad range of policy issues, with Dickinson often requesting that Logan put his ideas before one official or another. In two areas they shared the most concern. The first was promoting the scientific study of God's creation to foster political liberty. The second was maintaining good relations with France.

In the late 1790s, Dickinson published two documents that give insight into his ideas on religion and politics and demonstrate the correspondence of his ideas with Logan's. *A Fragment* (1796) was a piece of a larger manuscript on the religious instruction of youth, which ill-health prevented him from finishing. It was intended as a book of morality and ethics that would counter the pernicious effects of skepticism, which might "mislead or impair" the "Candor and Integrity in Young Persons."¹¹⁶ It is an enthusiastic celebration of nature, scientific learning, and obedience to the divine will. Young people are enjoined to view themselves as ministers and co-creators with God when they learn their letters, understand the solar system, exchange knowledge, cultivate the land, navigate the ocean, and love their fellow men. "These are the Works of Peace," says Dickinson.[117] Two years later, in 1798, Logan published his *Address on the Natural and Social Order of the World, as Intended to Produce Universal Good*, which contained many of the same themes and others Dickinson and Quakers cared about, such as eliminating oppression by magistrates, world peace, the perfectibility of man, and fair treatment of Indians. Logan took his ideas further than Dickinson could, putting them into practice on his experimental farm and in his promotion of agrarian democracy.[118] Of course, Dickinson was America's original "Farmer," having thirty years earlier captured the imagination of America with the ideal of the virtuous, disinterested freeholder studying and practicing the tenets of republican liberty.

Dickinson and Logan, both devoted Francophiles, also agreed on foreign policy. In 1797, as tensions rose between America and France, Dickinson wrote a second set of Fabius Letters, "in which," he summarized, "a just value for the Blessings of Peace is contrasted with the blind Rage for War, and the superior advantage of Negotiations over arms is stated."[119] His religious priorities came through clearly when he explored the concept of divinely implanted self-love. For Dickinson, there was a "system of affections" whereby God instilled self-interest in man, this self-love led naturally to "social affections," and then, by extension, friendships with foreign nations. "Our Creator never made individuals or nations, to be kind to themselves only."[120] They must "attend also to [the interests] of others."[121] He extolled the blessings of strong international alliances, explaining, "The friendships between nations comprehend more valuable objects, than those between individuals, such as national peace, prosperity, liberty, and safety."[122] France was our sister nation. Not only had the French "*first* acknowledged our *independence*," they followed the example we set in overthrowing a monarchy and establishing a republic.[123] Maintaining good relations was an obligatory expression of gratitude. Holding such convictions, and being as close to Logan as he was, it is difficult to imagine that Dickinson did not know of and encourage Logan's one-man peace mission to France in 1798. In a very Quakerly move, Logan took it upon himself to travel to France, meet with officials, and try to avert war. Some scholars have noted that his visit may have "turned the tide of American public opinion from war to peace."[124] The Federalist Congress, which immediately passed the Logan Act against such behavior, did not appreciate the effort.

Dickinson's most visible contribution to the American founding might indeed be as "Penman of the Revolution." His writings certainly prepared Americans for independence. But if we consider the intended message of not just his preindependence work but his entire life, we see something richer, broader, and more lasting than that. His was a constant voice of moderation that spoke for peace, unity, love and respect for divine creation, and liberty broadly defined. And he advocated these things insistently, even when it was unpopular to do so. Although ignored or rejected at first, his concerns, such as protection of rights for religious and political dissenters, the perpetual and amendable constitution, individual agency, civil disobedience, and abolitionism were subsequently adopted. They were the proverbial stones the builders rejected that became the cornerstones of the nation. These were not novel ideas. They had long been part of the Quaker tradition. Dickinson's other Quaker priorities, such as moderate discourse in domestic politics, humane treatment of prisoners, limiting the death penalty, rigorous education for all children, and peace as policy in foreign relations, are often touted as ideals, but rarely practiced with consistency. As we look to the founders for old solutions to current problems, perhaps Dickinson's greatest contributions are yet to come.

Notes

1. On Dickinson's life, see Charles J. Stillé, *The Life and Times of John Dickinson* (Philadelphia: Historical Society of Pennsylvania, 1891) and Milton E. Flower, *John Dickinson, Conservative Revolutionary* (Charlottesville: University Press of Virginia, 1983).
2. "Copy of a Paper Drawn up by Joseph Reed for W. Henry Drayton" [n.d.]. Maria Dickinson Logan Collection, Historical Society of Pennsylvania.
3. On his renown, see Carl F. Kaestle, "The Public Reaction to John Dickinson's Farmer's Letters," *Proceedings of the American Antiquarian Society* vol. 78, part 2 (1969): 323–359.
4. The appellation may have been given first by Moses Coit Tyler in *The Literary History of the American Revolution, 1763–1783*, 2 vols. (New York: G. P. Putnam's Sons, 1897), 2: 24.
5. Fredrick B. Tolles, "John Dickinson and the Quakers," in *"John and Mary's College": The Boyd Lee Spahr Lectures, 1951–1956* (Carlisle: Fleming H. Revel Co., 1951–1956): 67–88, 67.
6. Ibid., 76.
7. Jane E. Calvert, *Quaker Constitutionalism and the Political Thought of John Dickinson* (New York: Cambridge University Press, 2009).

8. In the late-eighteenth century, Quakers were the fourth largest religious denomination in the colonies, with a disproportionately large influence culturally, economically, and politically. At the time of the Revolution, most were concentrated in the Middle Colonies with Philadelphia having the largest Yearly Meeting at 30,000 members. See Edwin S. Gaustad, Philip L. Barlow, and Richard W. Dishno, *New Historical Atlas of Religion in America* (New York: Oxford University Press, 2000), 42–45.
9. John Dickinson [hereafter JD], "The Centinel. No. VIII," *Pennsylvania Journal*, May 12, 1768.
10. JD to Sarah Norris [1769]. R. R. Logan Collection, Historical Society of Pennsylvania [hereafter RRL/HSP].
11. JD to Samuel Miller, August 10, 1807. Photostat in J. H. Powell Papers, American Philosophical Society.
12. See Jane E. Calvert, "Pacifism," in Anderson and Herr, eds., *The Encyclopedia of Activism and Social Justice*, 3 vols. (Thousand Oaks, CA: SAGE Publications, Inc., 2007), 3: 1075–1078.
13. JD to Tench Coxe, January 24, 1807, cited in Flower, *John Dickinson*, 301.
14. The meaning of the word "traditional" will become apparent as the discussion progresses.
15. This much-abbreviated discussion is drawn from *Quaker Constitutionalism*.
16. The term *constitution* needs some explanation. Its primary definition was not, as it is for us, a written document codifying laws and principles. It did, however, mean the fundamental laws and principles, written or unwritten, by which a people lived. For early modern thinkers, *constitution* was also often synonymous with *government*. Most broadly, the word meant the composition of the people, the body politic. Within this last understanding, constitutionalism encompasses not just the structures, laws, and limits of government, but also how people, individually and collectively, interact with the government. Thus Quaker constitutionalism is not just a theory of structures, legal arrangements, and abstract ideas, but also a theory of popular civic engagement.
17. See, for example, Robert Filmer, *Patriarcha, or the Natural Power of Kings* (London, 1680) and Jonathan Boucher, *A View of the Causes and Consequences of the American Revolution* (London, 1797).
18. There is a vast literature on the Whig-Calvinist theory of revolution. See, most notably, Quentin Skinner, *Foundations of Modern Political Thought, vol. 2: The Age of Reformation* (Cambridge: Cambridge University Press, 1978) and John Locke's *Second Treatise of Civil Government* (London, 1690).
19. JD, *A Fragment* (Philadelphia: Thomas Dobson, 1796), 17.
20. JD, *The Letters of Fabius, in 1788, on the Federal Constitution; and in 1797 on the Present Situation of Public Affairs* (Wilmington: W.C. Smith, 1797), 26 [hereafter *Fabius '88* or *Fabius '97*].

21. *Fabius '88*, 29.
22. JD, *Letters from a Farmer in Pennsylvania, to the Inhabitants of the British Colonies* (Philadelphia: Hall and Sellers, 1768), 16.
23. JD, Notes on Politics and Religion [n.d.]. RRL/HSP. Dickinson's emphasis.
24. *Fabius '88*, 26.
25. Kaestle, "The Public Reaction to John Dickinson's Farmer's Letters," 326.
26. *Farmer's Letters*, 17, 67.
27. Ibid., 16.
28. Ibid., 67.
29. JD, *A Speech, Delivered in the House of Assembly of the Province of Pennsylvania* (Philadelphia: William Bradford, 1764), 15.
30. JD, "The Centinel. No. VIII."
31. JD, *A Speech*.
32. On the controversy in Pennsylvania and Dickinson's authorship of these three letters, see Richard J. Hooker, "John Dickinson on Church and State," *American Literature*, 16, no. 2 (1944): 82–98; and Elizabeth L. Nybakken, *The Centinel: Warnings of a Revolution* (Newark, NJ: University of Delaware Press, 1979).
33. JD, "The Centinel. No. VII," *Pennsylvania Journal*, May 5, 1768. On the American fear of Anglicanism in general, see Carl Bridenbaugh, *Mitre and Sceptre: Transatlantic Faiths, Ideas, Personalities, and Politics* (New York: Oxford University Press, 1962).
34. JD, "Reflections on the Flag of the Truce Trade," 25. John Dickinson Papers, Library Company of Philadelphia [hereafter JDP/LCP]. See also JD, *A Letter to the Inhabitants of the Province of Quebec* (Philadelphia: William and Thomas Bradford, 1774).
35. JD, "The Centinel. No. VI," *Pennsylvania Journal*, April 28, 1768.
36. JD to Samuel Miller, August 10, 1807.
37. The 1677 Quaker constitution of West Jersey provided for universal suffrage, and for a time in post-Revolutionary New Jersey, women had the vote until 1807. See *The West Jersey Concessions and Agreements of 1676/77: A Roundtable of Historians*, Occasional Papers, no. 1 (Trenton: New Jersey Historical Commission); and Judith Apter Klinghofer and Lois Elkis, "'The Petticoat Electors': Women's Suffrage in New Jersey, 1776–1807," *Journal of the Early Republic* 12 (1992), 159–193.
38. *Fabius '88*, 2.
39. JD, "An Essay Towards the Religious Instruction of Youth" [1796]. RRL/HSP.
40. JD, "Arguments against the Independence of these Colonies—in Congress." Gratz Collection, Historical Society of Pennsylvania [hereafter Gratz/HSP].
41. JD to John Jay, July 22, 1779. RRL/HSP.
42. *Fabius '88*, 2.
43. Ibid., 3–4.
44. *Farmer's Letters*, 4. The quote is from Alexander Pope's *An Essay on Man* (1734).

45. *Fabius '88*, 2.
46. Ibid., 3
47. JD to George Logan, January 23, 1805, in Deborah Norris Logan, *Memoir of Dr. George Logan of Stenton* (Philadelphia: The Historical Society of Pennsylvania, 1894), 149.
48. *Farmer's Letters*, 15.
49. Here Dickinson had initially written "religious."
50. JD, fragment of an essay [c.1774], RRL/HSP.
51. To be clear, not all breaking of the law is civil disobedience. It should not be confused with other forms of protest that involve breaking the law either violently or clandestinely. Moreover, civil disobedience also includes the responsibility of the disobedient to accept the punishment for breaking the law.
52. JD, *Friends and Countrymen* (Philadelphia: Franklin and Hall), 2.
53. JD, "Letters to the Inhabitants of the Colonies," *Pennsylvania Journal*, June 1, 1774.
54. John D'Emilio, *Lost Prophet: The Life and Times of Bayard Rustin* (Chicago: University of Chicago Press, 2003); Calvert, *Quaker Constitutionalism*, 329–333.
55. Philadelphia Yearly Meeting to Quarterly and Monthly Meetings (1776), cited in Richard Bauman, *For the Reputation of Truth: Politics, Religion, and Conflict Among the Pennsylvania Quakers, 1750–1800* (Baltimore: The Johns Hopkins University Press, 1971), 159; See also Calvert, *Quaker Constitutionalism*, 207–246.
56. Locke, *Second Treatise*, 457 (para. 235).
57. "Copy of a Paper."
58. JD to Samuel Ward, January 29, 1775. Gratz/HSP.
59. Michael J. Sheeran, *Beyond Majority Rule: Voteless Decisions in the Religious Society of Friends* (Philadelphia: Philadelphia Yearly Meeting, 1996), 66–67, 70.
60. JD to George Logan, December 13, 1804, in *Memoir*, 148.
61. Sheeran, *Beyond Majority Rule*, 67.
62. JD to President of Congress [John Jay], July 22, 1779. RRL/HSP.
63. Stillé, *Life and Times*, 204.
64. John Adams to Abigail Adams, July 3, 1776, in *Letters of Delegates to Congress, 1774–1789*, Smith et al., eds., 25 vols. (Washington, DC: Library of Congress, 1976–2000), 4: 376.
65. J. G. A. Pocock, *The Ancient Constitution and the Feudal Law: A Study of English Historical Thought in the Seventeenth Century* (Cambridge: Cambridge University Press, 1957), ch. 1.
66. *Fabius '97; Fragment*, 59.
67. James Bringhurst to Thomas Pole, July 1799. Bringhurst Letters, Friends Historical Library, Swarthmore College.
68. Jack D. Marietta, *The Reformation of American Quakerism, 1748–1783* (Philadelphia: University of Pennsylvania Press, 1984); Sydney V. James, *A People Among Peoples: Quaker Benevolence in Eighteenth-Century America* (Cambridge, MA: Harvard University Press, 1963).

69. Jack N. Rakove, *The Beginnings of National Politics: An Interpretive History of the Continental Congress* (Baltimore: Johns Hopkins University Press, 1979), 152, 153.
70. JD, Notes on the Articles of Confederation [1776]. RRL/HSP.
71. JD, Draft of the Articles of Confederation [1776], 2. RRL/HSP.
72. In an early draft of the Articles, Dickinson originally wrote "his or their" then changed it to "his or her." See JD, "Hints of a Confederation" [1776]. RRL/HSP.
73. See *Quaker Constitutionalism*, ch. 7.
74. See Nathan Kozuskanich, "'Falling under the Domination Totally of Presbyterians': The Paxton Riots and the Coming of the Revolution in Pennsylvania," in *Pennsylvania's Revolution* ed. William Pencak (University Park, PA: Pennsylvania State University Press, 2010), 7–35.
75. Quakers were denied their right to vote and hold office, fined, their property distrained, their stores looted, windows broken, soldiers quartered in their homes, and singled out for execution. In 1777, Congress and the Pennsylvania government colluded to arrest the leading Philadelphia Quakers and imprison them in Virginia for nine months without charge or trial. See Isaac Sharpless, *The Quakers in the Revolution* (1902; rpt. Honolulu: University Press of the Pacific, 2002); Robert F. Oaks, "Philadelphians in Exile: The Problem of Loyalty during the American Revolution," *Pennsylvania Magazine of History and Biography* [hereafter *PMHB*] 96, no. 3 (1972): 298–325; Peter C. Messer, "'A Species of Treason & Not the Least Dangerous Kind': The Treason Trials of Abraham Carlisle and John Roberts," *PMHB* 123, no. 4 (1999): 303–332.
76. JD, "At a Meeting of a large and respectable Number of the Citizens of Philadelphia...," *Pennsylvania Gazette*, October 23, 1776.
77. Ibid.
78. The matter of swearing or affirming allegiance in Revolutionary Pennsylvania is complicated where Quakers are concerned. They always refused to swear oaths and instead would affirm their allegiance when required to do so. Article One of their 1701 Charter required only "promises" of allegiance and fidelity to various powers "when lawfully required" by the king or earlier laws confirmed by the Assembly. In 1776 when Quakers turned neutral and decreed that members should closely circumscribe their political activities, that included the act of affirming allegiance (Bauman, 161). The issue is further complicated by the fact that Pennsylvania citizens were expected to declare allegiance not just to the state, but also to the constitution—the one neither created nor ratified by popular consent—and not just for officeholding, but also for voting, and even for businessmen and professionals to engage in their work. The Quakers' religious and political objections were thus closely intertwined. In effect, not only were they being compelled to break their vow of neutrality, they were being made to affirm a system that was born in opposition to them by people whom they knew were intolerant of their religious beliefs. See Harry E. Seyler, "Pennsylvania's First Loyalty Oath," *History of Education Journal* 3, no. 4 (1952): 114–1126. In this

matter, Dickinson, again, adhered to a more traditional Quakerism in which affirming allegiance was acceptable. But neither would he affirm the faulty 1776 constitution. As noted below, he affirmed allegiance to the state in 1782.

79. JD's copy of *The Constitution of the Common-Wealth of Pennsylvania* (Philadelphia: John Dunlap, 1776). LCP.
80. JD, *Essay on a Frame of Government for Pennsylvania* (Philadelphia: James Humphreys, Jr., 1776), 15–16.
81. *Minutes of the Council of the Delaware State, from 1776 to 1792* (Wilmington: The Historical Society of Delaware, 1887), 679.
82. JD, *By the President of the Delaware State, a Proclamation* (Wilmington: James Adams, 1781).
83. JD, Notes on Government [n.d.]. RRL/HSP.
84. Flower, *John Dickinson*, 203; *Pennsylvania Journal*, January 16, 1782.
85. The Society for Suppressing Vice and Immorality, which had Quaker leaders, petitioned the Pennsylvania legislature for another such act in 1798.
86. Kenneth R. Bowling, "New Light on the Philadelphia Mutiny of 1783: Federal-State Confrontation at the Close of the War for Independence," *PMHB* 101, no. 4 (1977): 419–450.
87. *Fabius '88*, 32.
88. G. S. Rowe, "Outlawry in Pennsylvania, 1782–1788 and the Achievement of an Independent State Judiciary," *American Journal of Legal History* 20, no. 3 (1976): 227–244, 244.
89. JD to George Read, April 28, 1786, in William Thomas Read, *Life and Correspondence of George Read* (Philadelphia: J. B. Lippincott & Co., 1870), 412–413.
90. One brief analysis of Dickinson's ideas during these years exists. Despite mistaking Dickinson for a Puritan, Susan M. Power gives an otherwise useful discussion in "John Dickinson After 1776: The Fabius Letters," *Modern Age* 16, no. 4 (1972): 387–397.
91. See Catherine L. Albanese, *Nature Religion in America from the Algonkian Indians to the New Age* (Chicago: University of Chicago Press, 1990); and J. Rixey Ruffin, *A Paradise of Reason: William Bentley and Enlightenment Christianity in the Early Republic* (New York: Oxford University Press, 2008), 76–77. There is no study of political Quakerism in the early Republic.
92. *Fabius '97*, 98.
93. JD, Notes on Religion [n.d.]. RRL/HSP.
94. JD to Samuel Miller, August 10, 1807.
95. Samuel Miller to JD, July 16, 1807. LCP.
96. *Fabius '97*, 156.
97. Until Dickinson's manuscripts are transcribed and published, the full picture of his philosophy and theology remains inaccessible. The John Dickinson Writings Project is working to make these texts available. See <http://www.uky.edu/DickinsonWritingsProject/>.

98. Max Farrand, ed. *The Records of the Federal Convention of 1787*, 3 vols. (New Haven, CT: Yale University Press, 1927), 1: 159.
99. Ibid., 1: 165, 169, 187; Jonathan Elliot, *The Debates in the Several State Conventions on the Adoption of the Federal Constitution*. 5 vols. (Philadelphia: J. B. Lippincott Co., 1863–1891) 2: 481, 5: 177; "Columbian Independence," *The Oracle of Dauphin and Harrisburgh Advertiser*, July 11, 1803.
100. Forrest McDonald, *Novus Ordo Seclorum: The Intellectual Origins of the Constitution* (Lawrence, KS: University Press of Kansas, 1985), 260.
101. *Fabius '88*, 19, 17, 8.
102. JD, Notes [n.d.]. RRL/HSP.
103. Ibid., 14.
104. Dickinson's copy of a letter from George Washington to John Vaughan, April 27, 1788. RRL/HSP.
105. *Fabius '88*, 23.
106. It is unknown whether he worked on abolition in Pennsylvania. A copy of the bill with his edits is in his papers at the HSP, but it is unclear when the edits were made. They are not reflected in the final version of the bill. The three manumission deeds are located, respectively, in RRL/HSP; Logan Papers, vol. 35, p.109, HSP; Kent County Delaware Deed Book y-1, p. 217, Delaware Public Archives. Copies are also at the John Dickinson Mansion, Dover, DE.
107. Note from Sally Norris Dickinson attached to the Manumission Deed, May 12, 1777. RRL/HSP.
108. JD, "An Act for the Gradual Abolition of Slavery in [Delaware]" [1786]. RRL/HSP.
109. Farrand, *Records*, 2: 372–373.
110. JD to Kinsman [Israel Pemberton?]. June 21, 1792. Gratz/HSP.
111. James Bringhurst to Thomas Pole, July 1799; Warner Mifflin to Henry Drinker, June 27, 1792, cited in Tolles, "John Dickinson and the Quakers," 77.
112. Deborah Norris Logan, in Stillé, *Life and Times*, 335.
113. Tolles, "John Dickinson and the Quakers," 78–79.
114. Ibid., 79–80.
115. Deborah Norris Logan, *Memoir*, 145.
116. *Fragment*, 6.
117. Ibid., 16.
118. Fredrick B. Tolles, *George Logan of Philadelphia* (New York: Oxford University Press, 1953).
119. JD to George Logan, August 6, 1805, in *Memoir*, 154.
120. *Fabius '97*, 115.
121. Ibid., 155.
122. Ibid., 157.
123. Ibid., 187.
124. Frederick B. Tolles, "Unofficial Ambassador: George Logan's Mission to France, 1798," *William and Mary Quarterly* 7, no. 1 (1950): 1–25, 5.

13

Isaac Backus and John Leland: Baptist Contributions to Religious Liberty in the Founding Era

Joe L. Coker

THE FIRST WEEKEND of the year 1802 was an unusual and momentous one in Washington, DC. It began with the astounding sight of a half-ton wheel of cheese being delivered to the doorstep of President Thomas Jefferson. It ended with the equally unprecedented sight of Jefferson attending a public worship service held in the nation's Capitol building. The cheese came as a gift from the residents of Cheshire, Massachusetts, who had spent months making the token of admiration for their president; the worship service that closed the weekend was led by the presenter of the "mammoth cheese," the Reverend John Leland of Massachusetts. During the course of the weekend another, less public event occurred: Jefferson composed a letter to a group of Baptists from Danbury, Connecticut. The Baptists there had written him a few months earlier seeking his support as they found their religious liberties violated by the Congregationalist majority in a state where "religion is consider'd as the first object of legislation."[1] Jefferson's response to the Danbury Baptists, wherein he used his now-famous metaphor of a "wall of separation" between the church and the state, would eventually become one of the most significant letters in the history of American politics, especially as it relates to how the First Amendment of the Constitution is to be interpreted and applied. At the heart of all these events—the cheese, the letter, and the preaching—were Baptists.

It is no coincidence that Baptists—and especially the Massachusetts preacher John Leland—are to be found in the middle of the events of that weekend, for Baptists played a crucial role in shaping early American attitudes regarding the relationship between church and state. Baptists like John Leland and Isaac Backus—a Baptist minister who by 1802 was in his waning years of life, but who had been the most prominent public face of Baptists in New England in the 1770s and 1780s—exerted both direct and indirect influence on the development of religious liberty principles in the post-Revolutionary era. While it may be possible to overstate the Baptist contribution (Baptist leader George W. Truett once proclaimed in a sermon that the separation of church and state in America "was preeminently a Baptist achievement"), no study of ideas about church/state separation in early America should neglect the significant role played by the Baptists.[2] Furthermore, any analysis of this Baptist contribution in the founding era must highlight the two leading Baptist activists for religious liberty at the time: John Leland and Isaac Backus. Both served as vocal advocates for full religious liberty in an era when ideas about the degree of separation between church and state in the nascent American republic were still in flux, and they represent the dynamic presence of Baptists in shaping American ideas about church/state separation.

Jefferson wrote to the Connecticut Baptists partly to express his solidarity with their opposition to religious establishments, but more importantly to explain his decision as president not to issue proclamations calling for days of prayer and fasting, a break with the practice of his predecessors. Indeed, Jefferson was even breaking with his own practice as governor of Virginia, where he did issue such proclamations. As president, however, he viewed the First Amendment as prohibiting the chief executive of the federal government—as opposed to a state official—from creating such religious entanglements. A main impetus for Jefferson's Danbury letter was to explain his conviction that it was inappropriate for the federal government to directly encourage religious practice or devotion. But fully understanding the implications of Jefferson's "wall of separation" has been an ongoing struggle in the realms of American politics, religion, and jurisprudence for the past two centuries. Especially in the twentieth century, this phrase played a central role in Supreme Court interpretations of the First Amendment's "establishment clause." Beginning with *Everson v. Board of Education* in 1947, the wall metaphor has served as the "organizing theme of church-state jurisprudence."[3] This chapter will examine how Isaac Backus, John Leland, and the Baptists they represented were leading advocates in early America for the ideas of liberty of conscience and religious disestablishment. It will also examine the degree to which these pioneers of religious liberty were prepared to embrace the Jeffersonian concept of a wall of separation between church and state. Despite occasionally being bolder in their ideas about separation of church and state than some Baptists at the time were comfortable with, Backus and Leland fairly represent the Baptists of early America and their commitment to religious freedom and disestablishment, as well as the spectrum of views within Baptist life regarding the degree to which religion should be separated from the state.

Baptists in Colonial America

As Baptists, Isaac Backus and John Leland were part of a Christian movement that had emerged in England in the early 1600s and was finally hitting its stride in North America. Baptists in America were slow to form large, organized denominational structures and bodies. In the colonial era, the most elaborate organizations of Baptist congregations were known as associations, which consisted of a small number of independent congregations that joined together. These associations did not exercise authority over the local congregation, but did provide opportunities for fellowship, cooperation, and solidarity.[4] The first such association was formed in Philadelphia in 1707 and served as the model for a number of Baptist associations formed in the mid-eighteenth century.

Despite this reluctance to form large denominational bodies, it is possible to speak of Baptists in the colonial and Revolutionary periods as falling into a handful of general groups. Robert Gardner has identified eleven such groupings, though the vast majority of Baptists in America in this era fall into a few main groups. The Particular Baptists were the first to establish a church in colonial America, in Rhode Island in 1639. Unlike the first Baptists to emerge in England in the 1610s, who held to a more Arminian understanding of atonement and salvation, these Baptists were strict Calvinists. Particular Baptist congregations grew very slowly throughout the seventeenth century, spreading to Massachusetts, New Jersey, and Pennsylvania. Baptist churches with an Arminian theology also emerged in the American colonies. One group, known as General Six-Principle Baptists (because of their adherence to the six foundational teachings enumerated in Hebrews 6:1–2), formed congregations primarily in New York and Rhode Island. Another strain of Arminian Baptists, known simply as the General Baptists, emerged around 1721 and was more inclusive (as opposed to the General Six-Principles, who made the laying on of hands a prerequisite for participation in communion). These Baptists, too, always remained numerically smaller than the Particular Baptists.[5]

When the revivals of the Great Awakening swept the colonies in the 1730s and 1740s, Baptists benefited. The new spirit and worship style of revivalism, however, led to a split in the Baptist ranks. The Separate (also sometimes known as "New Light") Baptists emerged in 1742, and though they were Calvinists like the Particulars, they placed greater emphasis on evangelism and revivalism than on defending Calvinist doctrine. In response, Particular Baptist congregations began to refer to themselves as "Regular" Baptists. Separate Baptists spread rapidly in the 1750s and 1760s, and made inroads into the southern colonies. There they established the Sandy Creek Association in North Carolina, which would play an important role in spreading the Baptist faith throughout the south.[6] Isaac Backus was part of this new Separate Baptist movement, joining the Baptists in 1756 and quickly becoming a leader of the Separate Baptists in Massachusetts and beyond.[7] Despite the differentiation between various Separate and Regular Baptists, the reality was that the theological distinctions between the two was not always particularly profound or noticeable, even to members of these movements. Backus and Leland epitomize the problem of trying to make too broad a generalization about the distinctions between the "Separates" and the "Regulars." While Regular Baptists generally disliked emotional revivalism, Leland was a Regular Baptist who preached tirelessly and dynamically on the revival circuit. And while Backus was a Separate Baptist, he demonstrated a commitment to promoting Calvinist orthodoxy that would have made any Regular Baptist proud.[8] Both Regular and Separate Baptists likewise held strong views about the separation of church and state.

By the 1770s the divisions between Separate Baptists and Particular/ Regular Baptists began to diminish, and these two largest groups of American Baptists began to reunite. This union coincided with the Baptists' greatest period of growth ever. Between 1770 and the end of the century, the Baptist ranks exploded. Though they had been present in American society since the late 1630s, and had experienced steady yet modest growth during the Great Awakening, it was during the final decades of the eighteenth century that Baptists hit a huge growth spurt. In Massachusetts, Baptist membership grew by 250 percent between 1700 and 1740, then by roughly another 250 percent between 1740 and 1770, but grew by 400 percent (from fifteen hundred to almost sixty-two hundred members) in the twenty years between 1770 and 1790. This growth would continue for the next generation, as Massachusetts Baptists grew threefold to nineteen thousand members by the early 1830s. Baptists in Virginia experienced an even faster rate of growth, increasing from less than one hundred members in 1740 to over two thousand in 1770, then growing tenfold over the next two decades to almost twenty-one thousand members in 1790. By the 1830s there would be over fifty-five thousand Baptists in the state. As this pattern suggests, the Great Awakening did much to spur the growth of the Baptist movement in America, but the most significant expansion did not occur until later in the century, around the time of the American Revolution.[9] Similar growth patterns were repeated in other states. Overall, Baptists in America increased from less than a thousand in 1700 to around sixteen thousand in 1770, and then expanded to over seventy-three thousand by 1790. By the 1830s, the overall Baptist population in America reached over 450 thousand.[10] In 1776 one out of every 264 Americans was a Baptist, and by 1800 this grew to one out of every 53 Americans. By 1830, it was one out of every 27.[11] Thus the Baptists were evolving from a fringe religious movement in America to a sizable, vocal, and increasingly influential religious minority in the period following the American revolution. Given this rapid expansion, Jefferson's letter to the Baptists in Danbury makes even more sense. By the time of his presidency, Baptists were a noteworthy voting bloc.

In addition to being a rapidly growing movement, the Baptists were heirs to a long tradition of advocacy for freedom of conscience and religious toleration. Thus it is no surprise to find them involved in the discussion of the proper relationship between the church and the state in the early years of the American Republic. The Baptist ancestors of Backus and Leland, both in America and England, earned a reputation as tireless advocates of liberty of conscience and as annoying critics of religious establishments. Thomas Helwys, leader of the first Baptist church established in England, famously wrote in his 1612 *Mystery of Iniquity* that "men's religion to God is betwixt God and themselves; the king shall not answer for it, neither may the King be judge between God and man. Let them be heretics, Turks, Jews, or whatsoever, it pertains not to the earthly power to punish them in the least measure." Helwys went further, sending a copy of his work to His Majesty King James I and penning a note inside its cover stating, "The king is a mortal man, and not God, therefore hath no power of the immortal souls of his subjects, to make laws and ordinances for them, and to set spiritual lords over them."[12] Shortly after penning these words, Helwys found himself imprisoned for his views and spent the rest of his days under arrest. His second-in-command, John Murton, picked up the banner and continued to give voice to the Baptist plea for religious freedom. In his 1615 work calling for religious toleration in England, Murton argued that the writings of the New Testament "teach no such thing as compelling men by persecutions and afflictions to obey the gospel."[13]

Three decades later and across the Atlantic Ocean, the ideas and writings of these early Baptists had a significant impact on Roger Williams, colonial America's most famous religious dissenter and advocate for religious freedom. Williams was arguably the founder of the first Baptist church in America. His famous 1644 treatise on religious freedom—*The Bloudy Tenent of Persecution for Cause of Conscience*—was perhaps the most important work on the subject written in the colonial period. Williams adds his own attack against state-coerced worship, stating that "an enforced uniformity of religion throughout a nation or civil state, confounds the civil and religious, [and] denies the principles of Christianity and civility." He continued even more bluntly: "forced worship stinks in God's nostrils."[14] Williams was also the first person in America to use the metaphor of a wall when speaking of the relationship between church and state. Over 150 years prior to Jefferson's 1802 letter, Williams advocated the idea that there should be a "hedge or wall of separation between the garden of the church and the wilderness of the world."[15] Williams' cofounder of the colony of Rhode Island, John Clarke, also became one of the earliest Baptists in North America after having been arrested in Massachusetts for taking part in an unauthorized worship service. In *Ill Newes from New England,* Clarke exposed the religious persecution taking place in the Massachusetts Bay Colony and appealed directly to King Charles II for "full liberty in religious concernments."[16] In the Revolutionary era, the ideals of early English and American Baptists would remain central to the theology and ideology of American Baptists, who would play an important role in advocating for full religious liberty in the new American republic. The Baptists were not, of course, the only religious minorities in colonial America. Presbyterians, Quakers, Lutherans, Mennonites, Moravians, Dunkers, and others likewise chafed under and complained about laws that used taxpayer money to fund the established clergy. Baptists, however, proved themselves to be the most consistently vocal and cantankerous of the dissenters in their denunciation of religious establishment.[17]

While other sects complained about such establishments, they nevertheless tended to comply with toleration statutes that allowed their preachers and meetinghouses to be licensed when such licensing was allowed by colonial officials. In Virginia, for instance, Presbyterians, Quakers, and others (including Regular Baptists) participated in such a system and applied for state licenses. But the Separate Baptists (those more influenced by the revivalism of the Great Awakening) refused to submit to such requirements, which they viewed as subjecting them to state regulation and approval.[18] As a result, Separate Baptist preachers were publicly punished for their opposition to religious establishments more frequently than ministers from any other dissenting group. Such persecution helped publicize and create sympathy for the cause of disestablishment. In Virginia, the refusal of Separate Baptists to conform to licensing requirements meant that they experienced public persecution in the form of fines, imprisonment, public lashings, and being dunked in water almost to the point of drowning.[19] Such persecution highlighted to some in the colony the injustice of the present religious establishment, and contributed to the growing demand in late eighteenth-century America to better articulate the concept of freedom of conscience and its implications for traditional religious establishments.

Most notable among those disturbed by the punishment of Baptists was James Madison, who remarked in 1774 that the "diabolical Hell-conceived principle of persecution rages among" the clergy in Virginia, leaving him with "nothing to brag of as to the state of liberty in my country." Madison specifically noted that "not less than five or six well-meaning men" were currently incarcerated "for publishing their religious sentiments which in the main are very orthodox."[20] These men being held "in close Goal" were Baptist ministers jailed for disturbing the peace by preaching without a license. The Baptists' nonviolent but very public resistance did much to turn public sentiment against state religious establishment regulations, especially in Virginia. Madison's commitment to religious liberty, fueled by his exposure to Baptist persecution, would bear fruit in the summer of 1776 when he successfully pushed for more specific language guaranteeing religious freedom in Article Sixteen of Virginia's Declaration of Rights.[21] He would later play a central role in the passage of the First Amendment to the Constitution of the United States.

While Baptists were representative of other religious dissenters in the era in terms of their opposition to state establishment of religion and demands for religious toleration, Baptists proved to be more vociferous in their attacks on the established clergy, more prone to civil disobedience in order to publicize their case, and therefore played a more public role in the push for religious liberty. Two of the most prominent Baptists in eighteenth-century America, Isaac Backus and John Leland, were at the forefront of that effort.

Life and Work of Backus and Leland

Isaac Backus was born into a wealthy and influential family in Norwich, Connecticut in 1724. Little is known about his early life, which he described as "careless," but it seems clear that he was not overly concerned with spiritual matters until the year 1741. It was then, in the midst of the Great Awakening sweeping across the American colonies, that Backus reports falling under "powerful conviction."[22] Jonathan Edwards had come to the area to preach in the late 1730s, and George Whitefield arrived in 1740. Backus attended two revivals in 1741, during which God began to "bring eternal things near [his] soul and show [him] the dreadful dangers of delay."[23] Shortly thereafter he was converted. Afterwards he affiliated with a Congregationalist church, but soon joined with several others who left to form a Separatist congregation, made up of Congregationalists who embraced the revivalism of the era.[24] Backus soon felt a call to enter the pastorate, and he began to preach despite local laws prohibiting preaching by anyone who was not a settled pastor of a recognized congregation or invited to preach by a settled pastor.[25] Like so many other New Light Congregationalists, he also began to question the practice of infant baptism and found himself more comfortable in the Baptist faith.[26] In 1756, Backus formed the first Baptist church in Middleboro, Massachusetts, where he would remain as pastor for over half a century. Most Baptist churches in the area at that time were of the "Old Baptist" persuasion and were unenthusiastic about the Great Awakening taking place around them, but Backus' Baptist congregation embraced both the revivalism and Calvinist theology of Jonathan Edwards. Backus was deeply concerned by the lax attitude towards Calvinism that he found in Baptist churches in New England, and his early years were spent visiting Baptist churches in the region and promoting a stronger Calvinist orthodoxy.[27]

Backus spent much of his energies building up his congregation in the late 1750s and 1760s, and promoting cooperative efforts with other congregations. In 1767, a group of Baptist churches formed the Warren Baptist Association, following the model of the Philadelphia association of

Baptists. Backus and his congregation joined, convinced that such extra-congregational organizations provided an opportunity to lobby the government and extend the influence of local Baptist congregations. Backus himself served as an agent of the Association for a number of years, representing Baptist views to the public and becoming a leading figure in New England Baptist life over the years. Though he received only a limited education, Backus wrote and published (according to his own claims) more than any other Baptist ever had.[28] These writings included the first history of Baptists in New England, as well as a multitude of pamphlets touching everything from Arminianism to liberty of conscience. The primary subject of many of the pamphlets he published for the Association was the disestablishment of religion in Massachusetts.

The bulk of Backus' public activity on behalf of disestablishment occurred during the formation of the Massachusetts constitution. The process began in 1778, though the first constitution drawn up by the legislators failed to be ratified by the people. Recognizing the significance of what the state was undertaking, Backus penned *Government and Liberty Described* to encourage his fellow Baptists—and the state legislators—to abolish the longstanding ecclesial establishment in the state. In 1779, the state legislature set up a process for local communities to elect representatives to assemble in Boston and write a constitution. Backus responded with *Policy as Well as Honesty*, wherein he quoted both scripture and John Locke to support his appeal to the legislators not to perpetuate the mistaken policy of the past that created religious establishment in Massachusetts. Backus likened religious establishment to taxation without representation.[29]

Backus was not elected as a delegate from Middleboro, but his close friend and fellow Baptist preacher Noah Alden was. Alden, who would be one of only five Baptists to serve as a delegate, asked Backus to provide him with suggestions for a Bill of Rights that might be incorporated into the constitution. Backus obliged, formulating a thirteen-point declaration of rights that included not only the "unalienable right to act in all religious affairs according to the full persuasion of his own mind," but also addressed property rights, criminal rights, and freedoms such as speech, press, bearing arms, and protection against illegal searches and seizure.[30]

When the Massachusetts Constitutional Convention convened in September 1779, Alden was asked to participate in the drafting of an article on religion. In its final form, the state's new constitution contained two statements regarding religion. Article Two affirmed the "right as well as the duty" to "worship the Supreme Being, the great Creator and Preserver of the Universe." It also guaranteed that "no subject shall be hurt, molested, or restrained, in his person, liberty, or estate, for worshipping God in the manner and season most agreeable to the dictates of his own conscience," as long as those practices do not disturb others. Article Three, at least to the minds of Backus and others like him, directly contradicted and violated the preceding Article by authorizing towns in the state to collect money from all citizens in order to fund "the institution of the public worship of God and for the support and maintenance of public Protestant teachers of piety, religion, and morality." The Article was founded upon the idea that "the happiness of a people and the good order and preservation of civil government essentially depend upon piety, religion, and morality," and that "these cannot be generally diffused through a community but by the institution of public worship of God and of the public instructions."[31] The new constitution stopped short of establishing a particular religious denomination, such as the Congregationalists, as the sole recipient of state funding. Funding would be based on the majority religious orientation of a particular area, and Christians who dissented from that denomination could direct their tax money to their church instead.

The inclusion of this article in the constitution when it was sent out for ratification infuriated Backus and other Baptists. He responded with *An Appeal to the People of Massachusetts State against Arbitrary Power*, complaining that the provision "asserts a right in the people of this State to make and execute laws about the worship of God, directly contrary to the truth which assures us that we have but ONE LAWGIVER in such affairs."[32] Backus' work likely contributed to the failure of Article Three to receive the two-thirds approval of the voters that was technically required for passage. Nevertheless, the convention ratified it in June of 1780, sending Backus back to his desk to launch a last-ditch appeal to the legislature to not accept the article as part of the constitution. This, too, failed to stop the state's march toward establishing a system of state-supported churches. Backus refused to give up the fight, and continued to write pamphlets restating the Baptist position on religious establishment and even urging Baptists to engage in civil disobedience by refusing to pay the tax or to buy the certificates that certified their dissenter status.[33]

Almost ten years after his efforts to prevent religious establishment under Massachusetts' new constitution, Backus was called upon to take part in the debate over the federal Constitution. Middleboro elected him as one of its four delegates to the state ratifying convention. Backus was one of twenty Baptist delegates at the convention, a voting bloc that made up roughly 10 percent of the delegates. The Baptists generally opposed ratification, but over the course of the convention Backus became convinced that the constitution's prohibition against religious tests for public office constituted a sufficient safeguard against religious establishment. Ultimately, he and two-thirds of his fellow Baptists voted in favor of ratification. His Baptist congregation back in Middleboro was less enthusiastic about the new constitution, though eventually Baptists embraced it more warmly.[34] In Backus' remaining years he continued to be a thorn in the side of the Standing Order in Massachusetts, though most of his energies were aimed at evangelistic campaigns across New England and into the south. Backus died in 1806, still over a quarter of a century shy of seeing Massachusetts finally renounce state establishment of religion.

The other major spokesman for Baptist views on church-state relations in the era of the early republic was John Leland. Born in Grafton, Massachusetts, in 1754, thirty years later than Backus, Leland represented a different generation of Baptists. His generation was to be deeply shaped not by the rigid Calvinism of the Great Awakening but more by the egalitarianism of the Revolutionary era and by the religious revivalism of the Second Great Awakening. Leland grew up in a Congregationalist church, but from a young age proved to be an intractable non-conformist. When the local minister showed up at the young Leland's house to baptize him at age four, the boy fled the house and had to be chased down. Ultimately the "reluctant subject" was dragged to the baptismal font with a bloodied nose and was baptized. The remainder of his childhood, Leland reports, was spent being "exceedingly attached to frolicking and foolish wickedness."[35] At age twenty, however, Leland underwent believer's baptism after being converted under the preaching of a Baptist evangelist. Like Backus, Leland soon felt called to preach, and in 1775 moved to Virginia to serve as an itinerant preacher.

Leland did not come of age in the midst of the Great Awakening, and his theology reflected a much lower level of commitment to Calvinism than did Backus.' At his ordination examination, Leland was asked: "Brother Leland, do you not believe that God chose his people in Christ before the foundation of the world?" Leland responded that he knew not "what God was doing before he began to make this world." When the moderator pressed Leland to state whether he believed that God "had a people from before the foundation of the world," Leland answered that "if he had, brother, they were not our kind of folks. Our people were made out of the dust, you know, and before the foundation of the world there was no dust to make them out of."³⁶ Such responses were characteristic of Leland's iconoclastic, irreverent, down-to-earth manner. He had little interest in defending an elaborate theological system and stated that the "theoretical principles of men have but little effect upon their lives."³⁷ Leland wrote that he knew both Calvinists and Arminians, and was "assured they are not all right in their systems," but that each has some element of truth.³⁸ He received no formal education, and harbored great disdain for educated, eloquent clergy.³⁹ The feeling was often mutual. Following his sermon to Congress in 1802, Leland was mocked by a Congregationalist (and Federalist) in attendance as "illiterate," "ignorant," and "clownish."⁴⁰

Leland's faith was highly individualistic, and his focus was on the relationship between the individual and God. He even deemphasized the importance of an organized church, and was cautious about anything that might come between a Christian and God.⁴¹ Leland was also suspicious of interchurch associations and any kind of extraecclesial organization, such as missionary societies and Sunday Schools. While Backus believed such associations provided opportunities for Baptist churches to influence the government, Leland saw them as dangerous instruments likely to become abused by the government. Preaching and baptizing were the only functions Leland felt comfortable performing, and one church dismissed him for his refusal to serve the Lord's Supper.⁴² Edwin Gaustad points out that Leland's ecclesiology makes particular sense "from the point of view of Jeffersonian democracy."⁴³ Jefferson, a leading thinker among the Enlightenment politicians, had argued that a government is best which governs least. Leland felt this principle also applied to the church, and that the fewer associations, organizations, and hierarchies a church is involved in, the better.

Leland was living in Virginia during the time when Massachusetts was drawing up a new state constitution, and thus he was not involved in the debates over Article Three as was Backus. Leland's time in Virginia led him to become engaged in politics there, though. In 1786, the Baptist General Assembly in Virginia appointed him as a lobbyist to the state's General Assembly. Leland's role in politics greatly increased two years later when Virginia was debating ratification of the federal constitution. Each county in the state was to elect a representative to attend the Virginia convention. In Orange County the two candidates for the position were John Leland and future President James Madison. Leland and the Baptist General Committee opposed the constitution's ratification because it contained no guarantee of religious freedom. Madison favored ratification without such provisions, but he feared that Leland would win in the heavily Baptist county. Madison was warned by Federalists in Virginia that the Baptists of that state must be won over in order to assure ratification. A meeting between Madison and Leland to discuss the issue supposedly took place at the latter's home prior to the election. Shortly thereafter Leland withdrew from the race, Madison was elected, and Virginia ratified the constitution.[44] Monica Najar has noted that Madison (as well as his father) intensely lobbied Leland and a few other prominent Baptist clergymen, and that Leland became key to winning supporters over to Madison. Once Leland and other Baptists were assuaged of their concerns about the Constitution, Madison reported to George Washington that opposition to ratification in Virginia had been put to rest.[45] Madison then went on to be the chief proponent of the Bill of Rights, introducing in the House of Representatives nine articles proposed as amendments to the constitution. The fourth of these articles forbade the establishment of a national religion as well as any infringement of the right of conscience, and eventually became the first amendment to the Constitution in 1791.

In addition to his indirect influence on the Bill of Rights, Leland was actively engaged in politics in Virginia and then Massachusetts. Some contemporaries felt he was too involved. G. N. Briggs, governor of Massachusetts and a friend of Leland's, recollected that "many thought he intermeddled too much in politics for a clergyman." Another contemporary said "that which probably interfered more than anything else with his usefulness as a minister was his almost mad devotion to politics." It was also said of Leland that "he magnified his office as a politician at the expense of lowering it as a Christian minister."[46] Regardless of such criticisms, Leland remained active in politics throughout his life. In 1791 he returned to New England and began agitating for a new constitution in Connecticut. The state's constitution funded the Congregationalists' Standing Order with tax money, allowed them to oversee education in the state, to preach election day sermons in the legislature, and enjoy other privileges. While the constitution did allow dissenters to obtain a certificate that exempted them from supporting the Standing Order, in 1802 Leland began to publish a series of pamphlets calling for more than just accommodations for dissenters. His works, published collectively under the title *A Connecticut Dissenter's Strong Box*, called for a complete overhaul of the constitution and fueled debate over the existing constitution. In 1819 the state would replace its constitution with a new one, which disestablished the Congregational Church.[47] Leland relocated to

Massachusetts and there continued the fight that had been launched by Backus to end the state's support of religion. In 1811 he was elected to the Massachusetts House of Representatives for one term.[48]

Leland experienced the greatest public notoriety, though, when chosen to escort the 1,235-pound cheese to President Jefferson. After arriving with the cheese and meeting with Jefferson, he was asked to preach in the nation's Capitol building on January 3, 1802. Compared to the stodgy, dogmatic, wig-wearing Backus, Leland was irreverent, sarcastic, and theologically eclectic. Backus diligently travelled from town to town trying to insure that Edwardsian Calvinism was faithfully being taught and adhered to by every Baptist congregation. Leland stated that both Calvinists and Arminians have some element of truth behind them, but that neither has a monopoly on it. Both preached and wrote extensively, but while Backus reflected the age of Jonathan Edwards, Leland reflected that of Lorenzo Dow. The key difference between Backus and Leland was generational. Backus was rooted in a previous generation that held to strict Calvinism, a firm attachment to order, and a fear of rebellion. Leland was from a new generation of evangelical Americans, untethered from traditional theological loyalties and more truly in line with the radicalism of Jefferson. The two knew one another and expressed great mutual admiration, though. In September of 1800, Leland was on a revival tour and preached for two days in Backus' church. Backus recorded in his diary that Leland preached "with much power" and that "great numbers" attended. Two people came forward after Leland's sermon, and Backus allowed Leland to baptize them.[49]

Backus and Leland on Liberty of Conscience

Both Backus and Leland were very conscious of their Baptist heritage and of their forebearers' commitment to religious liberty. Backus wrote the first history of Baptists in America, wherein Roger Williams and his advocacy of religious liberty played a key role. Leland also recognized the tradition he was part of, stating that "the principle, that civil rulers have nothing to do with religion in their official capacities, is as much interwoven in the Baptist plan, as Phydias's name was in the shield."[50]

Both Backus and Leland perpetuated this Baptist contention that freedom of conscience was an undeniable right. Underlying all of Backus' efforts at disestablishment in Massachusetts was the conviction that, in religious matters, every person has the right to choose for himself/herself. While in some areas of life we must give up some of our rights and appoint rulers over us, such is not the case with religious matters. "Our Lord has most plainly forbidden us either to assume or submit to any such thing in religion," he argued.[51] Backus quoted John Locke, who said that "a church is a free and voluntary society," meaning there should be no government compulsion to attend or financially support a given church. He argued that governmental efforts to remove this voluntary aspect of religion and impose religious conformity originated from Christians who were mislead by, what he calls, "the deceitful reasonings from the Jewish hand." By this Backus means that the early Puritans in America mistakenly appropriated practices from Israel in the Old Testament and applied them to their modern Christian commonwealth. As the Israelites were instructed to inflict punishment upon those who did not conform to their worship of God, the Christian leaders of Massachusetts had taken it upon themselves to enforce religious conformity. He proceeded to argue that "religion is voluntary obedience unto God which therefore force cannot promote," and that any attempt on the part of government to regulate worship "is as contrary to the laws of Christ as darkness is to light"[52]

Leland likewise argued forcefully and consistently for absolute freedom of conscience and against government intervention in one's religious choices. "The work of the legislature is to make laws for the security of life, liberty, and property, and leave religion to the consciences of individuals," he wrote.[53] Leland's eschatology shaped his conviction that every individual must be left free to follow his or her own conscience, as we will all stand as individuals before God for judgment:

> Every man must give an account of himself to God, and therefore every man ought to be at liberty to serve God in a way that he can best reconcile to his conscience. If government can answer for individuals at the Day of Judgment, let men be controlled by it in religious matters; otherwise, let men be free.[54]

Individual freedom to choose one's religion extended even to America's slave population, according to Leland, and he attacked masters who "whip and torture the poor creatures for going to meeting, even at night, when the labor of the day is over."[55]

Leland went so far as to reject the use of the word "toleration" as "despicable" because its usage implied that Protestants possessed the right and power to grant rights to others. "All should be equally free," he said, including "Jews, Turks, Pagans, and Christians."[56] Leland's explicit reference to non-Protestants reflects a distinction between his views and those of Backus. Backus frequently evoked the name of Roger Williams, but in his views concerning religious toleration he backed away from some of the demands made by Williams (and Williams's English Baptist predecessors) for full religious liberty and equality for all, even non-Christians. Backus assumed a certain privileged status existed in America for Protestant Christianity.[57] Leland, meanwhile, did not drop Williams's name in his writings the way Backus did (though he clearly seems to have read Williams), yet he perpetuated the traditional Baptist call for full religious liberty for both Christians and non-Christians alike.[58] Leland consistently and frequently enumerated Pagans, Deists, Jews, and "Turks" as equally deserving as Christians of religious liberty and freedom from religious taxation. He asked sarcastically about non-Christians being taxed to support Christian ministers,

> Is it the duty of a Deist to support that which he believes to be a cheat and imposition? Is it the duty of a Jew to support the religion of Jesus Christ, when he really believes that he was an imposter? Must the Papists be forced to pay men for preaching down the supremacy of the pope, who they are sure is the head of the church? Must a Turk maintain a religion, opposed to the Alkoran [sic], which he holds as the sacred oracle of heaven?[59]

Backus and Leland on Disestablishment

A corollary to the Baptist belief in freedom of conscience was their adamant stance against establishments of religion that coerced adherence and financial support for a certain breed of Christianity. As evidenced by his campaign against Article Three of the Massachusetts constitution, Backus staunchly opposed religious establishments and fought diligently to prevent them in the new American republic. He built upon his belief in liberty of conscience to attack religious establishments. "As no man can have a right to judge for others in soul affairs," he stated, "so they never could convey such a right to their representatives. Therefore all the taxes to support religious worship and judgments in such cases that have been among us were a taxing of us where we were not represented."[60]

Backus harkened back to the primitive Christian church and noted that Christ never made use "of secular force in the first setting up of the

Gospel-church, when it might seem to be peculiarly needful if ever." Thus no true minister of the gospel of Christ should ever seek "recourse to the kings of the earth to force money from the people to support him." Government intervention in religion is not only unbiblical, but also undermines the chief end of government, which is to promote the happiness of the people. Backus viewed the local church as a voluntary society of believers bound together by mutual covenant. Basing the church on covenant meant that "no person can be brought into it without his own consent."[61] By definition, then, a state church cannot be a true church because it forces people to belong against their will. Religion must be voluntary in order to be true.[62]

Like Backus, Leland argued that no church that received support from the state can be a true Christian church. Religious establishments serve only to defile and corrupt the church, and "metamorphose the church into a creature, and religion into a principle of state."[63] He further warned that "no national church, can, in its organization, be the Gospel Church." Using tax revenue to pay Christian ministers "turns the gospel into merchandise, and sinks religion upon a level with other things."[64] Sounding much like Roger Williams, who argued that emperors like Constantine had done more injury to Christ's kingdom than had emperors like Nero, Leland noted, "Persecution, like a lion, tears the saints to death, but leaves Christianity pure; state establishment of religion, like a bear, hugs the saints, but corrupts Christianity, and reduces it to a level with state policy."[65]

Upon his return to Massachusetts, Leland joined the Baptist clamor against religious taxation. He denounced Article Three of the state constitution in harsh terms, saying, "there remains no doubt, that the religious establishments of Massachusetts, and all state establishments of Christianity in the world, are all of them, ANTI-CHRISTOCRACIES."[66] Leland even went so far as to attack Article Two, which guaranteed religious freedom in Massachusetts, because the government took to itself the right to tell people that it is their duty to worship God. "This article would read much better in a catechism than in a state constitution, and sound more concordant in a pulpit than in a state-house," quipped Leland.[67]

Leland cited the recent outbreak of religious revival at Cane Ridge, Kentucky to demonstrate how religion could flourish completely free from government intervention, pointing out that "Kentucky had not laws to support teachers of piety, morality, and religion, and yet the Lord of Heaven has blessed them marvelously." He also sarcastically took a jab at his

Federalist opponents by noting that Kentucky is a state run by Democrats: "We are, therefore, reduced to the necessity of believing that Democrats can be religious, or that the accounts of the great reform in Kentucky are all false."[68] Leland admonished Massachusetts to follow the example of most every other state, which have no established religion and "yet they are not sunk with earthquakes, or destroyed with fire and brimstone." When speaking before the Massachusetts House of Representatives in 1811, he scolded them, saying, "Government should be so fixed, that Pagans, Turks, Jews, and Christians should be equally protected in their rights. The government of Massachusetts, however, is differently formed."[69]

Baptists and Jeffersonianism

Jefferson's letter to the Danbury Baptists was written with the intent of defending his refusal to issue proclamations of days of prayer and fasting, and to articulate his vision of a state free from entanglements with and meddling by the church. Jefferson no doubt expected to find in the Baptists a receptive audience for his wall metaphor, given the Baptist commitment to religious liberty as well as their high level of support for his presidency. During the presidential election of 1800, the Baptists of New England had strongly backed Jefferson. In places like Danbury, Connecticut, Middleboro and Cheshire, Massachusetts, and elsewhere in New England, they were vocal minority sect in a predominantly Congregationalist community and as Jeffersonians in a predominantly Federalist stronghold. While Federalists like Timothy Dwight engaged in fear-mongering predictions of Bible burnings and atheistic indoctrinations of children if Jefferson were to win the 1800 election, Baptists found in the Deist candidate a beacon of hope for religious liberty. Baptists feared that his opponent, John Adams, was predisposed to allow the establishment of Presbyterianism or Congregationalism as a national church supported by the government.[70]

Jefferson, while far from orthodox in his theology, had long proven himself to be fully "orthodox" in his views on church and state, as far as most Baptists were concerned. Theological differences between Jefferson and Backus notwithstanding, the two shared a similar understanding of the necessity of religious disestablishment and religious freedom. As Christopher Grenda has demonstrated, both Jefferson and Backus rejected a common assumption held by many Enlightenment thinkers: that religious toleration is good because religion promotes happiness in society.

This utilitarian assessment of religion simultaneously promoted religious freedom and justified state support of religious bodies. If religion promotes order in society, then the state should support religion. Indeed, this was the rationale for state funding of the Congregationalist clergy by the Massachusetts constitution, which stated: "the happiness of a people and the good order and preservation of civil government essentially depend upon piety, religion, and morality."[71] Backus objected to this by arguing that natural rights include our right to be happy, which he defined as freedom to follow God's revealed will voluntarily. Thus any establishment of religion was a violation of natural rights. Jefferson shared Backus' objection to the state's utilitarian calculation that establishing religion promotes public happiness. Though deeply influenced by European Enlightenment thinkers, he rejected the Enlightenment predisposition to discourage religious dissent based on the assumption that such dissent promoted discord in society.[72] Therefore Jefferson, Backus, and Baptists in general shared a common understanding of to the issues of natural rights, religious freedom, and religious establishments, despite their theological differences.

Prior to becoming president, Jefferson developed a lengthy track record of advocacy for liberty of conscience and disestablishment, as well as friendliness towards the Baptist movement. In 1777, he wrote a "Bill for Religious Freedom" to insure religious liberty and disestablishment of the Anglican Church in Virginia.[73] And by 1800 Jefferson enjoyed widespread support amongst Baptists north and south, an especially important constituency in the Federalist-heavy New England states since Baptists were growing at a rapid rate.[74] Backus strongly supported Jefferson, though he never met him. Leland knew Jefferson personally and greatly admired him. During Jefferson's presidency, Leland openly endorsed the administration. In a sermon to the people of Cheshire, he observed, "If we compare our present administration, with what preceded for several years, we shall see economy instead of extravagance . . . diminishing taxes . . . recalling foreign agents . . . a regard for the rights of the people."[75]

The bond between Baptists and Jeffersonian Republicans was thus a strong one, yet nevertheless awkward in some ways. Jefferson was shaped by Enlightenment principles, and while Backus often cited John Locke in his appeals for disestablishment, he was more influenced by the revivalism and piety of the Great Awakening than he was by the rationalism of the Enlightenment. Thus their motives for wanting religious liberty in America were different. Jefferson hoped it would lead to the demise of traditional forms of Christianity and the rise of a simpler, more rational religious/ethical consensus within society. Backus was confident that a free marketplace of religious ideas would inevitably fuel a revitalization of orthodox Calvinism in the country.[76] Leland, meanwhile, was somewhere between Jefferson and Backus, and was more influenced in his church-state views by the political philosophy of Jefferson and Madison than by Calvinism.[77] Leland's motivation for separation was not only to protect the church from corruption, as was Backus's, but also to defend true democracy.[78]

But Jefferson's introduction of the "wall of separation" concept into the mix of ideas surrounding religious liberty tested the limits of the Jeffersonian/Baptist alliance. Jefferson and the Baptists were in full agreement on issues of liberty of conscience and disestablishment, but Jefferson's rhetoric of a wall separating church and state was not readily accepted by Baptists. Likewise, Backus and Leland were not of exactly the same mind when it came to defining the exact nature of the proper relationship between church and state. While Backus saw a definite need for the presence of religion in government affairs, Leland wanted a greater degree of separation between the two. The difference between these two Baptist leaders reflected the diversity within the Baptist community in early America when it came to this third aspect of religious liberty, separatism.

Backus on Strict Separation

Despite Backus's many efforts fighting against the establishment of a state-supported church, he did believe that there could be an amiable relationship between the church and the state, and that the two institutions could be mutually beneficial to one another. "The necessity of a well-regulated government in civil states is acknowledged by all, and the importance and benefit of true Christianity in order thereto is no less certain," he wrote.[79] Backus rejected the idea of an absolute separation between church and state, believing instead that a "sweet harmony" ought to be sought between them. "Civil rulers ought to be men fearing God," Backus said, and "ministers ought to pray for rulers and to teach the people to be subject to them, so there may and ought to be a sweet harmony between them."[80] Backus's vision of "sweet harmony" between the church and the state grew out of his view that the two rely upon one another in some ways. Individuals need the state to protect their right to exercise their religious beliefs according to their conscience as well as to insure that they are not coerced into worshipping in any one particular way. By the same token, Backus saw religion as essential for democracy's survival. "Religion is as necessary for the well-being of human society," he argued, "as salt is to preserve from putrification or as light is to direct our way and guard against enemies, confusion, and misery." He saw Christianity as the key to America's future. "Piety, religion, and morality," he stated, "are essentially necessary for the good order of civil society."[81]

Because Backus believed that religion was essential to society's well-being, he had no objection to religious test oaths for state office-holders. In *A Door Open for Christian Liberty*, he noted approvingly that "no man can take a seat in our legislature till he solemnly declares, 'I believe the Christian religion and have a firm persuasion of its truth.'"[82] Backus wished to end tax-supported, state-favored religion but did not wish to create the high wall of separation between the church and the state that Jefferson envisioned.[83] In addition to test oaths, Backus was also comfortable with Presidents proclaiming days of prayer and fasting. Jefferson refused to follow the example of George Washington and John Adams, who had issued such proclamations during their presidencies. He instead agreed with James Madison that such proclamations by a president, even if they are only recommendations, imply that the government has some religious authority. Madison also cautioned that these proclamations "nourish the erroneous idea of a national religion."[84] Backus, however, believed that such proclamations were a prudent means of encouraging religious activity without favoring one group over another. He regularly read the proclamations from his pulpit and saw to it that his church observed the days of prayer, thanksgiving, and fasting.[85] Backus's approach to church-state separation, then, reflects what John Witte has called a "one-sided separation."[86] Backus's goal was to stop government control over religion yet allow religion to have a continued influence in the government. This one-sided separatism, Witte says, was typical of evangelical theologians of the eighteenth century who opposed an established state church but did not wish for religion to lose its privileges.

Leland on Strict Separation

Unlike Backus, and closer to Jefferson, Leland objected to the idea that there could or should be any type of healthy intermingling between the church and the state. He believed that Christianity had much to contribute to both private and public life in America, but was adamant that the state should not support the church in carrying out her work. Chaplains should be ministering to American soldiers and even lawmakers, Leland believed, but their salaries should not be paid by the government. Thus Leland's views are more in line with what Witte calls "two-sided separatism" than with the one-sided separatism of Backus.[87] Two-sided separatism is concerned not only with limiting the state's control over religion, but also with restricting the role religion plays in government. He agreed that the church needed a government that would protect individuals' right to free exercise, but rejected the notion that Christianity or even religion in general was essential to a well-ordered society.[88] "Moral maxims of right" are necessary for an ordered society, Leland said, but do not necessarily need to come from the Bible. To assert that Christianity is "essential to good government is far, very far, from being true."[89] Because Christianity was not essential to democracy's survival, Leland vehemently opposed religious test oaths for public officials. In a pamphlet entitled *Short Essays on Government,* he sharply criticized the same Massachusetts test oath that Backus had lauded. "The declaration is a good one for man to make when joining a Christian church," Leland wrote, "but in this place his Christian confession is prostituted to civil purposes."[90] Leland's views on test oaths were very similar to those of Thomas Jefferson, who wrote that forbidding someone to hold office until "he profess or renounce this or that religious opinion" not only violates his natural rights but "tends also to corrupt the principles of the very religion it is meant to encourage."[91] Leland also warned citizens to beware of political candidates who emphasize their religious beliefs.[92]

Leland's views on church-state separation went beyond those held by most Baptists of his time.[93] He objected to many church-state connections that others took for granted. For instance, Leland opposed having state-paid chaplains in the legislature or military. He called the paying of these chaplains "unconstitutional, inconsistent with religious liberty, and unnecessary in itself," and compared the state's actions to those of King George in England. "We cannot pay legal taxes for religious services, descending even to the grade of a chaplain for the legislature," he argued, lest religion be made a "creature of the state."[94] Leland said that if chaplains are felt necessary, they should be paid for with privately donated money.

Leland objected to other types of government accommodation of Christianity that most Americans and Baptists took for granted, as well.

When Congress expanded mail delivery to Sundays in 1810, American evangelicals reacted strongly and launched a "Sabbath protection movement" to promote the idea that America was a Christian nation. Leland became one of the most outspoken critics of the Sabbatarian movement.[95] He tied his opposition to Sabbath protection to his views on disestablishment, noting, "As it is not the province of civil government to establish forms of religion, and force maintenance for the preachers, so it does not belong to that power to establish fixed holy days for divine worship."[96]

Conclusion

The views of Backus and Leland reveal two things about these men and about the Baptists of the time period. First, a significant difference exists between the two men's conception of the proper relationship between church and state. Backus imagined a barrier between church and state that prohibited government from supporting one or even several religious groups through taxation of all members of society, but which still allowed religion to play a significant role in public life, including requiring public officials to affirm faith in the Christian God. Leland, on the other hand, strove for something much closer to Jefferson's wall between church and state, wanting to do away with anything that gave the impression that the government favored Christianity over other religions. The difference between these two reflects the diversity of opinion within early American Baptist life regarding just what it meant to implement full religious liberty in the new nation. Baptists universally wanted their fellow Americans to embrace the concepts of religious toleration and freedom of conscience, and they were leading critics of state establishments of religion. Baptists were less certain, however, about the degree to which they wanted to completely divorce religion from the political sphere. Leland seems to reflect the attitude of only the most progressive Baptists of his time, while Backus is more representative of mainstream Baptists in the founding era. Like Backus, they were generally diehard advocates of religious toleration, tireless critics of religious establishments, yet firmly convinced that religious institutions have a crucial role to play in sustaining social order and stability. Therefore, general acknowledgements and support of religion by the government was both permissible and necessary for sustaining a well-ordered society.[97]

An examination of Backus and Leland also reveals that despite their different views on church/state separation, neither embraced Jefferson's rhetoric of a wall of separation between church and state. Endorsement of the Jeffersonian interpretation of the First Amendment lay just beyond the limits of the Baptist/Jefferson alliance of the early nineteenth century. Backus and Leland reflect, to varying degrees, the conclusions drawn by Philip Hamburger regarding the reluctance of Baptists to fully embrace the idea of separatism that Jefferson proposed to the Danbury Baptists. As Hamburger points out in his important work, *Separation of Church and State*, Jefferson and his fellow Republicans introduced the idea of separatism largely as a tool to undermine Congregationalist ministers in New England who were supporting the Federalists from the pulpit.[98] He rightly draws attention to the response of the Danbury Baptists to the letter sent to them by the president of the United States. That response, essentially, was absolute silence. They did not publish the letter, mention it at their associational meeting, or in any other way acknowledge the president's response to them. Most importantly, they also refused to use the language that Jefferson had used—the "wall of separation"—in their continued attacks upon religious establishments.[99]

The vision of a wall separating church from state seemed too radical—even dangerous—to Baptists in Danbury and elsewhere in New England in 1802. Most held views similar to that of Isaac Backus, wanting religious liberty and disestablishment but still believing that good government is dependent upon the presence of religion in society and in government. Leland was definitely warmer to Jefferson's vision of a wall of separation than was Backus. Yet while the deep admiration that Leland displayed towards Jefferson on January 1, 1802, never diminished, Leland never invoked the kind of language that Jefferson had introduced later that day, either. The way in which that first weekend of 1802 ended is also instructive, and perhaps reveals that Jefferson was fully cognizant of the boldness of the proposal he had just posted to the Connecticut Baptists. Two days after Leland delivered the cheese and met with the president, he preached at a worship service in the US Capitol building. Jefferson attended the service, the first time for him to do so, and thereafter he attended Christian worship services in the Capitol building on a regular basis, a practice continued by his successor, James Madison. Daniel Dreisbach observes that Jefferson probably attended the service as much for public relations reasons as to hear his friend Leland preach.[100] The scene of Jefferson participating in an evangelical worship service that was taking place on government property most likely sent a reassuring message to his Baptist supporters, who would soon hear of his letter to their brothers and sisters in Danbury and might be concerned by his metaphor. Perhaps this provided a fitting ending to a significant weekend in Washington. It had begun with an impressive token of affection delivered by a prominent Baptist minister on Friday, continued with Jefferson penning his famous letter to the Danbury Baptist on the same day, and concluded on Sunday with the president attending a worship service in the Capitol building, allaying fears that he would pursue too radical a separation of church and state.

As leading Baptist spokesmen of revolutionary/early Republic eras, Backus and Leland brought long-held Baptist views regarding church and state into the national dialogue in ways that helped shaped American attitudes towards religious freedom. These Baptists were staunch advocates for absolute religious freedom and opponents of religious establishments in early America. Though these two—to varying degrees—balked at fully embracing Jefferson's metaphor of a wall of separation between church and state, they and their fellow Baptists did much to embed the principles of religious toleration and disestablishment into the fabric of American society. And though perhaps reluctant to embrace its language, Baptists provided a venue for Jefferson's introduction of an important new way of understanding and describing how church and state should relate—one that would have reverberations for centuries to come.

Notes

1. Danbury Baptist Association to Thomas Jefferson, October 7, 1801, in *The Sacred Rights of Conscience: Selected Readings on Religious Liberty and Church-State Relations in the American Founding*, ed. Daniel L. Dreisbach and Mark David Hall (Indianapolis, IN: Liberty Fund, 2009), 526.
2. Quoted in William D. Underwood, "The Metaphor of the Wall of Separation: Baptists and the First Amendment," *Baptist History and Heritage* 43 (Summer/fall 2008), 27.
3. Daniel L. Dreisbach, "The Mythical 'Wall of Separation': How a Misused Metaphor Changed Church-State Law, Policy, and Discourse." *First Principles Series* no. 6 (Washington, DC: The Heritage Foundation, nd.), 1.
4. Walter B. Shurden, "Associationalism among Baptists in America, 1707–1814" (ThD diss., New Orleans Baptist Theological Seminary, 1967), 9–14.
5. Robert G. Gardner, *Baptists of Early America: A Statistical History, 1639–1790* (Atlanta: Georgia Baptist Historical Society, 1983), 30–39, 52–55.

6. Ibid., 29–26.
7. T. B. Maston, *Isaac Backus: Pioneer of Religious Liberty* (Rochester, NY: American Baptist Historical Society, 1962), 28.
8. See Janet Moore Lindman, *Bodies of Belief: Baptist Community in Early America* (Philadelphia: University of Pennsylvania Press, 2008), 37, 47.
9. Considerable debate exists regarding the degree to which the evangelical revivals of the Great Awakening contributed to the rise of revolutionary sentiment among American colonists later in the eighteenth century. Alan Heimert, for instance, argues that the contours of American thought shaped by the ideas and practices of the Great Awakening profoundly impacted all areas of thought and activity later in the century, including support for revolution. Others see a less causal relationship between revival and revolution. Gordon Wood challenges the connections Heimert makes between mid-century revivalism and the subsequent growth of "Jeffersonian democracy and American nationalism." That being said, even Wood cautiously recognizes some connection between the two events, saying: "It seems evident that in one way or another the Great Awakening helped to prepare American society and culture for the Revolution, but of course not in any direct, deliberate, or intentional manner." While revivalists produced by the Great Awakening (like Isaac Backus) did not set out to spread a radical political ideology along with the gospel, they nevertheless contributed to the "new social and cultural circumstances out of which the Revolution arose," as Woods says. Backus and his fellow Baptists were deeply shaped by the revivalistic style of the Awakening, but their demands for freedom of conscience, for separation of church and state, and disestablishment had much deeper roots. In their advocacy for religious liberty, Backus and Leland were influenced more by the tradition of Thomas Helwys and Roger Williams than that of Jonathan Edwards and George Whitefield. Alan Heimert, *Religion and the American Mind: From the Great Awakening to the Revolution* (Cambridge, MA: Harvard University Press, 1966), viii; Gordon S. Wood, "Religion and the American Revolution," in Harry S. Stout and D. G. Hart, eds., *New Directions in American Religious History* (New York: Oxford University Press, 1997), 180–181.
10. Eighteenth-century numbers compiled from Gardner, *Baptists of Early America*, 34–36, 56–57, 71–76, 99–103. Figures for the 1830s are from F. A. Cox and J. Hoby, *The Baptists in America: A Narrative of the Deputation from the Baptist Union in England, to the United States and Canada* (New York: Leavitt, Lord, & Co., 1836), 471–472.
11. Henry C. Vedder, *A Short History of the Baptists* (Philadelphia: American Baptist Publication Society, 1907), 319 n.2.
12. Thomas Helwys, "A Short Declaration of the Mystery of Iniquity," in *The Life and Writings of Thomas Helwys*, ed. Joe Early, Jr. (Macon: Mercer University Press, 2009), 156, 209.

13. John Murton, "Objections Answered by Way of Dialogue," in Edwards Bean Underhill, ed., *Tracts on Liberty of Conscience and Persecution, 1614–1661* (New York: Burt Franklin, 1845), 120.
14. Roger Williams, *The Bloudy Tenent of Persecution for Cause of Conscience Discussed in a Conference Between Truth and Peace. Who, in all Tender Affection, Present to the High Court of Parliament (as the Result of Their Discourse) These, (Amongst Other Passages) of Highest Consideration*, Richard Groves, ed. (Macon, GA: Mercer University Press, 2001), 4; Roger Williams, "Letter to Major John Wilson and [Connecticut] Governor Thomas Prence," in Glenn W. LaFantasie, ed., *The Correspondence of Roger Williams*, vol. 2: 1654–1682 (Providence, RI: Brown University Press, 1988), 618.
15. Quoted in Leonard W. Levy, *The Establishment Clause: Religion and the First Amendment* 2nd ed. (Chapel Hill: The University of North Carolina Press, 1994), 249. It is unlikely that Jefferson ever read Williams directly, though a strong case has traditionally been made that he encountered Williams's ideas indirectly through the writings of John Locke, who does seem to have been influenced by Williams. LeRoy Moore, "Religious Liberty: Roger Williams and the Revolutionary Era," *Church History* 34 (March 1965), 65–68. Daniel L. Dreisbach has suggested that Jefferson borrowed the phrase from James Burgh, a dissenting Scotsman who urged the building of "an impenetrable wall of separation between things sacred and civil" and whose writings Jefferson greatly admired. Daniel L. Dreisbach, *Thomas Jefferson and the Wall of Separation between Church and State* (New York: New York University Press, 2002), 79–81.

    Whether Williams had in mind the same kind of wall that Jefferson did is unclear. Williams seemed to be concerned primarily with keeping the church pure. He wanted it kept separated from the corrupting influences of the secular realm, but did not specify whether he meant entanglements between the church and the state or simply the general sinfulness of the world outside the church. Elsewhere, however, Williams used the same garden metaphor when speaking of the corruption of Christianity after it became a state church in the fourth century. See also Perry Miller, *Roger Williams: His Contributions to the American Tradition* (Indianapolis: Bobbs-Merrill Co., 1953), 98.
16. Quoted in Thomas Bicknell, *Story of Dr. John Clarke, the Founder of the First Free Commonwealth of the World on the Basis of "Full Liberty in Religious Concernments"* (Providence, RI: by the author, 1915), 192.
17. Thomas E. Buckley, *Church and State in Revolutionary Virginia, 1776–1787*. (Charlottesville: University Press of Virginia, 1977), 14–15.
18. John Leland noted that the Separate Baptists were more "zealous" than their "solemn and rational" Regular Baptist counterparts. He also observed that the leadership of the Separate Baptist churches was home-grown: they were led by preachers from Virginia, while Regular Baptist churches were more often led by

northern preachers who had moved south. "The Virginia Chronicle," in *Writings of the Elder John Leland*, 105.

19. John A. Ragosta, *Wellspring of Liberty: How Virginia's Religious Dissenters Helped Win the American Revolution and Secured Religious Liberty* (Oxford: Oxford University Press, 2010), 30, 35.

20. James Madison to William Bradford, January 24, 1774, in *The Papers of James Madison*, eds. William T. Hutchinson and William M. E. Rachal (Chicago: University of Chicago Press, 1962), 1:106.

21. Madison succeeded in getting the wording changed from "all men should enjoy the fullest toleration in the exercise of religion" to "all men are equally entitled to the free exercise of religion . . ." He also attempted to have a clause approved that would forbid religious establishment in the state, but was unable to find the votes to get it inserted. See Buckley, *Church and State*, 18–19.

22. Isaac Backus, *The Diary of Isaac Backus*, William G. McLoughlin, ed. (Providence RI: Brown University Press, 1979), 3:1523.

23. Alvah Hovey, *A Memoir of the Life and Times of the Rev. Isaac Backus, A. M.* (Boston: Gould and Lincoln, 1858), 34–35.

24. William G. McLoughlin, *Isaac Backus and the American Pietistic Tradition* (Boston: Little, Brown, & Co., 1967), 20–22.

25. William Cathcart, "Isaac Backus," in *The Baptist Encyclopaedia: A Dictionary of the Doctrines, Ordinances, Usages, Confessions of Faith, Sufferings, Labors, and Successes, and of the General History of the Baptist Denomination in All Lands*, rev. ed. (Philadelphia: Louis H. Everts, 1883), 52.

26. Ironically, by moving to a Baptist congregation, these Separatists actually became victims of less persecution and prejudice against them, because Baptists were seen as an established dissenting movement while Separatist Congregationalists were not. Maston, *Isaac Backus*, 23.

27. Edwin S. Gaustad, "The Backus–Leland Tradition," *Foundations* 2 (April 1959), 132; McLoughlin, *Isaac Backus and the American Pietistic Tradition*, 89.

28. Maston, *Isaac Backus*, 30.

29. Isaac Backus, "Policy as Well as Honesty Forbids the Use of Secular Force in Religious Affairs," in William G. McLoughlin, ed., *Isaac Backus on Church, State, and Calvinism: Pamphlets, 1754–1789* (Cambridge, MA: Belknap Press of Harvard University Press, 1968), 381.

30. Isaac Backus, "Isaac Backus' Draft for a Bill of Rights for the Massachusetts Constitution, 1779," in *Isaac Backus on Church, State, and Calvinism*, 487.

31. "Articles I, II, and III of the Declaration of Rights of the Massachusetts Constitution of 1780," in Jacob C. Meyer, *Church and State in Massachusetts from 1740 to 1833: A Chapter in the History of the Development of Individual Freedom* (Cleveland: Western Reserve University Press, 1930), 234–235.

32. Isaac Backus, "An Appeal to the People of the Massachusetts State, Against Arbitrary Power," in *Isaac Backus on Church, State, and Calvinism*, 392.

33. Isaac Backus, "A Door Opened for Equal Christian Liberty: and No Man Can Shut It. This Proved by Plain Facts," in *Isaac Backus on Church, State, and Calvinism*, 436.
34. McLoughlin, *Isaac Backus and the American Pietistic Tradition*, 196–200.
35. John Leland, "Events in the Life of John Leland," in L. F. Greene, ed., *The Writings of the Elder John Leland: Including Some Events in His Life*, (New York: G. W. Wood, 1845), 10.
36. Quoted in J. Bradley Creed, "John Leland: American Prophet of Religious Individualism" (PhD diss., Southwestern Baptist Theological Seminary, 1986), 13.
37. Quoted in Gaustad, "The Backus–Leland Tradition," 135.
38. John Leland, "The Virginia Chronicle," in *Writings of the Elder John Leland*, 111.
39. Brandon O'Brien, "From Soul Liberty to Self-Reliance: John Leland and the Evangelical Origins of Radical Individualism," *American Baptist Historical Review* 27 (Summer 2008), 136.
40. Quoted in Dreisbach, *Thomas Jefferson*, 22.
41. Creed, "John Leland: American Prophet," 155.
42. Gaustad, "The Backus–Leland Tradition," 140.
43. Ibid., 145.
44. Edwin S. Gaustad, *Liberty of Conscience: Roger Williams in America* (Valley Forge, PA: Judson Press, 1999), 207. For Leland's account of this incident, see William B. Sprague, *Annals of the American Pulpit: or Commemorative Notices of Distinguished American Clergymen of Various Denominations* (New York: Robert Carter & Brothers, 1860), 178–180. The meeting between Leland and Madison has long been a part of Baptist lore. Some have questioned whether the meeting took place, since the only accounts of it stem from later recollections. There is evidence, though, that the meeting did take place roughly as described. Certainly Leland and Madison conferred over the matter. When Madison was elected as a Representative to the First Congress, Leland wrote to him asking to be kept informed "if religious liberty is anywise threatened" and expecting Madison to "stop by on your way to Congress," implying that Madison being a guest in his home was not unprecedented and that Leland had certain clearly stated expectations of Madison regarding religious liberty. Letter from John Leland to James Madison, 1789 (Library of Congress web site, http://memory.loc.gov/master/mss/mjm/03/0900/0940d.jpg, accessed September 25, 2011); H. Leon McBeth, *The Baptist Heritage: Four Centuries of Baptist Witness* (Nashville: Broadman Press, 1987), 282; O'Brien, 137–139.
45. Monica Najar, *Evangelizing the South: A Social History of Church and State in Early America* (Oxford: Oxford University Press, 2008), 129.
46. Sprague, *Annals of the American Pulpit*, 184–187.
47. Creed, "John Leland: American Prophet," 108–109.
48. Bernard H. Cochran, "John Leland: Advocate of Religious Liberty," *Religion and Public Education* 14 (Fall 1987), 379.

49. Isaac Backus, *The Diary of Isaac Backus*, William G. McLoughlin, ed. (Providence, RI: Brown University Press, 1979), 3:1459. Backus also noted that Leland had been traveling for three straight months, and in that time had preached almost one hundred sermons.
50. Leland, "The Virginia Chronicle," 118.
51. Isaac Backus, "An Appeal to the Public for Religious Liberty: Against the Oppressions of the Present Day," in *Isaac Backus on Church, State, and Calvinism*, 314.
52. Backus, "Policy as Well as Honesty," 371, 376–377.
53. John Leland, "Remarks on Holy Time—on Moral Law—On the Changing of the Day—on Sabbatical Laws," (1815), in *Writings of the Elder John Leland*, 441.
54. John Leland, "The Rights of Conscience Inalienable, and, Therefore, Religious Opinions not Cognizable by Law: or, the High-Flying Churchman, Stripped of His Legal Robe, Appears a Yaho," in *Writings of the Elder John Leland*, 181. Leland's eschatological emphasis was the continuation of a longstanding and unique Baptist way of viewing freedom of conscience, which has been recently documented in C. Douglas Weaver, "Early English Baptists: Individual Conscience and Eschatological Ecclesiology," *Perspectives in Religious Studies* 38 (Summer 2011): 141–158.
55. John Leland, "The Virginia Chronicle," 95. Leland's movement away from his abolitionist stance over the course of his life is explored in Bruce Gourley, "John Leland: Evolving Views of Slavery, 1789–1839," *Baptist History and Heritage* 40 (Winter 2005): 104–116.
56. Ibid., 118.
57. As evidenced, for example, by his support for test oaths for public office.
58. Leland seems to have either read or been exposed to the writings of Williams. Compare, for example, Williams's statement that "The unknowing zeal of Constantine and other emperors did more hurt to Christ Jesus' crown and kingdom than the raging fury of the most bloody Neros. In the persecutions of the latter, Christians were sweet and fragrant . . . But these good emperors, persecuting some erroneous persons . . . by this means Christianity was eclipsed . . ." with Leland's similar remark: "Experience, the best teacher, has informed us that the fondness of magistrates to foster Christianity has done it more harm than all the persecutions ever did. Persecution, like a lion, tears the saints to death, but leaves Christianity pure; state establishment of religion, like a bear, hugs the saints, but corrupts Christianity." Williams, *The Bloudy Tenent*, 112; John Leland, "The Government of Christ a Christocracy," in *Writings of the Elder John Leland*, 278.
59. Leland, "The Rights of Conscience Inalienable," 187.
60. Backus, "Policy as Well as Honesty," 381.
61. Isaac Backus, *A History of New England, with Particular Reference to the Denomination of Christians called Baptists*, 2nd ed., David Weston, ed. (Newton, MA: Backus Historical Society, 1871), 2:303–304.
62. Isaac Backus, "Government and Liberty Described: And Ecclesiastical Tyranny Exposed," in *Isaac Backus on Church, State, and Calvinism*, 351.

63. Leland, "The Rights of Conscience Inalienable," 183.
64. Leland, "The Virginia Chronicle," 118.
65. Leland, "The Government of Christ," 278.
66. Ibid., 280–281.
67. John Leland, "The Yankee Spy: Calculated for the Religious Meridian of Massachusetts, but Will Answer for New Hampshire, Connecticut, and Vermont, without any Material Alterations," (by Jack Nips, 1794), in *Writings of the Elder John Leland*, 220.
68. John Leland, "An Oration, Delivered at Cheshire, July 5, 1802, on the Celebration of Independence: Containing Seventeen Sketches, and Seventeen Wishes," in *Writings of the Elder John Leland*, 264.
69. John Leland, "Speech Delivered in the House of Representatives of Massachusetts, on the Subject of Religious Liberty, 1811," in *Writings of the Elder John Leland*, 355, 358.
70. Daniel L. Dreisbach, "Mr. Jefferson, a Mammoth Cheese, and the 'Wall of Separation Between Church and State': A Bicentennial Commemoration," *Journal of Church and State* 43 (Autumn 2001), 738. It did not help Adams's standing among Baptists like Backus that he had drafted the Constitution of Massachusetts and favored its "mild and equitable establishment" of religion. See John Witte, Jr., *Religion and the American Constitutional Experiment: Essential Rights and Liberties* (Boulder, CO: Westview Press, 2000), 36.
71. "Constitution of the Commonwealth of Massachusetts," *The 187th General Court of the Commonwealth of Massachusetts*, http://www.malegislature.gov/Laws/Constitution (accessed May 3, 2012).
72. Christopher S. Grenda, "Revealing Liberalism in Early America: Rethinking Religious Liberty and Liberal Values," *Journal of Church and State* 45 (winter 2003), 143–148, 156.
73. William Lee Miller, *The First Liberty: America's Foundation in Religious Freedom* (Washington, DC: Georgetown University Press, 2003), 48, noting that when writing his epitaph for his gravestone, Jefferson listed the writing of this bill as one of the three most important accomplishments of his life.
74. The number of Baptist churches in Massachusetts tripled between 1770 and 1790, while the number of Congregationalist churches experienced only modest growth. Meyer, *Church and State in Massachusetts from 1740 to 1833*, 96 n.17.
75. Leland, "An Oration," 262.
76. Peter Judson Richards, "'A Clear and Steady Channel': Isaac Backus and the Limits of Liberty," *Journal of Church and State* 43 (Summer 2001), 471; J. Judd Owen, "The Struggle Between 'Religion and Non-Religion': Jefferson, Backus, and the Dissonance of America's Founding Principles," *American Political Science Review* 101 (August 2007), 498.
77. Steven Hall Fennell, "Harmony or High Wall: A Comparison of the Views of John Leland and Isaac Backus Concerning Church-State Relations" (ThM

thesis, Southeastern Baptist Theological Seminary, 1989), 89. As William G. McLoughlin notes, Baptists after 1800 "found themselves politically aligned with the Jeffersonian party, but it is clear that they did not see it as a Revolutionary party so much as the fulfillment of certain premises of Christian liberty inherent in their new reformation." William G. McLoughlin, *New England Dissent 1630–1833: The Baptists and the Separation of Church and State* (Cambridge, MA: Harvard University Press, 1971), 2:751.

78. Creed, "John Leland: American Prophet," 134.
79. Backus, "Policy as Well as Honesty," 371.
80. Isaac Backus, "A Fish Caught in His Own Net," in *Isaac Backus on Church, State, and Calvinism*, 190.
81. Backus, *History of New England*, 2:321.
82. Backus, *Pamphlets*, 436. Backus's support for Massachusetts's test oath and the absence of references to non-Christians in his writings (noted above) imply that he was only comfortable with state accommodation of Christianity, not other religions.
83. The exact "height" of Jefferson's wall, of course, is an ongoing point of debate in American politics and jurisprudence. The first weekend of 1802 provides some insight into Jefferson's thinking, perhaps. Within twenty-four hours of introducing the wall metaphor, Jefferson was attending a Baptist revival service inside the nation's Capitol building. Some have suggested that Jefferson's attendance was motivated largely by his need to mitigate any fallout from his Danbury letter. Others argue that Jefferson was not simply making a one-time concession to Christian worship on government property. As noted below, Jefferson continued to attend such services throughout his presidency. Even later in life he would admire the arrangement in his own town of Charlottesville, Virginia: "The court house is our common temple, one Sunday in the month each. Here, Episcopalian and Presbyterian, Methodist and Baptist, meet together, join in hymning their Maker, listen with attention and devotion to each others' preachers, and all mix in society in perfect harmony." Thomas Jefferson to Doctor Thomas Cooper, November 2, 1822, as quoted in Richard Samuelson, "Jefferson and Religion: Private Belief, Public Policy," in *The Cambridge Companion to Thomas Jefferson*, ed. Frank Shuffelton (Cambridge: Cambridge University Press, 2009), 152.

Jefferson's openness to religious services held in public spaces, along with his other actions such as the use of federal money to build churches and support Christian missions working with Native Americans, creates a dilemma for those who construe his wall as "high and impregnable." Did he violate his own principles, or did he conceive of separation through the lens of federalism, restricting the federal government from religious entanglements but not state and local government? See Dreisbach, "The Mythical 'Wall,'" 2–3.

84. James Madison, "Detached Memoranda," in *James Madison on Religious Liberty*, ed. Robert S. Alley (Buffalo: Prometheus Books, 1985), 93.

85. McLoughlin, "Isaac Backus and the Separation," 235.
86. John Witte, Jr., "The Theology and Politics of the First Amendment Religion Clauses: A Bicentennial Essay," *Emory Law Journal* 40 (1991), 494.
87. Ibid., 495.
88. Creed, "John Leland: American Prophet," 130.
89. John Leland, "Which Has Done the Most Mischief in the World, The King's Evil or Priest–craft?," in *Writings of the Elder John Leland*, 489.
90. John Leland, "Short Essays on Government," in *Writings of the Elder John Leland*, 477.
91. Joseph Martin Dawson, *Baptists and the American Republic* (Nashville: Broadman Press, 1956), 41.
92. Leland, "An Oration," 267.
93. Creed, "John Leland: American Prophet," 131; Andrew M. Manis, "Regionalism and Baptist Perspective on Separation of Church and State,"*American Baptist Quarterly* 2 (September 1983): 213–227, arguing that while Leland's views were in the mainstream when he lived in Virginia, they seemed radical by New England standards.
94. Leland, "The Virginia Chronicle," 119; Leland, "Speech Delivered in the House," 355.
95. See J. Bradley Creed, "John Leland and Sunday Mail Delivery: Religious Liberty, Evangelical Piety, and the Problem of a 'Christian Nation,'" *Fides et Historia* 33 (Summer/fall 2001): 1–11.
96. Leland, "The Virginia Chronicle," 118–119.
97. See Philip Hamburger, *Separation of Church and State* (Cambridge, MA: Harvard University Press, 2002), 172–174.
98. Ibid., 149, 161.
99. Ibid., 163–165. McLoughlin likewise notes that no Baptist in this early era ever utilized the phrase "wall of separation" to describe his or her views on church/state relations and "despite their admiration for Jefferson as the spokesman for separation of church and state, the New England Baptists dissociated themselves from the deistic and anticlerical premises on which he based his stand." McLoughlin, *New England Dissent*, 2:1013.
100. Dreisbach, "Mr. Jefferson," 741.

Index

Abbot, Henry, 141*n*65
Abdrahaman, 93–95
Abraham (Bible), 188
Act of Union, 268
Adams, Abigail, 71–72, 231
Adams, John
　generally, 4–5, 21, 29, 54, 75, 87, 92, 106, 228
　Baptists and, 322, 335*n*70
　Bible and, 150, 153–154, 159–160
　Biblical Hebrew imagery and, 64
　Boudinot and, 262–263
　at Brattle Street Church, 231–232
　Congregationalism and, 34–35, 61*n*43
　Declaration of Independence and, 50, 288
　Deism and, 13, 22, 25, 229
　in Europe, 55*n*2
　on French Revolution, 92
　Hancock and, 244
　at Harvard, 65
　on Jesus, 29
　Judaism and, 65, 71–73, 77
　piracy and, 93–94
　prayer and, 325
　Reformed tradition and, 44, 229
　religion of, 204
　on religious liberty, 71–73
　Thanksgiving and, 262
　theistic rationalism and, 223*n*28
　Unitarianism and, 25, 35, 61*n*43
　Universalism and, 25
Adams, John Quincy, 92, 150, 168*n*26
Adams, Samuel
　generally, 5
　Bible and, 145
　at Brattle Street Church, 231–233
　Christianity and, 229
　Declaration of Independence and, 50
　Hancock and, 242–243
　Puritanism and, 44–45
　Revolutionary War and, 234
Adams, William Howard, 205
Address on the Natural and Social Order of the World, as Intended to Produce Universal Good (Logan), 297
Address to the Inhabitants of North America (Morris), 206
"An Address To Those Who Keep Slaves and Uphold the Practice" (Jones and Allen), 191
Adherence rates, 45–46, 56*n*3, 59*n*30
Affirmations, 291, 302*n*78
African-Americans
　generally, 89
　conversion of, 179–180, 184
　effect of demographic changes on, 180–181

African-Americans (*continued*)
    Great Awakening and, 182–183
    Jefferson on, 174–175
    Methodism and, 191
    slavery (*See* Slavery)
African Methodist Episcopal Church, 191–192
The Age of Reason (Paine), 19, 91, 149, 151, 257, 266
The Age of Revelation (Boudinot), 91, 257, 260, 265–266, 275n52
"Agrippa" (essayist), 132
Ahlstrom, Sydney, 35
Akers, Charles, 232, 243, 245, 246n11, 247n14
An Alarm to the Legislature of the Province of New York (Seabury), 109
Alciphron, or the Minute Philosopher (Berkeley), 17
Alden, Noah, 313
The Algerine Captive (Tyler), 97–98
Allen, Brooke, 22, 245n3
Allen, Ethan, 19, 21, 26, 151
Allen, Richard, 191
Amendability of constitutions, 281–283
American Bible Society, 146, 255, 258, 260, 267
American Colonization Society, 194
The American in Algiers (poem), 97
American Philosophical Society, 18
American Querist (Chandler), 109
American Revolution. *See* Revolutionary War
Ames, Fisher, 54, 133, 256
Andrews, Dee E., 191
Andrews, Samuel, 107
Andros, Edmund, 42
Anglicanism
    generally, 5
    Antifederalists and, 122
    bishops and, 47–48
    colonialism and, 102
    Declaration of Independence, signers of, 105
    Dickinson and, 284
    Great Awakening and, 102
    historical background, 39
    Islam and, 87
    Jefferson and, 34
    Loyalists and, 101, 105–116
    in Maryland, 2
    Morris and, 204, 217
    Native Americans and, 104–105
    in New England, 45
    Presbyterianism and, 47
    slavery and, 103–104, 117n16, 180
    in South, 46
    Toryism and, 282
    Washington and, 34
Anima Mundi (Blount), 16
Annapolis Convention, 277, 294
Antifederalists, 120–137
    generally, 6
    Anglicanism and, 122
    Baptists and, 122
    Bill of Rights and, 121
    Congregationalism and, 121–122
    establishment of religion and, 130, 132–135
    federalism and, 132–133, 136
    First Amendment and, 120
    Henry as, 121, 127, 134
    Islam and, 88–89
    prayer and, 143n99
    Presbyterianism and, 122
    Quakerism and, 122, 125
    religious affiliations of, 121–129
    religious liberty and, 125–131, 133–136, 142n85
    religious tests and, 124, 126–128, 130, 141n54, 142n78
    scholarly views of, 130–136
"Apostle to the Indians" (Eliot), 179

"Appeal to the People of Great Britain," 49–50
An Appeal to the People of Massachusetts State against Arbitrary Power (Backus), 314
Appleby, Joyce, 148
"Aristocrotis" (essayist), 140n41
Arminianism
    Baptists and, 307–308, 313, 316, 318
    Calvinism and, 28–29, 59n30
Articles of Confederation, 5, 149, 162, 203, 289–291, 294
Asbury, Francis, 190
Atheism, 21, 164
Auchmuty, Samuel, 113
Augustine (Saint), 56n7
Aurora (newspaper), 257

Bache, Benjamin Franklin, 257
Backus, Isaac, 305–329
    generally, 7, 122
    as Antifederalist, 138n10
    biography of, 312–315
    Calvinism and, 312, 318, 324
    Congregationalism and, 312
    on conscience, 317–320, 324–325
    at Massachusetts ratifying convention, 314–315
    on democracy, 325
    on disestablishment, 320–322
    on establishment of religion, 313–314
    Great Awakening and, 312, 323, 330n9
    Jefferson and, 322–324, 328–329
    on Jesus, 320–321
    Locke and, 313, 323
    Madison and, 324
    on Old Testament, 319
    overview, 305–307, 327–329
    on rationalism, 323
    on religious liberty, 318–320
    on religious tests, 334n57, 336n82
    on separation of church and state, 324–325, 328
    on taxation of religion, 134
Bailyn, Bernard, 110
Baird, Robert, 3
Baldwin, Abraham, 51, 54
Baptists
    generally, 6–7
    Antifederalists and, 122
    Arminianism and, 307–308, 313, 316, 318
    Backus and (*See* Backus, Isaac)
    Calvinism and, 46, 307–308
    in colonial America, 307–312
    Congregationalism and, 305, 322–323
    Danbury Baptists, 305–306, 309, 328–329
    establishment of religion and, 310–311
    General Baptists, 308
    General Six-Principle Baptists, 307–308
    Great Awakening and, 308–309, 311
    Jefferson and, 322–324
    John Adams and, 322, 335n70
    Leland and, 331n18 (*See also* Leland, John)
    Loyalists and, 116
    in Massachusetts, 308–309, 335n74
    in New England, 45–46
    New Testament and, 310
    Particular Baptists, 307–308
    persecution of, 311
    prevalence of, 308–309, 335n74
    Regular Baptists, 308, 331n18
    religious liberty and, 305–306, 309
    Separate Baptists, 103, 108, 308, 311, 331n18, 332n26
    separation of church and state and, 337n99
    slavery and, 104, 191, 198n44
    taxation of religion and, 134, 143n89
    in Virginia, 309

Barbary pirates, 93–94
Bartlett, Josiah, 50
Barton, David, 245n3
Bartram, John, 293
Battle of Bunker Hill, 243
Battle of Fallen Timbers, 193
Baxter, William, 241
Bayard, Samuel, 263
Beard, Charles A., 4
Beard, Mary R., 4
Bedford, Gunning, 51
Beecher, Lyman, 267
Benezet, Anthony, 184–185
Benson, Egbert, 54
Bentley, William, 293
Berkeley, George, 17, 25
Berlin, Ira, 191
Berman, David, 17, 31n12
Beverley, Robert, 18
Beza, Theodore, 38, 43–44
Bible, 144–164. *See also specific person*
  authority of, 223n31
  democracy and, 159–163
  Dickinson and, 149, 160
  discounting of influence of, 163–164
  Enlightenment, influence on founding compared, 144, 151, 163, 166n13
  federalism and, 163
  Founders and, 148–152
  Hebrew imagery and founding, 64–65, 264, 319
  Henry and, 145, 149, 156–157, 171n69
  influence on political ideas and institutions, 159–163
  Jay and, 145, 149
  Jefferson and, 146, 151–154, 159
  John Adams and, 150, 153–154, 159–160
  King James Bible, 145, 148, 153, 156, 163–164
  metaphors, use of, 152–159
  Morris and, 213–214
  New Testament (*See* New Testament)
  Old Testament (*See* Old Testament)
  Paine and, 145, 148, 151–153, 162, 168n40
  political use of text, 152–159
  rationalism contrasted, 144, 148, 151
  reading of, 148–152
  revealed knowledge in, 151
  role in founding, 43–45
  Samuel Adams and, 145
  secularism contrasted, 146–147, 164
  Sherman and, 145, 149, 162, 167n22
  slavery metaphor, 159
  Washington and, 150–151, 154–156, 161, 164, 170n66
  Witherspoon and, 145–146
Bible Society of Philadelphia, 146
Bill of Rights
  generally, 47, 53–54, 261
  adoption of, 129
  Antifederalists and, 121
  Boudinot and, 269
  Dickinson and, 295
  Hancock and, 244
  Leland and, 317
  Madison and, 317
Black Hoof (Shawnee), 193–194
Blacks. *See* African-Americans
Blackstone, William, 34, 86, 147
Blasphemy, 90
The Bloudy Tenent of Persecution for Cause of Conscience (Williams), 310
Blount, Charles, 16–17, 21
Blount, William, 51
Blumenbach, Friedrich, 182
Bonomi, Patricia U., 45–46
The Book of Common Prayer, 105, 108, 116, 206
Borden, Morton, 135–136
Boston Gazette, 44, 243
Boston Massacre, 234–236

Boston Tea Party, 106
Botein, Stephen, 23, 134–136
Boudinot, Elias, 253–269
    generally, 5, 8, 137
    Bible and, 146, 149–150
    Biblical Hebrew imagery and, 264
    Bill of Rights and, 269
    biography of, 255–258
    Christianity and, 229
    Congregationalism and, 259
    in Congress, 255–257, 271n13
    Constitution and, 269
    Continental Congresses and, 255
    Deism and, 262–263
    on electoral politics, 262–264
    on establishment of religion, 261
    as Evangelical, 258–259
    as Federalist, 255–256, 262, 269
    First Amendment and, 54
    on France, 263
    Great Awakening and, 258
    Islam and, 91–92, 98
    Jefferson and, 262–264
    John Adams and, 262–263
    on morality, 254
    on New Testament, 254
    on Old Testament, 254
    overview, 253–255
    Paine and, 257, 260, 265–267, 275n55
    Presbyterianism and, 253–254, 258–259, 268–269
    Reformed tradition and, 258–259
    religion of, 258–259
    "Righteous Republic," 261–267
    scholarly treatment of, 260–261
    on slavery, 264–265, 274n45
    Thanksgiving and, 261–262
    on theology, 165n6
    on voluntarism, 267, 269
    Washington and, 255, 257
    Witherspoon and, 268–269
Boudinot, Elias (Cherokee printer), 260
Boudinot, Susan, 266
Bourne, Benjamin, 54
Bowdoin, James, 231–232
Bowes, William, 233
Boyd, George Adams, 260, 269n1
Boyle Lectures, 28
Brandes, Paul, 245
Brant, Joseph, 105
Brant, Molly, 105
Brattle Street Church, 147, 230–233, 243, 246n11, 247n21
Briggs, G.N., 317
Brutus, Stephanus Junius, 38–39, 43
Buchanan, George, 38, 44
Buchanan, John, 247n17
Buell, Samuel, 85–86
Burgh, James, 331n15
Burke, Aedanus, 262
Burr, Aaron, Jr., 35, 71
Burr, Aaron, Sr., 255, 258
Butler, Jon, 14, 60n31

Caldwell, David, 129
Calhoon, Robert M., ix
Calvert, Jane E., ix
Calvin, John, 36–37, 43–44, 55n1, 231
Calvinism, 34–55. *See also* Reformed tradition
    generally, 5–7, 28–30, 230
    adherence rates, 56n3, 59n30
    Arminianism and, 28–29, 59n30
    Backus and, 312, 318, 324
    Baptists and, 307–308
    Brattle Street Church and, 231–232
    Catholicism and, 48–50
    Constitution, influence on, 51–53
    Declaration of Independence, influence on, 47–51
    defined, 55n1
    First Amendment, influence on, 53–54
    Hancock and, 229

Calvinism (*continued*)
  Leland and, 315–316, 318
  Morris and, 204, 214
  neglect of, 34–36, 54–55
  in New England, 46
  political theory of, 36–39
  role in founding, 45–46
  slavery and, 185
  Whiggism and, 282
Canada, Loyalists in, 114–115
Carroll, Charles, 229
Catholicism
  generally, 2, 7
  Calvinism and, 48–50
  Dickinson and, 283–284
  Federalists and, 135
  Islam and, 85, 87
  Jay and, 205
  Loyalists and, 114
  Morris and, 205–207, 213, 215–216, 218
  Native Americans and, 177
  Protestantism and, 28
  Reformed tradition versus, 36–37
  religious liberty and, 164
  slavery and, 180
  theistic rationalism compared, 209
Cato's Letters (Trenchard and Gordon), 86
"Centinel" (essayist), 125, 140n39, 284
Chandler, Thomas Bradbury, 108–110
Charles I (England), 42
Charles II (England), 114, 310
Chauncy, Charles, 25
Chernow, Ron, 66, 69–70, 78
Cherokee tribe, 181, 185, 194
Chopra, Ruma, x
Christ. *See* Jesus
Christianity. *See specific sect or topic*
Christianity as Old as Creation (Tindal), 17
Christianity Not Mysterious (Toland), 16
Christian nation, America as, 3, 327
Chubb, Thomas, 18
Church of England. *See* Anglicanism

Church-state relations
  generally, 5
  Antifederalists and, 134, 137
  Backus on, 325
  Baptists and, 306
  Deism and, 23
  establishment of religion (*See* Establishment of religion)
  Leland on, 315, 326
  separation of church and state (*See* Separation of church and state)
"Cincinnatus" (essayist), 128
Civil disobedience, 286, 301n51
Civil government, 56n7
Civil liberties, 283–284
Civil rights
  Dickinson on, 292
  Hancock on, 235
  Quakerism and, 284, 286, 290
Civil Rights Movement, 286
Clark, Abraham, 50
Clark, Barbara, 260
Clark, J.C.C., 46
Clarke, John, 310
Clarke, Richard, 231
Clarke, Samuel, 17
Clergy
  among Founders, 21
  Biblical Hebrew imagery and, 64
  colonialism and, 177
  Declaration of Independence and, 51
  Enlightenment and, 28
  establishment of religion and, 310–312
  Loyalists and, 102–104, 108–114
  in Massachusetts, 41
  slavery and, 180
  state support of, 323
Clinton, Bill, 76
Coercive Acts, 106, 110
Coke, Thomas, 190
Coker, Daniel, 177, 191–192

Coker, Joe L., ix
College of New Jersey, 35, 194
Collins, Anthony, 16–17, 21, 26
Collins, Isaac, 146
Colonialism
    Anglicanism and, 102
    clergy and, 177
    English colonialism, 177–179
    Puritanism and, 179
    Spanish colonialism, 177–178
Columbia College, 70
Columbus, Christopher, 177
Colwell, Stephen, 3
Commentaries on the Laws of England
    (Blackstone), 86
Committee of Safety, 228
Common law, 144, 164
Common Sense (Paine), 19, 87, 110, 162,
    168n40, 266
The Complete Anti-Federalist (Storing),
    122, 129–132
Condorcet (Marquis), 110
Confederate Constitution of 1861, 91
Confederation Congress, 63, 146,
    273n35, 277
Congregationalism
    generally, 28, 53, 87
    Anglicanism and, 47
    Antifederalists and, 121–122
    Backus and, 312
    Baptists and, 305, 322–323
    Boudinot and, 259
    establishment of religion and, 317
    Hancock and, 229 (*See also* Hancock,
        John)
    John Adams and, 34–35, 61n43
    Leland and, 315
    in New England, 45–46
    New Light Congregationalists, 6, 103,
        183, 312
    Old Light Congregationalists, 103, 230
    Presbyterianism and, 268

    prevalence of, 165n5
    Revolutionary War and, 234
    separation of church and state and, 328
    state support of, 41
Congregation Shearith Israel, 67, 73
Connecticut
    establishment of religion in, 53, 317
    General Court, 41
    ratification of Constitution, 126
Connecticut Compromise, 53
A Connecticut Dissenter's Strong Box
    (Leland), 317
Conscience, right of
    Antifederalists and, 124–136
    Backus on, 317–320, 324–325
    Baptists and, 307, 309–314
    Boudinot on, 261
    Dickinson on, 288–290, 293
    Hamilton on, 70
    Hancock on, 239
    Jefferson on, 75
    Leland on, 317–320, 325–327, 334n54
    Morris on, 205
    Puritanism and, 42
Constantine (Emperor), 334n58
Constitution
    secularism and, 34, 55
    Sherman and, 51–53
Constitutional Convention of 1787
    generally, 5, 125
    Backus at, 314–315
    Bible, influence of, 157–160
    Calvinists at, 55
    Dickinson at, 149, 277, 294–295
    Franklin at, 171n74
    Gerry at, 120
    Judaism and, 67
    Morris at, 203–204, 206
    Quaker constitutionalism and, 281
Constitution of 1787
    generally, 47, 149
    Boudinot and, 269

Constitution of 1787 *(continued)*
  Calvinism, influence of, 51–53
  federalism in, 52–53
  First Amendment (*See* First Amendment)
  Judaism and, 64
  limited government in, 52
  Morris and, 203–204
  ratification of, 125–129
  Reformed tradition, influence of, 51–53
  religious influence on, 51–53
  Thirteenth Amendment, 295
Constitutions
  amendability of, 281–283
  defined, 299n16
  permanence of, 281–282
  Quaker constitutionalism, 281–289
Continental Army, 150, 236, 244, 255
Continental Association, 111
Continental Congresses
  generally, 72, 146
  Boudinot and, 255
  Calvinists in, 55
  Declaration of Independence and, 50
  Dickinson and, 5, 149, 277
  Gerry and, 120
  Hancock and, 228, 244
  Judaism and, 64
  Loyalists and, 109, 111, 113
  Morris and, 203, 206–207
  Suffolk Resolves, 49
Conversion
  of African-Americans, 179–180, 184
  of Native Americans, 177–179, 184, 193
  of slaves, 179–180, 184
Cooper, James, 60n34
Cooper, John, 187, 189
Cooper, Myles, 108
Cooper, Samuel, 147, 231–232, 234, 243, 247n14
Copley, John Singleton, 231
Cornell, Saul, 122, 138n15

Cotton, John, 42–44
"A Countryman" (essayist), 129, 132
Crayen (Madame), 219
Creeds, 223n31
Creek tribe, 194
Crocius, Johannes, 188
Cromwell, Oliver, 114

Dalin, David G., ix
Danbury Baptists, 305–306, 309, 328–329
Daniel (Bible), 153
Daniels, Bruce, 46
Davenant, William, 114
Davenport, John, 42
"David" (essayist), 131
Davie, William, 51
Davies, Samuel, 1, 182
Davis, David Brion, 185
Death penalty, 292
Declaration of Independence
  generally, 47, 149, 255
  Anglican signers, 105
  Calvinism, influence of, 47–51
  clergy and, 51
  Dickinson and, 278, 287
  Hancock and, 228
  Jefferson and, 48, 50
  John Adams and, 50, 288
  Judaism and, 64
  Reformed tradition, influence of, 47–51
  religious influence on, 47–51
  Samuel Adams and, 50
  secularism and, 34, 55
  slavery and, 187
  Witherspoon and, 50–51
"Declaration of Rights and Grievances" (Dickinson), 5
"Declaration of the Causes and Necessity of Taking Up Arms" (Dickinson), 5

Defence of the Constitutions of the Government of the United States of America (Adams), 71
Deism, 13–30
  generally, 30, 89
  in America, 18–21
  Boudinot and, 262–263
  Dickinson and, 294
  in England, 15–18
  Founders and, 21–27
  Franklin and, 13, 18, 22, 26–28, 33n58, 229
  Hamilton and, 13, 22
  historical background, 15–21
  importance attributed to, 4–6
  Jefferson and, 13, 22, 24–25, 32n45, 229
  Jesus and, 16, 18
  John Adams and, 13, 22, 25, 229
  Judeo-Christian influence on founding contrasted, 13–15, 27–30
  Madison and, 13, 22–23
  militant Deism, 19–21
  Morris and, 204, 207–209, 229
  Paine and, 19–22, 26, 229
  rationalism and, 13
  secularism and, 13–15, 22–23, 27
  theistic rationalism compared, 208–210, 213–214, 216
  Washington and, 13, 22–24, 229
De Jure Regni (Buchanan), 44
De La Motta, Jacob, 75
De Lancey, James, 111
Delaware
  Constitutional Convention, 277
  ratification of Constitution, 125
Delaware tribe, 183
"Deliberator" (essayist), 125, 132
Democracy
  agrarian democracy, 297
  Backus on, 325

  Bible and, 159–163
  Islam contrasted, 86–87
  Leland on, 316, 324, 326
"Denatus" (essayist), 128
Den Hartog, Jonathan, ix, 273n34
Desbrosses, Elias, 111
De Veritate (Herbert), 16
A Dialogue Between a Virginian and an African Minister (Coker), 191–192
Dickerson, O.M., 241
Dickinson, John, 277–298
  generally, 4–5, 7
  Anglicanism and, 284
  Bible and, 149, 160
  Bill of Rights and, 295
  Catholicism and, 283–284
  Christianity and, 229
  at Constitutional Convention, 149, 277, 294–295
  Continental Congresses and, 5, 149, 277
  during Critical Period, 289–293
  Declaration of Independence and, 278, 287
  Deism and, 294
  on France, 297
  on French Revolution, 278, 288–289, 294
  implementation of Quaker policy and, 289–293
  influence in early republic, 293–298
  Jefferson and, 294, 296
  Locke and, 293
  on morality, 292–293
  on New Testament, 293
  overview, 277–279
  on pacifism, 280–281, 287–288
  Paine and, 294
  philanthropy of, 295–296
  philosophy of, 293–298, 303n97
  on popular participation, 283–286
  Presbyterianism and, 284

Dickinson, John (*continued*)
   Quaker constitutionalism, 281–289
   Quakerism and, 278–281
   on rationalism, 293
   religion of, 289–293
   on religious liberty, 289–291
   on religious tolerance, 283–284
   on resistance, 286–288
   Revolutionary War and, 289–293
   Rush and, 296
   on slavery, 294–295, 304n106
   on theology, 165n6
   Washington and, 294–295
Dickinson College, 296
The Dignity of Man (Emmons), 86
Diner, Hans R., 67
Discourse of the Grounds and Reasons of the Christian Religion (Collins), 17
Disestablishment, 320–322
A Dissertation on Liberty and Necessity, Pleasure and Pain (Franklin), 26
Dominican Order, 177
Dominion of New England, 42
The Dominion of Providence over the Passions of Men (Witherspoon), 268
A Door Open for Christian Liberty (Backus), 325
Dorchester, Lord, 115
Dow, Lorenzo, 318
Dowd, Gregory Evans, 181
Drakeman, Donald L., ix, 23
Dreisbach, Daniel L., ix, 8, 23, 43, 61n46, 81n75, 142n77, 328, 331n15
Drinker, Henry, 113
Dudleian Lectures, 28
Duffield, George, 72
Dunkers, 310
Dunmore (Earl), 184
Dutch Reformed Church, 108, 115, 165n5
Dwight, Timothy, 266, 322

"E" (essayist), 189
Early New England: A Covenanted Society (Weir), 40
Edwards, Jonathan, 1, 25, 29, 255, 258–259, 312, 318, 330n9
Egerton, Douglas R., 185
Eidsmoe, John, 245n3
Eisenstadt, Peter R., 45–46
Elcan, Marcus, 71
Election sermons, 40, 159, 161–163, 232, 243
Eliot, John, 179
Ellery, William, 50
Elliott, J.H., 177
Ellison, Keith, 98
Ellsworth, Oliver, 51–54, 165n6, 229
Elmer, Jonathan, 54
Emmons, Nathaniel, 86
English Civil War, 42–43
Enlightenment
   Bible, influence on founding compared, 144, 151, 163, 166n13
   clergy and, 28
   importance attributed to, 3–4
   Judeo-Christian influence on founding contrasted, 27–30
   Presbyterianism and, 29
   Protestantism and, 28
Environmentalism, 182
Episcopalianism. *See* Anglicanism
An Essay Concerning the Use of Reason in Propositions the Evidence Whereof Depends on Human Testimony (Collins), 17
An Essay on the Causes of the Variety of Complexion and Figure in the Human Species (Smith), 195
Establishment of religion
   Antifederalists and, 130, 132–135
   Backus on, 313–314
   Baptists and, 310–311
   Boudinot on, 261

clergy and, 310–312
Congregationalism and, 317
in Connecticut, 53, 317
disestablishment, 320–322
in First Amendment, 63, 116, 130, 132–135, 306, 317
in Georgia, 117n12
in individual states, 53
Islam and, 87–88
Judaism and, 63
Lutherans and, 310
in Maine, 53
in Maryland, 117n12
in Massachusetts, 53
Moravians and, 310
in New Hampshire, 53
in New York, 117n12
in North Carolina, 117n12
Presbyterianism and, 310–311
Quakerism and, 310–311
Reformed tradition and, 62n51
in South Carolina, 117n12
in Vermont, 53
in Virginia, 103–104, 117n12
Etting, Reuben, 74, 81n77
Evangelicals
  generally, 30
  Boudinot as, 258–259
  Native Americans and, 182

Fabius Letters (Dickinson), 5, 294–295, 297
The Faiths of the Founding Fathers (Holmes), 260
Faucette, John, 69
Fea, John, 144, 165n3, 276n67
"Federal Farmer" (essayist), 128, 141n60
Federalism
  Antifederalists and, 132–133, 136
  Bible and, 163
  in Constitution, 52–53
  Dickinson on, 294

in First Amendment, 132
The Federalist Papers, 5, 47, 52, 149
Federalists
  Catholicism and, 135
  French Revolution and, 269
  Jefferson and, 136
  Madison and, 136
  secularism and, 135
Feldman, Egel, 75, 77, 82n82
Filmer, Robert, 109
Finke, Roger, 45, 60n31, 117n10
First Amendment
  generally, 13, 23, 261
  Antifederalists and, 120
  Boudinot and, 54
  Calvinism, influence of, 53–54
  establishment of religion in, 63, 116, 130, 132–135, 306, 317
  federalism in, 132
  free exercise of religion in, 116
  Jefferson and, 62n50
  Judaism and, 64
  Madison and, 62n50
  Reformed tradition, influence of, 53–54
  religious influence on, 53–54
  separation of church and state in, 328
  Sherman and, 53–54
First Continental Congress. *See* Continental Congresses
First Federal Congress, 55
First Great Awakening. *See* Great Awakening
Flahaut (Madame), 219
Floyd, William, 50
Fort Hunter, 105
Fort Ticonderoga, 151
Fort Tiononderoga, 105
Foss, John, 95–96
Foster, Abiel, 54
Foster, Daniel, 243, 251n93

Foster, Herbert D., 43
Foucault (Madame), 219
Founders. *See also specific person*
    Bible and, 148–152
    clergy among, 21
    Deism and, 21–27
The Founders on God and Government (Dreisbach), 7
Fox, George, 180
A Fragment (Dickinson), 296
France
    Boudinot on, 263
    Dickinson on, 297
    Morris on, 210–212, 220
    support for Revolution, 50, 114
Franciscan Order, 177
Franklin, Benjamin
    generally, 4, 54–55, 87, 111, 228
    Bible and, 145, 147–148, 151–152, 157–160, 171n74
    Biblical Hebrew imagery and, 64
    at Constitutional Convention, 171n74
    cosmopolitan outlook of, 2–3, 34
    Deism and, 13, 18, 22, 26–28, 33n58, 229
    in Europe, 55n2
    Islam and, 84–85, 96, 98
    on Jesus, 152
    Native Americans and, 181
    religion of, 204–205
    theistic rationalism and, 223n28
Franklin, William, 108, 111
Franks, Isaac, 66–67
Frazer, Gregg L., x, 160
Freedom of press, 313
Freedom of speech, 283, 313
Free exercise of religion, 116, 332n21
Free Quakers, 287
French and Indian War, 231
French Revolution
    generally, 110, 256–257
    Dickinson on, 278, 288–289, 294

    Federalists and, 269
    Jefferson on, 24
    John Adams on, 92
    Reign of Terror, 203, 211
Freneau, Philip, 21
Frey, Sylvia, 117n16
Friendly Address to All Reasonable Americans (Chandler), 109
Friends. *See* Quakerism
"A Friend to Justice" (essayist), 187–188
"A Friend to the Rights of the People" (essayist), 127
Fundamentalists, 30

Gage, Thomas, 181
Gallatin, Albert, 296
Gardner, Robert, 307
Gaustad, Edwin, 316
Gehrt (Miss), 219
General Baptists, 308
General Six-Principle Baptists, 307–308
George III (England), 49, 51, 64, 159, 185, 234, 326
Georgia
    establishment of religion in, 117n12
    ratification of Constitution, 126
German Reformed Church, 165n5
Gerry, Elbridge, 5, 120–121, 123, 133, 137, 139n18
Gibson, Alan, 10n21, 173n97
Gilman, Nicholas, 51, 54
Gilsdorf, Joy, 40–41
Gilsdorf, Robert, 40–41
Glenn, Gary, 130–132, 141n68, 142n69
Glorious Revolution, 42–43
"God's Law," 42, 58n18
Golden Rule, 187, 192, 214
Goldman, Shalom, 65
Gomez, Michael, 84
Goodman, Christopher, 38
Gordon, George, 219
Gordon, Thomas, 86

Gorham, Nathaniel, 51
Government and Liberty Described
    (Backus), 313
A Grammar of the Hebrew Tongue
    (Monis), 65
Grant, Ulysses S., 76
Great Awakening
    generally, 6, 43
    African-Americans and, 182–183
    Anglicanism and, 102
    Backus and, 312, 323, 330n9
    Baptists and, 308–309, 311
    Boudinot and, 258
    Leland and, 315
    Moravians and, 183
    Native Americans and, 183
    political importance of, 1–2, 14–15
    Revolutionary War and, 330n9
Green, Ashbel, 268
Green Mountain Boys, 19, 151
Grenda, Christopher, 322

Haldimand, Frederick, 106
Hall, David D., 42
Hall, Lyman, 50
Hall, Mark David, x, 229
Hamburger, Philip, 328
Hamilton, Alexander
    generally, 4–5, 34, 54–55, 67, 204
    on conscience, 70
    Deism and, 13, 22
    Judaism and, 65, 69–71, 77–78
    on religious liberty, 69–71
    theistic rationalism and, 223n28
Hamilton, James, 69–70
Hamilton, Philip, 22
Hamilton, Rachel, 69–70
Hancock, Ebenezer, 242
Hancock, John, 228–245
    generally, 5, 8, 50
    Bill of Rights and, 244
    at Brattle Street Church, 230–233
    Calvinism and, 229
    on civil rights, 235
    Congregationalism and, 229
    Continental Congresses and, 228, 244
    death of, 243–244
    Declaration of Independence and, 228
    early life of, 229–230
    ethics and, 240–243
    as governor, 238–240
    on Jesus, 238
    John Adams and, 244
    lifestyle of, 240–243
    overview, 228–229, 243–245
    philanthropy of, 240–243, 251n87, 251n91
    Presbyterianism and, 229
    providentialism and, 236–238, 248n42
    Reformed tradition and, 229, 236, 239
    religion of, 229, 231–233, 245n3
    on resistance, 233
    Revolutionary War and, 233–235
    Samuel Adams and, 242–243
    on slavery, 240
    on state support of religion, 238–240
    Washington and, 244
    wealth of, 248n37
Hancock, John (father), 230
Hancock, John (grandfather), 230
Hancock, John George Washington, 233
Hancock, Nathaniel, 229
Hancock, Thomas, 230, 240–241
Harrington, James, 15
Harrison, William Henry, 194
Hart, John, 50
Hartford Convention, 211
Hartz, Louis, 52
Harvard College, 46, 65, 163, 230, 239
Hebrew Commonwealth, 161–163
Heimert, Alan, 14, 330n9
Heister, Daniel, Jr., 54
Helwys, Thomas, 309–310, 330n9
Henry, Jacob, 89

Henry, Patrick
  as Antifederalist, 121, 127, 134
  Bible and, 145, 149, 156–157, 171n69
  Christianity and, 229
  Islam and, 93
Henry VIII (England), 39
Herbert of Cherbury (Lord), 16–17
Hirschfeld, Fritz, 66
An Historical and Geographical Account of Algiers (Stevens), 96
History of Virginia (Beverley), 18
Hitchcock, Enos, 86
Hobbes, Thomas, 58nn19–20, 109
Holmes, David, 245n3, 260
Holyoke, Edward, 230
"Homo Sum" (essayist), 189
Hooker, Thomas, 40
Hopkins, Stephen, 21
Houston, William, 51
Huger, Daniel, 54
Huguenots, 48, 165n5, 204, 258
Hume, David, 15, 29, 34
Huntington, Benjamin, 54
Huntington, Samuel, 50
Hutchinson, Anne, 41
Hutson, James H., 45, 60n31, 121, 245n3

Ill News from New England (Clarke), 310
Illuminatism, 21
"Impartial" (essayist), 187
Independent Gazetteer, 91
Indians. *See* Native Americans
Individualism, 14, 316
Ingersoll, Jared, 51
Inglis, Charles, 104, 108, 110–113, 115
Institutes of the Christian Religion (Calvin), 37, 44
Iredell, James, 89
Iroquois tribe, 181
Islam, 84–98
  generally, 6
  Anglicanism and, 87
  Antifederalists and, 88–89
  anti-Muslim writings, 92–93
  blasphemy and, 90
  Boudinot and, 91–92, 98
  Catholicism and, 85, 87
  democracy contrasted, 86–87
  establishment of religion and, 87–88
  Franklin and, 84–85, 96, 98
  Henry and, 93
  Paine and, 87, 91
  perceived tyranny of, 86
  piracy and, 84–85, 93–95
  political imagery regarding, 91–92
  prophetic view of, 85–86
  religious liberty and, 88
  religious tests and, 88–91
  slavery and, 84, 95–98, 180
Israel, Jonathan, 17

Jackson, Andrew, 194
Jackson, James, 54
James, Sydney V., 113
James I (England), 109, 146, 309
Jamestown colony, 178
Jay, John
  generally, 5, 67, 267
  in American Bible Society, 146, 258
  Bible and, 145, 149
  Catholicism and, 205
  Christianity and, 229
  diplomacy of, 257
  Morris and, 218–219
  on theology, 165n6
Jay, William, 267
Jay Treaty, 257, 271n15
Jefferson, Thomas
  generally, 4–5, 21, 54–55, 87, 92, 98, 211, 228, 244, 305
  on African-Americans, 174–175
  Anglicanism and, 34
  Backus and, 322–324, 328–329
  Baptists and, 322–324

Bible and, 146, 151–154, 159
Biblical Hebrew imagery and, 64
Boudinot and, 262–264
on conscience, 75
cosmopolitan outlook of, 2–3
Danbury Baptists and, 305–306, 309, 328–329
Declaration of Independence and, 48, 50
Deism and, 13, 22, 24–25, 32n45, 229
Dickinson and, 294, 296
in Europe, 55n2
Federalists and, 136
First Amendment and, 62n50
on French Revolution, 24
on Jesus, 24, 146, 168n36
Judaism and, 65, 74–77
Leland and, 318, 322–324, 328–329
Locke and, 50
Morris and, 217, 221
Native Americans and, 174, 193, 336n83
on New Testament, 24, 146
on Old Testament, 24
piracy and, 93–94
political opponents of, 9n8
on race, 174–177, 186–187, 191–192, 195
religion of, 204–205
on religious liberty, 74–76, 81n75, 335n73
on religious tolerance, 82n82
on separation of church and state, 23, 27, 53–54, 130, 305–307, 310, 324–325, 328, 331n15, 336n83
on slavery, 175, 265
Thanksgiving and, 262, 273n36
theistic rationalism and, 223n28
Unitarianism and, 32n46, 75
Williams and, 331n15
Jeremiah (Bible), 156
Jesus

Backus on, 320–321
Deism and, 16, 18
Franklin on, 152
Hancock on, 238
Jefferson on, 24, 146, 168n36
John Adams on, 29
Leland on, 334n58
Morris on, 214–215
Paine on, 266
theistic rationalism and, 209, 214–215
Jethro (Bible), 160
Job (Bible), 153
John Dickinson Writings Project, 303n97
John Hancock Financial Services, Inc., 229
Johnson, Lyndon, 76
Johnson, Samuel, 108
Johnson, William, 104–105
Johnston, Samuel, 89–90, 98
Jones, Absalom, 191
Jones, Thomas, 111
Joshua (Bible), 72
Judaism, 63–78
generally, 2, 6, 89
in America, 63–64, 76–78
Biblical Hebrew imagery and founding, 64–65, 264, 319
Constitutional Convention and, 67
Constitution and, 64
Continental Congresses and, 64
Declaration of Independence and, 64
establishment of religion and, 63
First Amendment and, 64
Hamilton and, 65, 69–71, 77–78
Jefferson and, 65, 74–77
John Adams and, 65, 71–73, 77
religious liberty and, 164
Revolutionary War and, 78n1
in Rhode Island, 68–69, 76
Washington and, 65–69, 76–78

Judeo-Christian influence on founding
  Deism contrasted, 13–15, 27–30
  diversity of, 27–30
  Enlightenment contrasted, 27–30
Junto Club, 26
Jury trials, 292

Kenyon, Cecilia, 135
Kidd, Thomas S., x
King, Martin Luther, Jr., 286
King James Bible, 145, 148, 153, 156, 163–164
King Philip's War, 179
King's College, 70, 108, 204, 215
Kirk, Thomas, 241
Kirschke, James, 205–206, 217, 219
Knox, Henry, 193
Knox, John, 38, 43
Kramnick, Isaac, 45, 51

Lafayette (Marquis), 155
LaHaye, Tim, 245n3
Lambert, Frank, 4, 245n3
Langdon, John, 51, 54
Langdon, Samuel, 162–163, 234
Languet, Hubert, 38
Lansing, John, Jr., 51, 123
Lavien, Johann Michael, 69
"Law of Nature," 42, 58n18
The Law of Scottish Kingship (Buchanan), 44
Lee, Arthur, 128
Lee, Richard Henry, 5, 121, 124, 128, 131, 134
Leland, John, 305–329
  generally, 7
  Baptists and, 331n18
  Bill of Rights and, 317
  biography of, 315–318
  Calvinism and, 315–316, 318
  on church-state relations, 315, 326
  Congregationalism and, 315
  on conscience, 317–320, 325–327, 334n54
  on democracy, 316, 324, 326
  on disestablishment, 320–322
  Great Awakening and, 315
  on individualism, 316
  Jefferson and, 318, 322–324, 328–329
  on Jesus, 334n58
  Madison and, 316–317, 333n22
  overview, 305–307, 327–329
  on religious liberty, 87–88, 318–320
  on religious tests, 326
  Second Great Awakening and, 315
  on separation of church and state, 325–328
  Williams and, 334n58
Leslie, Charles, 109
Letters from a Farmer in Pennsylvania (Dickinson), 5, 283
Leviathan (Hobbes), 58n19
Liberalism
  Locke and, 36
  in Reformed tradition, 36
Liberty
  political liberty, 42–43
  religious liberty (*See* Religious liberty)
"The Liberty Song," 278, 283
"The Life and Morals of Jesus of Nazareth" (Jefferson), 146
The Life of Mahomet; or, The History of that Imposture Which was Begun, Carried on, and Finally Established by Him in Arabia (Anonymous), 92–93
Limited government, 52, 316
Lincoln, Abraham, 273n36
Linnaeus, Carl, 182
Lita (Madame), 219
Literacy, 56n6
Little Abraham (Mohawk), 105

Livingston, Philip, 50
Livingston, Robert, 205
Livingston, William, 51
Locke, John
　generally, 34, 44
　Backus and, 313, 323
　colonial America, influence in,
　　59n24
　on conscience, 319
　Dickinson and, 293
　environmentalism and, 182
　founding, influence on, 144, 163
　on individualism, 14
　Jefferson and, 50
　liberalism and, 36
　on natural rights, 58n20
　religion and, 17
　on self-preservation, 58n19
　on separation of church and state,
　　331n15
　on slavery, 265
　on social contract, 109
Logan, George, 296–297
Logan Act, 297
"A Lover of true Justice" (essayist), 177,
　188–190
Lowell, John, 231
Loyalists, 101–116
　generally, 6
　Anglicanism and, 101, 105–116
　Baptists and, 116
　Brattle Street Church and, 232
　in Canada, 114–115
　Catholicism and, 114
　clergy and, 102–104, 108–114
　Continental Congresses and, 109,
　　111, 113
　Lutherans and, 115
　Methodism and, 101, 115
　Moravians and, 116
　in New England, 105–108
　newspapers and, 111

　in New York, 105–108
　Presbyterianism and, 112, 115–116
　Quakerism and, 101, 113, 115–116
　resistance and, 107
　role of religion, 102–103
Luther, Martin, 37, 56n7, 86
Lutherans
　establishment of religion and, 310
　Loyalists and, 115
Lutz, Donald S., 146–147, 166nn9–10,
　166n13
Lyon, James, 92
Lyon, Matthew, 92

Madison, Dolley, 219, 228
Madison, James
　generally, 4–5, 52, 54–55, 116, 328
　Anglicanism and, 34
　Backus and, 324
　Bible and, 160
　Bill of Rights and, 317
　Deism and, 13, 22–23
　Federalists and, 136
　First Amendment and, 62n50
　on free exercise of religion, 332n21
　Leland and, 316–317, 333n22
　Morris and, 203–204
　piracy and, 94
　on prayer, 325
　Reformed tradition and, 35
　on religious liberty, 81n75
　on religious tolerance, 311
　on separation of church and state, 23,
　　53–54, 130
　on taxation of religion, 134
　Thanksgiving and, 273n36
　theistic rationalism and, 223n28
Main, Jackson Turner, 121, 130, 141n67
Maine, establishment of religion in, 53
Mandeville, Bernard, 33n58
Manis, Andrew M., 337n93
Manumission, 186

Marini, Stephen, 21–22, 138n13, 139n16
Martin, Alexander, 51
Martin, Luther, 44–45, 88, 124
Martin, Thomas, 35
Martin, William, 4
Martyr, Peter, 43
Maryland
　Anglicanism in, 2
　Catholicism in, 2
　establishment of religion in, 117n12
　ratification of Constitution, 126–127
　slavery in, 184, 192
Mason, George, 5, 121, 123
Mason, John Mitchell, 267
Massachusetts
　Baptists in, 308–309, 335n74
　Body of Liberties, 1, 41
　The Book of the General Laws and Liberties Concerning the Inhabitants of Massachusetts, 41
　clergy in, 41
　Constitution, 320–321, 323, 335n70
　Constitutional Convention, 313–314
　establishment of religion in, 53
　Provincial Congress, 228
　ratification of Constitution, 126
Massachusetts Bay Colony
　General Court, 40
　religious persecution in, 310
The Massachusetts Spy (newspaper), 19
Mathews, Donald G., 191
Matthiesen (Miss), 219
May, Henry, 86
Mayflower Compact, 1, 39–40
Mayhew, Jonathan, 51
McClurg, James, 51
McGuffey's *Eclectic Reader*, 3
McHenry, James, 51
McKean, Thomas, 50
McKinley, William, 76
McLoughlin, William G., 335n77, 337n99
McWilliams, Wilson Carey, 144, 165n2, 169n39

Mecom, Jane, 231
Memoir of the Rev. William Tennent (Boudinot), 257
"Memorial and Remonstrance" (Madison), 62n50
Methodism
　generally, 6, 45
　African-Americans and, 191
　Loyalists and, 101, 115
　slavery and, 104, 186, 190–191, 195
Meyer, Isidore S., 71–72
Middle Temple, 280
Militant Deism, 19–21
Mill, John Stuart, 36
Miller, Perry, 44
Miller, Samuel, 293
Mintz, Max, 205
Miracles, 16, 215–216
Miracles, no Violation of the Laws of Nature (Blount), 16
Missouri Compromise, 264–265
Mitchel, Jonathan, 58n18
The Moderator between an Infidel and an Apostate (Woolston), 18
Mohawk tribe, 104–105
Monarchies, 36
Monis, Judah, 65
Monroe, James, 218
Montesquieu (Baron), 15, 34, 86, 144, 146–147, 160, 163
Moore, R. Laurence, 45, 51
Morality
　Boudinot on, 254
　Dickinson on, 292–293
　Morris on, 219–220
Moravians
　generally, 116
　establishment of religion and, 310
　Great Awakening and, 183
　Loyalists and, 116
　Native Americans and, 185, 194
Mornay, Philippe du Plesis, 38

Morris, B.F., 3
Morris, Catherine, 212
Morris, Gouverneur, 203–221
  generally, 5, 8
  Anglicanism and, 204, 217
  Bible and, 213–214
  Calvinism and, 204, 214
  Catholicism and, 205–207, 213, 215–216, 218
  on conscience, 205
  at Constitutional Convention, 203–204, 206
  Constitution and, 203–204
  Continental Congresses and, 203, 206–207
  Deism and, 204, 207–209, 229
  on France, 210–212, 220
  Jay and, 218–219
  Jefferson and, 217, 221
  on Jesus, 214–215
  Madison and, 203–204
  on miracles, 215–216
  on morality, 219–220
  overview, 203–204
  on Prussia, 220–221
  Puritanism and, 204
  Quakerism and, 205–206, 215
  religion of, 204–205, 207–208
  on religious tests, 206
  on religious tolerance, 205–206
  on separation of church and state, 205–207
  sexual affairs of, 218–219
  Sherman and, 218
  theistic rationalism, 208–221
    (*See also* Theistic rationalism)
  Washington and, 218
Morris, Robert, 67, 71, 228
Morrison, Jeffry H., 151
Morse, Jedediah, 266–267
Morton, Perez, 219
Moses (Bible), 64, 153, 159, 161
Moses, Isaac, 70–71
Muhammad (Prophet), 92–93
Muñoz, Vincent Phillip, 68, 132–134
Murray, John, 184
Murton, John, 310
Muslims. *See* Islam
Mutiny of 1783, 292
Myers, Moses, 71
Myers, Samuel, 71
Mystery of Inquiry (Helwys), 309

Najar, Monica, 198*n*44, 317
National Gazette, 21
Native Americans. *See also specific tribe or person*
  Anglicanism and, 104–105
  Catholicism and, 177
  conflicts with, 179, 181–182
  conversion of, 177–179, 184, 193
  effect of demographic changes on, 180–181
  environmentalism and, 182
  Evangelicals and, 182
  Franklin and, 181
  Great Awakening and, 183
  Jefferson and, 174, 193, 336*n*83
  Moravians and, 185, 194
  in New England, 179
  in Pennsylvania, 179
  Presbyterianism and, 194
  Quakerism and, 179, 181, 183, 193, 289
  religion and, 181, 192–193
  Revolutionary War and, 185
  in Virginia, 179
Natural rights, 58*n*20
Navigation Acts, 241
Neem, Jonathan N., 275*n*61
Neolin (Delaware), 177, 181
New England. *See also specific state*
  Loyalists in, 105–108
  Native Americans in, 179
  Presbyterianism in, 46

The New-England Primer, 35
New Hampshire
    establishment of religion in, 53
    ratification of Constitution, 127
New Haven Gazette, 87
New Jersey
    Provisional Congress, 255
    ratification of Constitution, 126
    women's suffrage in, 300n37
New-Jersey Gazette, 186, 189–190
New Jersey Society of the Cincinnati, 253–254, 258
New Light Congregationalists, 6, 103, 183, 312
New Side Presbyterians, 6, 29, 258, 272n22
Newspapers, Loyalists and, 111
New Testament
    Baptists and, 310
    Boudinot on, 254
    Dickinson on, 293
    Jefferson on, 24, 146
    Paine on, 20
    slavery and, 188–192
Newton, Isaac, 17, 24, 86
New York
    Constitution, 205
    Constitutional Convention, 206
    establishment of religion in, 117n12
    Loyalists in, 108–110
    Provincial Congress, 203
    Provincial Convention, 203
    ratification of Constitution, 128–129
The New York Gazette, 112
New York Historical Society, 219
Ninety-Five Theses (Luther), 37
Noah, Mordecai Manuel, 73–74, 77
Nobles, Gregory, 252n105
Noll, Mark A., 29, 144, 165n4, 268, 276n63
Nones, Benjamin, 66
Norris, Mary, 280

North Carolina
    establishment of religion in, 117n12
    Presbyterianism in, 46
    ratification of Constitution, 129
    slavery in, 184–185
Northwest Ordinance, 63, 264
Notes on the State of Virginia (Jefferson), 174, 187, 192
Nott, Eliphalet, 267
Nowell, Samuel, 42

Oaths, 291, 302n78
"Objections to Signing the National Constitution" (Gerry), 123
"Objections to the Constitution of Government Formed by the Convention" (Mason), 123
Occom, Samuel, 183
Old Light Congregationalists, 103, 230
Old Testament
    Backus on, 319
    Boudinot on, 254
    Hebrew imagery and founding, 64–65
    influence on political ideas and institutions, 161
    Jefferson on, 24
    Paine on, 20
    political use of text, 153–156, 159
    slavery and, 188
"Old Whig" (essayist), 125, 140n38
Oliver, Peter, 51
Oracles of Reason (Blount), 16
Oren, Michael, 77
Orleans (Duchess), 211

Paca, William, 126–127
Pacifism, 280–281, 287–288
Paine, Robert Treat, 50, 149
Paine, Thomas
    generally, 4–5, 34, 54–55, 204
    Bible and, 145, 148, 151–153, 162, 168n40

Boudinot and, 257, 260, 265–267, 275n55
Deism and, 19–22, 26, 229
Dickinson and, 294
Inglis and, 110
Islam and, 87, 91
on Jesus, 266
on New Testament, 20
on Old Testament, 20
Painted Pole, 192
Palmer, Elihu, 20, 26
Palmerston (Lord), 218–219
Pareus, David, 38, 44
Parrish, John, 192
Parsons, Theophilus, 134
Particular Baptists, 307–308
Paterson, William, 51, 54
Paul (Bible), 147
Paxton Boys, 181–182
"Penman of the Revolution," 278, 298
Penn, William, 281–282
Pennsylvania
    Charter of Privileges, 284, 289–290, 302n78
    Native Americans in, 179
    Presbyterianism in, 46
    Quakerism in, 299n8
    ratification of Constitution, 125–126
    slavery in, 185–186
"Pennsylvania Farmer," 278
Pennsylvania Gazette, 18
The Pennsylvania Packet, 206
Pennsylvania Society for Promoting the Abolition of Slavery, 264
Persecution
    of Baptists, 311
    in Massachusetts Bay colony, 310
    of Quakerism, 41, 302n75
Pharaoh (Bible), 64, 159
Philadelphia Yearly Meeting, 184
"Philadelphiensis" (essayist), 125, 140n38

Philanthropy
    of Dickinson, 295–296
    of Hancock, 240–243, 251n87, 251n91
Phillips, Jonas, 67
Phillips, William, 168n41
"The Philosophy of Jesus of Nazareth" (Jefferson), 146
Pickering, Thomas, 193, 265
Pinckney, Charles, 5
Pintard, John, 265
Piracy, 84–85, 93–95
Pocahontas, 178
Policy as Well as Honesty (Backus), 313
Political liberty, 42–43
Pontiac's Rebellion, 104, 181
Power, Susan M., 303n90
Powhatan Confederation, 178–179
Poynet, John, 38, 44
Prayer, 143n99, 325
Presbyterianism
    generally, 34–35
    Anglicanism and, 47
    Antifederalists and, 122
    Boudinot and, 253–254, 258–259, 268–269 (*See also* Boudinot, Elias)
    Congregationalism and, 268
    Dickinson and, 284
    Enlightenment and, 29
    establishment of religion and, 310–311
    Hancock and, 229
    limited government and, 52
    Loyalists and, 112, 115–116
    Native Americans and, 194
    in New England, 46
    in North Carolina, 46
    in Pennsylvania, 46
    prevalence of, 165n5
    Revolutionary War and, 51
    slavery and, 191
    in South, 46

Press, freedom of, 313
Price, Richard, 87
Prideaux, Humphrey, 91–92
Priestley, Joseph, 24–25, 32nn46–47, 293
"Princeton Circle," 268, 276n63
Princeton College, 22, 29, 44, 255, 258, 268
Princeton Seminary, 268
Principles of Nature (Palmer), 20
Proclamations, 325
Proctor, Donald J., 252n107
The Prospect (newspaper), 20
Protestantism. *See also* Reformed tradition; *specific sect*
   Catholicism and, 28
   Enlightenment and, 28
   prevalence of, 165n5
Providentialism, 236–238, 248n42
Prussia, Morris on, 220–221
Pufendorf, Samuel von, 205, 216
Puritanism
   generally, 1, 37
   in America, 39–43
   Brattle Street Church and, 231
   colonialism and, 179
   conscience and, 319
   historical background, 39–43
   Morris and, 204
   prevalence of, 165n5
   Revolutionary War and, 234
   Samuel Adams and, 44–45
   slavery and, 180

Quaker Constitutionalism and the Political Thought of John Dickinson (Calvert), 279
Quakerism
   generally, 5, 7, 30, 89
   Antifederalists and, 122, 125
   constitutionalism, 281–289
   Dickinson and, 278–281 (*See also* Dickinson, John)
   establishment of religion and, 310–311
   Free Quakers, 287
   Loyalists and, 101, 113, 115–116
   Morris and, 205–206, 215
   Native Americans and, 179, 181, 183, 193, 289
   in Pennsylvania, 299n8
   persecution of, 41, 302n75
   prevalence of, 299n8
   slavery and, 180, 183–185, 189–190, 195
Quebec Act of 1774, 48–49

Race, 174–195
   African-Americans (*See* African-Americans)
   conceptions of, 176
   Jefferson on, 174–177, 186–187, 191–192, 195
   Native Americans (*See* Native Americans)
   religion and, 177
   slavery (*See* Slavery)
Rakove, Jack, 34
Ramsay, David, 168n40
Randolph, Edmund, 5, 21, 123–124, 127
Rationalism
   generally, 4, 6
   Backus on, 323
   Bible contrasted, 144, 148, 151
   Deism and, 13
   Dickinson on, 293
   theistic rationalism (*See* Theistic rationalism)
Rawls, John, 36
Reagan, Ronald, 76
Reason: The Only Oracle of Man (Young), 18–19
"Reasons of Dissent" (Yates and Lansing), 123
Reason the Only Oracle of Man, or A Compenduous System of Natural Religion (Allen), 151

The Reformation of Rights (White), 58n20
Reformed tradition, 34–55. *See also* Calvinism
    adherence rates, 45–46, 56n3, 59n30
    in America, 39–43
    Boudinot and, 258–259
    Catholicism versus, 36–37
    Constitution, influence on, 51–53
    Declaration of Independence, influence on, 47–51
    defined, 55n1
    establishment of religion and, 62n51
    First Amendment, influence on, 53–54
    Hancock and, 229, 236, 239
    historical background, 39–43
    John Adams and, 44, 229
    liberalism in, 36
    literature of, 43–45
    Madison and, 35
    neglect of, 34–36, 54–55
    political theory of, 36–39
    prevalence of, 165n5
    resistance and, 38–39, 42, 44
    role in founding, 43–45
    Sherman and, 50, 229
    Witherspoon and, 44, 229
A Reforming People: Puritanism and the Transformation of Public Life in New England (Hall), 42
Regular Baptists, 308, 331n18
Reign of Terror, 203, 211
Religion of Nature Delineated (Wollaston), 18
Religious liberty
    Antifederalists and, 125–131, 133–136, 142n85
    Backus on, 318–320
    Baptists and, 305–306, 309
    Catholicism and, 164
    Dickinson on, 289–291
    Hamilton on, 69–71
    Islam and, 88
    Jefferson on, 74–76, 81n75, 335n73
    John Adams on, 71–73
    Leland on, 87–88, 318–320
    Madison on, 81n75
    restrictions on, 164
    Unitarianism and, 164
    Washington on, 66–69
Religious tests
    Antifederalists and, 124, 126–128, 130, 141n54, 142n78
    Backus on, 334n57, 336n82
    in Constitution, 52, 61n46, 91
    Islam and, 88–91
    Leland on, 326
    Morris on, 206
Religious tolerance
    Dickinson on, 283–284
    Jefferson on, 82n82
    Morris on, 205–206
    in New England, 41
Remarks on the Slavery of the Black People (Parrish), 192
Resistance
    Bible and, 144–145
    Boudinot on, 268
    Declaration of Independence and, 47–48
    Dickinson on, 283, 286–288
    Hancock on, 233
    Loyalists and, 107
    Reformed tradition and, 38–39, 42, 44
Restoration, 42–43, 114
Revelation
    generally, 3
    in Bible, 151
    Deism and, 15–19, 22–24, 28
    Dickinson on, 293
    theistic rationalism and, 208–209
Revere, Paul, 49
Revival, 321–322. *See also* Great Awakening

Revolutionary War
  Congregationalism and, 234
  Dickinson and, 289–293
  Great Awakening and, 2, 330n9
  Hancock and, 233–235
  Judaism and, 78n1
  Native Americans and, 185
  Presbyterianism and, 51
  Samuel Adams and, 234
  slavery and, 176, 184–185
  Witherspoon and, 234
Rhode Island
  Judaism in, 68–69, 76
  ratification of Constitution, 129
Richter, Daniel K., 178, 181–182
Ridgway, Whitman H., 138n10
"Righteous Republic," 261–267
Right of conscience. *See* Conscience, right of
Rights of Magistrates (Beza), 44
Rivington, James, 109
Roberts, Kenneth, 107
Robertson, David Brian, 52
Robertson, Donald, 35
Rodney, Caesar Augustus, 296
Rolfe, John, 178
Roman Catholicism. *See* Catholicism
Roosevelt, Theodore, 206–207, 221
Rousseau, Jean-Jacques, 110
Rowlandson, Mary, 179
Rowson, Susannah, 96
The Royal Gazette, 112
Royal Georgia Gazette, 112
Rush, Benjamin, 5, 77, 146, 149, 167n20, 229, 293, 296
Russell, Philip Moses, 66
Rutherford, Samuel, 36, 38
Rutledge, John, 5

Sabbath, observance of, 229, 235, 239, 290, 327

Salomon, Haym, 67
Samson (Bible), 154
"Samuel" (essayist), 126
Sandy Creek Association, 308
Sarna, Jonathan D., 63–64, 68
Sassi, Jonathan D., x
Saul (Bible), 161
Schureman, James, 54
Schuyler, Philip, 54
Scottish Covenanters, 165n5
Scriptures. *See* Bible
Seabury, Samuel, 108–109
Seal of United States, 159
Search and seizure, 313
The Second Advent (Boudinot), 92, 258
Second Continental Congress. *See* Continental Congresses
Second Great Awakening, 315
Second Treatise on Government (Locke), 44
Secularism
  generally, 3–4
  Bible contrasted, 146–147, 164
  Constitution and, 34, 55
  Declaration of Independence and, 34, 55
  Deism and, 13–15, 22–23, 27
  Federalists and, 135
  slavery and, 186
Secular millennialism, 86
Sedgwick, Theodore, 256
Sedition Act, 92
Seixas, Gershom Mendes, 67–68, 70–71, 80n30
Self-preservation, 58n19
Separate Baptists, 103, 108, 308, 311, 331n18, 332n26
Separation of church and state, 23, 27, 41, 53–54, 130
  Backus on, 324–325
  Baptists and, 337n99
  in First Amendment, 328

Jefferson on, 23, 27, 53–54, 130, 305–307, 310, 324–325, 328, 331n15, 336n83
Leland on, 325–328
Locke on, 331n15
Williams on, 310
Separation of Church and State (Hamburger), 328
Sequerya, John de, 66
Seven Years' War, 43, 48
Sewall, Jonathan, 106
Shain, Barry Allan, 42–43
Shawnee tribe, 181, 192–194
Shay's Rebellion, 240
Sherman, Roger
  generally, 5
  Bible and, 145, 149, 162, 167n22
  Christianity and, 229
  Constitution and, 51–53
  First Amendment and, 53–54
  Morris and, 218
  Reformed tradition and, 50, 229
  on theology, 165n6
Sherwood, Samuel, 48
Short Essays on Government (Leland), 326
Short Treatise on Politike Power (Poynet), 44
Silverman, David J., 183
Simon (Madame), 219
Singletary, Amos, 88–89
Six Discourses (Woolston), 18
Skinner, Quentin, 39
Slavery
  abolition of, 185–186
  Anglicanism and, 103–104, 117n16, 180
  Baptists and, 104, 191, 198n44
  Boudinot on, 264–265, 274n45
  Calvinism and, 185
  Catholicism and, 180
  clergy and, 180
  conversion of slaves, 179–180, 184

Declaration of Independence and, 187
Dickinson on, 294–295, 304n106
effect of demographic changes on, 180–181
Hancock on, 240
Islam and, 84, 95–98, 180
Jefferson on, 175, 265
Locke on, 265
manumission, 186
in Maryland, 184, 192
Methodism and, 104, 186, 190–191, 195
Missouri Compromise and, 264–265
New Testament and, 188–192
in North Carolina, 184–185
Old Testament and, 188
in Pennsylvania, 185–186
Presbyterianism and, 191
Puritanism and, 180
Quakerism and, 180, 183–185, 189–190, 195
religion and, 177, 186–191
Revolutionary War and, 176, 184–185
secularism and, 186
in South Carolina, 240
in Virginia, 180, 184, 190, 192
Slaves in Algiers (Rowson), 96
Smith, Adam, 231
Smith, Gary Scott, x
Smith, James, 50
Smith, Melancton, 141n60
Smith, Samuel Stanhope, 194–195, 268
Smith, William, Jr., 54, 111–112, 115
Social contract, 109
Social Contract (Rousseau), 110
Society for Alleviating the Miseries of Public Prisons, 296
Society for Suppressing Vice and Immorality, 303n85
Society for the Propagation of the Gospel in Foreign Parts, 102, 104–107, 112

Society of Friends. *See* Quakerism
Socinianism, 23
Solomon (Bible), 153–155
Some Considerations on the Keeping of Negroes (Woolman), 184
South. *See also specific state*
　Anglicanism in, 46
　Presbyterianism in, 46
South Carolina
　establishment of religion in, 117n12
　ratification of Constitution, 127
　slavery in, 240
Spain, colonialism in, 177–178
Sparks, Jared, 206
Speech, freedom of, 283, 313
The Spirit of the Laws (Montesquieu), 86, 146
Spring, Gardiner, 267
Staloff, Darren, x
Stamp Act, 47, 185, 255, 287
Stamp Act Congress, 5, 277
Stark, Rodney, 45, 60n31, 117n10
State support of religion
　clergy and, 323
　Congregationalism and, 41
　Hancock on, 238–240
Stevens, James Wilson, 96
Stiles, Ezra, 26, 45, 76, 159
Stillingfleet, Edward, 28
Stockton, Hannah, 255
Stockton, Richard, 50, 255
Stone, Geoffrey R., 4
Stoner, James R., 7
Storing, Herbert J., 122–123, 126, 129–132, 138n15, 140n42, 143n88
Stout, Harry S., 35, 46
Strong, Caleb, 51, 54
Strong, Rowan, 102
Stuart, John, 105
Suffolk Resolves, 49
Swanwick, John, 88

Syllabus of an Estimate of the Merit of the Doctrines of Jesus (Jefferson), 76–77
Synod of Dort, 188

Taft, William Howard, 76
Taxation of religion, 134, 143n89
Taylor, N.W., 267
Tea Act, 110
Tecumseh (Creek), 194
The Temple of Reason (newspaper), 20
Tennent, Gilbert, 258
Tennent, William, 257
Tenskwatawa (Creek), 194
Tests. *See* Religious tests
Thacher, Peter, 243, 251n91
Thanksgiving, 261–262, 273n36
Thanksgiving Proclamations (Hancock), 237–238
Theistic rationalism, 208–221
　active God in, 210–213
　adherents of, 223n28
　Catholicism compared, 209
　Christianity compared, 208–209
　Deism compared, 208–210, 213–214, 216
　Franklin and, 223n28
　Hamilton and, 223n28
　intervention of God in, 210–213
　Jefferson and, 223n28
　Jesus and, 209, 214–215
　John Adams and, 223n28
　Madison and, 223n28
　revelation and, 208–209
　Washington and, 223n28
Theocracies, 41
Theology, 165n6
Thirteenth Amendment, 295
Thirty Years' War, 112
Thomson, Charles, 146
Thornton, Matthew, 50
Tillotson, John, 28

Tindal, Mathew, 16–18
Toland, John, 16–17, 21
Tolerance. *See* Religious tolerance
Toleration Act of 1689, 15
Tolles, Frederick, 279
Toryism, 282
Touro Synagogue, 68
Travels in England, France, Spain and the Barbary States (Noah), 73
Treaty of Paris, 237, 260
Treaty of Utrecht, 102
Trenchard, John, 86
Tripoli Wars, 93–94
The True Interests of America (Inglis), 110
The True Nature of Imposture Displayed in the Life of Mahomet (Prideaux), 91–92
Truett, George W., 306
"Truth et Justice" (essayist), 189
Tryon, William, 112
Tucker, Thomas Tudor, 137, 262
Turner, Charles, 126, 131, 142n78
Two kingdom doctrine, 56n7
Two Treatises of Government (Locke), 109
Tyler, Moses Colt, 298n4
Tyler, Royall, 97–98

Unger, Harlow G., 233, 240–241, 245, 248n36, 252n101
Union College, 267
Unitarianism
　generally, 24, 27, 30
　importance attributed to, 4
　Jefferson and, 32n46, 75
　John Adams and, 25, 35, 61n43
　religious liberty and, 164
　Washington and, 23
Universalism
　generally, 30
　John Adams and, 25

Valley Forge, 66

Van der Kemp, Francis, 72
VanDrunen, David, 56n7
Vermont, establishment of religion in, 53
Vindiciae, Contra Tyrannos (Brutus), 38–39
Virginia
　Articles, Laws, and Orders, 1
　Baptists in, 309
　Convention, 156
　Declaration of Rights, 123, 311
　establishment of religion in, 103–104, 117n12
　First Charter, 1
　General Assembly, 316
　Native Americans in, 179
　ratification of Constitution, 127–128, 316–317
　slavery in, 180, 184, 190, 192
　Statute for Establishing Religious Freedom, 62n50, 63, 74, 81n75, 88, 116, 323, 335n73
Voltaire, 27, 72
Voluntarism, 267, 269, 275n61

Wadsworth, Jeremiah, 54
Waldman, Steven, 76, 245n3
Wall of separation. *See* Separation of church and state
Walters, Kerry, 32n45
War of 1812, 94, 176, 194, 267
War of Independence. *See* Revolutionary War
Warren, James, 153, 242
Warren, Joseph, 231, 243
Warren, Mercy, 131
Warren Baptist Association, 312–313
Washington, George
　generally, 4–5, 54–55, 153, 193, 217, 228, 236, 317
　Anglicanism and, 34
　Bible and, 150–151, 154–156, 161, 164, 170n66

Washington, George (*continued*)
  Biblical Hebrew imagery and, 64, 72
  Boudinot and, 255, 257
  Deism and, 13, 22–24, 229
  Dickinson and, 294–295
  faith and, 3
  Hancock and, 244
  Judaism and, 65–69, 76–78
  Morris and, 218
  prayer and, 325
  on religious liberty, 66–69
  Socinianism and, 23
  on taxation of religion, 134
  Thanksgiving and, 262
  theistic rationalism and, 223*n*28
  Unitarianism and, 23
Washington, Martha, 66
Washington, Patsy, 66
"A Watchman" (essayist), 126
Webster (Lady), 219
Weems, Mason Locke, 3
Weir, David A., 40
Wenger, Beth S., 67
Wesleyans, 185
West Jersey Constitution, 300*n*37
Westtown School, 296
Wheatley, Phillis, 174–175, 182
Wheelock, Eleazar, 183
"A Whig" (essayist), 187
Whiggism, 101, 110, 282, 288
Whipple, William, 50
White, John, 58*n*20
Whitefield, George, 1, 182, 255, 258, 278, 312, 330*n*9
White Haven Church, 149
Whitten, Mark Weldon, 159
Williams, Roger, 41, 310, 318, 320–321, 330*n*9, 331*n*15, 334*n*58

Williams, William, 50, 126
Williamson, Hugh, 51, 54
Willis, Samuel, 40
Wilson, James, 5, 50–51, 223*n*28, 229
Wilson, John F., 143*n*98
Wingate, Paine, 54
Winthrop, John, 36, 40, 239
Wiswall, John, 106–107
Witherspoon, John
  generally, 5, 22, 52, 255
  Bible and, 145–146
  Boudinot and, 268–269
  Christianity and, 229
  at College of New Jersey, 35
  Declaration of Independence and, 50–51
  Reformed tradition and, 44, 229
  Revolutionary War and, 234
  on theology, 165*n*6
Witte, John, 325–326
Wolcott, Henry, 40
Wolcott, Oliver, 50
Wolf, Eva Sheppard, 190
Wollaston, William, 18
Women's suffrage, 300*n*37
Wood, Betty, 117*n*16, 330*n*9
Wood, Gordon S., 4, 29, 153
Woolman, John, 183–184
Woolston, Thomas, 15, 18
Wynkoop, Henry, 54

Yale University, 46
Yamasee War, 104
Yates, Robert, 51, 123
Young, Thomas, 18–19, 31*n*23

Zilversmit, Arthur, 198*n*35
Zionism, 65, 77
Zubly, John Jacob, 112

CPSIA information can be obtained
at www.ICGtesting.com
Printed in the USA
BVHW041728161122
652137BV00004B/14